THE BUSINESS OF
MEDICAL PRACTICE

David Edward Marcinko, MBA, CFP, is a practicing board certified surgeon, from Temple University in Philadelphia, who has authored more than 150 publications and four major medical and business textbooks, in two languages. He received his undergraduate degree from Loyola College in Baltimore, his business degree from the Keller Graduate School of Management, in Chicago, his financial planning diploma from Oglethorpe University, in Atlanta, and his board certification from the Certified Financial Planners, Board of Standards, in Denver. His corporate managerial experience includes owning and operating an ambulatory surgery center and serving as president of a regional physician practice management company, in the midwest, that aborted its IPO roll-up due to adverse market conditions last year. He is a member of the Financial Planning Association and is founder of the privately held practice management and financial planning firm, Marcinko Business Associates Inc. in Norcross, Georgia. He is a consultant for numerous medical, financial, and insurance companies and lectures extensively in a witty and entertaining style throughout this country and Europe. Dr. Marcinko possess a general securities license, multiple insurance licensees, and is a registered representative of Sun America Securities and a registered agent for the American International Group (AIG). He is also a registered investment advisor who can be reached at 770-448-0769 (voice)/770-939-7393 (fax) /www.marcinkoadvisors.com (Web site).

THE BUSINESS OF MEDICAL PRACTICE

Profit Maximizing Skills for Savvy Doctors

David Edward Marcinko, MBA, CFP

Editor

 **Springer Publishing Company**

Springer Publishing Company, Inc.
536 Broadway
New York, NY 10012-3955

Acquisitions Editor: Bill Tucker
Production Editor: J. Hurkin-Torres
Cover design by James Scotto-Lavino

03 04 / 5 4 3

Library of Congress Cataloging-in-Publication Data

The business of medical practice: profit maximizing skills for savvy doctors / David
    Edward Marcinko, editor.
        p.   cm.
    Includes bibliographical references and index.
    ISBN 0-8261-1311-7 (hardcover)
    1. Medicine—Practice.   2. Physicians—Finance, Personal.   I. Marcinko, David E.
(David Edward)
    [DNLM: 1. Practice Management, Medical—economics.   W 80 B9787 2000]
R728.B877   2000
610'.68—dc21   99-054299
                                                                                 CIP

Printed in the United States of America

The economic, financial, business, reimbursement and management information contained in this book is not to be construed as a standard of fiscal analysis or reimbursement for any medical or surgical practice. Its content does not reflect the policy of the American Medical Association (AMA), American Dental Association (ADA), American Podiatric Medical Association (APMA), American Chiropractic Association (ACA), American Optometric Association (AOA), American Society of Actuaries (ASA), American College of Surgeons (ACS), Marcinko Business Associates (MBA), Medical Group Management Association (MGMA), the American College of Physician Executives (ACPE), Planned Financial Consultants (PFC), or any other affiliated organizations, trustees, staff, or members. Certain figures and statistics were obtained from the Hoechst Marion Roussel Managed Care Digest Series 1998, and were used with permission. Please consult a financial accountant (CPA), managerial accountant (CMA), business expert (MBA), certified financial planner (CFP), attorney (JD), registered investment advisor (RIA), or private practice management firm with health care experience, for more individualized information.

Examples are generally descriptive and do not purport to be accurate in every regard. The health care industry is evolving rapidly, and all information should be considered time-sensitive.

Dedication

This textbook is dedicated to its contributing authors who crashed the prototypical product developmental life cycle and produced time sensitive material in an expedient manner.

It is also dedicated to all the finance, accounting, calculus, securities, insurance, information technology, legal, business and graduate school professors who taught me about the new health care economics. Especially noted are: Randy Arrowood, RIA, CFP, Robert Button, CMA, CPA, Martha Buxton, MBA, Jackson Collins, MBA, Charles "Chick" Finn, ChFC, CLU, Paul Folger, MBA, Herbert E. Garner, RIA, William T. Ginn, Jr., MBA, MSFS, ChFC, CLU, CFP, Dean Arlis "Al" Head, Rex A. Huber, MBA, Steven McGee, JD, Nancy Messegge-Downey, MBA, John Kochikowski, MBA, Rachel Pentin-Maki, MHA, Larry Rager, MBA, PhD, Joel Rosenberg, MBA, and Russell Robinson, MBA, CFA, who then encouraged me to teach those of the medical profession.

Above all, this book is dedicated with love to my mother Cecelia, father Edward, brother Ed, sister Teresa, brother-in-law Julio, uncle Stosh, aunt Helen, wife Hope, and daughter Mackenzie.

David Edward Marcinko, MBA, CFP
Editor

Contents

SECTION TWO: QUANTITATIVE ASPECTS OF MEDICAL PRACTICE

SECTION THREE: CONTEMPORARY ASPECTS OF MEDICAL PRACTICE

Contributors

Bridget Bourgeois, CPA, is a professional hospital, clinic, and medical practice appraiser for the health care consulting division of Ernst & Young. Prior to joining the firm she was a member of the health care mergers and acquisitions team of the American Appraisers Associates. Her specialty functions included long-term care; home health; assisted living; and general, acute, and psychiatric hospital valuations. She is also involved in similar activities within the physician practice management industry. She can be reached at 404-817-5765 (voice) or 404-817-4341 (fax)

Dr. Gary Bode, MSA, is a surgeon who retired to earn his master's degree in accountancy. He then founded Comprehensive Practice Accounting, a nationally based firm limited to health care practitioners. He uses proactive tax planning and strives to make individual practice parameters and medical statistics intuitively useful for office managerial purposes and profit enhancement. Dr. Bode writes for nine health care journals and can be reached at 800-839-4763 or E-mail: cpa@wilmington.net.

Render S. Davis, MHA, CHE, is a certified health care executive. He served as assistant administrator for General Services, Policy Development, and Regulatory Affairs at Crawford Long Hospital of Emory University from 1977 to 1995. He is currently an Administrator for Special Projects and Co-Chair of the Ethics Committee of Crawford Long Hospital and an independent health care consultant in the areas of policy and ethics. He is a founding board member of the Health Care Ethics Consortium of Georgia and has served on the consortium's executive committee, advisory board, Futility Task Force, and Strategic Planning Committee and has chaired the Annual Conference Planning Committee since 1995. He may be reached at (404) 256-0264 voice/fax, or by E-mail: rendavis@mindspring.com.

Dr. Charles F. Fenton III, JD, is a board-certified surgeon-attorney who practices health care law in Atlanta, Georgia. He is a founding member of The Health-Law Group and author of several medicolegal publications for physicians and the bar. His clients include health care practitioners involved in Medicare/Medicaid audits and recoupment actions, as well as physicians involved in disputes with insurance or managed care companies. He can be reached at (voice) 404-233-5937, (fax) 404-231-0853 or E-mail: medlawyer@sprintmail.com.

Eric Galtress is a Senior Account Executive, Business Development, for Medical Management Consultants, Inc. (MMC), the leading Professional Employer Organization (PEO) specializing in health care. With expertise in government compliance, contract management, and business development, he held executive positions at three PEOs, each having its own area of market specialization. He has developed and provided instruction in client needs analysis and the proposal process in the field of human resource management and is also active in the implementation of tailored services and client retention. He can be reached at (voice): 800-899-6624, (fax): 800-322-6624, or E-mail: erichrservices@earthlink. net.

Dr. Harry Goldsmith is the physician director of Medical Review Consultants. He serves as a liaison for the AMA's CPT Coding Committee and is a member of the American College of Medical Quality. He lectures nationally and writes about issues related to medical reimbursement and related issues. He can be reached at 562-923-0789 (voice), 562-809-3311 (fax), or E-mail at 102637. 3524@compuserve.com.

Allan Gordon specializes in managed care consulting to providers and health plans, including managed care contracting and network development, market and competitive analysis, physician network review, and contract negotiations. He has 15 years industry experience in health plan operations and network development and has served as a network advisor on health plan site audits with medical groups and IPAs. Mr. Gordon recently merged with Phoenix Healthcare Consulting, LLC. He can be reached at 888-PHC-6252 (voice) or 310-379-0916 (fax).

Angela Herron, CPA, has professional experience that includes financial management and advisory services to health care clients, including business planning and advisory services on transactions for health care companies and business ventures. She works with physicians to prepare for managed care contracts and with PHOs to structure and implement integrated managed care delivery systems. She is a founding member of Phoenix Healthcare Consulting, LLC, and a graduate of the University of Northern Iowa. She can be reached at 888-PHC-6252 (voice) or 310-379-0916 (fax).

Hope Rachel Hetico, RN, MHA, received a master's degree in health care administration from the College of St. Francis, Joliette, Illinois. Prior to joining Marcinko Business Associates, Inc., she was a senior corporate health care executive for Apria Healthcare in Costa Mesa, California. She is a well-known reimbursement specialist and nationally known expert in infection and utilization review, as well as NACQA, HEDIS, and JCAHO rules and regulations. She can be reached at 770-448-0769 (voice) or 770-939-7393 (fax).

Jeanne Hogan, MPH, is a founding member of Phoenix Healthcare Consulting, LLC, and has over 20 years of health care consulting experience. She specializes in business and strategic planning for health care providers, and works extensively with medical groups and hospital executives to anticipate and plan for the changes caused by the expansion of managed medical care. She can be reached at 888-PHC-6252 (voice) or 310-379-0916 (fax).

Thomas A. Knox, MBA, is vice-president for provider partnerships at Delta Dental Plan of Minnesota, which owns half interest in a privately held dental practice management company. For twenty years, he has held senior leadership positions in several different health care organizations and implemented various joint ventures, partnerships, and alliances in a variety of medical organization. He can be reached at 612-829-8434 (voice), 612-944-4193 (fax), or E-mail: knox@unidi-al.com.

Frederick William LaCava, PhD, JD, also known as "Duffy," earned his BA degree from Emory University, Atlanta, a PhD in English from the University of North Carolina, Chapel Hill, and a JD from Indiana University School of Law, Blooming-ton. He practices health law at the LaCava Law Firm in Indianapolis and can be reached at 317-577-2249 (voice) or 317-577-1320 (fax).

Dr. O. Kent Mercado, JD, is a board-certified surgeon from a family of physician-surgeons, who practices health care law in Chicago. He is a nationally known author and lecturer and advocate for physicians' rights. He can be reached at the Mercado Medical and Legal Center-West, 708-383-6800.

Edward J. Rappaport, JD, LL.M, graduated from the University of Georgia School of Law and received his LL.M degree in taxation from the University of Florida. He has a tax, estate, and general business planning practice in Atlanta and represents closely held business interests. He lectures regularly at legal seminars and is a frequent author, whose most recent work appeared in *Estate Planning* magazine. Mr. Rappaport is President of the North Atlanta Tax Council and is active in the Atlanta Tax Forum and the Fiduciary Law Section of the State Bar of Georgia. He can be reached at: Robinson, Rappaport, Jampol, Aussenberg & Schleicher, LLP 770-667-1290 (voice) or 770-667-1690 (fax).

Dr. William P. Scherer, MS, is a board-certified surgeon in Fort Lauderdale, Florida, and an Internet designer for many Web page applications in the medical and nonmedical sectors. He is widely published in medical and information technology journals and several textbooks and is a journalist and photographer who contributes extensively on issues related to the new electronic media. He can be reached at (voice) 954-776-0200, (fax) 954-776-2396, or E-mail: DrScherer @aol.com.

Eugene Schmuckler, PhD, CTS, is Coordinator of Behavioral Science at the Georgia Public Safety Training Center and a licensed psychologist. He is on the board of directors of the Association of Traumatic Stress Specialists and is a certified trauma specialist. Dr. Schmuckler is an international speaker and author, with publications translated into Russian and Dutch. He is Chairman of the Department of Psychology, Keller Graduate School of Management, in Atlanta. He can be reached at 770-589-1927.

Foreword

President Clinton's health care plan of 1992 may have died an ignominious death, but changes ushered into the landscape during the past eight years are profound and here to stay. Because of them, the onus on today's medical practitioner is to survive in the new reality of the 21st century. To accomplish this goal, traditional medical knowledge must be merged with contemporary business information and disseminated to physicians in a useful manner. Dr. David Edward Marcinko, and his stellar team of contributing authors, have accomplished this goal by condensing the full gamut of accounting, financial, insurance, legal, managerial and leadership skills into a single enlightening volume. The insights contained in this book will assist all independent medical professionals redefine their thinking and re-engineer their practices, to the benefit of the communities they serve.

When I entered medical school, the number of books written about practice enhancement were few and far between. Those that did exist were rudimentary. Most available today, market driven. The truth is, this book should be part of every medical school, dental school, and health care administration business curriculum. Personally, it was only through the arduous completion of graduate school did I become familiar with the principles distilled herein. Under the current system, however, this information is reserved for insurance entities controlling the health care industrial complex, not practitioners. This lost opportunity, due to myopic medical educators, has fueled the managed care crisis. It is now up to us to refocus the health care debate on quality care, efficient processes, and the bottom line.

Still, how often have we heard that medicine is different from other businesses and that it is impossible to provide a lower cost and higher quality service? Arguably, this is true to some extent, but the realist cannot ignore examples from the business world. The fate of industrial giants, such as GM, IBM and Kodak were almost sealed by attitudes that declared their industries somehow different and exempt from the pressure to provide more cost competitive products. History demonstrated this erroneous philosophy, as nimble foreign competitors, began doing exactly what the American giants said was impossible; producing better and less costly products. Today, this same demand is being forced on medical services, and those who refuse to evolve will undoubtedly suffer fates similar to their industrial counterparts. For, it seems certain that those physicians who lack the competitive business and management skills presented in this book, will do so at their own peril.

For example, how often have we heard passive colleagues speak of the time when "the pendulum will swing back," referring to the second coming of the golden age of medicine? This is, of course, a frequent topic of hospital doctor's lounge conversation, along with the routine vilification of managed care companies. While I would agree that there will be some "correction" in the health care market, the "golden age" of medicine is over. In truth, I say good riddance. I say this not from the taste of sour grapes, but because what we have lost as a society is a system that was riddled with inefficiency and waste. In short, it was a system that was not sustainable. As a result, physicians find themselves collared with illogical and often ridiculous restrictions imposed by individuals with little understanding of what is actually required to care for patients. The fact of the matter is that we have no one to blame but ourselves for failing to see the future, and refusing to seize a position of leadership in our own industry. As a result, we have entered the realm of disgruntled followers. Encouragingly, Dr. Marcinko admonishes us to regain our stature, but only after we have a thorough understanding of the forces at work, as presented in this eloquent business tome.

Dr. Marcinko, a prolific educator from the next generation of young physician executives, has emerged to create a book that fills a much needed and important medical niche, from one of the very best publishing houses in the field. *The Business of Medical Practice* is well researched, up to date, and written in an easy to read fashion with examples, spreadsheets and illustrations to enhance reader understanding and interest. It is a virtual medical-economics page-turner that describes in nontechnical language, the creative techniques which can be understood by any practitioner willing to devote the time and resources to implement their use. Moreover, he is not just an ivory tower academic. As a surgeon, founder of an ambulatory surgery center, and past president of a regional physician practice management corporation, he is, above all, an aggressive pragmatist who helps us answer such real-life question as:

"Should I sign this managed care contract and what I am to earn based on its underlying economic assumptions?"

"When is my practice most efficient, least efficient, and where do I really earn my money?"

"How can I reduce my costs, increase revenues, and decrease my operating assets?"

"What financial, accounting and managerial skills do I need most?"

"How can I help my patients in an honest and ethical fashion, and still be successful?"

"How can I practice medicine with joy and enthusiasm, again?"

Dr. Marcinko is to be congratulated on the completion of this major, and much needed addition to the vital new field of professional business management. This book is destined to become the classic practice management textbook for all physicians and is a must-read for the nation's, more than two million, independent health care providers and their related business advisors. Indeed, it will be time very well spent.

Antonio Silva, MD, MBA
Emory-Northlake Regional Medical Center
Emory University-Goizueta School of Business
Atlanta, Georgia

Preface

In the current health care insurance crisis, *The Business of Medical Practice: Profit Maximizing Skills for Savvy Doctors* is a textbook of specific value to all medical practitioners, since declining reimbursement, increasing expenses, federal regulations, and even Wall Street are all raising havoc with physician income and patient care. Contrary to conventional wisdom, we do not believe that draconian free market competition will dramatically reduce health care costs, for three reasons. First, it is difficult to define medical quality. Second, a perfectly competitive marketplace does not exist. Thirdly, American society is not ready for the brutally rational efficiencies of the business world. *Above all else*, medicine is a uniquely personal experience.

On the other hand, we are pragmatic and realize that practicing health care providers of all independent degree designations (allopathic, osteopathic and podiatric physicians, dentists, optometrists, chiropractors, psychologists, physician assistant's, physical therapists and nurse practitioners), must learn to better compete in the next decade. Ultimately, practitioners who seek to be clinically *and* economically responsible are the wave of future. It is the physician-executive with MBA or managerial training, who can best direct future systems of autonomous care, with improved outcomes for patient, payer and physician alike.

The information in this text will help achieve this goal and is most applicable to the solo or small group practice; or for those who aspire to be decision makers. For the employed physician or resident, it will also serve as a blueprint for what can still be achieved. And, for the practice administrator, it will serve as a guide to the next generation of medical networks, IPAs or more complex large group management endeavors.

The Business of Medical Practice: Profit Maximizing Skills for Savvy Doctors is written in prose form, using nontechnical jargon, without the need to document every statement with a citation from the literature. This allows a large amount of information to be condensed into a single and practical volume. It also allows the reader to comprehend an important concept in a single reading session, and a deliberate effort has been made to include germane examples with updated information. The interested reader is then able to research selected topics. Overlap of material has also been reduced, but important concepts are reviewed for increased understanding.

The textbook is divided into three major sections, written by 20 contributing authors, with the concepts developed in Section Two (quantitative) and Section Three (contemporary) building on those of Section One (qualitative). Each section is then divided into multiple parts, for a total of 25 logically progressive yet stand-alone chapters.

Chapter 1 briefly reviews the history of health care economics in the United States; from the days of private pay to indemnity insurance and the "golden era of medicine" to contemporary managed care. Chapter 2 discusses the uses and abuses of restrictive covenants in physician employment contracts, since more than 40% of the nation's contemporary physicians are now employees rather than independent practitioners. Chapter 3 focuses on office labor cost reduction tactics through permanent outsourcing and co-employment options, as human resource management is the major expense driver of any medical practice. Chapter 4 surveys the management information technology (hardware and software) required for the modern digital office, while chapter 5 extols nuances of proper CPT coding and documentation in a skeptical payer climate. The basics of capitation contracting econometrics are examined in chapter 6. Chapter 7 provides strategies for effective managed care relations by understanding, obtaining, negotiating, and servicing managed care contracts, and chapter 8 represents a legal discourse on nonclinical risk management issues, as Section One is concluded.

Section Two begins the quantitative aspects of the book, as chapter 9 investigates the perils of indiscriminate cash flow control in rising, declining, and neutral growth environments. Chapter 10 presents basic concepts of fixed and variable office cost behavior, among others, while chapter 11 dissects the discipline of activity-based costing which is a watershed concept to most physicians that has become the costing method of choice in the hyper competitive environment. Chapter 12 explores advanced cost-volume accounting techniques, emphasizing the nontraditional contribution margin approach to the income statement, with numerous spreadsheet examples to enhance understanding. Chapter 13 introduces vital financial methods to calculate and augment return on office investment and its resulting residual income. Chapter 14, on financial ratio analysis, represents the economic benchmarking equivalent of the clinical outcomes chapter and surveys the typical office for lost sources of profit. Chapter 15 highlights the business philosophy required to create real practice equity value in an era of health care mergers and acquisitions, while chapter 16, on practice valuation techniques, concludes the section and emphasizes the discounted cash flow method of appraisal, since bricks and mortar are becoming increasingly worthless. It is an important chapter for the retiring practitioner in the quest for a proper payoff after years of hard work.

Section Three begins with chapters 17 and 18 and provides utilization review and case management and clinical benchmarking information, respectively. Chapter 19 discloses the contentious issue of medical antitrust and the ERISA managed care exemption. Chapter 20 offers a sobering musing on change management and the new role of the physician as follower, rather than leader, of the health care revolution. Chapter 21 critiques Wall Street's newest security machination, the physician practice management corporation; the initial euphoria, debacle, and future of this business model is discussed, using real-life examples. Chapter 22 redefines the standard of medical care to incorporate insurer financial restraints, while chapter 23 similarly opines on the ethical and moral issues of managed medical care. Chapter 24 presents important asset protection strategies useful in an increasing litigious atmosphere, and chapter 25 rightly concludes the third section, and the book, with a discussion on choosing the business management advisor who represents the best fit for both the office milieu and individual practitioner.

In conclusion, as you read, study, and reflect on this challenging textbook, remember the guiding philosophy of Eric Hoffer: "In a time of drastic change, it is the learners who will inherit the future. The learned find themselves equipped to live in a world that no longer exists."

INSTRUCTIONS FOR CONDENSED READING AND REVIEW

To the new physician, mid-career practitioner, or seasoned health care provider or to those practice managers who find that mastering business topics is a difficult endeavor, this book is a useful source of information even if you recoil at the thought of cost-volume profit analysis or contribution margins in conjunction with a medical practice.

If you are of this ilk, I urge you to begin your reading with chapters 1, 2, 3, 5, and 7, which will encourage you to learn the basics of management theory as it relates to the practice of medicine today. Then, after reading this much of the book, you are sure to find enough business material communicated in Section One, that you will want to give the mathematical portions of the book another try. All theories are explained in plain language with easily understood spreadsheet calculations and tables to reinforce vital concepts, in Section Two. Chapters 10, 11, 12, 13, and 14 are the most difficult of the book, but they are also the most worthwhile; especially to larger group practices. Moreover, chapters 17, 18, and 19, of Section Three offer case and outcomes management reviews and legal ruminations in the face of an economically driven society. Likewise, the philosophic promulgations of chapters 22 and 23 are both mentally caustic, so take your time and read slowly to consider and digest the material thoroughly.

Finally, study and enjoy the remaining chapters of the book at your leisure. There is something in them for all medical professionals, regardless of specialty or degree designation. The effort will be well rewarded with enhanced revenue, decreased personal stress and improved patient care; the ultimate goal of any contemporary health care reform or futuristic medical business model.

Your thoughts, suggestions, and opinions after reading *The Business of Medical Practice: Profit Maximizing Skills for Savvy Doctors* are most appreciated and welcomed.

Good medicine, good business, and good day!

David Edward Marcinko
Hope Rachel Hetico

Qualitative Aspects of Medical Practice

## CHAPTER 1

Health Care Economics in the United States: Evolution or Revolution?

The Insurance Payment Paradigm Shift

David Edward Marcinko and Hope Rachel Hetico

> We are now entering the Age of Unreason, when the future, in so many areas, is there to be shaped by us and for us—a time when the only prediction that will hold true is that no prediction will hold true; a time, therefore, for bold imaginings in private life as well as public; for thinking the unlikely and doing the unreasonable.
>
> —Charles Handy, *The Age of Unreason*

A basic but hardly promoted premise of all health care economics is imprecision. Nevertheless, we may define traditional health care economics as how the medical-industrial complex allocates its limited resources (cerebral input, equipment, technology, infrastructure and monetary assets) to the insatiable appetites of the US consumer, through the natural laws of supply and demand. This occurs because physicians are willing to sell and patients are willing to buy their services. At some point of equilibrium, supply equals demand, for a price known as *market equilibrium*.

For example, let's take a look at the medical practice of Dr. Jane Smith and her competitor Dr. Harry Jones. When the price of a noncovered Medicare service is lowered by Smith, her patient load increases, and Dr. Jones's volume slows. Conversely, if she raised her fees, Dr. Jones's practice would flourish. This phenomenon, illustrated by market forces (the "invisible hand" of Adam Smith), can be reviewed from the traditional, contemporary, and futuristic health care economic perspectives outlined below.

TRADITIONAL HEALTH CARE ECONOMICS

Demand Side Considerations in Medical Care

Medical care may be defined as the examination and treatment of patients. Implicit in this definition is the fact that the lower the direct out-of-pocket price offered to the patient (all other factors held constant), the greater the number of units of medical commodity the patient will demand. In this relationship, *demand* is defined as the set of service quantities (outputs) demanded at various prices, and the *quantity demanded* is the amount of care requested at a specific price. Changes in demand occur as a result of personal income and tastes, physician shortages and surpluses, personality and perceptions, and a host of other factors. A graphic representation of this relationship is the classic downward-sloping demand curve, and the rationale behind the curve lies in the possibility of substitution, because very few, if any, commodities are absolutely identical and necessary. (See Figure 1.1.)

Supply Side Considerations in Medical Care

Historically, physician suppliers were motivated to maximize their profits by augmenting services and minimizing costs. Implicit in this definition is the fact that physician suppliers will endeavor to provide as many services as possible. In

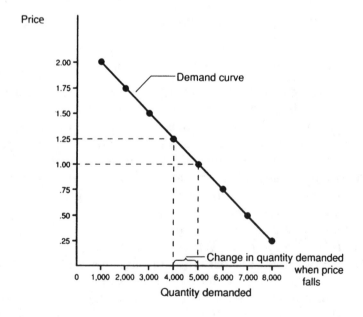

FIGURE 1.1   Typical downward sloping demand curve for health services.

this relationship, *supply* is defined as the set of services quantities (outputs) provided at various prices, and the *quantity supplied* is the amount of care rendered at a specific price. Changes in supply occur as a result of similar but opposite factors, as found in the demand relationship. A graphic representation of this relationship is the classic upward-sloping supply curve; equilibrium is reached when the supply and demand curves intersect at the historic *usual, customary, and reasonable* price point. (See Figures 1.2 and 1.3.)

Marginal Revenues and Cost

If a doctor has the opportunity to see even a single additional patient at a profit, he or she will rationally do so. The *marginal revenue* (MR) from the extra office visit exceeds the *marginal cost* (MC) of the visit. Once the cost of the visit equals the revenue it produces, the incentive to see more patients is lost. In other words, no additional profit is left at the point where MR = MC. This is a standard business concept that always hold true, absent situations such as monopolies or oligopolies. Once satisfied, health care gratification, or *utility*, diminishes, and more care has a lower return on health and productivity.

Marginal Utility and Medical Price Elasticity

If utility is a word used to describe the value of medical service to a patient, then *marginal utility* (MU) is the value of treating one additional patient. At some

FIGURE 1.2 **Typical upward sloping supply curve for health services.**

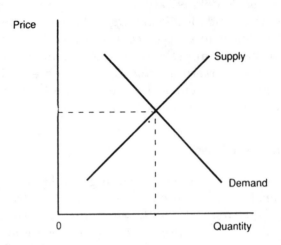

FIGURE 1.3   Market equilibrium for health services.

point the treatment plan is completed, the patient is satisfied, and additional services are of no value. Another example of this is the inadvisability of having two offices in the same neighborhood, rather than in different geographic locations. The marginal utility of the second neighborhood office is often negligible.

In our initial example of Dr. Jane Smith, some patients may not decide to leave her practice despite the fee increase. Patients may consider such intangibles as demeanor, location, or quality of service and elect to continue their relationship with her. When this occurs, we say patient demand is *inelastic* to price change or price increases. On the contrary, if patients quickly go to Dr. Harry Jones, demand is said to be *elastic* to price pressure, and some studies show that a mere $10–$12 monthly increase in out-of-pocket costs is enough to send patients elsewhere. Medical service elasticity is affected by such things as deductibles, copayments, and coinsurance, as well as physician reputation and communication skills. When an industry becomes more competitive, as in health care today, fees tend to become more elastic, and patient volume becomes very sensitive to even small changes in price. In a managed care environment, every noncovered service will have its own level of pricing elasticity, and every doctor should estimate that level for all fees, in order to achieve optimum patient volume. Traditionally, medical services and food were inelastic to price changes; automobile sales are very elastic to price sensitivity. This relationship is rapidly changing, and there is even a mathematic equation stating this phenomenon in ratio form:

$$\text{Elasticity of Medical Supply} = \frac{\%\ \text{Change in Total Revenue}}{\%\ \text{Change in Price}}$$

For instance, if a 20% increase in an office visit charge resulted in a 30% increase in quantity of services supplied, the price elasticity would be 30/20, or 1.5. Therefore, a high elasticity coefficient equates to a high price elasticity.

Generally, a coefficient greater than 1 is considered elastic; a coefficient less than 1 is inelastic. Interestingly, exact unity prevails when elasticity of supply is exactly equal to 1.

In addition to price elasticity of demand, the competitive marketplace drives supply and prices. For example, there is usually more medical competition in large metropolitan areas than in rural areas. Prices tend to rise and fall, and the market is more sensitive to price fluctuation because of this structure. In the traditional medical community, this led to the development of four basic medical marketplaces types.

The Four Traditional Models of Medical Competition

In a discussion of competitive medical models, assumptions must include normal demand quantities, many fully informed patients, and the fact that physicians cannot directly influence demand for care. These assumptions, although fluid, also preclude that the number of patient buyers is large enough to have any influence over price and results in the following structures:

In a *pure monopoly* there is only one provider with a unique service. The doctor is a "price maker" and charges whatever he or she wishes.

In an *oligopoly* there are a few physicians who provide similar services. For example, when it becomes clear to Dr. Smith and Dr. Jones that neither can win the price war, oligopolists return prices to prior, still inflated levels.

In *monopolistic competition* there are many providers with differentiated services. For example, should Dr. Jones decide to have evening hours, she may charge a premium for her fees if Dr. Jones does not follow suit.

Finally, when *pure competition* occurs, there are many physicians providing similar and substitutable services. Marketing and advertising do not affect fees, and prices are determined by supply and demand. The doctors become "price takers" by accepting fees arrived at by practicing competitively.

Externalities Defy Traditional Medical
Supply-and-Demand Economics

The marketplace structures listed above, although efficient, are not necessarily timely. This is particularly true in medicine and is attributed to various "externalities" that seemingly deter competition. Formally, *externalities* are defined as the costs or benefits of market transactions that are not directly reflected in the price that buyers (patients) or sellers (doctors) use to make their decisions. They represent defects, or inefficiencies, in the pricing system and can be either positive or negative. Pertinent externalities for the physician and health care practitioner include but are not limited to the following:

1. *Barriers to entry:* Physicians and other "learned health care professionals" receive an extended formal education. This not only ensures competence and protects the public but also reduces competition.

2. *Competitive advantage:* Once school is over, holding a medical degree is an effective strategic advantage over a nondegreed practitioner.
3. *Monopsony and oligopsony:* These conditions occur when discounts are extracted from health care providers because of supply and demand size inequalities and may run afoul of antitrust laws.
4. *Barriers to exit:* The increased cost of doing business effectively precludes many physicians from terminating practice until all fiscal investments are recouped. Observe that few doctors can practice "part time" and still afford their overhead.
5. *Mortal turpitude:* Since physicians take the Hippocratic Oath, they are expected to place patient welfare above their own. This is not necessarily true of business entities, which must adhere to legalities only.
6. *Moral hazards:* All know that smoking, dietary indiscretions, drinking, drug use, and promiscuous behavior are unhealthy. Yet many pursue this lifestyle that drives up health care costs for society as a whole.

Other externalities that drive up the cost of health care are well known but not easily changed. First, most Americans have group insurance through their employment; they don't buy it, which makes them fairly indifferent to the cost of or need for individual health care purchases. Second, acquiring health insurance is not like buying a commodity; it is difficult for a lay person to know what purchases make sense and at what price. Third, most health insurance purchasing decisions are made by the doctor (i.e., refer to a specialist or have surgery), not the patient consumer, and hence there is a vested interest in increasing service demand. Finally, what well-informed person would be a tough bargainer when his or her health is at stake? Who is going to negotiate with a neurosurgeon?

During the so-called Golden Age of Physicians, 1965–1985, Medicare, Medicaid, and the factors mentioned above worked to isolate American medicine from financial reality. More recently, however, the private sector is demanding cost containment by negotiating prices for medical services.

Medical Profit Maximization

Now that something about marketplace inefficiencies has been reviewed, it is time to consider how these externalities are applied to the medical marketplace. This is done by realizing that the previously imperfect (fee-for-service) marketplace is becoming more perfectly competitive (efficient) in the current managed care environment. For example, consider the following economic scenarios.

1.   A glut of physicians causes them to become price takers, selling a homogeneous (commoditized) service. An appendectomy is an appendectomy! Or is it? Financially, many doctors are taking what they're given (by HMOs), because they're working for a living. Younger doctors, under 40, are especially inclined to work for less because they have had little exposure to fee-for-service compensation. Perhaps providers need to differentiate themselves from the competition?

Ponder the MD versus DO controversy: one of the fastest-growing areas of specialization is osteopathic family medicine. Or physician (MD and DO) versus health care extender (RN, CRNA, CNM, PA) dilemma. Want another example? Estimate the degree of service differentiation by becoming a sports medicine doctor, dermatologist, pediatrician, surgeon, or invasive radiologist. Finally, consider that according to the American Geriatrics Society (AGS) only 8,000 of the country's 670,000 physicians are formally certified in geriatrics, yet the reason for the shortage in this subspecialty is unclear. Moreover, according to Dr. Mike Wasserman, president and chief medical officer for Gerimed of America, a geriatric medical management company based in Englewood, Colorado, "managed care plans have misunderstood how to manage the senior population."

2.   Physicians have an increasingly smaller share of the medical marketplace because of extended care providers. Does this help or hinder them? Price information is freely available to all MCOs because of computerization. Recall all the fee schedule surveys popular several years ago? What impact does this knowledge have on medical care today?

3.   Doctors have been defeated in their ability to influence the marketplace by selling a quality but nevertheless standardized service. Consider the economic effects of practice guidelines in this light.

4.   As medical care becomes efficient, each doctor is a perfect substitute for the another. Patient demand becomes perfectly elastic at the HMO's capitated set price. This being the case, there is no incentive to lower fees in an attempt to attract more patients, because doctors would not be able treat any more patients. The price decrease just lowers income but has no effect on number of patients treated. It simply decreases profits.

5.   Since marginal revenue is the fee obtained from seeing one extra patient, marginal revenue becomes equal to HMO price, and marginal profit is zero when marginal revenue just equals marginal cost. Will the MD still want to wait another hour just to see that last late HMO patient?

6.   A profit-maximizing office will operate at a short-term loss as long as its minimum average cost is less than its minimum possible average variable cost. But just how long is "short term," anyway?

7.   Efficiency prevails when medical services are made available just up to the point that marginal benefits equal marginal costs. When efficiency is achieved, it is not possible to make more money without decreasing another doctor's income in a capitated risk pool situation. *Voila!* Managed competition, anyone? It is estimated that more than a quarter of all physicians may leave practice by the year 2005!

Regardless of the technical nature of the above arguments, practical attention must be directed toward the possibility of governmental (national health care) intervention or marketplace (HMO) intercession, relative to two other concepts that directly affect medical practices: price ceilings and price floors.

Price ceilings are maximum legal charges and always result in shortages when they are set below market equilibrium prices. How long is the wait at a local charitable hospital versus that at a local for-profit medical center? Price ceilings often result in an underground black market economy that exceeds legal limits. Non-price-rationing (i.e., free medical care), on the other hand, distributes available services to patients on a basis other than ability to pay. The most common non-price-rationing device is "first come, first served." Finally, *price floors* establish minimum prices, which often result in surpluses when they exceed equilibrium price levels. The minimum wage is a good example of a price floor.

Price ceilings and floors benefit certain groups but impair the distribution of goods and services by the price system in free competitive markets. Government intervention interferes in the functioning of competitive markets and is likely to result in "resource allocation" problems. Remember Keynesian macroeconomic philosophy. In evaluating managed care price controls, the gains to beneficiaries of price ceilings and floors must be weighed against the resulting allocation problems. Alternative methods that will make the gainers just as well off, without impairing the rationing function of medical prices, can be considered as ways to increase efficiency in the medical economy.

Traditional Methods of Health Care Delivery

Prior to 1970 the health care reimbursement system was not a monolithic complex, and most Americans received their health care through one of five third-party organizations: (1) Blue Cross/Blue Shield (prepaids), (2) commercial insurance (private) companies, (3) Medicare (federal-elderly), (4) Medicaid (state-poor), and (5) CHAMPUS (military).

The four participants in this fragmented system were the patient (consumer), the physician (provider), the employer (buyer or payer), and the third-party intermediary. Moreover, the doctor-patient relationship was often muddled by the third parties, who became brokers between MD and patient, both of whom merely sought to understand (a) who was responsible for payment, (b) how the MD would assist the patient to obtain reimbursement, and (c) how to establish the ultimately responsible party.

In the meantime, commercial insurance medical costs were accelerating at a rate greater than the Consumer Price Index. There was no single reason for this cost escalation, but many economists believed the following circumstances conjoined at one point in time to increase health care costs dramatically:

1. Law of supply and demand (increasingly too many doctors chasing too few patients). For example, a recent study commissioned by the American Academy of Orthopedic Surgeons (AAOS) and conducted by the Rand Corporation, determined that 19% fewer residencies are needed next year. A similar study by the American Physical Therapy Association (APTA) projected an 11% surplus by the year 2000. Even Milliman & Robertson, an actuarial firm, estimates that only 300,000 of 450,000 physicians actively practicing medicine in the United States are necessary. The same situation is true for other health care employees. Mergers, acquisitions, outsourcing, closings, and consolidations have only exacerbated the situation.

2.   The US federal budget deficit is about $3.4 trillion: income is about $1.6 trillion, and outflow is about $5 trillion. On the other hand, does a budget surplus exist, as many politicians would have you believe? Additionally, the federal budget further demonstrates the severity of the health care cost problem as a percentage of the national budget: Social Security, 21%; national debt interest, 20%; Medicare and Medicaid, 16%; defense spending, 15%; domestic spending, 15%; miscellaneous spending, 11%; and international spending, 2%.

3.   Increased administrative costs and advancements in technology. The primary use of new technology has been in the areas of diagnosis and treatment. However, HMOs also use technology to increase operational efficiency and reduce costs. The price paid is in the loss of jobs or reduction in the skill level needed to perform certain tasks, formerly done by trained technicians, nurses, or physicians.

4.   Malpractice phobia, misinformed patients, hungry trial lawyers, and class action lawsuits. A recent issue of *Jury Verdict Research* contained statistics for 1996 jury awards for medical malpractice claims. The median award for all medical negligence claims increased by 14% over 1995 and in childbirth cases was $1.3 million, more than double the median for any other type of medical malpractice verdict. Other median awards were

- $621,000 for medication errors.
- $508,000 for misdiagnosis cases.
- $250,000 for surgical negligence.
- $250,000 for nonsurgical treatment cases.
- $250,000 for cases involving doctor/patient relations.
- $568,000 median award for all medical malpractice cases.

5.   Cultural and socioeconomic timing (i.e., medical care is a right, not a privilege) as some patients or employers may not be willing to pay the price for good medical care. According to Steven Wetzell, of the St. Paul, Minnesota, employer-initiated Buyers Healthcare Action Group (BHCAG), even seemingly small health care premium amounts matter. For example, the difference between his group's high- and low-cost health care plan was only about $19 per member/per month, yet every one of his low-cost provider groups gained enrollment last year, whereas all high-cost providers lost enrollment, up to 18%. It was the BHCAG experience that price was the driver of health plans enrollment, even more than patient satisfaction.

Domestic Productivity Crippled by Exploding Health Care Costs

Traditional organizations, except for the military, provided a type of insurance known as *indemnity insurance*, which has the following features: (a) the insured individual has the ability to choose the physician and the hospital he or she wants to visit and (b) Medical providers are paid a separate fee for every service provided, as long as it is covered by the patient's benefit plan. Under the system of indemnity (fee-for-service) reimbursement, the implication was that it was the doctor's fault if he or she was not paid, and it was the doctor's problem if the medical needs of the patient were not met.

Although confusing, the system gave patients great freedom and give MDs great incentive to supply care, but insurers had little control over the care that was rendered and its associated costs. Health care costs skyrocketed to more than $900 billion, or 15% of GNP, by 1999–2000, crippling US productivity. For example, consider that Medicare in 1999 costs $250 billion and is projected to be fiscally insolvent by 2008, when health care spending will have reached $2 trillion, or 17%–18% of US GDP. Currently, it has enough to "pay" medical benefits for about 10 months, but in reality it cannot pay anything. This creates a rising burden on the young, who subsidize treatment for the old and middle-aged. Workers under 65 pay most taxes, and even among workers there are generational subsidies. In 1998, workers 45–64 years old with employer-paid insurance had health costs twice those of workers 18–44, since the young have wages reduced because of elders' insurance costs. Moreover, consider that since 1963, in the Medicare system alone, the following happened:

1. Workers contributing to the system decreased from 6:1 to 2:1.
2. Enrollees increased from 20 million to 37 million, and the total is still climbing.
3. The elderly population increased from 9% to 13% of the US population.
4. The average life span increased from 70 to 77 years.

The Medicare Trust Fund increased from $3 billion to $132 billion. (This is not really a trust fund but actually an accounting fiction; technically, the fund holds interest-earning US government bonds, representing a $200 million accounting surplus of payroll taxes collected in 1998 minus benefits paid. But these are very special bonds as the trustees cannot sell them on Wall Street and can only hand them back to the US Treasury. This does not increase the size of Uncle Sam's wallet because every trust fund asset is a Treasury liability. For the government as a whole, the asset and liabilities net out to zero, and if the trust fund were abolished, there would be no effect on private bondholders or economic activity. The government would not be relieved of any existing obligations or commitments. The bonds are essentially IOUs the government has written to itself.)

Furthermore, the rising cost of health care can also be attributed to wide variability in treatment patterns that could be ascribed only to style and not to patient differences. For example, studies by John (Jack) Wennberg, MD, in the early 1970s at Dartmouth Medical School, shocked the health care community when he discovered that differences in hysterectomy, tonsillectomy, and prostatectomy rates in one county were 30%–50% higher than rates in adjacent counties. By the early 1980s, Wennberg's studies concluded that new physician incentives were needed if doctors were to provide appropriate care at acceptable costs. Nevertheless, iatrogenic factors contributing to health care cost escalation continued into the 1990s, despite rising physician incomes. For example, it is now estimated that

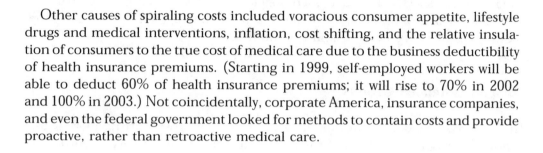

1. 53% of all surgeries may be unnecessary.
2. 36% of medical office visits may not needed.
3. 35% of all hospital admissions may be iatrogenic.
4. Medication errors abound.

Other causes of spiraling costs included voracious consumer appetite, lifestyle drugs and medical interventions, inflation, cost shifting, and the relative insulation of consumers to the true cost of medical care due to the business deductibility of health insurance premiums. (Starting in 1999, self-employed workers will be able to deduct 60% of health insurance premiums; it will rise to 70% in 2002 and 100% in 2003.) Not coincidentally, corporate America, insurance companies, and even the federal government looked for methods to contain costs and provide proactive, rather than retroactive medical care.

Medicare Cost Containment Policies

In the past, Medicare controls to stymie the cost spiral included (1) increasing medigap premium taxes, making copayment and deductibles more expensive and discouraging enrollees from obtaining first-dollar insurance coverage on medical expenses; (2) increasing supplemental medical insurance (SMI) premiums, copayments, and deductibles (cost sharing); (3) lowering physician assignment fees; (4) screening out unhealthy patients ("cherry picking" and "adverse selection"); (5) reducing beneficiary benefits (rationed care); (6) incorporating utilization review (prospective, concurrent, and retrospective) programs; (7) precertifying hospital admissions; (8) increasing the use of second opinions for surgical procedures; (9) implementing the case management of expensive disease processes; (10) organizing corporate self-insurance; (11) using direct employer contracting; (12) pushing back the age of eligibility to 67; (13) increasing the use of prepaid managed care organizations; and (14) as of January 1, 1999, the promotion of Medicare HMOs, known as Medicare+Choice plans.

Needless to say, the above cost-reduction attempts were largely ineffective, and now the Medicare/HMO precursors and their 7 million enrollees are still projected to lose money and benefits. Moreover, as the US Congress tinkers with future budgets to augment the measures noted above, there is always the potential for the incorporation of onerous medical practitioner user fee(s), as proposed below:

- $1 fee on any medical claim not submitted electronically.
- Fees for unprocessable "dirty" medical claims submissions.
- Provider registration fees.

Additionally, until about 15 years ago, traditional fiscal output-maximizing models were used by most hospitals to maximize reimbursement, according to something like the following formula.

$$\text{Hospital Cost} = \text{Costs per Service} \times \text{Services per Patient/per Day}$$
$$\times \text{Days per Admission} \times \text{Number of Admissions}$$

That is to say, third parties reimbursed hospitals for expenses already incurred, on some retrospective formula based on a lower of cost or charges (i.e., *cost-plus*) basis. Regardless of how costs were defined, this encouraged hospitals to expand, adding facilities, technology, and expenditures.

Diagnosis-Related Groups

In 1983–84, the federal government introduced a new prospective payment system known as diagnosis-related groups (DRGs) for Medicare patients. According to this system, all charges were reimbursed on a per diem diagnosis case basis. The model suggested that hospitals would minimize costs because they were at risk for any expenses incurred above the given reimbursement rate and would strive to reduce costs to an efficient level. This was unlike any hospital behavior reimbursable under the older retrospective system, and recognizing that the model predicted a tendency for hospitals to maximize the number of patients admitted, Medicare regulations made provisions for professional review to determine the necessity of care.

Under current reimbursement rules, the Health Care Finance Administration (HCFA) mandates that patients must now stay the national average length of stay for the specific DRG in order for hospitals to earn a full DRG payment. Hospitals that normally discharge faster than average have two choices: (1) retain the patient until the national average is reached (most likely), or (2) discharge the patient earlier (least likely) to incur the full cost of treatment and get a serious reduction in revenue.

Unfortunately, not being an all-payer system, hospitals shifted services and costs to non-Medicare patients, so the DRG system had system-wide ramifications beyond its intended population. Additional modification made the DRG system increasingly unwieldy, and ultimately, this cost-containment strategy was not enough. Therefore, even prior to the 1973 HMO Act, it was apparent that the health care delivery system needed more dramatic changes. A new strategy, known as *managed care*, which is an approach that links the delivery and financing of health care in order to coordinate care, was adopted.

This new approach caused insurers and providers to renounce the traditional incentives of indemnity insurance, to control costs and eliminate inefficiencies. The ideology produced what is known as the *medical reimbursement paradigm shift* because it was a dramatically different way of thinking about medical care payments. Whether this lofty goal has indeed been achieved, however, is still debatable. Nevertheless, the following types of formal and informal models exist in the managed care system, and they must be understood in order to economically survive as a business unit into the next millennium.

CONTEMPORARY HEALTH CARE ECONOMICS

> Currently, MCOs have few incentives to provide quality healthcare. Instead, incentives are in place to compete by offering the lowest possible premium or price, while providing only a minimal level of care.
>
> —Warren Greenberg, PhD, Professor of Health
> Economics, George Washington University

The physician activist Dr. Paul Ellwood aggressively advocated for and actually coined the term health maintenance organization (HMO). An HMO is a group responsible for both the financing and delivery of health services to an enrolled population. Managed care is a prospective payment method (providers, hospitals, surgical centers, vendors and ancillary care givers) whereby medical care is delivered, regardless of the quantity or frequency of service, for a fixed payment in the aggregate. It is not the individual care of the traditional indemnity insurance. It is essentially utilitarian in nature and collective in intent. Prepaid medicine is not new but rather was promoted extensively by the precursors of today's managed care revolutionaries, the so-called Four Horsemen of the Apocalypse (Walter McClure, Clark Havighurst, Alain Enthoven, and Paul Ellwood, MD). Since passage of the act, the growth of HMOs and other managed care organizations (MCOs) have increased their enrollment to more than 72 million enrollees. This represents an increase of 14% within the past year, with a 19% commercial growth rate in the prior year. The Pacific region accounts for one-fourth of all HMO members, followed by the Mid-Atlantic (18%) and the South-Atlantic (16%) regions. Individual states with the most HMO penetration are Oregon (48%), Massachusetts (45%), California (44%), and Utah (41%). States with the least penetration are Alaska (1%), Vermont (1%), Wyoming (1%), North Dakota (2%), Mississippi (2%), Montana (3%), South Dakota (3.5%), and Idaho (4%). Medicaid is one of the fastest-growing HMO products as enrollment in this field increased 34% in 1998. Medicare enrollment also grew more slowly and is expected to accelerate in the future. (See Figure 1.4.)

In fact, according to one recent study, Table 1.1 represents the percentage of reimbursement rates given to today's HMO commercial providers, by type.

According to Alain Enthoven, PhD, of Stanford University, the term *managed care* covers a wide range of options that differ dramatically in incentives offered to physicians and the methods used to control utilization and expenses.

Structurally, HMOs are often divided into two types and six subtypes. The two basic HMO types include the *command control* and *empowerment* models. In the former it is assumed that doctors must be strictly controlled, dominated, and micromanaged because they will not take responsibility for managing the quality and cost of medical care. The latter HMO type assumes the exact opposite of its physicians, giving them more latitude for independent thought and decision-making skills. The six traditional HMO subtypes are listed below.

A *staff model* HMO is the most restrictive plan, for both doctors and patients. It requires that physicians be employees and that they treat only the HMO's own members, who must be seen at centralized locations and with a closed panel of

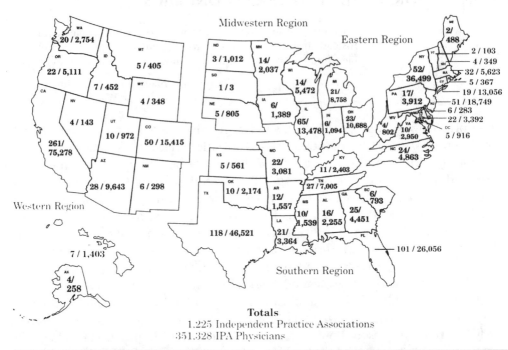

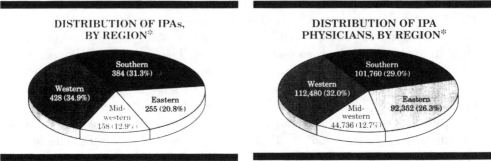

FIGURE 1.4   Distribution of IPAs and IPA physicians.

*Eastern Region consists of Connecticut, Delaware, District of Columbia, Maine, Maryland, Massachusetts, New Hampshire, New Jersey, New York, North Carolina, Pennsylvania, Rhode Island, Vermont, Virginia, and West Virginia.

Southern Region consists of Alabama, Arkansas, Florida, Georgia, Kansas, Kentucky, Louisiana, Mississippi, Missouri, Oklahoma, South Carolina, Tennessee, and Texas.

Midwestern Region consists of Illinois, Indiana, Iowa, Michigan, Minnesota, Nebraska, North Dakota, Ohio, South Dakota, and Wisconsin.

Western Region consists of Alaska, Arizona, California, Colorado, Hawaii, Idaho, Montana, Nevada, New Mexico, Oregon, Utah, Washington, and Wyoming.

NOTE: According to TIPAAA, "an independent practice association (IPA) is a group of independent private practice physicians who have created an incorporated entity for contracting with managed care organizations or performing other managed care functions. IPAs are also known as individual physician associations."

Data source: Physician Groups & Networks Database, Center for Healthcare Information and The IPA Association of American © 1998.

From *1998 Hoechst Marion Roussel Managed Care Digest Series.* Reprinted by permission of the publisher, Hoechst Marion Roussel, Inc.

TABLE 1.1 HMO Commercial Providers' Reimbursement Rates

PCPs	All	Staff	IPAs	Networks	Groups
Capitation	47%	8%	40%	77%	51%
Fee Service	29%	7%	40%	21%	2%
RVS	8%	0%	9%	2%	0%
Salary	7%	85%	0%	0%	36%
Other	9%	0%	11%	0%	11%

Source: Medical Interface, Bronxville, New York, September 1998.

providers. It is in market decline because of its lack of flexibility. In a *group model* the doctors are not employees but may treat non-HMO members and work out of private offices. In a *network model*, the HMO contracts with the MDs, who may or may not have an exclusive relationship with it and may be in a closed or open panel. An *independent practice association (IPA) model* is built around a group of independent physicians who retain the right to see other patients. They comprise an open panel in which doctors retain their own separate self-administered offices. In a *direct contract* HMO the provider's practice is similar to the IPA model, but the HMO administrators have a direct contract with each participating MD, who may or may not retain the right to see non-HMO patients and practice in a variety of settings. Finally, the least restrictive, the *mixed model*, HMO, represents a combination of the above five HMO types.

Employee Retirement Income Security Act

When dealing with the major medical programs, one must be cognizant of the Employee Retirement Income Security Act of 1972 (ERISA—IRC 404[c]), which determines whether the third party is an insurance company or an ERISA organization; state laws through the Freedom of Choice acts (FCA) preclude discrimination on the part of insurance companies. Since ERISA programs are covered under federal law, they are not subject to the act. Generally, patients can sue health plans and employers in federal court, though not in state court, for the cost of a denied benefit, legal fees, and court costs but not for compensatory or punitive damages. They can also sue doctors for malpractice in state court. Federal employees may sue the Office of Personnel Management (OPM) in federal court only for the amount of denied coverage, plus attorney and court costs. If it loses, the OPM can obtain a court order to require the insurer to pay. Thus, ERISA has shielded nongovernmental health plans from punitive and compensatory damages in state courts. This is known as the ERISA exemption and has allowed MCOs to flourish.

Recently, cracks seem to be starting in the exemption. In 1998 a US district judge upheld a Texas law allowing patients to sue a managed care plan for medical malpractice. The judge's decision did limit lawsuits to cases in which negligence occurs in the actual performance (commission) of medical services, not necessarily the withholding (omission) of services. To date, no cases have been brought under it.

Preferred Provider Organizations

A *preferred provider organization* (PPO) is a bridge between traditional indemnity insurance and an HMO. There are several different types that attempt to feature the provider choices seen in indemnity insurance with the cost reductions seen in HMOs. Two similar entities, known as an *exclusive provider organization* (EPO) and a *point of service* plan (POS) or *swing out* plan (SOP), consist of an exclusive provider panel that has agreed to accept a deep discount in medical fees in return for the volume of patients the plans can provide. A combination of these models has been very successful for many employers and is not restricted by the HMO Act. A payment time line for a typical PPO may look something like the following: Health care provider bills PPO → PPO bills company → company pays PPO → PPO pays provider.

Changes in Medical Payment Delivery Models

As payments have shifted from the older fee-for-service model to the newer managed care capitation model, the following differences have been observed (see Figure 1.5).

Traditional (Fee-for-Service) Methodology

Characteristics include the following:

1. Full fee for service rendered as medical payment.
2. Illnesses and diseases treated, retroactively.
3. Individual patients treated.
4. Active and acute diagnoses made.
5. Medical care rendered in the office or hospital setting.
6. Referrals to specialist made in difficult cases.

Contemporary (Managed Care-Capitation) Methodology

The per member/per month (PM/PM) medical capitation model requires the payment of a fixed sum of money to a medical provider to cover a defined set of health care services for an individual enrollee over a defined period of time. Under PM/PM capitation the doctor assumes the risk for the incidence (utilization rate) of medical conditions requiring procedures specified in the MCO contract. Characteristics are listed below:

1. Discounted payment from HMOs and MCOs.
2. Illnesses prevented proactively.
3. Population cohorts treated collectively, not individually.
4. Chronic disease intervention before acute disease exacerbates.
5. Care rendered in networks, the home, or other subacute care facility.
6. Outcomes evaluated on the basis of results, not specialty care.

GROUP PRACTICES WITH HMO/PPO CONTRACTS

SIZE (# of FTE Physicians)	Type of Managed Care Contract				
	PPO	IPA HMO	Network HMO	Group HMO	Staff HMO
10 or fewer	85.1%	49.8%	52.2%	37.8%	16.1%
11–25	80.5	43.4	48.7	40.7	19.5
26–50	79.6	44.9	51.0	42.9	20.4
51–100	85.2	63.0	66.7	29.6	14.8
101 or more	70.4	44.4	48.1	29.6	11.1
SPECIALTY COMPOSITION					
Single Specialty	87.2%	53.6%	56.0%	41.4%	19.3%
Multispecialty	80.2	44.2	45.7	33.8	14.3
ALL GROUPS	**83.6%**	**48.9%**	**50.8%**	**37.6%**	**16.8%**

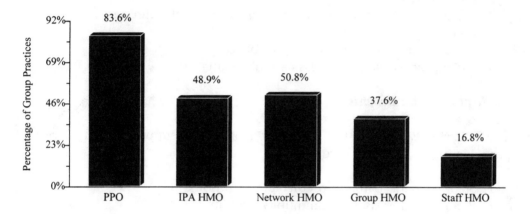

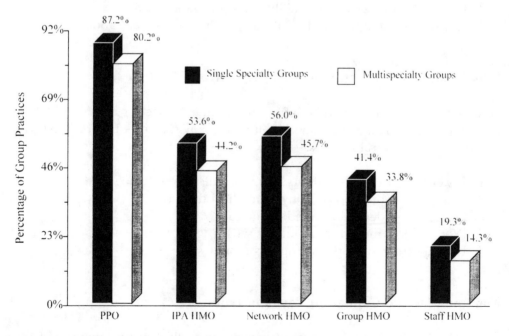

FIGURE 1.5   Group practices with HMO/PPO contracts.

Data source: Medical Group Management Association Member Database, 1997 © 1998.
From *1998 Hoechst Marion Roussel Managed Care Digest Series.* Reprinted by permission of the publisher, Hoechst Marion Roussel, Inc.

Under PM/PM capitation, the MD is at risk for (a) utilization and acuity, (b) actuarial accuracy, (c) cost of delivering medical care, and (d) adverse patient selection.

MCO Carrier Benefits

Some of the benefits for corporate America (payers), which supplies the majority of health insurance to its employees (insureds), are listed below:

1. Known medical expenses (fixed, not variable, costs) to companies.
2. Risks and benefits of patient compliance borne by MD/providers, not corporate America.
3. Fewer administrative staff needs because medical claims are no longer reviewed.
4. Costs reduced through economies of scale.
5. Patients controlled and MDs carefully managed.

Medical Provider Benefits

The following is a brief list of the benefits physicians supposedly may derive by participating in managed care plans.

1. Stable patient load and predictable cash flows.
2. Potential referrals and community visibility.
3. Reduced office expenses, liability, and utilization review.
4. Reputation equivalency (i.e., all doctors in the plan are good).

Why Health Care Practitioners Are Disenfranchised

Despite the above purported benefits, anecdotal evidence suggests that MDs are less happy about managed care and their profession, than ever before (see Figure 1.6). There are several reasons:

1. Fewer fee-for-service patients and more discounted patients.
2. More paperwork and scrutiny of medical decisions.
3. Lost independence and medical morale.
4. Profession of medicine no longer satisfying.
5. Health care providers making less money.

Manipulating the Capitation Payment Numbers

Since MCOs pay a fixed amount of money, regardless of the quantity of care provided (i.e., capitation), we can begin to explore how reimbursement issues have been dramatically changed under this new payment paradigm.

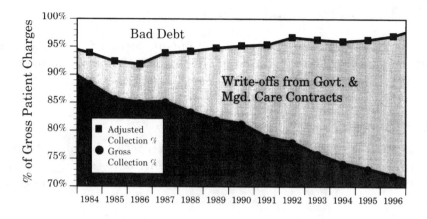

FIGURE 1.6 Why health care practitioners are disenfranchised: bad debt, write-offs from government and managed care contracts, and gross fee-for-service collections.

Data source: Medical Group Management Association Cost Survey: 1997 Report Based on 1996 Data © 1997. From *1998 Hoechst Marion Roussel Managed Care Digest Series*. Reprinted by permission of the publisher, Hoechst Marion Roussel, Inc.

Example

For simplification, suppose, as a chiropractor, Dr. Kosmicky received an MCO contract to evaluate, and the following numbers were supplied to him by the MCO:

- Capitation Range = 5 per 125 cents ($1.25) per member/per month (PM/PM)
- 10,000 Lives @ 30 cts./pt/month/year
- 5% Patient encounter rate (range = 2.5–7.5%)

The following is the financial yield possible from this contract:

- $10,000 (5%) = 500 visits/yr. or 41 visits/mo. or 10/week
- $10,000 × .30 = $3,000/month or $36,000/year
- $72 average per new patient (NP)

NP = 3 visits/year average = $24 per old patient visit.

Now, a capitation analysis might evolve to look something like the following, if the doctor is able to treat the numbers of patients given in the example below, by accepting additional similar contracts.

- $24/patient × 3 patients/hour = $72 hour
- 72 patients × 8 hours = $576/day
- $576 × 5 days/week = $2,880/week
- $2,880/4 weeks/month = $11,520/month

- $11,520 \times 12$ months = $138,240/year

In other words, the provider becomes a quasi-employee of the HMOs and is reduced to an hourly worker; even though he may yield increased compensation, at the indicated volume demonstrated below:

6 patient/hours/48 day = $276,480 per year
9 patient/hours/72 day = $414,720 per year

Also realize that many times the doctor does not even derive the full $72 economic benefit from new patient visits, since most patients have already been in the existing practice. *The result is simply an across-the-board wholesale fee reduction for the practice.*

Dr. Kosmicky also recognizes that this rate is based on averages, and he will receive no additional payment if all members of a single contract visit him more than three times a year; nor is his payment reduced if they don't visit him at all. The rate is reasonably close to his normal office fee of $30, so he accepts the financial risk of the contract.

To further illustrate the contentious point of physician compensation reduction, consider the September 11, 1998, AMA-sponsored lawsuit by the Medical Association of Georgia on behalf of its physicians when Blue Cross and Blue Shield of Georgia reduced reimbursement rates on its indemnity insurance plan, affecting 13,480 doctors. In effect, older methods of compensation are being made obsolete by capitation. These include the following:

- Productivity-based systems (majority of practices).
- Fixed salary system.
- Equal distribution of revenue among partners.
- Individual contracts for each MD.

A recent study by the Medical Group Management Association confirmed that neither primary care physicians nor specialists appear immune to the downward compensation trend in medicine, as seen in Table 1.2.

Point of Service Plans

Capitation offers the same advantages to POS ("unmanaged care") plans as it does to HMOs, but it is more risky for the provider. The main reason for the

TABLE 1.2   Percentage Change in Medical Physician Compensation (1993–97)

Year	1993–94	1994–95	1995–96	1996–97	93–97
All primary care	2.7 %	4.46%	1.42%	0.86%	9.26%
All specialties	2.34%	1.79%	2.58%	−0.48%	6.34%

discrepancy is medical risk acceptance without considering POS peculiarities. For example, these plans, unlike HMOs, allow out-of-network services, and POS managers and providers must pay the unmanaged outside contractors in addition to the discounted in-service physicians. Reinsurance is useful, but these plans tend to be chronically short of capital, and as a result, 7%–10% higher operating costs than traditional HMOs should be expected.

Physician Hospital Organizations

A physician hospital organization (PHO) is a blend of private doctors and hospitals, maintaining its concentration and control of surgical rather than medical care. Ownership may be divided by a governing board according to a pro-rata basis, with the larger partner having most organizational strength and bargaining power in the corporate structure. Typically, this favors the hospital. From a strategic standpoint, most MDs are still not currently aligned with PHOs, because surgical care is increasingly being delivered in private offices or ambulatory surgery centers (ASCs). Additionally, PHOs may become potential MD competitors, often lack managed care contracting experience, have inflexible provider networks, and may require MD exclusivity in their organization. (See Table 1.3.)

Medical Networks and IPAs

In an attempt to increase market share and augment profits, some doctors contemplate forming independent physician associations (IPAs). The benefits of these organizations include the following: (1) there are marketing and advertising benefits with reduced equipment costs through economies of large scale for equipment, (2) the network pays the MD/DO directly, (3) there is no need for individual negotiations, (4) a patient and cash flow stream is available, and (5) a collective group autonomy exists.

On the other hand, potential risks include the fact that the MD/DO is not capitated but the physician pool likely will be. This merely means that the per unit price of each medical intervention will likely decrease as individual doctors in the pool compete for its limited resources ("managed competition"). Other

TABLE 1.3 Functions of PHOs, by Percentage

54% negotiate managed care contracts
45% negotiate on all health insurance contracts
40% serve as an MSO
27% establish own insurance product(s)
22% employ doctors and support staff
12% consolidate and acquire physician practices
05% acquire alternative medical practices

Modified from *Modern Physician*, October 1998.

disadvantages are (1) variable income due to the managed competition described above; (2) 10%–20% administrative fee, payable in cash, to the IPA managers; (3) reduced and discounted fee schedules; and (4) lost personal autonomy.

Obviously, signs of insolvent networks include (1) delayed data entry, (2) telephone or facsimile delays, (3) slow payment schedules, (4) poor expense tracking, (5) insufficient MIS and software, and (6) sparse interest statements or financial information.

Management Service Organizations

Most management service organizations (MSOs) for doctors are organized as IPAs. Under such plans, the MDs make the rules, regulations, and medical care guidelines, and MSO administrators (MBAs, CPAs, MHAs, CFPs, and CMAs) administer those policies. Centralized data are collected, and the organization is responsible for utilization review, quality control, and eligibility verification and payment. The MSO is more of a broker, working for the physicians in the plan—marketing, selling, and running it on a daily basis. This leaves the MDs unfettered to provide patient care, for a price that is typically 10%–18% of net patient revenues per month.

A practitioner may be a candidate for an MSO organization if he or she possesses most of the following characteristics: excellent medical education; management and leadership skills; practice in a large, multidoctor group with rising net income; possession of current management information and technology systems with gross margins exceeding 50%–55%; ancillary services such as a wound care center or ambulatory surgery center; age under 45 years; and desire to practice medicine into the future. Finally, the provider should have some business savvy and practice in an area with relatively weak MCO market penetration. Any provider should also consider joining an MSO if his or her future professional outlook is optimistic and positive.

FUTURISTIC HEALTH CARE ECONOMICS FOR THE NEW MILLENNIUM

> The most important reform we can make to the US healthcare system is not a new set of laws or regulations, but a fundamental change in attitude.
>
> —William C. Steere Jr., CEO, Pfizer, Inc.

Uwe Reinhardt, PhD, James Madison Professor of Political Economics at Princeton University and an opponent of MCO liability, opined that in the near future there will be a three-tier system of medical care in the United States. The bottom tier will consist of the uninsured and uninsurable (45 million as of July 1999), the middle tier will be served by MCOs, and the top tier will continue to demand traditional (indemnity) fee-for-service medicine. Regardless of the future model(s) of care, the goals of any optimal health care economic policy should include the following characteristics: (1) low-demand barriers of price, travel, wait time, referral ease and paperwork; (2) adequacy of supply regarding medical personnel, clinics, drugs, and equipment; (3) technical efficiencies such as service mix; (4) public expenditure control with tax reductions; and (5) quality of care for the common social good. The following machinations might prove useful in the future.

More Medicaid Cost-Containment Policies

Some state governments have applied for and received special waivers from the federal government (Department of Health and Human Resources) forcing more than 22 million Medicaid enrollees to various managed care risk plans. The resulting fixed payment methodology is usually varied, with states using a "take it or leave it" or "bid" payment methodology to further reduce costs. Under the former method, states offer the same payment structure to all HMO plans. Under the latter method, HMO plans submit a proposed payment schedule within the state's predefined range, preventing lowball underbidding (promoting underutilization) or overbidding (promoting excessive profits). Pricing floors and ceilings are effectively created in this manner.

UTILIZATION OF MEDICARE PRIVATE ACCOUNTS

According to Texas A&M health care economists Thomas R. Saving and Andrew J. Rettenmaier, today's young people could replace Medicare with private insurance if they saved about $600/year (2% average earnings) in private accounts. For each dollar deposited into the account, the Medicare payroll tax could be reduced by a dollar. The government would deposit the difference for those not able to afford the contribution. The accounts would be conservatively invested to grow with the economy as a whole. Upon retirement, participants could then choose from options such as traditional or managed Medicare, HMOs, PPOs, or whatever model existed at the time of enrollment. This private account option would secure health benefits if begun now. If not, according to Boston University economist Laurence Kotlikoff, Medicare payroll taxes could be increased up to 55% (probably uncollectable), and/or severe rationing would occur for the future elderly.

Spread of Specific Episode Capitation

Under the specific episode of care (SEC) capitation model, MD providers deliver care for covered enrollees with a specific medical condition or for those who require a particular treatment intervention on a fixed basis per episode. Many believe this concept will grow in the future.

Adoption of Full-Risk Capitation

For many physicians, the future might include full-risk medical care contacts. In this payment system, the participant agrees to provide "all" of the care for a given patient population or contract. In other words, the MD would have to include services such as diabetic management, traumatology, radiology, emergency care, pediatric immunizations, geriatrics, home I.V. antibiotics, DME (durable medical equipment) and all specialty care in the consideration of this full-risk contract. Of course, increased benefits accompany the increased risk. The risks: all medical and surgical care necessary for the contracted population. Since there is the potential for more reward but with much more risks, the physician business executive must carefully consider these contract types and maintain the following relative contingencies:

1. Stop-loss reinsurance.
2. 15–50-mile coverage radius.
3. Subcapitated medical specialists with deep discounts.
4. 25–100 providers in the network.
5. 100–250,000 patient population or more (more patients mean less risk).
6. Subcapitated hospitals, surgical centers, pharmacies, and DME vendors with discounts.
7. Encompass a small (< 20%–25%) portion of the practice.

Certainly, this system does not bode well for the solo practitioner or even for small medical group practices.

Development of Social HMOs

Social HMOs offer extended coverage for some of the unconventional expenses associated with senior health care, such as transportation and in-home day care, that are not covered by traditional MCOs. One such plan is Elderplan, in Brooklyn, New York. According to the American Association of Health Plans (AAHP), social HMOs provide coordinated services by uniting federal and state funds and services to benefit the elderly.

Proliferation of Fraudulent Silent ("Mirror") Health Care Models

A silent, *faux*, or "mirror" PPO, HMO, or other provider model is not really a formalized MCO at all! Rather, it is simply an intermediary attempt to negotiate practitioner fees downward, by promising a higher volume of patients in exchange for the discounted fee structure. Of course, the intermediary then resells the packaged contract product to any willing insurance company, HMO, PPO, or other payer, thereby pocketing the difference as a nice profit. Sometimes these virtual organizations are just indemnity companies in disguise. Physicians should not fall for this ploy, since pricing pressure will be forced even lower in the next round of "real" PPO negotiations!

Occasionally, an insurer or bold insurance agent will enter a market and tell its practitioners that they have signed up all or many of the local major employers. Then they'll go to the employers and give them the same story about signing up all the major providers. The real case is that they haven't signed up either, and a Ponzi-like situation is created! Providers should be on guard for silent HMOs, MCOs, and any other silent insurance variation, because these virtual organizations do not exist except as exploitable arbitrage situations for the middleman.

Use of the "Hospitalist" or Hospital-Based Medical Groups

Inpatient care in this country has usually meant hospitalized patients cared for by their primary care or admitting physician. Although this model has the advantage of continuity and perhaps personalization, it often suffered because of the limited knowledge base of the physician as well as lack of familiarity with the available internal and external resources of the hospital. Furthermore, the limited time spent with each individual patient prevented the physician from becoming the quality leader in this setting. These shortcomings have led hundreds of hospitals around the country to turn to the hospitalists as dedicated inpatient specialists. The National Association of Inpatient Physicians (NAIP) now estimates that there are approximately 3,000 hospitalists in America, and future projections estimate that full adoption of the model could result in up to 30,000 hospitalists nationally by 2001.

The term *hospitalist* was coined by Dr. Robert M. Wachter of the University of California at San Francisco in 1996. It denotes a specialist in inpatient medicine. At its center is the concept of low cost and comprehensive broad-based care in the hospital, hospice, or even extended care setting. If well designed, hospitalist programs can offer benefits beyond the often cited inpatient efficiencies they bring. For example, the average length of stay for patients on the medical service of UCSF's Moffitt-Long Hospital fell by 15%, compared to concurrent and historical controls adjusted for case mix. There was no reported decrease in patient satisfaction or clinical outcomes. However, a recent coalition of 23 specialty medical organizations urged all managed care organizations to oppose mandatory programs, as established in Florida, Maryland, Missouri, and Texas. Led by the Washington-based American College of Physicians and the American Society of Internal Medicine, the movement has legitimate concerns regarding buy-in, compensation, communication, liability and logistics, which must be answered before wholesale benefits of the hospitalist concept can be realized.

Similarly, another integration model is on-site employee affiliations, which represent an adjustment of the hospitalist concept. This redeployment of existing MDs into the workplace (factory, police station, office building) or retail setting (Wal-Mart) is another exciting challenge in heath care today. The keys to success are thoughtful implementation and a commitment to measure the results of change and use the data to produce further changes.

Increased Physician Union Clout

Health care practitioners of all types have accused both their national and state societies of being slow to respond to their changing needs. In 1962, for example, 82% of physicians belonged to the American Medical Association. Today the figure is about 43%. Now, fully 42% of contemporary physicians are employees and are therefore no longer as dependent on traditional medical societies for credentialing, quality review, practice management, or malpractice assistance. Thus, the strength of medical societies is diminishing, and as practitioners move into employment positions, the enhanced role of unionization has arisen. Although the AMA has removed barriers to collective bargaining, it is still adamantly opposed to strikes. Traditional constraints, under the National Labor Relations Act and other antitrust laws are being litigated, and prominent unionization campaigns are occurring across the country. Congress has even recently hosted a plenary panel of leaders from the country's most significant physician unions, representing about 45,000 union members.

For example, unions, like the Federation of Physicians and Dentists (FPD), an 8,000-member Tallahassee, Florida–based affiliate of the AFL-CIO, can represent fee-for-service physicians as third-party negotiators, but current laws prohibit independent contractors from collective bargaining on their behalf.

On the other hand, in a recent example of federal strength, the National Labor Relations Board, in Philadelphia, rejected a labor union's (Local 56—United Food and Commercial Workers, Pennsauken, New Jersey), request to represent a group of 400-plus New Jersey physicians in negotiation with a Mount Laurel, New Jersey–based HMO. The physicians would have been the first private-practice independent practitioners to gain that right, which is limited to salaried doctors at large HMOs and public hospitals. Currently, the decision is under appeal.

Most recently, the American Osteopathic Association (AOA) and the American Chiropractic Association (ACA) has decided to avoid the union fray, and the DOs and DCs have not joined the ranks of their allopathic union brethren. A similar union for podiatrists (doctors of podiatric medicine) is the First National Guild for Healthcare Providers of the Lower Extremity (Local 45), which is under the umbrella of the Office and Professional Employees International Union (OPEIU). It is attempting to unite the nation's DPMs and other specialists under the AFL-CIO banner and currently has more than 22,000 affiliated members in 16 states.

Although the number of unionized physicians is still low, unionized nurses (RNs) are commonplace, and nurses are also not timid about striking (Grady Memorial Hospital, Atlanta, and Kaiser Permanente, Los Angeles). As with physicians, grievances include staff reduction and care quality issues.

Professional Practice Management Corporations

Many experts believe that HMOs may have reached a limit in their ability to squeeze physician compensation. The past few years have seen the birth of a new industry known as professional practice management corporations (PPMCs). In PPMCs, physicians join together to regain clout in their dealings with MCOs. PPMCs provide management services to private practices and attempt to acquire and consolidate individual practices in selected geographic markets. PPMCs provide comprehensive long-term management, as well as administrative, financial, information, and service solutions, to successfully navigate the challenging health care environment. Although the MD controls the practice, the PPMC provides important products and services, such as electronic connectivity; management support; cost, quality, and outcomes reporting; payer contracting; nonmedical support; long-term strategic and joint venture development; and marketing, public relations, and advertising capacities. All are beyond the scope of the solo practice, and the economies of scale generated can be significant.

PPMCs come at some cost, however, typically on a pro-rated gross or net revenue basis, often in excess of 20%–35%. Some lost independence occurs as well. Still, many economic and business authorities believe that local or regional, rather than national, consolidation of the profession, through an integrated business model, is the next logical generation of development. This appears true (despite many multispecialty and national PPMC economic debacles in the last half of 1998) if doctors are to regain their rightful place as "conductors of the nation's health care symphony."

Patient Bounty Hunters

Under a new program from the Health Insurance Portability Accountability Act, the Department of Health and Human Service (HHS) began a new Incentive Program for Fraud and Abuse Information in January 1999. Under this program, HHS will pay $100–$1,000 to Medicare recipients who report abuse in the program. To assist patients in spotting fraud, HHS has published examples of potential fraud, which include the following:

- Medical services not provided.
- Duplicate services or procedures.
- More expenses services or procedures than provided (upcoding/billing).
- Misused Medicare cards and numbers.
- Medical telemarketing scams.
- Nonmedical necessity.

To discourage flagrant allegations, regulations require that reported information directly contribute to monetary recovery for activities not already under investigation. Nevertheless, expect a further erosion of patient confidence as they begin to view themselves as "bounty hunters."

Managed Care "Backlash"

According to a recently published national study by the MEDSTAT Group and JD Power and Associates, which surveyed nearly 30,000 physicians participating in 150 health care plans and located in 22 different markets, nearly 7 of 10 physicians considered themselves "anti-managed care." Dissatisfaction with financial reimbursement was the leading factor, but four other major factors drive physicians' rating of health plans, as listed below:

42% dissatisfaction with financial reimbursement

26% administration

11% policies impacting on care quality

11% support of clinical practice

10% limits on care

Nevertheless, do not think that HMOs will be unresponsive to this managed care backlash. In 1998, managed care companies and their allies fought against restrictive new proposed regulations and spent $112,000 per lawmaker to lobby Congress. This $60 million outlay was four times the $14 million plus spent by medical organizations, trial lawyers ($1 million), unions ($1.4 million), and consumer groups ($8 million) to press for passage of the so-called Patients' Bill of Rights. The $60 million lobbying tab is 50% higher than the $40 million that tobacco interests spent to kill legislative attempts to raise cigarette taxes to curb teenage smoking!

Globalized Managed Care?

It is generally acknowledged that US health care technology is the envy of the world. However, many other countries feel that too much emphasis is being placed on efficiency rather than care, and citizens who can afford indemnity insurance still prefer the traditional model of delivery. According to Mark H. Tabak, CEO of International Managed Care Advisors, Inc., it would be good if MCOs could change this image, especially in the global health care community. For example, many experts feel that managed care inroads can be made in South America, Western Europe, Eastern Europe, Asia, and other places where the telecommunications, airports, power generators, or transportation infrastructures are already in place. These nations "have overlooked the most basic and fundamental infrastructure item, which is access to healthcare." "If you can really change your image, and put health on the top priority instead of costs, it is good for the US and it is also good for the international perception." Since managed care is becoming dramatically restrained and the exponential growth rate of the past is over, many companies are looking overseas for revitalization of the industry.

According to Rachel Pentin-Maki, RN, MHA, a health care advisor based in Lantana, Florida, "The globalization of managed care represents the next paradigm shift in healthcare economics."

Concluding Remarks ("Stay the Course")

As can be seen from the above, it is important for health care providers to stay informed and current as to the volatile direction that health care is taking in this country. It is vital for every physician to learn as much about medically related business and financial topics as possible. Several medical schools have even initiated business certification and degree programs; and other medical colleges, along with the private sector, will do the same. This will allow the profession to make the transition from a supply-based medical system to a demand-driven one. It will also ensure that practices are operated as a strategic business unit (SBU) and not like the "home office" medical practices of the past.

In fact, according to Dr. Regina E. Herzilinger, professor of healthcare economics at Harvard Business School, the trend in managed care now appears to be moving toward giving control back to physicians who "stay the course" and continue to practice medicine. For example, of 800 small business executives surveyed in 1998 by the Kaiser-Harvard Program on Public and Health Social Policy, 89% favored legislation requiring health plans to divulge operating information, an independent appeals process was favored by 88%, and 61% believed that patients should be able to sue health plans for malpractice, regardless of the ERISA exemption. More important, this espousal of health care legislation manifests in executive willingness to pay some of the increased premiums for improved coverage.

However, many physicians, nurses, and health care workers don't see it this way and become depressed. Pragmatically, the future health care industrial complex will offer great opportunities to change medicine for the better. One way to accomplish this goal is to master the concepts of third-party reimbursement and learn the new language of business, accounting, negotiation, marketing, information technology, and capitation finances. The remaining chapters of this book will assist in the endeavor.

REFERENCES AND READINGS

American Osteopathic Association, (312) 202-8191 or www.am-osteo-assn.org.

APMA Alert, November 23, 1998.

Beamon, K. Navigating uncharted waters (a tale of seniors, MCOs and Medicare managed care). *Managed Healthcare News*, 14(10), 1998.

Coppola, N. M., Croft, T., & Leo, E. Understanding the uninsured dilemma. *MGM Journal*, September 1997, p. 72.

DeNelsky, S. J. And then came the hospitalists. *Managed Healthcare News*, 14(10), 1998.

Dunevitz, B. Physician compensation stays flat for second year straight. *MGMA Update*, October 1998.

Ellwood, P. Models for organizing health services and implications for legislative proposals. *Milbank Memorial Fund Quarterly*, 50:73–100, 1972.

Enthoven, A. Why not the Clinton health plan? *Inquiry*, summer 1994, pp. 129–134.

Gallagher, A. On their own: Bucking the trend to join groups, some doctors are staying solo. *Modern Physician*, November 1998.

Glavin, M. J. Healthcare in a free society. *Journal of Hillside College*, 4:1–9, 1995.

Goodman, J. C. Why your grandchildren may pay a 55% payroll tax. *WSJ*, October 7, 1998.

Green, J. Americans polled favor market driven delivery system reform. *American Hospital Association*, 5:1, 1994.

Greenberg, W. Market failure in managed care. *Managed Healthcare News*, 14(10), 1998.

Henderson, L. Those who do, teach. *Managed Healthcare News*, 14:8, 1998.

Hilsenrath, P. E., & Destigter, M. Oligopsony, health insurance and anti-trust. *MGM Journal*, March 1996.

Hultman, J. *Here's how, Doctor.* Los Angeles: Medical Business Advisors Publishing, 1995.

Jacobs, P. *The economics of health and medical care*, 3rd ed. Gaithersburg, MD: Aspen Publishers, 1986.

Kaiser Foundation. Document 1403, 1998.

Kurtz, E. *Managed Healthcare News*, November 1998.

Lewin, L. S. A paler shade of gray (or, returning the physician to the center of healthcare). *MGM Journal*, September 1998, p. 60.

Marcinko, D. E. A brief history of healthcare economics in the US. Data Trace Publishing. *Foot and Ankle Quarterly*, Volume 12, No 1, 1999.

Marcinko, D. E. *Profit maximization and reimbursement.* Columbus, OH: Anadem Publishers, 1998.

McGinley, L., & Cloud, D. J. US takes aim at HMO fraud in Medicare and Medicaid. *Wall Street Journal*, October 19, 1998.

Modern Physician. August, September, October, 1998.

Moore, P. L. MCO liability harmful for long term growth. *MGMA Newsletter*, October 1998.

On health. Price Waterhouse newsletter, spring 1998.

Peele, R. Podiatric medicine and the guild. *APMA News*, December 1998.

Piturro, M. Changing the game. Steve Wetzell of BHCAG offers a new twist on healthcare. *Managed Healthcare News.* November 1998.

Rabinowitz, E. Calling all geriatricians. *Managed Healthcare News*, November 1998.

Salant, J. D. Managed care reform foes spend $60 million. *AJC*, November 28, 1998.

Shalmali, P. Market dynamics shake up demand for specialist. *Biomechanics*, October 1998.

Shea, W. F. Managed care's people problem. *Managed Healthcare News*, November 1998.

Starr, P. *The logic of healthcare reform.* Knoxville, TN: Whittle Direct Books, 1992.

Sterling, J. The seven deadly sins of physician practice management. *MGM Journal*, September 1998, p. 17.

Sturm, M. G. Recent Medicaid payment developments. *MGM Journal*, September 1998, p. 8.

Swartzberg, M. J. Employee assistance program. *MGM Journal*, March 1996.

Targovnik, D. It's a small managed care world. *Managed Healthcare News*, 14:9, 1998.

Wachter, R. M. *Hospital medicine.* Baltimore: Lippincott/Williams and Wilkins, 1999.

Wachter, R. M., & Goldman, L. The emerging role of hospitalists in the American health care system. *NJM*, 335:154–157, 1996.

Wilkerson, J. D., Devers, K. J., & Given, R. S. *Competitive managed care: The emerging healthcare system.* San Francisco: Josey-Bass Publishers, 1998.

## CHAPTER 2

Restrictive Covenants and Practice Non-Compete Agreements

Are They Still Necessary or Worthwhile?

Frederick Wm. LaCava

> The greatest peril to American healthcare today lies not in one reform, but in one grand strategy.
>
> —Professor Richard A. Epstein, University of Chicago

T he angriest individuals I have ever met in my life are parties to litigation over covenants not to compete. Not medical malpractice cases, not even divorces, produce the fury, the expense, the feelings of betrayal and fraud that infect doctors fighting over whether, if, and how a paragraph in what was once a friendly business deal should be interpreted. The anger and grief probably spring from a failure of the parties to achieve a mutual understanding at the time the agreement was negotiated. These covenants are still necessary, but overreaching by one side or the other leads to terrible legal conflicts.

DEFINITION

The covenants in question are agreements that in certain circumstances one of the parties is committing himself or herself not to practice his or her profession for a period of time within a geographical area or with members of a defined population. They arise in two sets of circumstances: sale of a practice or as a term of an employment agreement. The law treats the two types quite differently, favoring agreements as part of the sale of a practice and entertaining challenges to covenants in employment contracts.

A covenant not to compete is legally based on preservation of a protectable interest in goodwill. Though goodwill is an intangible property right, it is very much a real one. Accountants and the IRS have recognized methods of quantifying it. The federal government's Fraud and Abuse enforcement arm is very interested in making sure that it is not in fact a disguised kickback, and divorce lawyers love it when divorce prompts an evaluation of marital property. Goodwill is the value attributed to an ongoing practice's name recognition, location, telephone numbers, business names, and all those things that would make a potential patient come to one doctor's office rather than another's. The law recognizes that a practitioner has the right to protect that value from a competitor who unfairly tries to appropriate it.

COVENANTS IN THE SALE OF A PRACTICE

Goodwill should be protected in the sale of a practice because much of the value of such a practice is encompassed by the element of goodwill. A practice may include a building or suite of offices, either owned or leased; the equipment, furniture, and supplies on hand; records of patients; and other financial interests. But the biggest value of a practice is the propensity of existing patients to come to that location for medical services. The goodwill has been created by the practitioners who have provided those services in the past. To the extent that patients have liked Dr. Washington and have been satisfied with his medical treatment, they will tend to come to his office after Dr. Adams has acquired the practice. A large part of what Dr. Adams has paid for is the likelihood of transfer of that patient loyalty from Dr. Washington to him. A *necessary* part of the sale of the practice, then, is a commitment from Dr. Washington not to compete with Dr. Adams in that location or nearby for some reasonable amount of time. If Dr. Adams were not to require such a commitment from Dr. Washington, Dr. Washington would be free to open a new office across the street from the old one and attract the patients who were loyal to him to come to the new office. Unless Dr. Adams only bargained for some secondhand equipment and shopworn office space, he would not have gotten the goodwill he paid for.

Covenants not to compete that are incident to the sale of a practice are favored by the law, almost universally enforced, and play a logical and necessary part of the sale or transfer of goodwill. Disputes and litigation over these covenants arise when the seller tries to find a way to get around the commitment.

For example, "Yes, I signed the covenant not to compete with Dr. Adams, but my wife, Dr. Martha Washington did not. She can start up a competing practice across the street from the old office. She doesn't use the business name 'Washington Internal Medicine Associates' that I sold to Dr. Adams; she uses 'Dr. M. Washington Internal Medicine, P.C.' I don't practice medicine in any way at her office; I just sit out in the waiting room and drink coffee and chat with the patients."

Sellers who try such tactics usually lose. In negotiating the sale of a practice, either as seller or buyer, use an attorney who is expert in the area of covenants not to compete. Don't use a real estate lawyer, your tax attorney, or your divorce attorney. Don't use your brother's former college roommate just because he would do it cheap. You would never have a psychiatrist set your broken leg, so pay for the appropriate specialist. Make sure that the terms of the covenant are reasonable. A covenant whose terms are draconian may be voided by a court, leaving the purchaser with no protection at all.

COVENANT AS PART OF EMPLOYMENT CONTRACT

A covenant not to compete that is part of a contract of employment (or part of a stockholder's agreement) is far more likely to result in litigation because such covenants are far more likely to be used or avoided unfairly. Many an employer would like the covenant to function to punish an employee who would dare to leave a job with an ongoing practice and compete with it in any conceivable fashion. Many an employee has signed an employment contract without ever giving thought to the possibility that the covenant would be enforced against him or her, or worse, thinking that the covenant *could not* be enforced. If the covenant is drafted to be reasonable, it will be enforced and should be enforced. The reasons are easy to see.

Young associate, Dr. Johnson, joins elder practitioner, Dr. Lincoln, in an ongoing practice, with goodwill created by Lincoln. Dr. Johnson gets to know Dr. Lincoln's patients and impresses them with his own abilities. Dr. Johnson and Dr. Lincoln do not agree on an extension of the employment contract, and Dr. Johnson is notified that he may not practice medicine within the terms of the covenant not to compete contained in his employment contract. Dr. Lincoln has a protectable interest in the goodwill of his practice that Dr. Johnson should not be allowed to appropriate and use against his former employer as a competitor. If the covenant is reasonably drafted, it will do no more than protect that defined interest belonging to Dr. Lincoln. The problem is defining what interest may be reasonably protected.

"REASONABLE" TERMS OF THE COVENANT

A covenant not to compete will not be upheld by a court if its effect is to go beyond the interest that Dr. Lincoln has in his goodwill. Patients who have a current relationship of trust with Dr. Lincoln should be recognized as a legitimate interest. But what about persons who have never been patients of Dr. Lincoln's, patients who may never have heard of Dr. Lincoln? What about patients who have not seen Dr. Lincoln in years and who may no longer have any tendency to consult with him on a new problem? The courts have struggled with this concept, and decisions can be found that both enforce and strike down covenants that cover future or possible patients.

The covenant must be for a reasonable amount of time. How long is there a reasonable expectation that a patient would come back to a doctor who treated him or her earlier? Covenants up to 2 years have been almost uniformly upheld; covenants longer than that period have had varying fates.

The covenant must extend over no more than a reasonably necessary geographical area to effectuate protection of the legitimate interest. That geographical area may be far wider in a rural area than within a metropolis. The size of the geographical area may also vary with the kind of business interest being protected. In some cases an area of a whole county is too big, while in others an area of 12 states is deemed reasonable. The definition of the geographical area is many times given little review by a court; instead, another covenant with protection of one county or a 50-mile radius is cited, with a conclusion that an area of similar size is also reasonable. A more particular examination of the facts of the case may distinguish it from another case.

An alternative to a geographical limitation is a specification of certain persons whose business may not be solicited by the former employee, usually a designation of current patients or customers who have been served by the employer within the time of the associate's employment. In these cases, there is no geographical area of coverage; the patient or customer may reside anywhere. Courts approve of these current customer limits.

A covenant may be declared unenforceable if one of its terms is unreasonable and cannot be separated from the remainder of the covenant. The law will not apply a "blue pencil" to rewrite the terms of a covenant to bring it within the scope of reasonability, but it will strike down a term that is unreasonable and that can be isolated from the other terms of the covenant. However, a covenant may contain a *cy pres* clause (medieval French for "as close"), which directs the court to enforce the covenant within the limits of the law as close to the meaning of the parties as possible.

REMEDIES (THE LEGAL RX)

No, a "remedy" at law is not a medical prescription; it refers to the things that courts can do to protect or compensate a person who has been harmed by violation of a covenant not to compete. The possible remedies are (1) an award of actual damages proven after the fact (i.e., how much monetary loss can be attributed directly to the unfair competition of the former employee), (2) liquidated damages calculated in advance at the time the covenant was drafted, and (3) injunction (i.e., a court order that the former employee stop violating the covenant immediately). The first remedy is almost never used and is included in this analysis to show why the other two remedies are used instead. Actual damages after the fact requires that the whole period of the covenant run before any remedy can be considered. Employers argue that they could be put out of business before they ever got to be heard in court. Employers also argue that it would be so difficult as to be impossible to calculate. I have my doubts about how impossible it would be, but it is not very practical. I will come back later to liquidated damages and why they are far more appropriate for physicians.

An injunction is an order by the court (i.e., the government) that a doctor not practice his or her area of medicine within the area and time limits of the covenant. In order for a court to issue an injunction, the court must find that the damages that may be done to the former employer are irreparable (i.e., that no amount of money that can be reasonably calculated can compensate the former employer for the harm done by the former employee's competition). Further, the court must determine that it is in the public interest to issue the injunction. Very frequently, an employment agreement containing a covenant not to compete will have recitations in it that the parties agree that damages to the employer would be irreparable and that it would be in the public interest that an injunction be issued to enforce the covenant (i.e., that the covenant try to supply these necessary areas of proof by incorporating them into the language of the covenant). No court is bound by such recitations. It is only the court that determines the public interest, not the parties, and it is only the court that can determine that an alleged damage is or is not irreparable.

There are a million arguments and counterarguments between medical practitioners over whether the financial damages that may occur between them can or cannot be calculated. However, once a court turns to damages that may be done to patients, arguments tend to be more one-sided. Courts are beginning to pay serious attention to the public interest, which may be affected by the issuance of an injunction in circumstances in which it may be shown that an injunction would endanger members of the public who may need a particular specialty of medicine or even the ability to perform a specific procedure within that area of specialty—for example, by having physicians available to make full use of a particular facility in a community hospital that would otherwise suffer.

Arguments also have been made that a covenant between doctors is or should be against public policy because the enforcement of such an agreement forbids a patient from seeing the physician he or she prefers without allowing the patient any say in the matter. The opinions of the Council on Ethical and Judicial Affairs of the American Medical Association (1986), sec. 9.02, provides for agreements restricting medical practice.

AGREEMENTS RESTRICTING THE PRACTICE OF MEDICINE

The Council on Ethical and Judicial Affairs discourages any agreement between physicians which restricts the right of a physician to practice medicine for a specified period of time or in a specified area upon termination of employment or a partnership or a corporate agreement. Such restrictive agreements are not in the public interest.

I am unaware of the AMA giving any practical support against covenants not to compete. Courts in some states have taken the position that the covenants are void because they are against public policy. You must consult with an attorney to find out the legal handling of covenants not to compete, between physicians, involving injunctions.

Liquidated damages are specifications within a contract, in advance of any breach, which reasonably determine what monetary damages are likely to result from a breach of the covenant not to compete. The liquidated damages may set a specific figure or provide a certain formula for calculating the damages, based on specified elements such as collections at a particular office. If the covenant is for longer than a year, the contract may provide that liquidated damages for breach during the first year will be this amount, and a breach after 1 year will be that amount. The law highly favors liquidated damages because the two parties have calculated the amount in advance and thus relieve the court of having to determine damages from the many different ways by which they can be calculated.

It is my own position that a specification of liquidate damages in a contract eliminates the claim for injunctive relief as well. The basic argument for injunctive relief is that a monetary award cannot compensate for the injuries done. Liquidated damages specify that amount and eliminate that claim. Some courts, however, have granted both damages and injunctive relief, perhaps because the parties did not raise the logical conflict before the court. I personally advise my clients to seek or offer provisions for liquidated damages because I personally find it repugnant to use the power of the state to tell a patient that he or she may not seek medical treatment from Dr. Kennedy or Dr. Nixon. The patient's choice is not to be sacrificed for a business concern, while the monetary damages will protect the loss of any goodwill that may be suffered.

Liquidated damages, however, have their own set of abuses. The amount of the damages may not bear a logical relationship to any reasonable way to calculate damages. An amount that is obviously in excess of such an estimation is legally a penalty on the person violating the covenant rather than compensation of injuries sustained by the complaining party. The law will not enforce a penalty or private punishment. An employer who overreaches may find himself or herself with no protection at all.

CONCLUSION

When faced with the prospect of drafting or of signing a covenant not to compete, consult a lawyer experienced in that area of law. Such a covenant is a reasonable and appropriate protection for the legitimate property right of goodwill, but such covenants will lead to bitter conflict if they attempt to restrict competition beyond what is legitimately protectable.

REFERENCES AND READINGS

Dick v. Geist, 107 Idaho 931, 693 P.2d 1133 (App. 1985).
Duffner v. Alberty, 19 Ark.App. 137, 718 S.W.2d 111 (1986).
Ellis v. McDaniel, 95 Nev. 455, 596 P.2d 222 (1979).
Lowe v. Reynolds, 75 A.2d 967, 428 N.Y.2d 358 (1980).
Wagler Excavating Corp. v. McKibben Const., Inc., 679 N.E.2d 155 (Ind.App. 1997).

## CHAPTER 3

Human Resource Options for the Harried Physician

Don't Sweat It . . . Outsource It, and Reduce Office Overhead Costs

Eric Galtress

> Very little is needed to make a happy life.
>
> —Marcus Aurelius

In this chapter we will provide the medical practitioner with an overview of the human resources (HR) requirements of the employer, including a brief history of employment and labor laws, government compliance issues, increased costs, and the alarming upsurge in employee litigation. The last poses an extraordinary level of liability to the physician, second only to that of medical malpractice.

We will also present supporting information on an innovative alternative available to the practitioner: being able to delegate (*outsource*) most of the HR burden and the employee-related liabilities. Simply put, instead of the practitioner being the "employer of record" of the workplace employees, this responsibility is outsourced to an off-site professional employer organization (PEO) that specializes in labor management and cost control. You retain functional control of the employees, and the PEO handles the HR issues.

The PEO can provide these same services *more cost effectively* by combining your employees with the employees of the many other practices they already serve. It's a matter of simple economics. The PEO relationship is not to be confused with a physician practice management firm (PPM). The PEO has *no financial interest or ownership* whatsoever in the practice but merely is there to provide valuable assistance with regard to employee issues.

DEFINITIONS

Outsource: To have someone else take responsibility *and* much of the liability to perform a service for you because

1. They can do it cheaper and/or faster.
2. They can do it better because of their expertise and experience.
3. They have all of the required professional staff and/or facilities.
4. They take all or part of the risk and the liability to do it right.
5. They save you the time of doing it yourself or having one or more of your key staff members distracted from the priorities of the practice.
6. It benefits all parties.

Human resource management: Generally speaking, HR management consists of the activities, responsibilities, and issues of any business, corporation, partnership, or practice that comes as a result of having employees (independent contractors are not considered employees). Some of these requirements are mandatory, such as minimum wage; other aspects and their related administrative functions can be at the discretion of the owner(s) of the practice, such as sponsoring health benefits for employees.

There are a multitude of federal, state, and local laws and regulations that must be complied with by all business entities with employees. These govern how employees must be treated and paid, as well as ensuring that their rights in the workplace are protected.

HUMAN RESOURCE COMPONENTS

Human Resource Administration: employee handbook, guides and regulations, posters, procedures for recruiting, hiring, reviews, discipline, termination, and labor law expertise.

Payroll Processing: Employer tax administration, record keeping, reporting, payroll calculations/deductions, paycheck printing and distribution, W2s, W4s, quarterly reports, unemployment administration, management reports, time-off utilization and accruals.

Labor and Liability Issues: Unemployment, sexual harassment, wrongful termination, employee separation (forms DE1101, DE1545), discrimination, employee rights, costs of labor disputes and litigation, personnel record keeping (I-9, W4, DE4, etc.), government compliance with ADA, EEOC, COBRA, immigration and other government regulations.

Workers' Compensation Coverage: Insurance premium and full legal coverage, claims filings, management and administration, fraud investigation and defense, audits and loss control, communication with injured employees, return-to-work procedures.

Safety: Establish and implement an illness and injury prevention program (IIPP) in accordance with the requirements of Senate bill 198 (SB198). Provide all required general and specific safety training as well as all required personal protective equipment.

Benefits: Administration of mandatory employee benefits such as overtime pay, work breaks, unemployment insurance, and the like as well as additional benefits and employee incentives that may be provided by the owner(s) of the practice, such as health insurance, pension plans, vacations, paid time off, sick leave.

EMPLOYEE RELATED OVERHEAD COSTS

Typically, *employee related overhead costs* are tracked by expressing the applicable costs as a percentage of the total gross wages of the practice, *excluding* the physician's compensation. Figure 3.1 provides a breakdown of the primary activities, which amount to 22% of gross wages as a national average. (Source: Survey Human Resource Management—Bureau of National Affairs (SHRM-BNA) Survey).

Take note that this 22% *does not* include the cost of health insurance or pension plans for the employees, since this varies as to whether the practice will sponsor

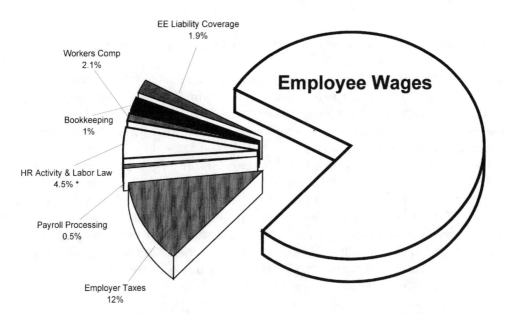

Employee Related Overhead Costs
(National Average as a Percentage of Gross Wages - 22%)

EE Liability Coverage
1.9%

Workers Comp
2.1%

Bookkeeping
1%

HR Activity & Labor Law
4.5% *

Payroll Processing
0.5%

Employer Taxes
12%

Employee Wages

FIGURE 3.1   For every $1,000 of employee salary, each employee costs you an additional $220 (22%), exclusive of health insurance costs.

*Based on Bureau of National Affairs report.

these benefits for the employees, the age of the employees, the type of insurance plan (HMO, PPO, POS), the size of the practice, and the geographic location.

A general outline of HR components and the employee-related overhead costs has been shown previously. However, you should note that each area has within it far more detailed procedures and management requirements than the outline may suggest. A comprehensive listing of all HR activities within the major components is shown in Table 3.1.

The listing is arranged so that one can see the activities that are the responsibility of the practice without the PEO and which of these same activities are assumed by the PEO once the practice subscribes to a PEO service.

QUESTION

Should the harried physician take on the human resources responsibility and the related liabilities of being the employer and hope for the best, or should the physician focus on building the practice and delegate (outsource) most of these activities (headaches to most practitioners) to a PEO?

The practitioner *has a choice* in dealing with human resources today.

Let's take a look at the typical small practice today and find out how the HR responsibilities may be handled. We will also take a look at how this same practice may utilize the added value provided by the PEO and be relieved of most of the hassle and administrative burden as well as much of the liability.

Alternative 1: The Practice Performs the HR Responsibilities

The typical practice will hire a sharp office manager or administrator who has experience with personnel issues, has lots of common sense, will consult with the practitioner, will be backed by a labor attorney on retainer and a bookkeeper and/or CPA. The practice may also purchase employee liability insurance protection as an added cost.

The practice then deals with possibly six or seven service providers, brokers, and consultants for payroll, employer tax administration, workers' compensation insurance, health programs, pension plans, employee labor law issues, and so on.

Each of these business entities has its own agenda and has no connection or vested interest in any of the others' activities. Each vendor bills the practice in accordance with its own billing period, which means perhaps hundreds of invoices to reconcile and just as many checks to write throughout the year.

This same office manager or administrator (or as often is the case, maybe even the practitioner) may also take on the tasks of researching, developing, and distributing an employee handbook; office hiring and selection procedures; compensation policies; job descriptions; and implementing and maintaining compliance with ongoing government regulations. The HR activities outline shown previously covers all of these areas and, of course, includes dealing on a daily basis with employee issues, both personal and work-related.

TABLE 3.1   MMC, Inc. Comprehensive Human Resource Services Program

	With MMC		Without MMC
	MMC	Client	Client
Human Resource Management			
Personnel records administration	X		X
Unemployment claims administration	X		X
Government regulations and compliance	X		X
DOL Dept. of Labor, EDD Employment Development Dept.	X		X
Sexual harassment program implementation	X		X
ADA Americans with Disabilities	X		X
COBRA insurance continuance	X		X
EEO equal employment opportunity	X		X
FMLA Family and Medical Leave Act	X		X
INS immigration requirements	X		X
OSHA safety regulations	X		X
Other governmental compliance issues	X		X
Personnel policies and protocol	X		X
Hiring, qualification, selection consultation	X		X
Proper termination procedures	X		X
Disciplinary procedures	X		X
Documentation procedures	X		X
Employee administration consultation	X		X
Wage/hour law consultation	X		X
Complaint procedures	X	X	X
Employee counseling	X	X	X
Wrongful termination consultation	X		X
Employee recognition program administration	X		X
Employee handbook	X		X
Workers' Compensation • Safety Program • Cost Management Loss • Control			
WC insurance provided	X		X
Claims processing and filing	X	X	X
Claims management	X		X
Loss control program	X	X	X
Fraud awareness program	X		X
Legal responsibility for audits and defenses	X		X
Communication with injured employees	X		X
Employee liability insurance (embezzlement, dishonesty)	X		X
ADA Americans With Disabilities compliance	X		X
SB198 Senate Bill 198 compliance	X	X	X
Safety Management Program	X	X	X
OSHA Records Administration	X	X	X
Payroll Administration • Employer Tax Responsibilities			
Payroll processing and delivery	X		X
Employer tax routing to all agencies	X		X
Quarterly report preparation and responsibility	X		X
W-2, W-4 preparation	X		X
Payroll deductions	X		X
Reconciliation of payroll accounts	X		X
Payroll management reporting	X		X
Legal responsibility for audits	X		X

(continued)

TABLE 3.1   *(Continued)*

	With MMC		Without MMC
	MMC	Client	Client
Flexible Employee Benefits Program			
Administration of Benefit Program	X		X
Rate Negotiations With Health Care Providers	X		X
Selection of Comprehensive Major Medical Plans	X		X
Dental plan available	X		X
Vision plan available	X		X
Employee assistance plan included (24 hr/365 days)	X		X
Group term life insurance	X		X
Long-term disability insurance	X		X
Discount legal plan	X		X
Credit union	X		X
Group membership discount programs	X		X
Family entertainment discount programs	X		X
Video library, employee self betterment	X		X
Audiocassette library, employee self betterment	X		X
Section 125/127 cafeteria tax benefits programs	X		X
401(k) retirement savings plan administration	X		X
Optional Services Available at Nominal Cost			
Recruiting, selection and hiring responsibility	X	X	X
Management and supervisorial training programs	X	X	X
Recruiting, interviewing, qualifying, selecting, hiring	X		X
Pre-entrance screening	X		X
Employee performance reviews	X		X
Disciplinary situations, file documentation	X		X
Customer service	X		X
Basic supervisory skills	X		X
Other key aspects of employee administration/ management	X		X
Predictive index testing for key hiring decisions	X		X
Candidate assessment and qualification criteria	X		X
Background checks	X		X
Reference checks	X		X
Drug testing program	X		X
Employee turnover reduction program	X		X
Job descriptions, salary surveys	X		X
Job qualification and assessment	X		X
Employee time keeping/benefits accrual software	X		X

Finally, this individual will also be expected to contribute time to help ensure a smooth operation at the practice, keep the trust and confidence of current patients and add new patients, increase and maintain employee productivity from a medical standpoint, and help in the practitioner's long-term plan for growing the practice.

This approach has, for the most part, been the most widely used in the past; however, *it no longer allows the practitioner to focus on the priorities of the practice*, the ones that *increase the bottom line.*

Years ago, when each practice was "just like a family" there were no managed care challenges, nor did there exist the mountain of employment legislation and government compliance issues to deal with. In recent years, the explosion of new legislation and a highly litigious society has created an environment in which the physician must continue to seek alternatives to best manage the employee-related overhead costs as well as the liabilities of being the employer.

Liabilities of Being the Employer

Woven into the employee-related overhead costs are the *liabilities, risks, and exposures* of being the employer. *While employees can be the practitioner's greatest asset, next to malpractice, employees can be the practitioner's greatest liability.*

Figures 3.2 and 3.3 illustrate the impact of the increasing number of employment laws as well as the increasing costs of employee-related litigation.

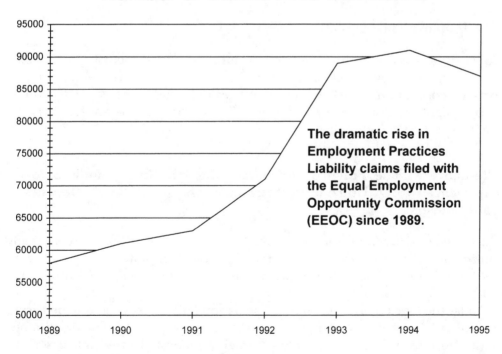

FIGURE 3.2 *Source: PEO Insider Magazine*, Feb. 1998 issue, article by Robert Jurgel, RPLU.

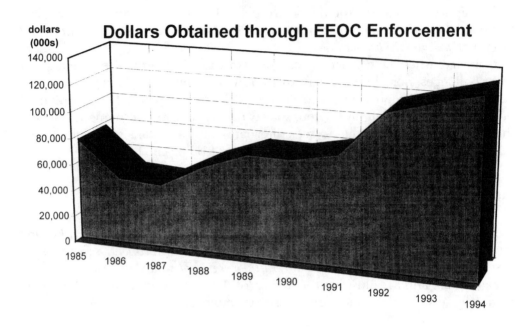

FIGURE 3.3 *Source: PEO Insider Magazine*, Feb. 1998 issue, article by Robert Jurgel, RPLU.

New Employment Legislation

Congress, at any given time, has several hundred employment legislative bills pending. How many will become law is anyone's guess, but the workplace can expect a continuum of new employment laws and regulations as a reflection of today's highly litigious society (see Figure 3.4). A copy of current legislation is available at www.mmchr.com.

Alternative 2: The Practice Outsources the HR Responsibilities to an Experienced PEO, Utilizing Professionals Who Specialize in the Health Care Industry

Outsourcing of functions that traditionally fall within the HR domain is already utilized on a very large scale by more than 62% of all employers today, including the health care industry. Payroll processing is just one example (Source: 1997 SHRM-BNA Survey #62).

Today the harried physician must build a foundation to concentrate on caring for patients, being highly productive, and growing the practice. The practitioner must also attract and keep in place a highly motivated professional staff of employees that are dedicated to these same principles. This becomes an ongoing challenge in today's highly competitive and dynamic managed care environment.

Enter the PEO industry, which has come to be recognized as a viable HR services alternative for virtually all small to midsize companies, including medical

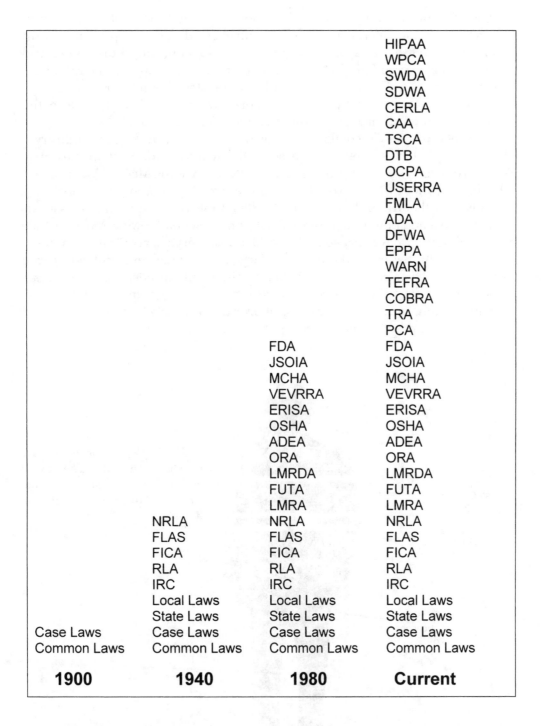

1900	1940	1980	Current
			HIPAA
			WPCA
			SWDA
			SDWA
			CERLA
			CAA
			TSCA
			DTB
			OCPA
			USERRA
			FMLA
			ADA
			DFWA
			EPPA
			WARN
			TEFRA
			COBRA
			TRA
			PCA
		FDA	FDA
		JSOIA	JSOIA
		MCHA	MCHA
		VEVRRA	VEVRRA
		ERISA	ERISA
		OSHA	OSHA
		ADEA	ADEA
		ORA	ORA
		LMRDA	LMRDA
		FUTA	FUTA
		LMRA	LMRA
	NRLA	NRLA	NRLA
	FLAS	FLAS	FLAS
	FICA	FICA	FICA
	RLA	RLA	RLA
	IRC	IRC	IRC
	Local Laws	Local Laws	Local Laws
	State Laws	State Laws	State Laws
Case Laws	Case Laws	Case Laws	Case Laws
Common Laws	Common Laws	Common Laws	Common Laws

FIGURE 3.4   The upward climb in government regulations. Staying in compliance with the rising number of government regulations requires a full-time effort. (Source: NAPEO)

practices. In prior years, the terms "employee leasing" and "staff leasing" were the most common references used for similar but different approaches in this industry, but these terms can leave one with a misconception of the depth of services a highly credible PEO can bring to an organization. Specialization and tailored services and benefits, along with the transfer of employer liabilities, are more accurately conveyed by the contemporary term *outsourcing*. Therefore, that term has been used throughout this chapter. (See Figure 3.5.)

PEOs became fully recognized as a growing force in the staffing industry in the early 1980s. In 1983, for example, according to information obtained from the Aegis Group, there were approximately 20 PEOs, including Medical Management Consultants, Inc. (MMC). Not all have grown steadily or stood the test of time, but it is clear that this industry has multiplied itself consistently and dramatically year after year and now numbers over 2,000 companies nationwide. More recently, the PEO industry has engaged in consolidations, mergers, acquisitions, and specialization. This has created several very large PEOs, some being publicly traded.

However, bigger isn't necessarily better when you consider that the primary benefactor of the PEO services program is the small to midsize practice or business. Often, large companies cannot provide the specialized services or quick response these practices need. (See Figure 3.6.)

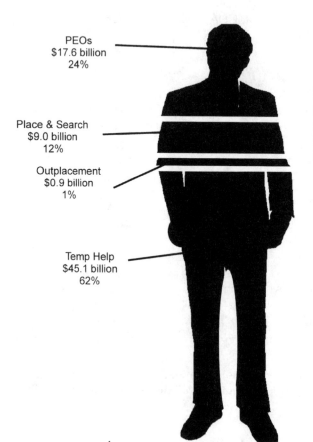

PEOs
$17.6 billion
24%

Place & Search
$9.0 billion
12%

Outplacement
$0.9 billion
1%

Temp Help
$45.1 billion
62%

FIGURE 3.5   Major segments of the staffing industry. The PEO industry has now grown to one fourth of the entire staffing industry.

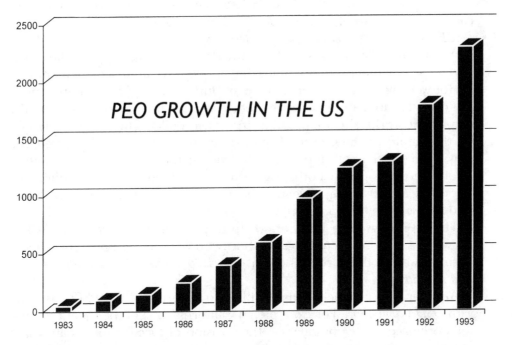

FIGURE 3.6 **The PEO industry has grown dramatically year after year—from just a handful of companies in 1983, to over two thousand today. (Source: The Aegis Group)**

Among the more experienced PEOs are those that specialize in various market segments, such as manufacturing, transportation, light industry, health care, and others. These PEOs come to know the unique aspects of their respective marketplaces and use their experience and expertise most effectively. This can be critical in an environment where employers face so many exposures, not only in running their businesses but in coping with the escalation in employment laws and related litigation.

WHAT ARE THE ADVANTAGES OF OUTSOURCING?

How can the PEO's integrated services benefit all parties in the relationship?

For the Practice

Outsourcing allows for more focus in providing care to patients and growing the practice.

- *It controls and reduces hard and soft dollar costs.* Outsourcing consolidates the activities and costs of a multitude of service providers and vendors into a single and highly specialized services provider. Only one check per pay period need be issued for these HR services. A summary of examples of each of these types of costs is contained in Table 3.1.

- *It reduces the liabilities of being the employer.*

  Among these liabilities is the Exclusive Remedy Law as applied to *workplace injuries*, which, in most states, holds that employees cannot sue their employers for workplace injuries, since their "exclusive remedy" for required medical care, rehabilitation, wage benefits, and so on, is contained in the employer's workers' compensation insurance policy. Further, liability falls on the employer (employers' insurance carrier) who has the injured employee on the payroll and who is providing the workers' compensation insurance coverage. In both cases, this is usually the PEO, although the workplace employer may have some liability if "gross negligence" contributed to or caused the workplace injury.

  These findings have been drawn from guidelines laid down by Arthur Larson, a highly respected legal authority on workers' compensation insurance, as well as those contained in *California Workers' Compensation Claims and Benefits.*

  Another area in which some liability is transferred to the PEO has to do with *OSHA compliance*. For example, in California, one of the toughest states for workplace safety compliance, the Division of Occupational Safety and Health issued their policy as applied to *dual-employer* (temporary help, employee leasing, PEOs, etc.) situations. It said in part: "The company supplying the employee is referred to as the *primary* employer" (PEO), "and the company supervising the employee at the workplace is referred to as the *secondary* employer" (the practice). Of course, the workplace employer is generally responsible for maintaining a safe workplace, and in the medical profession this is usually not a problem.

  A third area of transferred liability relates to *payroll administration and management*. As the employer of record, the PEO takes responsibility for proper compliance with all federal and state agency requirements for payroll taxes and records management of the employees. This is because it is the PEO's federal and state ID's that are used in the filings. State requirements, however, do require that the workplace employers maintain copies of their time-keeping records for a specified period of time.

- *It provides more cost-effective and better employee benefits options.* This allows the practice to attract and retain the best employee candidates and reduces the huge costs, loss of productivity, and disruption associated with employee turnover (see Figure 3.7).

- *It reduces the time spent on employee and government compliance issues for both the practitioner and key staff members.* This enables them to focus on patient care and their own priorities and not be distracted by nonproductive personnel and compliance issues.

- *It provides peace of mind.* Outsourcing insures that the stringent compliance requirements and government regulations are being handled by experienced professionals with the required expertise and a vested interest in ongoing compliance.

Annual Per Person Cost of Job Turnover/
Percent of Companies (206 companies responded)

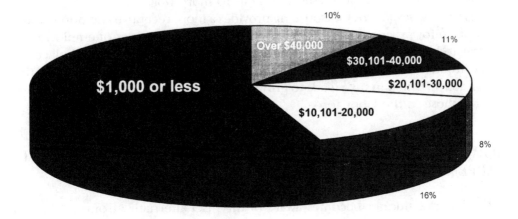

FIGURE 3.7   **Factor in lost productivity from a vacancy, search fees, management time used to interview and training costs for a new hire. Source: Data-William M. Mercer, Inc.,** *Business Week Magazine,* **April 20, 1998.**

For the Employee

Outsourcing increases morale, productivity, and job fulfillment.

- *It protects their rights.* Outsourcing helps to foster an environment in which the employee's as well as the owner/practitioner's rights in the workplace are respected.
- *It offers better benefits.* Outsourcing provides employees with greater access to more affordable (big company) health and other benefits options, more selectivity, and a means to participate in self-funded or employer-matched retirement plans and tax savings opportunities.
- *It addresses and resolves problems.* Outsourcing puts in place a means to help identify and resolve employee issues and concerns that may otherwise escalate.
- *It results in increased job stability.* Outsourcing provides for a potentially more stable employment relationship, career growth, and self-betterment opportunities by means of specialized employee programs offered by the PEO, such as training.

For the Government

Outsourcing offers more assurance of compliance and enhanced communication.

- *It consolidates requirements.* Tax filings and collection of employer payroll taxes from many practices through a single PEO entity reduces administration costs.
- *It brings health care to more workers.* Outsourcing provides options to the owner/practitioner to extend medical benefits to more workers.
- *It improves compliance.* Outsourcing provides a more receptive and noninvasive option for practices to comply with the increasing volumes of employment-related laws, regulations, and legislative requirements in the workplace.
- *It reduces unemployment.* Outsourcing promotes higher productivity at the practice, which in turn leads to growth and more employment opportunities for those in the labor force.

HOW DOES THE PEO RELATIONSHIP GET STARTED AND WHAT HAPPENS NEXT?

1. The practitioner becomes aware of the PEO alternative from

   - Word of mouth from another colleague who is a PEO client.
   - Membership in a particular association or fraternal organization.
   - Trusted advisors such as an attorney, CPA, financial planner, or business consultant.
   - A special education course in which he or she is participating.
   - Recommendation of a governmental agency; Employment Development Department (EDD).
   - Endorsement by an affiliation of physicians or a medical group to which he or she belongs.
   - Enduring the pain and anguish of a major employer/employee-related problem.

2. *PEO selected.* The practitioner seeks out a candidate PEO utilizing the selection procedure outlined in the latter part of this chapter ("How Should You Select a PEO for Your Practice?"). The two parties agree to meet to review the PEO program. During this initial meeting it is important that the practitioner be prepared to ask questions and have his or her concerns addressed.

3. *Data provided to PEO.* The PEO representative will need copies of cost information relating to workers' compensation, payroll, and administration costs and must know whether employee health benefits are desired and what, if anything, the practice may have in place in the area of employee handbook, OSHA program, and other HR-related procedures. This information will allow for a very productive dialogue between the practitioner and PEO.

4. *Needs analysis developed.* The practitioner should also be prepared to *be forthright* with any concerns he or she may have regarding employees in the workplace, whether these are simply concerns for the future or are happening now. Reputable PEOs do not increase their fees but, on the contrary, are able to best integrate and deliver the required services cost-effectively by getting the

full picture at the outset. Nothing in the workplace comes as a surprise to a seasoned PEO—they've seen it all and have the expertise and experience to deal with it.

Examples may include sexual harassment issues, concerns about firing a particular employee, unresolved employee issues, suspected fraudulent workers' compensation claims for difficult-to-prove cases such as "stress," difficult employees, hostility in the workplace, the total absence of government compliance requirements, and so on.

Of great concern to a small practice is high turnover. This is a *huge time bomb of cost* to the physician who spends valuable time training the employee and, for whatever reason, the employee moves on to what they deem to be a better opportunity with better benefits, now that they're fully trained. The practitioner then has to start all over and hope for the best. Other employees are disrupted to "cover" the workload, and morale goes down. It's a continuous cycle of negativity. An experienced PEO can assist the client in reversing this turn of events.

5. *Proposal developed.* When the practitioner and the PEO are satisfied that the "needs profile" has been fully understood, the resultant analysis is used to develop a proposal tailored to the practice. This is the most meaningful way to go through the process—a proposal based on real data, real events, real concerns, and real needs.

6. *Proposal presented.* The proposal is presented to the practitioner and should address not only the needs of the practitioner but also the benefits available to the workplace employees. Take note that even though some practices choose not to sponsor health benefits for their employees, there are other benefits made available by the PEO at no cost, as we have noted previously (retirement plan, tax savings programs, credit unions, discount memberships, family entertainment, etc.).

7. *Proceed, modify, or wait.* Any remaining issues are clarified, and the practitioner decides to proceed or wait. Hopefully, after this process, it is clear to the practitioner that the benefits outweigh other considerations. A program timetable is reviewed and agreed on. The PEO program can then be up and running in as short a period as 1 week for urgent situations, but it is best to allow about 3 weeks from the time that the decision is made for a smooth transition.

8. *Conclude service agreement and employee orientation.* A service agreement summarizing the terms of the arrangement is reviewed and signed by the practitioner and PEO. The employees are given an orientation on the services and benefits available to them as a result of the program. In addition, the employees have the opportunity to ask questions and have the PEO address any concerns, and then the paperwork is completed. This fulfills all of the necessary administrative requirements and results in the many advantages noted previously.

The PEO becomes the employer of record for the practitioner's employees, and the practitioner remains as the workplace employer, retaining functional control of the employees. What results is referred to as a *co-employer* or *dual employment* relationship, extending the benefits of the arrangement to all parties (see Figure 3.8).

9. *Program benefits begin.* Prior to each payday, the practice reports hours worked to the PEO. Since the PEO already has all employee and wage data in

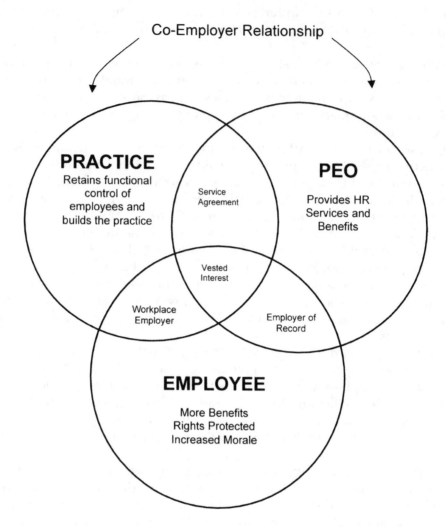

FIGURE 3.8 **The co-employer relationship between the practice and the PEO benefits all parties. (Source: NAPEO)**

their automated system, an invoice is generated quickly. The invoice includes wages, employer taxes, workers' compensation insurance, health benefits if applicable, HR services, and the pre-agreed service fees for the pay period.

The invoice is paid by the practice, and the PEO has the payroll checks printed and delivered to the workplace and/or performs a direct deposit for those employees who have requested this feature. Take note that the payroll checks are issued *from the PEO's own accounts*. This is an important distinction as viewed by government authorities and the IRS and provides a measure of liability protection for the practice.

Sounds simple, and it can be. A well-established and highly reputable PEO will take a much deeper and *vested interest* in the specific needs and requirements of the practice from the beginning. Once in place, the PEO will assume most of the responsibility for the HR elements and this becomes a cooperative effort with the practice. This co-employer relationship can be generally summarized by the division of responsibilities seen in Figure 3.9.

ADDED VALUE DERIVED FROM THE PEO RELATIONSHIP

What you will receive is the full complement of services discussed above but with a great deal of *added value*, depending on the PEO you choose and, of course, their ability to deliver the added value that would be meaningful to your practice.

Examples

Although the basic HR elements are the same, each client has a particular workplace atmosphere, along with specific needs, requirements, and priorities that are meaningful to that client. Perhaps it is a brand-new practice with no HR policies whatsoever in place. It may need access to salary and benefits surveys so that it can attract the best employee candidates and remain competitive with other practices in the area.

Some practices may be having problems with a high rate of employee turn-over—a very costly situation to deal with and one that requires a concerted and directed effort to overcome. In either of these situations, the program of services offered by an experienced PEO can include procedures to correct the problem or put in place the required support.

As a standard procedure, experienced PEOs, such as MMC, perform an individual *client needs analysis* to address any specialized requirements. These may include a training curriculum to help develop managers and supervisors, medical billing seminars, or a tailored pension plan. Payroll is another area that can bring special needs.

Case 1

In a recent program developed for an MMC client, there was a need for a PC-based time-clock system that would also be used for tracking the accrual of vacation and sick leave hours. This would save a lot of time for the person in charge, who had been performing these tasks and preparing the relevant reports manually.

MMC researched candidate vendors and alternative software packages to do the job. After reviewing the operational aspects with MMC, the client company made the selection and MMC integrated the software program within their own payroll management system. The client company was delighted to gain not only the benefits of the expanded payroll function but also a great reduction in the hours spent on the manual, error-prone, time-keeping system they had been using.

The more obvious concern to the practitioner is the area of *employer liability*. The following cases are actual examples that have occurred at MMC clients in

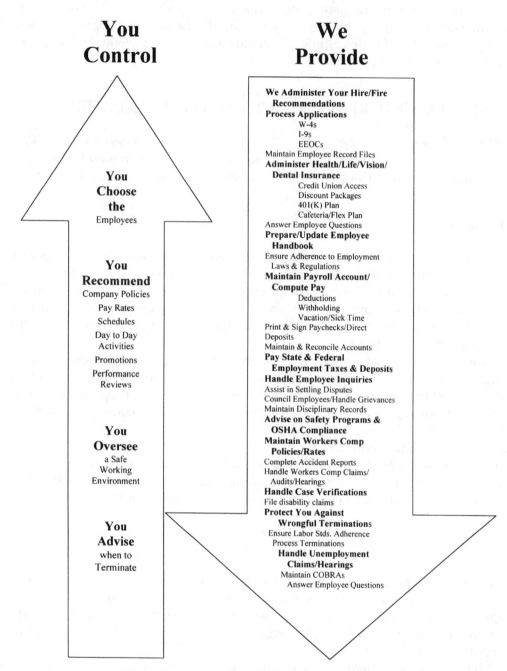

FIGURE 3.9　Division of responsibilities between the PEO and the practice.

the past 3 years. These cases convey the importance of a *swift and appropriate response* to workplace issues that can literally close a practice if not handled properly.

Case 2

Complaints were made of sexual harassment against a physician by female employees and patients. When the MMC client manager became aware of the problem, MMC sent one of their labor law representatives to meet with the employees.

After consultation with the physician, the offending doctor was warned, and a policy was developed and signed by the doctor, to the effect that he would not be in an examination room alone with a female patient or employee at any time. Through immediate follow-up and assistance from MMC's Labor Law Department, all offended parties agreed to drop their accusations, and the physician was grateful to have the issue resolved without legal action. Without MMC, a lawsuit would have been filed against the physician.

Case 3

A doctor wanted to terminate an employee but was concerned that the employee might react violently. The office manager was afraid to confront the employee, and the doctor didn't want to face a disaster during office hours or possible harm after hours.

A client support consultant from MMC went to the office, presented the employee with her final check and conducted an exit interview to make sure her feelings were heard and her rights were protected. The situation was resolved peacefully, and business continued without incident.

Case 4

An administrator determined that one their billers was incapable of handling the duties she was performing and, so as not to look bad, was burying paperwork instead of giving it to a supervisor who offered to help. She decided to terminate the employee and told MMC she had a paper trail of memos to the employee, showing poor performance.

Reviewing the paperwork, MMC found that, in fact, the employee had been told that she was doing a "great job." Termination would have resulted in an immediate claim. The employee's manager really felt that this individual was a nice employee. Thus, MMC helped compose a letter of warning, and the employee was reassigned to less vital work that needed to be done. The employee had a chance to improve, litigation was avoided, a considerable amount of time was saved, and the owner, manager, and employee were happy with the arrangement.

Case 5

This particular example focuses on one of the more vulnerable aspects of a small medical practice and conveys another major advantage of selecting a PEO that specializes in this field.

A doctor discovered that one of his staff members had been embezzling money over the course of a number of months. The doctor did not have any insurance coverage for embezzlement, but fortunately for him, MMC's Comprehensive Services Program automatically included this important benefit.

MMC assisted in the investigation and prosecution of the employee. MMC's insurance carrier made payment to the doctor on the claim, and the employee was arrested. The doctor is very happy about the protection he received. Without MMC he would not have been able to recover any of the stolen money.

These examples clearly illustrate just how powerful and meaningful the element of added value can be when the practice forms a trusting relationship with a well-established and highly specialized PEO. Without the experience and close working relationship that MMC had formed with its clients, the practitioners would have spent a lot of time, effort, and mental anguish trying to resolve these issues alone and/or with the assistance of costly legal counsel.

The key element in these examples was that MMC's services personnel had already formed a close working relationship with the practitioner clients. When a PEO incorporates a friendly staff of field representatives, it gains a critical familiarity with the work force from the employee's perspective and collectively holds a vested interest in the resolution of any employee-related issues, exposures, and liabilities.

WHAT ARE THE DISADVANTAGES OR CONCERNS OF OUTSOURCING?

In reviewing the many advantages presented above, one would think that there are no disadvantages or reasons why the practitioner would not move forward. After all, the proposal presented by the PEO conveys the specific advantages and the corresponding added value that can be gained from the PEO relationship.

If there is any hesitation, it is usually because of one or more of the following general reasons, often referred to as the 4 C's: cost, control, culture, and commitment. Let's explore each.

Frequently Asked Questions

Cost Concerns

Perception. With a full HR professional staff at my disposal, transfer of liability, labor law and government compliance assistance, Fortune 500 benefits and employee administration support, aren't the services very expensive for a small practice?

Reality: The PEO is cost-effective and brings added value. As part of the proposal development process, MMC and other experienced PEOs perform a careful analysis, taking into consideration the various current costs (in both hard and soft dollars) of the practice. This analysis also includes important feedback on other areas of added value that the PEO program can bring. Not surprisingly, the PEO is usually in a better position to provide these important services more cost-effectively, by improved economies of scale, than the practice is.

Control Concerns

Perception. If the practice becomes a co-employer with the PEO and the PEO becomes the employer of record, wouldn't I lose control of all employee- and compliance-related matters?

Reality: The PEO brings greater control to the practice and employee issues. Creating an alliance with a PEO that can provide your practice with the HR expertise you do not presently have actually increases your effectiveness in handling the medical priorities of your practice. The PEO enhances the level of confidence and assuredness at the practice by dealing with the daily employee-related issues, giving the practitioner greater control in this important area.

When the PEO becomes the employer of record, it takes on major responsibility and liability relating to the workplace employees. The PEO is now charged with ensuring that the practice is in full compliance with all employee-related government requirements and labor law regulations.

Culture Concerns

Perception. If the PEO becomes the co-employer and employer of record, the employees may feel that they no longer work for the same organization, that the relationship will not benefit them, and this may affect their morale.

Reality: The PEO relationship benefits the employees. MMC and other long-standing PEOs are very sensitive to this perception and for this reason make it a point to meet and come to know all employees at the practice, both as a group and individually, during the employee orientation procedure. The PEO representative will also be pleased to meet with employees prior to the service agreement period to address any concerns.

Interestingly, some or all of the physicians themselves become "employees" of the PEO to enjoy the many benefits available to them. The workplace employees are soon reassured, once they understand that they will continue to perform the same daily workplace duties, with the same individuals, with virtually no change and that the relationship further protects their own rights. The employees also recognize the benefits to the practice, which can serve to form a more stable workplace for them and enhance their own well-being, and view the relationship positively.

In addition, when the employees can gain access to a wider variety of benefits—an employee assistance plan, a retirement plan, a tax savings plan, credit unions, discount movies, self-betterment opportunities, and so on—they can only view this as beneficial to them. And they have the owner/practitioner to thank for bringing these added benefits to them as part of the PEO relationship.

Commitment Concerns

Perception. With so many administrative and liability responsibilities delegated to the PEO, doesn't the service agreement with the PEO require a long-term commitment in which I must be bound by strict terms and conditions?

Reality: An experienced and reputable PEO will include a termination clause with no penalty as part of the services agreement. Many PEOs require a 1-year service commitment. However, PEOs that have gained credibility over the years, with a loyal following of clients, will include a termination clause or similar arrangement to allow for an easy transition out of the agreement. These PEOs will have a service agreement that is clear and user-friendly, and this clause can be acted on with no questions asked. Ordinarily, a termination request may result when a practice closes due to retirement, merger or buy-out, and so on.

In some cases, even though the program is running smoothly, the practitioner may choose not to abide by certain labor laws, such as paying overtime when required. He or she may not follow other recommendations made by the PEO in the best interests of the practice regarding labor law issues. In cases such as this, the PEO may choose to terminate the relationship for its own protection. This rarely happens but can occur when practices merge or new owners/partners are added who do not fully understand the advantages and compliance benefits afforded to PEO clients.

How Will My Current Costs Compare with Those of a PEO?

As in most service businesses, there are a variety of approaches used by PEOs to establish their costs for servicing their clients' needs and to calculate their fees. For simplicity, PEOs generally express their overall fees as a percentage of gross wages, stating what is included in this comprehensive fee.

Many cost factors enter into each practice. Remember, there are both *hard and soft* dollar costs. The *hard dollar costs* are straightforward and easily determinable. These may include actual costs for existing workers' compensation insurance coverage, payroll processing, health programs, and so on.

In reviewing the comprehensive listing of HR services areas broken down by function (Table 3.1), you can readily see that the vast majority of the costs are *soft*. This means that they are time-consuming in nature and involve interpretative analysis; thus, they pose some difficulty in arriving at an actual dollar cost. The more HR activities performed by the practitioner or key staff member, the more costly they become.

Another example of a soft dollar cost that is not fully understood and rarely tracked is employee turnover. For this reason, we must rely on extensive surveys performed by the Bureau of National Affairs and other employment reporting organizations to gain some understanding of what these employee overhead costs really are.

All things being equal and based on national averages that incorporate both hard and soft dollar costs, PEOs are beneficial. Most of the time, the PEO can reduce the overall employee-related overhead costs of the practice when you consider both hard and soft dollars.

In cases where the practitioner does not sponsor a health insurance plan for the employees, for example, there is no substantial opportunity to reduce cost in this area. In this instance the PEO can deliver its services at minimal cost impact, which may average from 2%–3% of payroll costs.

But What about the Savings in Your Time Spent on These Nonproductive Issues and Your Concerns about Liability?

Even when there is a small cost involved, virtually all practices stand to benefit in the areas noted previously. This is particularly true when the practitioner and/ or key staff members are burdened with these time-consuming responsibilities and problems themselves and are held accountable to perform them in compliance with the applicable regulations. With the transfer and sharing of liabilities, the PEO brings real value and a cost-effective and meaningful alternative for the practice and the employees.

How Should You Select a PEO for Your Practice?

We'll assume that you, the practitioner, have reviewed the benefits available to your practice as well as to the employees and have found that this alternative is worth your consideration. Now you are ready to take the next step and seek a PEO worthy of your trust and confidence. This simply means that you will take the initial steps to go through the needs analysis process and subsequently receive a formal proposal as outlined previously.

1. *Check the length of time the PEO has been in business, its credibility, and its reputation.* This can be easily performed by contacting the candidate PEO(s) for client references, endorsements, and other performance indicators such as steady growth. Has the PEO been audited by the IRS, and if so, were any changes required?

2. *Make sure that the PEO has the scope of services that can meet your requirements.* This may include a wide selection of health benefits from well-established providers, a retirement plan, a tax savings plan, a 24-hour employee assistance plan, and additional insurance protection, such as employee liability coverage.

Some PEOs refer their clients to an outside insurance broker for health coverage, which has its disadvantages. It can be far more desirable for many reasons, including cost, management, and tax benefits for the employees, to have the health benefits fully available and administered by the PEO itself.

3. *Be sure that the PEO has the financial resources and professional staff in place to support your needs.* If possible, a visit to the PEO's corporate location can be a very good indicator. Although virtually all services can be performed from the corporate location, certain PEOs have a professional staff of field representatives who regularly visit their clients in the local community.

4. *Seek a PEO that carefully maintains written details and documents the ongoing service relationship with its clients and workplace employees.* Many PEOs simply maintain a verbal dialogue or rough notes, but in today's highly litigious society *this is not good enough.* This aspect is often the difference between having to endure a long court battle as opposed to the accusing individuals withdrawing a claim once they realize there exists an accumulation of written documentation that may disprove their initial assertions.

5. *Confirm payment of taxes and insurance.* Ask for assurance that payroll taxes and the relevant insurance premiums have been paid by the PEO on a timely basis. Quarterly audits can be reviewed as an example.

6. *Require a termination clause.* Make sure that the service agreement includes a termination clause that provides a means to end the agreement with no penalties.

7. *Select a PEO that specializes in dealing with the health care industry.* Because of the stringent agency requirements, health care professionals can be among the most educated and sophisticated individuals in the work force. In a typical small practice, the employees not only interact with one another but virtually all of these employees also interact in some way with the patients and physicians as well, even if it just involves basic courtesy and a professional and friendly demeanor. This presents a different exposure level with regard to employee issues.

This is quite different from what may occur in a typical small, non-health-care business, where the employees interact only with other employees and their supervisors. For this reason, a PEO that handles a variety of industries may not be as suitable for a practitioner as one that specializes in health care.

Choosing a PEO with health care specialization can also be beneficial in other areas, including the availability of training opportunities and a seminar curriculum geared toward the needs of the practice. Available topics may include the following:

- Customer service and patient relations.
- Achieving success in a managed care environment.
- Medical billing procedures.
- Limiting malpractice liability.
- Maintaining a healthy practice.

Some PEOs can also offer other subjects such as basic supervisory skills, stress reduction in the workplace, and time management and organizational skills, which have a more universal application.

8. *Verify licensing requirements.* Some states require a PEO to be licensed or registered. If your state requires this, be sure that the PEO meets the proper requirements.

9. *Association membership.* The national trade association of the PEO industry is NAPEO. Members share a commitment to ongoing education, professional development as service providers, and their own as well as the association's code of ethics.

Note: *The information contained in this chapter has been compiled and presented from experience gained in this industry and familiarity with the many benefits that the PEO relationship can bring. This information does not necessarily represent the opinion of all PEOs and is not intended to be used as legal advice.*

REFERENCES AND READINGS

Larsen, A. *The Law of Workmen's Compensation.* New York: Matthew Bender, 1990.
O'Brien, D. W., & Eggleston (O'Brien), B. M. *California Workers' Compensation Claims and Benefits*, Tenth Edition. New York: Lexis Law Publishing, 1999.

## CHAPTER 4

Management Information Systems for the "Wired" Medical Office

Computer Hardware, Software, Applications, and the Internet

William P. Scherer

> Do spend money on medical MIS, but not spend it needlessly on gadgets that do not add value to your practice.
>
> —Hope Rachel Hetico, Health Care Consultant

Since the invention of the personal computer (PC), physicians have transformed their paper-and-pencil office management systems into real-time digital data powerhouses. There is no question that computers have become a ubiquitous part of daily practice in the modern-day medical office. With the tremendous increase and complexity of paperwork required by Medicare, Medicaid, health maintenance organizations (HMOs), and preferred provider organizations (PPOs), computers can no longer be considered luxury items. Additionally, computers have started a medical information revolution in telecommunication, using the Internet, World Wide Web, and on-line services.

The impact of computers in the physician's office has been nothing short of revolutionary. Tasks that used to require days of work by hand can now be accomplished within minutes with the aid of a computer. The old-style pegboard system of accounting has rapidly been replaced by sophisticated medical office manager programs. In addition to providing exact accounts receivable, to the penny, most medical software allows the user to generate unlimited financial reports with a breakdown of patient demographics and trends.

It should be noted that computers can't do anything magical that an average secretary can't perform by hand. However, the speed and accuracy of machines allow physicians precise control over their bookkeeping and medical documentation. Computers are also excellent tools to eliminate repetitive, time-consuming tasks like typing operative reports, composing referral letters, and completing HCFA 1500 insurance forms. A computer doesn't replace human beings, but it does help them to do their jobs faster and more efficiently. Computers have no innate intelligence; they can't think, reason, or create. They are totally dependent on a human operator and must be told what to do, step by step. An old computer adage "garbage-in, garbage-out" means that if the information entered into a computer is inaccurate, then the reports that are produced are worthless.

NEEDS DETERMINATION

Before purchasing a computer system, you must determine if you really need a computer. Physicians who use billing services to process their insurance claims or independent practitioners who are employed by an HMO or medical clinic may never feel the need for a computer in their practice. However, most new practitioners and large multidoctor practices can expect significant increased productivity when computers are properly applied to automate their offices.

Purchasing a computer system for your office can be an extremely confusing and overwhelming experience for both the novice and the seasoned professional. The practitioner needs to carefully and intelligently evaluate a variety of choices and prices before deciding on a specific system to meet their individual needs. Investing a little time and effort to research the available options will allow the physician to make a true informed decision.

Once a decision is made to computerize an office practice, the physician must make a personal commitment to understand "computerese." It is not advisable to assign your office manager or staff secretary the job of deciding which computer system you need. Too many physicians rush out to buy a computer system simply because their colleagues have done so. Since the monetary penalty for making a poor choice can be in the five-figure range or more, it is evident that the physician must personally become an educated consumer. It is advisable to buy a few different magazines that specialize in computers, such as *PC Magazine* or *Macworld*, to help understand certain topics. Reading the ads in newspapers and magazines can also be an educational experience.

The local library can also be an excellent source of information for physicians, and most libraries have current subscriptions to the popular computer magazines. Although most computer books become dated within 1 year of publication, there are quite a few outstanding buyer's guides that are published on a yearly basis. There is even an annual computer buying guide published by *Consumer Guide* that features best-buy recommendations for many categories of computers, software, and peripherals.

One of the best ways to become computer literate is to sign up for an introduction to computers class at a local high school or community college. Prices for these courses are usually less than $100, and they are given at night to accommodate working adults. Local computer stores and even specialized computer consultants also offer instructional courses and usually provide more flexibility in time and day selection than the public schools do.

Even though modern computers have become extremely easy to use compared to the first-generation systems, no system is completely "user friendly." A basic understanding of some technical terms is necessary to allow you to learn, use, and carry on a reasonable conversation about computers. Like medicine, computers have their fair share of confusing jargon and specialized acronyms and seem incredibly complex when looked at as a whole. Once the basics are understood, most people find computers to be not so mysterious and actually enjoy discussing new applications.

POINT OF PURCHASE

There are many places to purchase a computer system, ranging from discount mail order companies to the local Office Depot or a medical software vendor. Even though price is usually the first feature most shoppers look for, the quality of the hardware and the support provided are the most important options doctors should consider. Research the company by reading current medical and computer magazines or ask colleagues what they think of their present systems.

If you are looking to selectively upgrade your present system to include all of the latest bells and whistles, you may have to go to a local computer specialist to help you install the necessary parts. If you check the Yellow Pages, you can even find that there are computer professionals who, like many physicians, will make house calls to help you fix or upgrade your present system.

A solo practitioner can obtain state-of-the-art hardware and some basic medical and managed care software programs for about $10,000–$12,000; a small to medium-sized group practice, for about $30,000–$50,000; and a large group practice with multiple satellite offices, for about $50,000–$100,000.

Accordingly, in order to create the ideal management information systems (MIS) configuration for your wired medical office, the following hardware, software, and peripheral items should be considered, either by the practitioner or an information technology (IT) consultant.

COMPUTER HARDWARE SYSTEM CONFIGURATIONS

All computer systems are composed of two parts: the hardware and the software. The hardware includes the tangible parts of the computer, such as the monitor, disk drive, and keyboard. The programs that run the hardware and allow the user to interact with the computer are known as software. These two parts work synergistically to impart speed, accuracy, and flexibility.

When computers were first invented, they were composed of vacuum tubes and were larger than an operating room. They used large amounts of electricity, gave off a lot of heat, and required a full-time technician. Then came the invention of transistors, which did the same job as the vacuum tubes but much better and faster and used less space. Scientists later discovered that by modifying the transistors to multiply their number and by miniaturizing the electronic components, they could produce even more efficient and varied devices.

The new generation of electronics were termed microchips, integrated circuit chips, and finally microprocessors. Currently, microprocessors are used to control modern-day computers and are even starting to appear in many electronic devices, ranging from automobiles to microwave ovens. Every year newer, faster, smaller, and more sophisticated microprocessors are introduced into the computer marketplace. The end result is the development of extremely powerful computers at very reasonable cost.

Data Configurations

Computer microprocessor performance is based on whether miniature electronic switches are turned on or off, assigning the number 1 to switches that are turned on and 0 to those that are switched off. Computers perform their complex functions by using a simple mathematical formula called the binary system. Computer memory consists of electronic or magnetic cells, each of which contains information on whether the switch is open or closed.

The smallest piece of electronic data that can be processed by a computer is called a bit. A bit is a binary digit that occupies a memory cell and is either a 1 or a 0. The cells, or bits, are usually linked together in a 8-bit sequence of adjacent binary digits that the computer considers a unit, called a byte. One byte of memory represents one character, either a number, a letter, or a space. For example, it takes one byte of computer memory to store the letter *F;* it takes four bytes of memory to store the word *hand.*

Microprocessor Speed

To make large amounts of memory easy to describe, thousands of bytes of memory are described as kilobytes (KB or K) and millions of bytes are referred to as megabytes (MB). Thus, 256KB would represent 256,000 bytes, and 8MB would represent 8,000,000 bytes. Technically, because of the binary nature of computer memory, 1K actually represents 1,024 bytes, and 1MB ends up as 1,048,576 bytes.

One of the many factors that determine the computing power of a microprocessor is the clock speed, recorded in megahertz (MHz). The clock speed is determined by utilizing the frequency of the vibrations from a quartz crystal to regulate data transfer. The clock rate is a measurement of the millions of cycles per second the microprocessor executes. Thus, the larger the MHz, the faster the computer can process information.

Bus Size

Bus size refers to the number of bits of data the computer can send or receive. The first-generation Intel 8088 microprocessors used an 8-bit data bus, whereas the latest Intel Pentium microprocessors utilize 64-bit data paths. A 64-bit data bus can process eight times the amount of data as a 8-bit bus operating at the same clock speed. High-speed memory cache can also be used like a turbocharger for microprocessors and can double the processing power of most non-cached computers.

Random Access Memory

All computers contain random access memory (RAM), system memory, or simply memory. RAM is a superfast temporary holding place for data and computer code that is loaded from a floppy disk or hard disk and has a great impact on computer performance. RAM is measured in megabytes (MB) and is equivalent to 1 million characters of storage. The bare bones minimum amount of system RAM for any current computer is 16MB; however, most systems contain 64MB of RAM, and top-of-the-line computers have 128MB. Users will notice improvement in system performance with a RAM of 64MB for Windows or Macintosh-based computers.

Floppy Disk Drives

Because RAM is only a temporary storage for computer data, users need the ability to save their files on a more permanent medium. The most popular types of data storage are the floppy disk and the hard disk drives. Most floppy disks contain a 3.5-inch diskette that can store 1.44MB of data and allow the user to easily transport data between two locations. Zip drives (really cartridges) ($100), by Iomega, can hold up to 100 MB more; the newest drives, up to 250MB of data. Floppy disks are formatted to either a PC or a Macintosh format for data storage. Macintosh computers can read disks created with Macs or PCs, but PCs can't read Macintosh diskettes.

HARD DISK DRIVES

Hard disk drives are located inside the computer system case and provide rapid access to your computer files; they have much greater storage capacity than floppy diskettes. Look for a minimum of 10GB (gigabyte) capacity for the PC and Macintosh. Enhanced integrated drive electronics (EIDE) drives are used in the PC; small computer system interface (SCSI) drives are used in the Macintosh. The speed of hard disk drives are measured in milliseconds (ms), and users should purchase drives with a speed rating of around 10ms.

Physicians who currently have a computer and are interested in upgrading their hard disk drives can expect significant improvement in their overall system performance. Most medical office management software is data-intensive and requires a speedy disk drive to process time-consuming tasks like monthly accounts receivables and detailed practice analysis reports. In addition to increased performance, larger hard disks will allow the user to store more information than an older drive will.

A hard disk drive is one of the few moving parts in a computer system, and physicians should be aware that, for a variety of reasons, their hard drive could wear out and damage or possibly lose valuable data. Even though most hard disk drives are rated to last at least 100,000 hours of use, even a small sector error could result in a program malfunction. The best method to secure and archive computer data is to perform a daily backup of the hard disk drive with a tape backup device or a high-capacity removable cartridge disk drive.

Hard Drive Back-up Systems

Unfortunately, archival backup systems, one of the most important computer peripherals, are not considered a standard feature on any computer system available today. There are a variety of inexpensive tape backup devices, such as the Colorado series, made for the PC and Macintosh, that allow a user to copy all of the information from a hard disk drive to a streaming tape for security or to use in another location.

Additionally, new removable hard disk cartridge devices are available that attach to the serial or parallel port and offer a faster backup method than tapes.

Monitors and Video Cards

Two of the most expensive components of a computer system are the monitor and video graphic card. These are also the only parts of a computer that have not gotten less expensive over the past few years. The average computer screen for most physicians is a 15-inch color monitor. One of the deceptions in a computer advertisement is that a 15-inch monitor, in reality, has less than a 14-inch viewable image. Power users who want to take full advantage of Windows or System 8.5 or 9.0 graphical user interfaces should consider purchasing a 17-inch or 19-inch monitor.

IBM-COMPATIBLE MACHINES VERSUS MACINTOSH SYSTEMS

Although there are thousands of brands of computers, they all are based on a few different microprocessor types. The most popular styles of microprocessors for the medical office and home environments are Intel and PowerPC. Intel microprocessors are used by IBM-compatible PCs; PowerPC microprocessors are used by the Apple Macintosh line of computers.

Making the right choices for purchasing a computer system is a major concern for all physicians. Before shopping, the decision must be made on what the computer will be used for and what microprocessor family, peripherals, and accessories will be needed. It is essential that these questions are considered before shopping and that the purchaser remain uninfluenced by sales pressure, seasonal rebates, two-day closet sales, or local price wars. In the end, you can expect years of faithful service from whichever system you choose to buy.

Computer systems, like Medicare rules and regulations, are constantly evolving, making it difficult for the average doctor to keep up with the almost weekly changes. The good news for the profession is that the cutthroat competition within the computer industry provides users with more power and features that cost less than last year's system. If you purchased a computer more than 2 years ago, it is time to reevaluate your components to determine if you can benefit from selected upgrades or an entirely new system. Even though you may be perfectly content with your present system, the cost benefit of new purchases can produce improved productivity. If you are in the minority of physicians who still do not own a computer system, this chapter will help you become an informed consumer.

There are two main choices for computer purchasers: the PC (aka IBM-compatible) or the Macintosh. The PC, based on an Intel microprocessor, dominates the marketplace with a estimated 85% market share of office and home computer systems. Most PC's use an operating system designed by Microsoft: Disk Operating System (DOS), Windows 3.1, Windows 95/98/2000, or Windows NT. The Macintosh, made by Apple, represents a much smaller market share than PCs have but has a very loyal and dedicated following. The Macintosh System 8.5 or 9.0 operating system is famous for its ease of use and efficiency.

The Intel microprocessor has been the brains behind PCs since it was introduced in 1981. There are six generations of Intel microprocessors, with increasing computer power, in models that include 8086, 80286, 80386, 80486, Pentium, Pentium Pro, and Pentium II and III. Physicians shopping for a new computer system should purchase a system based on a Pentium III microprocessor with a clock speed faster than 450MHz. If you own a computer based on an Intel 80486 or slower, you can expect a significant improvement in computer processing speed with a Pentium motherboard upgrade or a new system.

Depending on which model of Intel microprocessor you may own, upgrading an existing PC can be either a complete waste of money or a viable alternative to purchasing a new computer. If you own a computer based on an 8086 or 80286 microprocessor, it would be impractical to upgrade, and you would be better off purchasing an entirely new system. If your system is based on a 80386 or 80486, upgrading your microprocessor to a Pentium while keeping the original hard disk, RAM, disk drives, keyboard, computer case, and monitor can save hundreds of dollars compared to buying a new system.

The Macintosh computer used to be based on a Motorola microprocessor that included the 6800, 68020, 68030, 68040, and 68060. The current Macintosh systems are now based on the PowerPC 601, 603e, or 604 microprocessor, which offers greater performance than the older Motorola microprocessors. If you are looking to purchase a Macintosh, look to the Power Macintosh 7200 as the minimum system or the top-of-the-line Power Macintosh 9500.

Of course, the new iMac is currently very popular, having sold more than a million units last year and bringing Apple back from the brink of obscurity ($1,500). It features plug-in-lay compatibility and immediate Internet access. One disadvantage is its lack of a floppy disk drive, which can be added separately. Other add-ons include an iView video camera from Ariston ($120); the USB pen partner from Wacom ($100); the Image Mate digital film card reader from San Disk ($90); and the Smart One 56-k modem, from Best Data ($100). Upgrading an older Macintosh can be accomplished by replacing the logic board or adding a card to certain machines.

LAPTOP AND NOTEBOOK COMPUTERS

Laptop and notebook computers are among the fastest-growing segments in the computer industry. Physicians who have multiple offices or nursing homes can take their laptop computers along with them on the road. A few notable physicians are even giving national lectures and presentations from their laptops at many of the medical seminars. Shopping for a laptop computer is similar to that for desktops except that you will pay a premium of around 50% more for a computer with the same features.

There are many important considerations that need to be made when shopping for a laptop or notebook computer. Price, weight, memory, hard disk size, screen display, expandability, ruggedness, and keyboard styles are just a few of the many features that separate one portable computer from another. If you are interested in a Macintosh, the PowerBook packs a PowerPC microprocessor, 32MB RAM, 1 GB hard disk, and a 10.4-inch dual scan color monitor in an ergonomically designed portable case for under $2,500. The Toshiba Satellite has an amazing Pentium II microprocessor, 64MB RAM, 5 GB hard disk, and a 10.4-inch active matrix monitor that sells for under $2,000.

COMPUTER RELATED PERIPHERAL DEVICES

Modems

The information superhighway, Internet, World Wide Web, and commercial on-line service providers have gotten tremendous attention within the past year. These computer networks can be accessed by anyone with a PC and a modem. A computer modem (modulation-demodulation) allows a computer to communicate with another computer over ordinary analog telephone lines. Modems can be internal or external to the system case and are rated in speeds of bits per second (bps).

Modems are one area of technology where it is crucial to have the fastest device to take full advantage of the information superhighway. Physicians should purchase only a modem that is rated at 56,000 bps or faster and should incorporate fax capabilities as well as voice mail. If you currently own a slower modem, with a speed of 14,400, 9600, or 2400 bps, upgrading to a 56,000 bps modem will cost around $150 but will quickly pay for itself when you can get more information in substantially less time than with an older modem. Also, realize that bandwidth (measure of information in bits) is more important than modem speed for high speed Internet access. The following three broadband services are currently available in most areas of the country.

    Cable Modem: Analysts expect cable modems to become the dominant form of Internet access because of existing telephone line connections. Top speed for a cable modem is about 30 million BPS.
    Route: Ordinary telephone lines.
    Advantage: Pre-existing television cables.
    Disadvantage: The more doctors, or neighbors who log on, the slower it is.

    DSL Line: Digital subscriber lines do not interfere with voice traffic and can be downloaded at 384 kilobits per second, to 1.54 megabits per second.
    Route: Ordinary telephone lines.
    Advantage: Guaranteed speed of data connections.
    Disadvantage: Office must be near a phone switching station.

    Satellite Dish: Speeds of up to 400 kbps to 45 mbps may be possible in this potentially ubiquitous services.
    Route: Transmissions go to a dish antenna.
    Advantage: No cable wires are necessary.
    Disadvantage: Fast speeds apply only to downloading. Still needs a phone line for sending mouse commands to the satellite and dish.

Many consumer software titles take advantage of multimedia computers to display music, video, and animation. In order to handle this increased software demand, multimedia computers must be equipped with a CD-ROM, sound card, and external speakers. The Macintosh has built-in sound capabilities, whereas a PC needs a separate sound adapter installed. Sound cards for the PC should be compatible with the Sound Blaster standard, made by Creative Labs, Inc. Additionally, the best-quality sound cards use wavetable synthesis rather than the older FM synthesis to create sounds. The choice in speakers ranges from an inexpensive $25 pair made by Radio Shack to $800 concert-quality Bose surround-sound speakers.

CD-ROMs

Virtually every computer system purchased today comes equipped with an internal CD-ROM (compact disk-read only memory), even though most physicians do not have the need for one in their office practice. CD-ROM drives provide the most efficient means to transfer large software titles onto the computer's hard disk drive. Previously, users would have to load their programs from as many as 20 floppy disks that can now be replaced with one CD-ROM. The computer industry has also embraced CD-ROMs as an effective method of preventing software piracy.

    CD-ROM drives are rated on rotation speeds, compared to standard audio-only CD players. The first CD-ROM drives that were introduced to the consumer marketplace in 1990 were rated 1X, which had a spin rotation equal to an audio CD player. The 1X drives proved to be very slow, compared to relatively fast hard disk drives and faster 2X, 4X, 6X, 8X, 10X, 20X, 24X, and even 32X and 40X drives, which were introduced to overcome the original limitations of 1X players. The current recommendation is to purchase a CD-ROM with at least a 20X–24X speed rating or a 10X DVD player.

Printers

Choosing a printer is dependent on what you intend to print and how much you want to spend. The three most popular types of printers are laser, dot matrix, and inkjet. Laser printers offer the best print quality at the fastest available speeds and generally cost more than any other type of printer. Dot matrix printers are the only type of printer that can print multipart forms like the HCFA-1500, but they are very noisy and produce the lowest print quality of the three types of printers. Inkjet printers are almost as good as laser printers in terms of print quality but are about one-quarter the speed, and the printed page can smear if it gets wet. Inkjet printers are also the only type of printer that can offer color printing at a reasonable price.

WANs and LANs

Many medical offices have multiple computers attached together to form a local area network (LAN) or wide area network (WAN). A LAN or WAN allows multiple staff members to access and share patient files, printers, hard disk drives, and CD-ROMs. Apple includes a basic peer-to-peer network capability as a standard feature on all Macintosh computers. PCs, on the other hand, have to install specialized Ethernet network cards and network software like LANtastic or Windows to run a network.

Surge Protection

Protecting a computer investment with the proper surge protection and uninterruptable power supply (UPS) is one of the most overlooked features among shoppers. A simple surge protector can be purchased for approximately $20 and will provide basic protection from unpredictable power spikes and surges. A better choice for the office environment is a UPS device that costs around $200 that will supply 5 to 30 minutes of emergency power in the event of a total blackout as well as protecting against spikes and surges.

INTEGRATED BUSINESS OFFICE SOFTWARE SUITE SYSTEMS

Over the past 10 years, the advances in software have been nothing short of revolutionary. In 1987 physicians were limited to individual DOS-based programs that had to be purchased separately and would cost several thousand dollars. With the advent of Windows and Macintosh graphical user interfaces, integrated software suites rapidly replaced individual programs and provide the most cost-effective way to purchase office productivity software.

Software suites are a relatively new category of software that integrates several of the most popular office applications into a single seamless package. Currently there are three suite packages, including Microsoft Office, Corel Office Professional, and Lotus SmartSuite. While the Corel Office is popular with WordPerfect Users and Lotus SmartSuite is popular with Lotus 1-2-3 users, Microsoft Office is the undisputed leader, with a 90% market share and superior application integration. Therefore, the individual components that make up this best-selling suite will be addressed.

Microsoft Office

With over 60 million users, Microsoft Office is an amazing software package that is offered in many different versions for the Windows 95 and 98, Windows 3.x, and Macintosh operating systems. The flagship version, designed for Windows 95, is Office 97 Professional Edition ($300), which includes: Word, a word processor; Excel, a spreadsheet; PowerPoint, presentation graphics and slide show producer; Access, a database; Outlook, a desktop information manager; Publisher, a desktop publisher; Internet Explorer, a popular Internet browser; and Bookshelf Basics, a set of on-line references. The Standard Edition ($200) is similar to the Professional Edition but does not include Access, Publisher, or Bookshelf Basics. The Small Business Edition ($200) includes two programs not found in the other versions: AutoMap Streets Plus and Small Business Financial Manager but does not include Access, PowerPoint, Internet Explorer, and Bookshelf Basics.

Microsoft's objective for the Office 97 suite is to make it easier for people to get their work done by designing and building the best desktop applications in the world. Microsoft invested more than 25,000 hours of research in the designing of Microsoft Office 97 to gain an understanding of how users expect and want their software to work. "Our investment in understanding the needs of customers and our continued ability to deliver exciting enhancements are the cornerstone of Office's ongoing success," said William H. Gates III, CEO of Microsoft. "Customers will be very pleased with Internet integration, the new collaboration capabilities of Outlook 97, and the IntelliSense technology featured in Office Assistant."

Microsoft Word gives physicians everything they need to create professional looking documents, transcribe their SOAP (subjective, objective, assessment, and plan) notes, create letters of medical necessity, and share information on the printed page or on the Internet with other health care providers. Word includes many useful features to help users create and edit documents. The Letter Wizard structures the layout of a letter and inserts dates and addresses automatically, and Grammar Check proofreads documents for grammatical and spelling errors in real time as users type. The Web Page Wizard makes it easy for doctors to create documents with imbedded hyperlinks, graphics, and tables for rapid publication on the Internet.

Microsoft Excel is one of the easiest spreadsheet programs to learn how to use and incorporates several analysis tools that can turn raw numbers into valuable forecasting data. Physicians can keep track of CPT codes, relative value units (RVU), capitation rates, follow-up days, Medicare allowables, Medicaid allowables, and managed care percentage rates. Once the initial information is entered, the power of spreadsheets can then be utilized. As an example, if you are debating weather you should sign up for an HMO contract that reimburses physicians on a certain percentage of Medicare or certain dollar amount per RVU, you can forecast the impact on your practice by changing one number in the spreadsheet. New web technologies such as Web Queries and URLs in Formulas bring information from the Internet into Excel for rich analysis and presentation.

For instance, as a participating provider, you can calculate what you can collect from Medicare, as seen in Table 4.1. The number in the first column might represent the amount that Medicare estimates that the UCR "should be." The rules state that they will allow the MD to collect only 80% of that UCR, which is the participating amount. Of that 80% the patient must pay 20% up to their deductible, and Medicare will pay the remaining 80% of the 80%. The third column would list what Medicare will pay, and the fourth column, what the patient must pay you.

To create your own similar spreadsheet, take the participating amount that Medicare allows. For example, if for Procedure A, the actual Medicare allowable charge is 47.20 (second column). Medicare allows MD providers to charge 80% of what they consider the fee should be, in this case $59.63 (first column). To calculate the first column, multiple the actual Medicare participating amount by 1.2 to give a figure for the first column.

Remember, Medicare actually reimburses 80% of what you are allowed to charge. So multiply the figure in column 2 by 0.8 to obtain the amount of what the Medicare payment will be. Subtract this figure from the figure in column 2 to estimate what the patient payment is.

Microsoft PowerPoint is used by many physicians to organize and develop presentation slides for lecturing at national, state, and regional medical meetings. PowerPoint delivers numerous innovations that enable presenters to easily organize, illustrate, and promote their research in the office, at a seminar, or on the Internet. There are numerous animation effects, sound effects, clip art, drawings,

TABLE 4.1   Participating Provider Spreadsheet

UCR	Actual Medicare	Medicare Payment	Patient Payment	Procedure
59.63	47.70	38.16	9.54	A
83.01	66.41	53.13	13.28	B
50.18	40.14	32.11	8.03	C
64.11	51.29	41.03	10.26	D
27.68	22.14	14.71	4.43	E
28.40	22.72	18.18	4.54	F

and charting samples included on the CD-ROM to help bring presentations to life. Keeping with the Internet integration theme, the HTML Wizard automatically creates complete Web presentations, including navigation controls, frames, and animations that take advantage of the PowerPoint Animation Player browser extension. Physicians can even record and add their own voice to their on-line presentations.

Microsoft Access builds on its rich tradition of innovation by extending the role of desktop databases to the Web. Traditional database applications in medicine include surgical logs, office inventory control, CME courses, DME logs, membership directories, and keeping track of blood or urine cultures for CLIA certification. Access can also integrate data from a wide variety of sources, including HTML pages from the Internet. Physicians can even create Web pages that contain live views of their data so that Web browsers can interactively query, update, or add information to their databases.

Microsoft Outlook is the newest addition to Office. It is designed to make it easier to communicate with others by integrating E-mail, scheduling, contacts, tasks, and access to documents. An innovative E-mail function, such as AutoPreview, displays the first three lines of each E-mail message so that users can quickly prioritize which messages to read or delete. Message Flags allow users to mark E-mail messages to help prioritize follow-up actions.

Stedman's Spellchecker and Dictionary

The major limitation of software-based spellcheckers, no matter what word processor you may use, is the inability to recognize medical terminology. Unfortunately, when you create a medical document such as a SOAP note or a research paper, the spellchecker flags any word it does not recognize and forces you to verify or correct the spelling. Stedman's Plus ($99.95), by Williams & Wilkins (800-527-5597), is the most comprehensive and powerful medical spellchecking software on the market and provides a solution for medical professionals.

Stedman's Plus, Version 5.0, contains more than 432,000 up-to-date medical, pharmaceutical, and bioscience terms. In addition, there are over 30,000 trade and generic drug names from the PDR generics database, 63,000 eponymic terms, 73,000 medical/surgical instrumentation, and over 60,000 bioscience terms from the *International Dictionary of Medicine and Biology*. The software works as an add-on to DOS, Windows, and Macintosh versions of WordPerfect, Microsoft Word, Lotus AmiPro, and WordPro word processors, and no medical office should be without it.

Stedman's Electronic Medical Dictionary 3.0 ($79.95) is the computerized version of the famous 100,000-word *Stedman's Medical Dictionary*, 26th edition. This software enables you to find the definition of any medical word or phrase from within any application. For example, if you are entering charges in your office practice management software and want to look up the definition of "tenosynovitis," pressing a hotkey combination (Control + Left Shift + D) will bring up the definition, pronunciation, etymology, and hyphenation of the word.

The best part of using the electronic dictionary rather that the printed version is the ability to perform a variety of searches. You can browse for words based on an index, which displays the term you want, the definition and an alphabetical listing of the terms following it. The "Search On" option lets users search for terms within the definitions and anagrams of other words in the dictionary. However, the greatest feature of the software is the ability to search for terms using wildcard characters to stand for a letter in a word. This is useful when you can't remember exactly how to spell a word or are stuck on a crossword puzzle. Ever since the first version of Stedman's Electronic Medical Dictionary was released several years ago, it has earned a permanent place in most physicians' office computers.

Quicken and QuickBooks

According to a national Quicken Survey, managing money is so stressful that 34% of Americans develop physiological symptoms such as moodiness, anger, headaches, insomnia, upset stomach, backaches, and rashes as a result. Additionally, 28% of Americans do not currently know how much money they have in their bank accounts and 15% have bounced at least one check during the past year. There is no question that, next to your office practice management software and a word processor, business accounting software is a must-have for doctors to maintain complete control over their personal and business finances.

Quicken ($49) and QuickBooks ($99), by Intuit, are the most popular personal and small-business financial software in the computer industry. With a 70% market share and leading in the development of on-line banking, Quicken has become synonymous with computerized checkbook accounting. "Our goal is to lift the burden of financial hassles from individuals and small businesses. Our products and services organize users' financial matters and help them understand their finances with a click of a mouse," said Scott D. Cook, chairman of Intuit. "We're working toward the day when users will receive and act on all financial matters electronically—without paper transactions."

Quicken is designed mainly to organize personal finances and is like a checkbook on steroids. To get started using Quicken, you must first set up your bank and credit card accounts by entering information from your latest statements. Once your basic account information is set up, Quicken manages every dollar deposited, every check written, every item purchased with your credit cards, and your investment interest. By using the built-in calendar, you can schedule your bills to be paid and the software reminds you when they are due. In addition, you can create budgets, reports, and graphs to show you where your money goes and to simplify tax planning for your accountant.

The cornerstone of Quicken is an intuitive mouse-driven interface organized the way people think and work rather than as the traditional menu-driven approach. Unlike conventional icon bars, which take users from one place to another in a program without explanation or options, Quicken's activity bar presents multiple choices of related activities and explains them in plain English instead of cryptic computer terminology. The activity bar is located at the bottom of the screen and allows users to jump between different accounts and reports without having to navigate through multiple menu screens.

To ease the transition to computerized bookkeeping for new users and financial novices, Quicken provides active help at every step and a multimedia overview that includes step-by-step instructions for getting started. Audio assistance and on-screen written instructions throughout the program always make it clear what to do next. To further prevent customers from making frustrating mistakes, Quicken anticipates customers' most frequent errors, intercepts them with on-screen messages before they go astray, and guides them back on track. Of interest to recent graduates, the interactive Debt Reduction Planner can help physicians develop an action plan for getting out of debt sooner and save money on interest charges.

QuickBooks is a project-tracking and small-business accounting package that is based on the ease of use of the original Quicken program. Most physicians would benefit from QuickBooks' additional features because it incorporates a complete payroll tracking function. QuickBooks automatically calculates earnings and deductions; prints payroll voucher checks; creates 940s, 941s, W-2s, W-3s, and 1099 tax documents; and includes built-in tax tables. One of the most useful features is the inventory tracker that shows what items you are overstocked on and what supplies you need to order.

The most exciting feature of QuickBooks is the integrated on-line banking and payment option. For the first time, doctors do not have to leave their desks or pick up a phone to see which checks have cleared, view the current balances for all their bank accounts, or transfer money between accounts. Paying monthly bills, while never a enjoyable experience, can easily be performed on-line without having to write a check—much less sign or mail them. To pay bills, simply schedule when you want to send a payment to a vendor, click a button on the mouse, and the process is done. Physicians may be skeptical about sending and receiving their financial data on-line, but QuickBooks is extremely secure and reliable; all transactions are handled through a private network using state-of-the-art encryption technology.

WinFax Pro

According to Davidson Consulting, over 336 billion pages will be faxed worldwide this year. Although most of these faxes are sent and received by traditional fax machines, a small percentage of professionals have been using the power of a computer to control their fax documentation. Since 1994 most computer modems have had built-in fax capabilities, and new software has been created to virtually replace stand-alone fax machines. Symantec's WinFax Pro ($99) is the world's best-selling fax software. It enables users to fax a document from any Windows program and to receive and manage all their fax communications from their computer.

Aimed at general business users and professional organizations, WinFax Pro provides increased quality and convenience over stand-alone fax machines. Faxes that originate from a computer require no scanning, don't have to be printed before faxing, and don't require you to leave your seat to transmit. WinFax Pro has an intelligent fax transmission engine that is able to detect transmission failures, auto-correct, and auto-configure, for improved reliability. Advanced telephony features like TalkWorks take advantage of the new "voice-enabled" modems and add voice answering machine, speakerphone, automatic speed dialing, caller ID, and fax on-demand functions.

State medical associations can take advantage of WinFax Pro's optional Fax Broadcast feature to send the same fax to 1 or 10,000 people, virtually simultaneously. With a click of a mouse button, the Fax Broadcast receives your phone list and document directly from your computer and then guarantees that the last person on the list receives your message at virtually the same time as the first person. You can even schedule faxes to work around international and regional time differences to take advantage of lower telephone rates outside peak business hours.

MEDICAL PROGRESS NOTES SOFTWARE

Most physicians would agree that one of the least enjoyable aspects of practice is the time and effort involved in producing medical records of patient encounters. While handwriting has stood the test of time and doesn't incur any direct expenses, it can be very time-consuming and may require transcription if a referral letter is needed by another doctor or an insurance company. Dictating patient notes into a tape recorder is extremely easy and fast but can involve a significant expense that may be hard to justify as the health care dollar shrinks.

Your medical records are a permanent recording of your patient treatment encounters and can be audited by Medicare, reviewed by managed care organizations, and even subpoenaed by an attorney. By now every physician has heard the famous statement, "If it's not documented in the chart, you didn't do it." Maintaining high-quality, legible medical records is no longer a luxury physicians can afford to do without.

MediNotes

MediNotes Corporation (515-277-1500) has created a Windows-based software program designed to help ensure Medicare compliance by allowing physicians to generate notes through its intuitive interface and robust selection of findings. They have even licensed all the CPT and ICD-9 codes directly from the American Medical Association to ensure users that the most current codes are available to link to different billing software packages.

MediNotes is based upon the popular SOAP note format that is used by most medical professionals. There are several options available when you want to create a patient note, depending on whether it is for a new or an established patient. Templates allow you to create a note using predefined wording for common conditions such as hypertension and diabetes. Rather that using canned templates, doctors use an interactive fill-in-the-blanks form to create a custom report. In addition, you can create a new note from a previous note for the same or a different patient, or build a note from scratch.

As you create your patient's progress note, MediNotes allows you to use point-and-click findings for each section of the SOAP note. As you click various findings, they will appear in a text box that represents your note dictation. Drag-and-drop findings can also be utilized for particular conditions by clicking on a subjective or objective finding and dragging it onto a photograph of a patient or radiograph. The patient's record is automatically updated with the exact location of their pathology, which can be modified according to each user's needs.

"Patient medical records are easily and accurately entered into your computer where they can be saved or printed. By using an electronic patient folder, Medi-Notes Deluxe can store photographs, x-rays, videos of gait, and conversations," said Scott Leum, president. "Imagine clicking one button to review your patient's medical history and allergies in chronological order. MediNotes Deluxe is the most flexible product available allowing you to enter patient medical records using the terminology preferred in your practice."

As the result of their physician user input, innovative ideas are continually being added to the program, making it more powerful and easier to use. Medi-Notes makes use of IBM's Voice Type Dictation for doctors who would rather dictate than type or click certain findings. Built-in medical spell-checking adds a professional appearance to your notes and referral letters. On-demand fax capabilities allow you to fax your notes directly from within the software to another physician's office. Customized patient instructions are also included and can be given to each patient as he or she leaves the office. An optional "Scheduling Simplified" module can track physician scheduling and tie together all of the daily office appointments in a single window.

To use MediNotes, you must have a PC with at least a 486 CPU, 8 MB RAM, Windows 3.1, and a printer. Prices for MediNotes start at $995 for the Lite version and $1,995 for the Deluxe version. The IBM Voice Type Dictation Version 3.0 is an extra $699, and the incredible Norand 6622 Pen Based Computer is a $3,995 option. While the Norand 6622 Mobile Computer may be on the expensive side for most doctors, it represents the most advanced solution to creating patient notes this side of *Star Trek*. This revolutionary data collection tablet must be seen to be believed. It allows physicians to create SOAP notes in real time while the patient is sitting in the treatment room!

Quick Notes

Since starting the computerized medical record revolution in 1989, Quick Notes, Inc. (800-536-6683, http://www.quicknotes.com) has become the granddaddy in our profession. Quick Notes starts at $1,795 and is the only medical system to utilize a hand-held bar scanner device to create progress notes from a wall chart or desk chart containing prewritten statements.

While holding the small fiberoptic wireless scanner, a physician can create complete and precise patient notes, narratives, and various reports. Documentation is accomplished by scanning words, numbers, phrases, or report bar codes located on the well-organized wall or desk chart. For example, a note could be created by scanning the following bar codes: scan "The patient presented with a chief complaint of" scan "severe" scan "and" scan "constant" scan "pain when walking." Scan "These symptoms are" scan "due to an athletic injury that occurred on" scan "6/30/97." The doctor will get immediate feedback that the bar code has been read properly by the audio tone emitted and the lighting of the LED on the scanner after it has moved across the bar code in either direction.

The scanner can be inserted in the downloader unit at any time of the day, after 1 or over a 100 patients. At the touch of a button the bar code information is fed into the computer. The computer then transcribes and stores the bar codes, forming words and phrases that create complete sentences and paragraphs. Within a few minutes, an entire day's records are transported into the computer and are available for immediate access, editing, storage, or printing.

The optional Quick Notes +Plus ($595) software package gives the physician the ability to go into greater detail for specific textbook-style descriptions with a single bar code scan. Quick Notes +Plus also contains a built-in word processor, which offers physicians an easy way to incorporate their own referral letters, template reports, or descriptions of common diagnosis with their daily notes in minutes. There is also an optional Quick Reports ($695) module that will allow you to scan your own consent forms, history and physicals, and operative reports with a single swipe of the scanner.

HotDocs

The least expensive solution to improve the efficiency of your progress notes is to create your own macros in a word processor or use specialized macro creation software to automate the way you currently write or dictate your documentation. HotDocs Pro (800-500-3627, http://www.capsoft.com) is a $99 software program that significantly reduces the time spent producing repetitive, routine documents, such as histories and physicals, oral examinations, and osteopathic, podiatric, or chiropractic manipulations.

Physicians can use HotDocs to create master forms based on their own word processor documents. The master form displays customized dialogues that ask questions and then uses the answers to create a unique document. HotDocs master forms not only speed document production, they also improve the quality of finished documents by ensuring that pronouns, verb tenses, plurals, dates, and so on are correctly merged and formatted throughout the document. Hot-Docs runs inside most major word processors, including WordPerfect, DOS and Windows versions; Microsoft Word; and Ami Pro.

HotDocs allows users to move backward and forward through dialogues in case a previous selection needs to be changed. This feature is a major advantage over basic macro systems included in word processors, which don't allow backing up to change selections. Users can also attach a script to a dialogue based on a condition so that they will take effect only if the user enters a certain answer.

For example, if a patient has diabetes, HotDocs can require the doctor to enter specific information on his or her medical condition. However, if the patient doesn't have diabetes, HotDocs can hide the extra diabetic questionnaire so that it won't appear to the user.

There is a library within HotDocs where users can create folders to organize master forms. This allows physicians to create folders like "new patient," "follow-up," or "postop." HotDocs has a drag-and-drop expression-building utility that enables nonprogrammers to write sophisticated rule-based expressions. This feature is a powerful tool for building "if, then, else" expressions, for determining the correct insertion of pronouns, verb tense, computed numbers, date values, and optional and conditional languages.

MANAGED CARE AND MEDICAL CARE SOFTWARE

Managed care software is not the same as medical care software. Most physicians use some of the patient-driven business management software programs, described above, to generate insurance claims, assist in patient scheduling, document encounters, and bill insurance companies. However, medical care software is a type of executive decision support system (EDSS), with database, that is used in the diagnosis and treatment of illness and disease.

Purkinje Systems

For example, Purkinje (210-476-0030) has developed a complete electronic charting, medical care, and clinical documentation system that has been used at such institutions as Johns Hopkins University, Harvard Medical School, and the Stanford Medical School. It is a type of clinical knowledge–based (CKB) software, and its Dossier of Clinical Information (DCI) has an extensive database of more than 300 customizable templates to provide the tools physicians need to access patient data, make diagnoses, document clinical encounters, and formulate treatment plans, according to HCFA evaluation and management (E/M) guidelines.

Managed care software, by distinction, is profit-based and measures such things as office financial ratios, E/M codes, CPT codes, capitation disbursements, and utilization rates, and it identifies and tracks cost trends for each patient encounter. Its purpose is to provide managerial and cost accounting information to maximize time and profits.

Selecting the Right Managed Care Software

The managed care software guide, *CTS Guide to Medical Practice Management Software*, for offices, groups, MSOs, PSOs, clinics, and physician networks is a good place to start. This software evaluation program is a source of objective reviews that analyze the strengths and weaknesses of leading management systems; such as: Medical Manager, PCN, QSI, IDX, +Medic, R/2000, SpectraMED, and others. It incorporates easy-to-read charts to rate the quality performance of more than 700 features for each system, as well as its ease of use, set-up speed, reporting calculations, documentation, and a host of other items. It also provides a comprehensive critique of key applications, such as patient personal identification information, financial accounting, scheduling and routing, billing, and managed care functions. CTS has been publishing medical management and managed care software selection tools since 1983, and this program includes all the requirements you will need to quickly rank and select the practice management software that best fits your individual practice, priorities, and needs (800-433-8015 and www.ctsguides.com).

For example, the Medical Manager software has been used by more than 110,000 health care providers to reduce costs, improve patient care, and manage practices in a more efficient manner. This program comes with a sophisticated suite of products for office management, managed care, electronic connectivity, medical records, and enterprise management. Its modular component integration system allows additions to functionality as the growth and needs of your practice dictate (800-222-7701, www.medical manager.com).

Another company, NDC Health Information Services, assists clients in meeting the challenge of providing practice management software solutions across the entire continuum of the health care community. Available products include (a) physician and dental practice management services and network systems; (b) pharmacy and pharmaceutical sales, research, and contact management programs; (c) physician, hospital, payer, and MCO financial services and claims management systems; (d) compliance management; and (e) accredited clearinghouse services (800-852-0707).

Capitation Software

Capitation software is yet another type of managed care software that allows the practitioner to monitor and manage member enrollment and fixed payments and to make distributions to subcapitated providers who represent fixed liabilities. Pamela Waymack, of Phoenix Services Managed Care Consulting of Evanston, Illinois, gives the following tips, which have been modified to help the small-group practitioner choose the right package.

1. Know your budget and stick to it. It will assist you in making buy or lease decisions.
2. Know your hardware platforms and software restrictions.
3. Know your office needs or perform a needs assessment.
4. Invite referrals and request for proposals (RFPs) from multiple reliable vendors.
5. Study and review all vendor RFPs.
6. Ask for a demonstration or trial subscription.
7. Obtain a cost report with estimate and variance.
8. Negotiate the best possible price
9. Know your timetable requirements.
10. Include support and training in your package deal.

A currently popular software program for analyzing the capitation and cost accounting details of a medical practice is the Physician Services Practice Analysis (PSPA) program developed by the Center for Research in Ambulatory Health Care Administration of the MGMA (303-397-7880). The program is based on CPT-4 codes and uses resource based relative value scale (RBRVS) values as the unit of analysis. Costs are determined on the basis of the practice's historical managerial accounting information, and the software is updated periodically by the HCFA

Summary reports include the information on physician FTEs, total number of patients seen, total procedures performed, total charges submitted, charges per procedure, charges per patient, procedures per patient, procedures per FTE physician, charges per FTE physician, and percentage of practice total charges, among other benchmarks. This allows the efficient practice to determine charges per patient per month (PM/PM), costs per PM/PM, adjusted charges per PM/ PM, adjusted costs per PM/PM, project capitation contract income, project dollar and percentage variances, and produce collection and purchased service percentages for the practice. Thus, physician service, practice analysis PSPA and similar programs allow you to: measure, negotiate, identify, develop, calculate, track, analyze, and extract cost data to maximize office profitability.

MOBILE PRACTICE MANAGEMENT SOLUTIONS

The Compendia clinical practice management system from Physix (800-749-2585), is a functional, fully integrated, clinical electronic medical record that combines mobility and point-of-care management with administrative flexibility and power. A simple point-and-click design allows the physician to access and add to a myriad of comprehensive information repositories within the computerized chart. It offers the following features:

- electronic charting and SOAP format note taking
- digital drug and medical references
- ICD-9/CPT billing codes
- improved productivity
- expanded communications and decision-making capabilities
- elimination of redundant processes
- optimized level of patient care
- mobility at the point-of-care

ELECTRONIC MEDICAL CLAIMS SUBMISSION

The Medicare Transaction System (MTS) took effect in January 1998 as a single, government-owned national claims processing system. Federal insurance reform is also pushing for electronic data interchange (EDI), forcing most MDs to participate in the network. According to principal Steven Findly, "We're processing almost four million Medicare claims annually, with 87% filed electronically. Three years ago, that number was only half." Therefore, medical offices must prepare for the current shift from the more traditional but expensive paper claim filing system to the less costly electronic claim filing system (see Table 4.2).

The electronic process begins when a medical claim is keyed into the system as each patient is seen or a file is created by the software's office manager to produce the HCFA claim form. The claim file is submitted directly from the office computer to the insurer, or clearinghouse. A clearinghouse, such as Synergistic Office Solutions, Inc. (http://www.sosoft.com), is a company that files the claim from the billing program. The clearinghouse checks the claim for errors; if there are any, the claim is returned within a day via modem. The clearinghouse enables the claim to meet the different requirements of varying insurers before it is sent to specific companies. Sometimes a floppy diskette can be submitted instead of using the phone lines. The entire process takes 1 to 3 days. The claim can be viewed and corrected on the computer screen without ever having to print a copy. Once the claim is submitted to the insurer, it is given an ID number, which ensures that it has been received. The ID number is analogous to being sent by certified mail. After the claim is given an ID number, there is almost no reason that it should ever need to be tracked again. However, if it is necessary to check its status, additional communication software is available. The insurance company can then respond with notes or any requests for information within days.

Electronic Claims Paperwork

There is virtually no paperwork when filing electronically. The movement of business formation from paper to bits not only reduces the amount of paperwork but makes the information more valuable. According to Marlon Miller, of MTS, this provides several advantages: (1) the information can be shared and accessed electronically and reused across multiple departments, with no copying required; (2) data can be automatically extracted from a database, pulling out only the information that is desired at specific times; (3) electronic information packages can be routed in a business process, cutting cycle time and improving accuracy.

TABLE 4.2 **Paper Claim Filing Costs Per Month**

	Price	Per month	Total per month
Employee time (getting claims mailed out)	$10/hr. (avg.)	40 hours/month	$400
Price per claim (paper and postage)	$0.60	$0.60 × 1000	$600
Follow-up on claims	$10/hr. (avg.) 50 hours/month	50 hours/month	$500
Total per month			$1,500

Costs of Electronic Claims

The cost of sending claims electronically is more difficult to understand than the electronic filing process. Costs are broken down into categories, such as software, technical support, and cost per claim. Clearinghouses often claim low costs in one area of service, but may charge higher prices in other areas.

The software that must be purchased for and/or installed into the existing office management information systems can be very expensive. American Medical Software (http://www.americanmedical.com) offers very basic packages, from $995 to more complex packages costing up to $5,995. Some clearinghouses even offer software at little or no cost. Usually, when a contract exists between a clearinghouse and a medical office, the per claim charge is higher. Technical support is also important since poor follow-up can make an elaborate software package virtually useless to an office.

The variable cost-per-claim is the most expensive item in electronic claims submission, with ranges from $1–$4 per claim. It can be difficult to get a definite cost per claim because many clearinghouses base their cost on how many claims are sent out of the office, the average charge of each claim, the specialty of the practice, and in some cases, the complexity of each claim. Table 4.3 is helpful in this regard.

DEVELOPING A MEDICAL INTERNET (WWW) SITE

It seems that everyone is "surfing the Net" and participating in the latest computer information revolution. Almost every major corporation in America has developed a World Wide Web site on the Internet, and thousands of individuals and organizations are creating new Web sites every day on the information superhighway. Accordingly, some time should be spent focusing on how physicians and medical associations can take advantage of this new technology to promote our profession in cyberspace.

The Internet is actually the name for a group of international computer networks or worldwide information resources; the World Wide Web (Web for short) is the graphical user interface that makes navigating the Internet as easy as pointing and clicking a button on a mouse. The Web is the fastest growing and most exciting part of the Internet because it contains multimedia capabilities.

TABLE 4.3   The Network Group Electronic Claim Filing Prices Per Month

	Price	Per month	Total per month
Software	$125 per month	$125	$125
Technical support	$300 per day	$300/month (avg.)	$300
Price per claim	$0.25	$0.25 × 1000	$250
Total per month			$675

The multimedia features of the Web include graphics, text, sound, video, animation, pictures, voice communication, and three-dimensional virtual reality environments.

By now, you may wonder how physicians and medical associations can take advantage of this unique opportunity to join the estimated 30 million people on the information superhighway. There are many reasons for a state association or organization to have an Internet presence, including providing a cost-effective means of communication to the members; increasing the visibility of the state organization and medical profession with the Internet public; 24-hour information access for members that can include state publications and directories; current officers and committees directory; practice parameters; listing membership benefits and services; and publishing state bylaws, a comprehensive membership directory with complete addresses and phone numbers; and an E-mail directory of members with on-line addresses.

Individual physicians who want to use the Internet as an advertising tool for their practice may want to create a Web site to include information similar to that in their office brochure. Physicians can create dynamite Web sites that might include a color photograph of the doctor, staff, and office; educational background and residency training; hospital affiliations; board certification; copies of published articles; video presentations of pathologies; x-ray changes preop and postops; equipment selections; directions to the office and hours of operation; HMO and PPO insurance participation lists; patient educational handouts; answers to commonly asked questions; and typical office forms that patients could fill at home rather than in the waiting room.

Some of the challenges physicians and medical associations face in setting up a Web site are physicians' lack of experience and expertise with advanced computer technology and Hypertext Markup Language (HTML), the programming language of the Internet. HTML is a complex scripting language that tells software browsers how to display the various elements of a Web page, such as links, body text, header text, graphics, tables, and frames. Fortunately, there are a variety of software tools that put simple and basic Web site development well within the reach of most computer-literate individuals who want to spend a few weeks to learn how to program. The possibilities of using the Internet are limited only by imagination, programming, content, and the cost of running a site.

The basic unit of every Web site is a page of information. The information on a page can be in the form of text, images, video, sound, links, forms, frames, and tables. Text on Web pages is formatted so that words appear in different styles (bold or italics) and different type sizes. As in most documents, the text in Web documents is organized into body text and several levels of headers, which organize what you read.

There are several kinds of images on a Web page: In-line images form part of a page and can be integral to its design. Background images allow Web designers to use colors and regular patterns as design elements at their site. Downloadable images are separate files that are external to a page. Users can download these images and save them on their hard disk, then view them at a later time, even when not using a Web browser. In addition to external images,

Web pages can point to external sound and video files. A link, or hyperlink, takes users to another page or to a graphic or other related file. Links can be text, images, sound, or even a different location in another country. If a link consists of text, it is underlined and is a different color from the rest of the text. Most browser software will tell you when your mouse cursor is on a link because it turns from an arrow into a pointing finger. Clicking with the mouse takes you to the page or graphic "pointed to" by the link.

Forms can be text boxes or other screen "objects" in which you can type text, choose from a list, make a selection using radio buttons and check boxes, and in general supply information to the Web site. Frames were introduced by Netscape and allow Web designers to present information in several windows on a single page. This feature is especially useful when the same information, such as a table of contents, is useful in many places across a large and complex site. Pages with frames are called framesets and can be saved and printed only one frame at a time. Tables enable Web designers to present structured information more compactly and more effectively, by allowing you to see data that has been formatted in rows and columns. A table can contain text, images, and hyperlinked text or images.

A home page is the first page users see when they log into a Web site. In a complex site it is the "doorway" to the rest of the site or the starting point for exploring the site. Sometimes it is the place where you'll find the equivalent of a table of contents. America Online (AOL) offers its members the ability to create their own basic home page on the World Wide Web without ever needing to know HTML. AOL's Personal Publisher is an easy web publishing tool. It allows you to fill in a few blanks, add pictures, format text, and publish your pages to the Web quickly and easily. AOL gives members 2 megabytes of server space (a server holds your pages and allows others to access them on the Web) per screen name to create pages. While this is sufficient for individual physicians to promote their practices, it is too limited for medical associations.

Web sites have long and intimidating-looking names called uniform resource locators (URLs). A URL has several parts: The first part is the protocol (http in this case), which is a set of rules computers observe to exchange information; "http" stands for the hypertext transfer protocol, the Web's own protocol. Next you'll see a colon, two forward slashes, and "www," which is short for World Wide Web. A computer address, or domain name, comes next and is used by computers in routing data across the many networks that make up the Internet. Finally, you often see a directory path at that computer plus a file at the end of the path: "http://www.ama.org/register.html." Web pages usually end in "html," for Hypertext Markup Language, or sometimes just "htm." This directory path is optional, because URLs can take you to the "top level" page of a site (e.g., http://www.ama.org/) or they can be more complex and take you to a specific page at that site (e.g., http://www.ama.org/subscribe).

INTERNET HEALTH CARE SITES FOR PATIENTS

For doctors wishing to see what their patients are reading on the internet, the following are popular medical internet sites for the general population of net surfers:

(1) http://igm.nih.gov/
This site is a project of the National Institutes of Health and the National Library of Medicine. It allows users to search the Medline, with its more than 9 million biomedical journal citations, as well as other health care resources.
(2) www.kidshealth.org/
This site, from the Nemours Foundation and its related hospitals, clinics, and centers, it is a good resource on pediatric health care for children, teens, and parents.
(3) www.hon.ch/
This site is sponsored by the Health on the Net Foundation in Switzerland. It is dedicated to improving medical information for patients on the Web.
(4) www.ama-assn.org/
This is the office site of the AMA and its journal, *JAMA*. It also includes helpful medical information for consumers.

WORLD WIDE HEALTH CARE SOLUTIONS

Since the key to immediate data access, managed care coordination, patient satisfaction, and insurance claim information is now global in reach, Passport Health Communications (615-661-5657) has developed programs to assist in the growing benefits of on-line medical communication with these three services:

1. Passport One Source offers providers and insurers a single source for eligibility, claims status, benefits and formulary data, secure access to administrative information, cost effect data interchange, and accurate and timely physician referrals.
2. Practice.Net helps physicians to develop a customized Web site, allowing patients to access general information about the practice, obtain educational materials, make appointments, refill prescriptions, even complete patient satisfaction surveys.
3. Internet Consulting enables physicians to develop long-term communication strategies on the Internet and to access marketing opportunities and provide consulting services using nontechnical terminology.

CONCLUSION

In the contemporary hypercompetitive environment the correct understanding and use of the preceding MIS tools, applications, and configurations will greatly assist the medical practitioner in gaining a strategic competitive advantage over those providers not using such "wired" electronic systems.

REFERENCES AND READINGS

Bader, B., & Matheny, M. Understanding capitation and at-risk contracting. *Health System Leader*, March 1994.

Capitation Management Report, February 1998. (800) 597-6300.

Scherer, W. P. The computerized physician. *Physician Management*, 14:59 (August 1996).

Scherer, W. P. Developing a World Wide Web site on the Internet. *Physician Management*, 16:75 (April 1997).

Scherer, W. P. Internet resources for infection information. In Marcinko, D. E. (Ed).: *Infections of the foot: Diagnosis and management*. St. Louis: Mosby-Yearbook, 1998.

Scherer, W. S. Medical management information systems. In Marcinko, D. E. (Ed).: *Profit maximization and reimbursement*. Professional business and financial skills for the hyper competitive healthcare environment. Columbus, OH: 1998. Anadem Publishers, 1998.

Scherer, W. S. Practice management software: A decade of innovation, 1987–1997. *Physician Management*, 16:69 (August 1997).

## CHAPTER 5

Effective Insurance Coding and Billing Guidelines

Get Paid for Your Services . . . Leave Nothing on the Table

Harry Goldsmith

> Physicians have only themselves to blame for managed care. For the last 20 or more years, we have been our own first priority—our own self-worth and bank accounts. We have lost sight of the ball, that patients are our first priority.
>
> —Burton Lee, MD

Effective coding results not only from an understanding of the details found within the pages of various billing guidelines but also from an appreciation for the overall philosophy of third-party reimbursement. This chapter is designed to assist the health care professional to better appreciate the "whys" and "therefores" of billing and reimbursement methodology leading to more accurate and effective coding.

MEDICAL AND SURGICAL FEES

Determining your professional fees may, in fact, be one of the last entrepreneurial acts afforded the physician in the highly regulated health care system in which we practice. In the "old days" the physician's fees were based on his or her determination of what the service was worth or how it was valued. In many cases, the evaluation, examination, and management services, as well as minor procedures, were lumped by primary care physicians under a single office visit fee. Patients were expected to pay their doctor's fees at the time of service. Third-party payers primarily covered large-ticket major medical items such as surgery and hospitalization.

Things have changed. While indemnity insurance types still exist, they are endangered and fading away as an option. Over the years, managed care has replaced usual, customary, and reasonable fee for service with a contracted fee schedule. Essentially under managed care, you can charge just about anything you want, but the managed care organization (MCO) will reimburse only up to its maximum contractual allowance as determined by a set fee schedule. The greater the difference between your charge and the allowable reimbursement, the more you will eventually write off your artificially inflated accounts receivables.

So is it worth your time and effort to determine the procedure and service fees?

Absolutely. Despite changes in insurance models, a health care provider's fees should reflect what the doctor feels his or her services or procedures are worth. The type of insurance that the patient has should not play an influencing factor in either the fee determination or services rendered. Additionally, fees should not vary according to the patient's insurance type or what the patient's managed care contract determines is the maximum payable allowance.

Determining a professional fee for a given service takes into account many factors, including the professional work performed, nonclinical work performed, unusual skills required, time for service, practice expenses (e.g., staff salaries and benefits, disposable items, rent, utilities, etc.), and risk, as well as direct (surgical global care) and indirect (communicating with other health professionals, laboratory finding evaluation, review of x-rays, etc.) follow-up care. In establishing professional fees, the operative phrase is "provider determined." While the input from knowledgeable, experienced staff is certainly desirable, the ultimate responsibility for determining fees rests on the shoulders of the health care professional providing the service. Of course, the medical treatment administered and for which reimbursement is sought is assumed to be performed on the basis of necessity and effectiveness.

Why are reasonable fees and reimbursement for services important? Well, medicine is a business whether physicians like to admit it or not. Businesses that are not profitable do not remain businesses for long. Today, most health care professionals will admit that they are working harder and for more hours, seeing more patients to maintain practice revenues. Even so, in many cases expense increases are outpacing revenue increases. In an age of managed care even Marcus Welby, MD, would have to work harder.

Medical fees must be reasonable. How is fee reasonableness determined if physicians are not allowed to sit down and discuss specific fees (collusion, price fixing)? A good rule of thumb is to take the Medicare allowance and multiply it by a million. Just kidding.

Actually reviewing the annual Medicare rules and regulations found in the year-end *Federal Register* is a good place to start. That issue, printed between November 1 and December 15 of each year, lists all the current procedure terminology (CPT) codes and their Health Care Financing Administration (HCFA)–determined relative value units (RVUs). The RVUs are procedure-comparable. You can assume that if, for example, a free muscle flap procedure using microvascular techniques is valued at 68.65 total RVUs, it would be a relatively more complicated procedure than a simple repair of a small laceration at a total of 4.34 RVUs. You would price your procedure fees accordingly. Generally, if a managed care allowance exceeds what you have billed, your fee is unreasonably low. The true test of reasonableness is your comfort (emotional as well as economic) level in charging the cash patient the same fee. If you feel it is in the reasonable range and you are not consistently writing off 98% of your charges, it probably is reasonable. Under a managed care fee schedule, the service billed amount generally has significance only when the fee charged is less than the contract allowance. In that case, the MCO allowance is reduced to the lesser amount billed.

Medical fees must cover the practice overhead. MCOs as a rule prefer "a few good men/women" rather than wholesale acceptance when contracting with health care professionals. Credentialing of providers is one means to limit the number of health care professionals under contract; forming exclusive provider networks is another. In populous urban areas it is not uncommon for health care providers to sign any and all managed care contracts presented to them in order to ensure an adequate volume or pool of patients in the practice—especially in light of expected reduced reimbursement. Unfortunately, many providers fail to read or analyze the MCO contracts they sign. A few practitioners may reason that some managed care money is better than no money at all. But that is not always the case. A careful review of your practice's financial health may determine that, in fact, you may be losing money for each patient seen and treated under some managed care contracts. Not being able to cover your overhead is not a good practice and should be avoided.

Understand how services or procedures are coded for third-party billing purposes. The only reason the billing codes exist is for use in third-party reimbursement. Providers certainly do not have to use CPT codes to bill cash patients. The universality and acceptance of standard third-party billing and coding systems, such as the AMA's health care provider CPT, the HCFA's Health Care Financing Administration Common Procedure Coding System (HCPCS) for supplies, orthoses, prostheses, and so on, and the International Classification of Disease, 9th Revision, Clinical Modification (ICD-9-CM), have contributed immeasurably to refining claim submission and adjudication. Not only were codes developed for billing purposes, but each manual contains a wealth of information, rules, and guidelines to aid in making the reimbursement process universal, or reasonably so—or somewhat reasonably so.

Unusual circumstances and higher fees: On occasion, a significant modification on the part of the health care provider may be necessary in the performance of a service or procedure. This significant service or procedure, if not defined under another more or less comprehensive service, may warrant an increase or decrease in a "standard" fee for the "standard" service. This valuation variation is commonly coded with a CPT modifier reflecting the unusual circumstances. There is no guarantee that a third-party payer will approve additional reimbursement for the provided service or procedure. The medical record or operative report would have be very clear and detailed in distinguishing a usual and customary modification of a procedure from a significant unusual variation in a service or procedure.

MEDICAL PAYMENT REIMBURSEMENT

First-party reimbursement is defined as the direct financial relationship between the patient and the provider of services. Second-party reimbursement involves a guardian or guarantor of the patient being legally responsible for service payments. Third-party reimbursement removes the obligation for payment of the incurred health care cost payment from the patient to a third party (e.g., an insurance company, government agency, self-insured trust, administrator, etc.). Seventy-five years ago, first- and second-party reimbursement dominated health care payment in the United States; today third-party reimbursement is the predominant means of health care cost payment.

Third-party payers determine the cost of the health care insurance (to the employer, taxpayers, or beneficiary) based on a set benefit package and reimbursement allowance. While some payers, such as MCOs, require the health care provider to submit claims for services on the patient's behalf, others give the beneficiary the option of assigning the rights to the payment of the claim directly to the provider. The act of assignment obliges the payer to deal directly with the practitioner who is acting on behalf of the patient. Reimbursement generally follows the assignment of the claim.

With third-party reimbursement comes a whole host of rules, regulations, definitions, and restrictions. Some of these are universal, but many more vary from third-party payer to third-party payer. Unfortunately, this variation often leaves the health care provider wondering what rules and restrictions apply to the particular patient currently being treated. It is impractical for the provider's office to keep copies of the most current insurance policies their patients have in order to avoid errors in claims submission. Understanding this, each provider's office must develop a standard protocol for capturing practical and available information important for managing third-party reimbursement. Much of this information is available on the beneficiary's health insurance card and driver's license, both of which should be copied at the time of the initial office visit. The important information includes the following:

1. A photo and name of the beneficiary (this prevents fraudulent use of health insurance benefits by nonbeneficiaries).
2. Current beneficiary address (or an opportunity to update the address by the front office staff).
3. The name of the insurance plan.
4. Policy, group, contract, and/or identification numbers.
5. Customer service telephone number(s).
6. Possible assigned medical group or primary care physician name and telephone number.
7. Possible assigned hospital.
8. Possible benefit (e.g., prescription benefits) listing.
9. Possible co-payment requirements.
10. Instructions on card use.

The provider of services must keep in mind that possession of an insurance card is not a verification that the health insurance benefits are in effect. A critical function of the front office is to call the customer service number and verify that the insurance is in effect. As long as the office staff has the insurance representative on the telephone, they should ask either if there is a list of general benefit limitations or requirements that can be faxed directly to the office or if the representative can list any specific benefit limitations or requirements of particular interest for that office or specialty (e.g., physical therapy preauthorizations and limitations, MRI preauthorizations and assigned radiology locations, hospital versus ambulatory surgical center site of service requirements, etc.). If you are fortunate enough to receive a faxed list, make two copies: one for the patient's chart and the other for a folder filed by insurance or payer companies containing similar plan benefit limitations and/or requirements.

Policy benefit limitations or exclusions are absolute and not debatable or appealable. These are plainly issues of plan reimbursement and not medical necessity. Often the denied benefit (because of a policy exclusion) may be medically necessary, but because of the way the original insurance premium was structured and plan benefits developed, that particular service, item, or procedure was specifically excluded from reimbursement. Payment for that excluded service, item, or procedure would be the responsibility of the patient (unless the provider's managed care contract specifically forbids billing the patient), not the third-party payer.

The reimbursement allowance is the third-party payer's payment obligation based on the submitted claim for service and tempered by actuarial determinations, negotiated benefit allotments, policies, guidelines, and other influencing factors. The levels of reimbursement can vary from contract to contract, from third-party payer to third-party payer for the same services. Regardless of the insurance model, maximum reimbursement allowances are determined by the third-party payer. Under an indemnity insurance model, fee-for-service reimbursement may seem to be open-ended but, in fact, is limited by usual, customary, and reasonable (UCR) allowance profiling. Under most managed care models, a fee schedule limits the allowances per service or procedure. The health care provider, under managed care, agrees to accept a discounted version of usual and customary indemnity reimbursements in exchange for the opportunity to see and treat patients under the managed care contract.

Regardless of the fee schedule limits, health care providers should continue to bill services at consistent fees regardless of the third-party payer type. Obviously, the greater the disparity between the billed amount and the contract allowance, the greater the accounts receivables appear—but the amount may have no basis in reimbursement reality. When the explanation of the medical benefit (EOMB or EOB) statement is received, the receivable "write-offs" may be considerable. Fortunately, most medical computer software automatically adjusts differences in office fees and known payer allowances.

DEDUCTIBLES, CO-PAYMENTS, AND PATIENT DISINCENTIVES

To reduce the prospect of beneficiaries casually seeking medical attention that may generate unnecessary costs, especially when the problem is minor or very self-limiting, third-party payers built "first dollar payment" requirements into their health care plans. The patient would be responsible for deductibles and co-payments; some financial responsibility is thereby extended to the patient. In their own way they allowed the patient to determine the need to seek professional care by creating a financial disincentive for the patient.

The deductible is an annual amount that the patient (or beneficiary family) must first pay out-of-pocket in order to activate third-party reimbursement benefits. The co-payment is a similar patient first-dollar contractual obligation, but it occurs with each patient–health care provider encounter that utilizes insurance for benefit reimbursement purposes. There may be minimal exceptions to the demand for co-payment, depending on the individual insurance policy language, such as instances of multiple encounters with the same provider in a single day or in cases of true emergency services.

Studies have shown that the higher the deductible and co-payment amounts, the more reluctant patients were to casually take advantage of their insurance benefits. With these financial disincentives in place, the patient is put in a position of making the initial determination of professional medical necessity: should they try to treat a cough with over-the-counter (OTC) medications, or should they go directly to the doctor for examination and treatment? One would assume that if the deductible and co-payments were high enough, only patients with persistent or truly worrisome health problems would end up in the doctor's office. But reality does not always follow theory. Unfortunately, there are many examples of patient concern over the costs of the deductible or co-payment, resulting in delay or failure to seek medically necessary professional care. The results can range from the escalation of a moderately simple problem to a severe—even life threatening—one. One would think that reasonably high deductibles and co-payments would be made to control managed care costs, but due to the competitive nature of the business, many MCOs have severely reduced or eliminated deductibles or co-payments as beneficiary inducements to seek care by contracted health care providers.

Health care providers who routinely waive their patients' deductibles and co-payments are contributing to the patients' sidestepping mandated insurance policy requirements. Without financial disincentives in place, it has been shown that billing abuse and overutilization of services drive up the overall cost of health care. The National Health Care Anti-Fraud Association has stated that in some cases it may be billing fraud for health care practitioners to routinely forgo the collection of deductibles or co-payments.

Interestingly, and again for competition reasons, some capitated health maintenance organizations (HMOs) have utilized television, radio, and print advertisements to induce patients to join their plans. Some of the benefits, according to the ads, include no paperwork, no balance billing by doctors, and no deductibles or co-payments Because these reimbursement models are based on a capitated scheme (a single amount is paid per member per month to the provider regardless of services utilized), no direct increase in provider costs are generally realized. Yet the capitated providers may see increased numbers of patients with seemingly minor complaints and not appreciate a dime more of compensation. In some providers' offices, the deductible and co-payment amounts add up to sizable amount of money over the year.

MEDICAL CODING DEFINITIONS

The American Medical Association's *Physicians' Current Procedural Terminology* manual (commonly known as the CPT manual) is the recognized coding manual used by health care providers to bill third-party payers. No quantitative values are assigned to the codes in the CPT manual. Each third-party payer determines a value, whether a direct dollar or unit value, for each CPT code. Each CPT code represents a service, procedure, test, or study. The CPT manual attempts to define each of the codes specifically by individual descriptive phrases and by generally utilizing guidelines, rules, and definitions related to code groupings: medical, surgical, pathological, and diagnostic services. Third-party payers develop additional protocols, guidelines, rules, and definitions for internal use.

The value assigned to each CPT code is based on a determined amount of work, practice expense, and risk inherently bundled into the service or procedure. Each procedure or service is further defined as a body of work made up of multiple lesser components, all valued within the main CPT code. As an example, if the surgical lengthening of a leg tendon is the main procedure to be performed, it would be assigned a unique CPT code. Within the tendon lengthening code definition and assigned value would be included (bundled or "packaged") seemingly obvious lesser procedures available to the surgeon in achieving the ultimate goal of the tendon lengthening. These lesser procedures include the incision itself, retraction of vital structures, tying off small vessels, suturing the tendon in a lengthened position, closing the soft tissue in layers, suturing the skin, applying a dressing, and applying a posterior splint. Although some surgeons in particular cases may not need to tie off small vessels because no vessels interfered with the surgical exposure, or maybe they had to tie off two more vessels than is usually necessary, or they may elect not to apply a posterior splint, or the procedure may take 20 minutes longer because a required instrument falls on the floor and has to be resterilized, the overall code value of the tendon lengthening procedure does not change. Essentially, with exception of minor modifications one way or another, the main procedure remains the same. Those minor modifications or variations in technique would be included in what would be called the global surgical description and allowance. Not all potential secondary or minor procedures must be performed to fully reimburse the primary procedure.

The fragmentation or breakdown or unbundling of the main or primary procedure through the billing of each secondary procedure is billing abuse at best, intentional double billing at worst. Health care providers intentionally billing for the purpose of unwarranted financial gain may be committing fraud (see Figure 5.1).

THE MOST COMMON PROCEDURES OF MEDICAL GROUP PRACTICES*

CPT-4 CODE	Medicine Description	% of Total	CPT-4 CODE	Surgery Description	% of Total
95004	Allergy Skin Test	12.0%	36415	Drawing Blood	4.2%
99001	Specimen Handling	11.6	54240	Penis Study	2.0
90925	ESRD Related Services	6.2	66984	Remove Cataract; Insert Lens	0.8
92014	Eye Exam and Treatment	4.4	52000	Cystoscopy	0.7
92015	Refraction	3.1	43239	Upper GI Endoscopy; Biopsy	0.6
CPT-4 CODE	Radiology Description	% of Total	CPT-4 CODE	Pathology/Laboratory Description	% of Total
77430	Weekly Radiation Treatment	13.3%	86215	Deoxyribonuclease; Antibody	7.7%
77413	Radiation Treatment Delivery	10.7	88157	TBS Smear (Bethesda System)	7.0
77414	Radiation Treatment Delivery	7.7	85030	Automated Hemogram	5.3
77336	Radiation Physician Consult.	5.0	88313	Special Stains	5.2
70450	CAT Scan of Head or Brain	4.7	85024	Automated Hemogram	4.7
CPT-4 CODE	Evaluation and Management Description	% of Total	HCPC CODE	HCPCs** Description	% of Total
99213	Office/Outpatient Visit, Est.	11.1%	J2405	Ondansetron HCl Injection	10.6%
99212	Office/Outpatient Visit, Est.	5.6	J0730	Chlorpheniramine Maleate Inj.	10.0
99214	Office/Outpatient Visit, Est.	2.7	J1561	Immune Globulin Injection	5.4
99231	Subsequent Hospital Care	1.7	G0001	Drawing Blood for Specimen	3.7
99232	Subsequent Hospital Care	1.7	J0585	Bolulinum Toxin a per 100 u	1.8

THE SIX MOST COMMON PROCEDURES OF MEDICAL GROUP PRACTICES

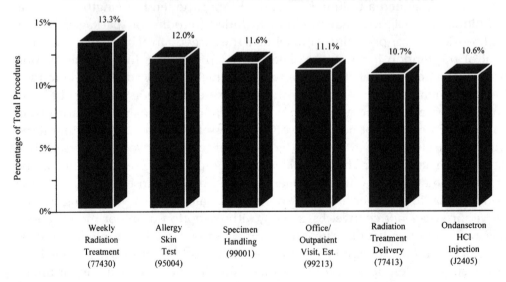

FIGURE 5.1   The most common procedures of medical group practices.*

Data source: CRAHCA Physician Services Practice Analysis Comparison, January–June, 1997 Medians © 1997. From *1998 Hoechst Marion Roussel Managed Care Digest Series.* Reprinted by permission of the publisher, Hoechst Marion Roussel, Inc.

COMMONLY PERFORMED PROCEDURES, AS A PERCENTAGE OF TOTAL RVUs[1,2]

CPT-4 CODE	Family Practice (167.91 FTEs) Description	% of Total	CPT-4 CODE	Internal Medicine (200.55 FTEs) Description	% of Total
99213	Office/Outpatient Visit, Est.	12.03%	99213	Office/Outpatient Visit, Est.	13.23%
99214	Office/Outpatient Visit, Est.	5.73	99212	Office/Outpatient Visit, Est.	0.25
99212	Office/Outpatient Visit, Est.	3.13	99214	Office/Outpatient Visit, Est.	6.04
95165	Supervision/Prov. of Antigens	0.16	99232	Subsequent Hospital Care	0.07
95024	Intracutaneous Tests	0.09	99391	Periodic Preventive Medicine	1.06
CPT-4 CODE	Allergy/Immunology (15.12 FTEs) Description	% of Total	CPT-4 CODE	Pediatrics[3] (90.44 FTEs) Description	% of Total
99213	Office/Outpatient Visit, Est.	9.98%	99212	Office/Outpatient Visit, Est.	3.68%
93010	Cardiography Interpret, Report	0.54	99213	Office/Outpatient Visit, Est.	5.05
99214	Office/Outpatient Visit, Est.	5.44	99202	Office/Outpatient Visit, New	2.01
99212	Office/Outpatient Visit, Est.	2.51	99203	Office/Outpatient Visit, New	2.39
99232	Subsequent Hospital Care	2.48	72100	Radiologic Examination, Spine	0.70
CPT-4 CODE	General Surgery (48.05 FTEs) Description	% of Total	CPT-4 CODE	Orthopedic Surgery (130.13 FTEs) Description	% of Total
99213	Office/Outpatient Visit, Est.	8.45%	99213	Office/Outpatient Visit, Est.	9.40%
99214	Office/Outpatient Visit, Est.	4.14	99214	Office/Outpatient Visit, Est.	4.72
99212	Office/Outpatient Visit, Est.	2.83	99212	Office/Outpatient Visit, Est.	2.57
95165	Supervision/Prov. of Antigens	0.15	95165	Supervision/Prov. of Antigens	0.34
95024	Intracutaneous Tests	0.08	95024	Intracutaneous Tests	0.22
CPT-4 CODE	Diagnostic Radiology (29.63 FTEs) Description	% of Total	CPT-4 CODE	Hematology/Oncology (38.82 FTEs) Description	% of Total
99213	Office/Outpatient Visit, Est.	7.99%	99213	Office/Outpatient Visit, Est.	9.44%
99214	Office/Outpatient Visit, Est.	4.21	99214	Office/Outpatient Visit, Est.	4.85
99212	Office/Outpatient Visit, Est.	3.28	99212	Office/Outpatient Visit, Est.	2.70
95165	Supervision/Prov. of Antigens	0.22	95165	Supervision/Prov. of Antigens	0.29
71010	Radiologic Examination, Chest	0.36	95024	Intracutaneous Tests	0.17
CPT-4 CODE	Invasive Cardiology (49.36 FTEs) Description	% of Total	CPT-4 CODE	Noninvasive Cardiology (38.30 FTEs) Description	% of Total
99213	Office/Outpatient Visit, Est.	3.60%	99213	Office/Outpatient Visit, Est.	8.64%
99214	Office/Outpatient Visit, Est.	4.24	99214	Office/Outpatient Visit, Est.	2.26
99212	Office/Outpatient Visit, Est.	1.86	99212	Office/Outpatient Visit, Est.	5.40
95165	Supervision/Prov. of Antigens	0.19	99232	Subsequent Hospital Care	2.16
95024	Intracutaneous Tests	0.12	99231	Subsequent Hospital Care	1.00

FIGURE 5.2 Commonly performed procedures, as a percentage of total RVUs.

[1,2]Data Source: CRAHCA Physician Services Practice Analysis Comparison © 1997.
[1]"RVUs" refers to total Relative Value Units reported in the specialties listed in the first six months of 1997.
[2]"Est." in some of these CPT-4 code description represents "established patient."
[3]"Pediatrics" excludes subspecialty pediatrics such as pulmonology, neurology, gastroenterology, and endocrinology.
From *1998 Hoechst Marion Roussel Managed Care Digest Series*. Reprinted by permission of the publisher, Hoechst Marion Roussel, Inc.

COMMONLY PERFORMED PROCEDURES OF MEDICAL GROUP PRACTICES

CPT-4 CODE	Digestive System Procedures	Average Number of Procedures per 1,000		Median Number of Procedures per 1,000	
		Commercial	Senior	Commercial	Senior
43234–43259	EGD Endoscopy	4.59	29.71	4.48	23.58
45378–45385	Colonoscopy	5.37	41.18	5.57	32.38
49495–49525	Inguinal Hernia	1.67	4.87	1.48	4.92
74150–74170	CT Abdomen	3.99	25.25	3.56	19.05
74270–74280	Barium Enema	5.53	34.37	4.70	28.94

CPT-4 CODE	Reproductive System Procedures	Average Number of Procedures per 1,000		Median Number of Procedures per 1,000	
		Commercial	Senior	Commercial	Senior
56356	Endometrial Ablation	0.15	0.42	0.12	0.43
58150–58200	Total Abdominal Hysterectomy	1.76	1.81	1.32	1.26
58260–58285	Vaginal Hysterectomy	0.61	1.19	0.40	1.01
59400–59410	Vaginal Delivery	12.95	—	12.08	—
76805–76816	Obstetric Ultrasound	32.08	0.40	22.92	0.08

CPT-4 CODE	Miscellaneous Procedures	Average Number of Procedures per 1,000		Median Number of Procedures per 1,000	
		Commercial	Senior	Commercial	Senior
29870–29889	Knee Arthroscopy	3.28	3.82	3.72	3.15
31622–31656	Bronchoscopy	0.58	6.64	0.72	4.66
47600–47620	Cholecystectomy	0.39	2.71	0.25	2.06
56340–56342	LAP Cholecystectomy	1.73	4.31	1.86	4.42
66830–66984	Cataracts	1.38	33.23	1.30	40.74

FIGURE 5.3   Commonly performed procedures of medical group practices.

From *1998 Hoechst Marion Roussel Managed Care Digest Series.* Reprinted by permission of the publisher, Hoechst Marion Roussel, Inc.

MEDICAL DOCUMENTATION

Most physicians, third-party payers, and legal consultants agree that the medical record represents a real-time document evidencing pertinent facts, findings, and observations regarding (1) the nature of the presenting medical problem, (2) a patient's medical history, (3) the clinical examination findings, (4) the doctor's medical decision-making considerations, (5) diagnostic impressions, and (6) any resulting physician actions. The medical record chronologically documents the care of the patient. The medical record facilitates the ability of the physician to evaluate and plan the patient's treatment, to monitor the patient's health status over time, to readily access information necessary to communicate to other health care providers involved in the patient's care, and to act as a testament validating medical necessity and evidencing the performance of services.

Medical record legibility, accuracy, and thoroughness are fundamental elements required to validate third-party payer reimbursement. How much information to chart seems to be the topic of endless debates. Generally, it is the quality, not the quantity, of the information that is important. The physician, in his or her best judgment, must determine if the patient's medical "story" is adequately documented so that another health care professional could pick up the chart and understand the patient's course of medical events. Poor record keeping may have a profoundly negative impact, not only on issues of reimbursement but on the care of the patient. The quality of the medical record does play a significant role—either positive or negative—in circumstances involving questions of legal liability.

Often, the question arises as to ownership of the medical records: Are they the property of the health care provider or the patient? Whereas the physical record is the sole property of the provider, the content of the medical record is not. The information contained in the patient's medical record documents medical status, progress, and future actions, some or all of which may be of considerable value, for example, to (1) the patient transferring care—for whatever reason—to another health care provider, (2) doctors covering the practice of a vacationing physician, (3) an insurance company requesting record copies, or (4) a consulting health care specialist. Doctors should have established administrative protocols for allowing release of information from a patient's medical record. Although a third-party payer may require direct copies of progress notes for specified dates of service, the patient requesting records to be transferred may, at the election of the doctor, be given either a complete photocopy of the chart or a detailed summary letter containing relevant portions abstracted from the medical record. It would be a breach of patient confidentiality to casually allow protected information to be sent to unauthorized parties. The physician has a paramount obligation to release patient medical information only on receipt of a written and duly signed authorization from the involved patient or guardian.

Although styles of record keeping may differ, there are general principles that must be kept in mind.

Completeness

The medical record should reflect pertinent and essential medical information related to the patient's condition and treatment. Basic data should include subjective, historical, and objective findings; treatments; prescriptions; diagnostic findings (laboratory, x-ray, etc.); and reports. An incomplete medical record may fail to validate the performance of services and/or procedures. Consequently, claimed medical treatment may not be reimbursable.

Clarity

The patient record must be organized in a manner allowing for quick review of previous notations. Shortcuts in record keeping, allowing for assumptions on the part of the reader, can be dangerous. Illegible handwriting and the use of "personal" rather than universal abbreviations and special codes are not considered to be consistent with the standards of the medical community.

Precision

Inappropriate terminology, misspelled words, and vague conclusions are negative reflections on the precision of the chart. The medical record should not be subject to multiple interpretations.

Consistency

The physician has a duty to be consistent in charting the medical record. Clinical workups should follow accepted documentation standards. Objective and subjective findings, test results, and treatment programs should be presented in a logical fashion.

Objectivity

The health care provider has a responsibility to present clinical facts as observed. These facts, when combined with the patient's subjective statements and medical history, should represent as accurate as possible a picture of the patient's medical status. The doctor must maintain objectivity throughout the process of gathering and interpreting the facts surrounding a medical case.

Appearance

The medical record should read as though written for a third party: another health care provider, an insurance company, or an attorney. The handwriting should be legible. Typed notes are preferred, although not mandatory. If a mistake in documentation occurs, the error should be struck through once and initialed. The physician should avoid erasing parts of the record, scratching out sections, writing in the margins of the chart, and documenting patient encounters out of chronological order. The chart should appear clean and professional.

SUBMITTING REIMBURSABLE "CLEAN" CLAIMS

The service and procedure billing codes and fees are submitted on universal claim forms or on electronic forms. The current standard paper form is known as the HCFA 1500. Although this form is accepted by the vast majority of third-party payers, including government agencies, there are still some payers that, for whatever reason, choose to mandate use of their unique forms. Fortunately, these third-party payers are few in number. Universal claim forms allow for transmitting essential information in a consistent format. Third-party payers can more accurately adjudicate claims, thereby reducing the chances for processing and payment delays. The universal claim form has been widely accepted by both providers and payers because of its ready adaptability to computer-generated billing programs.

Electronic Claims

Electronic claims submission follow standard protocols requiring special computer access and software. Each claim is electronically checked for accuracy prior to adjudication. The benefits of electronically submitted claims include both increased processing speed and quicker payment receipt. It is probable that the electronic format will be mandated by most third-party payers in the next 10 years.

Accuracy is essential when submitting a claim for review. The practitioner is well advised to include all relevant information requested on the form. For a more efficient processing of the claim, office staff should consider the following:

- Forms should be typed for easier adjudication and faster payment.
- Patient information should include birth date, policy numbers, social security numbers, and a listing of any secondary insurance.
- If the condition was the result of employment or accident, the appropriate area on the form should be checked.
- The date that the illness, injury, or first symptom was noted must be entered, along with the date that the patient first consulted the physician for the condition.
- The most specific descriptive ICD-9 codes should be listed in order of relevancy and linked to their related CPT codes.
- Each service or procedure claimed should be listed individually, along with date of service, place of service, CPT code, and an appropriate modifier.
- Fees should be specifically listed for each independent service or procedure performed.
- Supplementary supportive information (e.g., pathology report or operative report) should be included to expedite claim processing and reduce the chances of payment delays.

Superbills

The complexities of medical practice as well as the need for communication and improved efficiency among the health care provider's office, the patient, and the third-party payer has led to the development of the "superbill." Originally, superbills, which were forms containing vital practice, patient, service, and diagnostic information, were attached to a minimally completed HCFA 1500 claim form and submitted to third-party payers. Because generally the same information requested on the HCFA 1500 form was contained in the superbill, many insurers agreed to accept their use. Unfortunately, over the past 20 years, submission of multiple varieties (in terms of sizes, fonts, colors, and layouts) of superbills led to increasing payer refusal to process superbill-submitted claims. As a result, offices have limited superbill use to that of an internal patient charge ticket. This allows for billing information to be accurately directed to the office insurance staff. The amount of information contained on a completed well-designed superbill is generally sufficient to allow the office insurance staff to complete either the HCFA 1500 claim form or most electronic billing formats, without repeatedly interrupting the health care provider for additional information.

The two most obviously important sections of a superbill are the CPT (service, procedure, supply, etc.) coding area and the ICD-9 (diagnosis) coding area. Both sections should contain the practitioner's most commonly utilized codes. Evaluation and management codes should include the entire range of service levels and not be limited to only the upper levels. If possible, procedure or service fees should not be preprinted on the superbill, but they can be serially numbered to prevent loss.

GLOBAL SURGICAL SERVICES AND MULTIPLE-FEE RULES

Surgeons commonly perform multiple independent surgical procedures during a single surgical session. As a consequence, over the years, third-party payers have developed "multiple-fee rules," which allow reimbursement of the primary procedure at 100% but may discount or reduce the value of any lesser or secondary procedures performed. This reduction in secondary procedure allowance is reasonably justified because there does exist an overlap of global services—work, practice expense, and malpractice—among procedures performed during a single surgical session. As an example, if hand surgery performed on the left hand included a carpal tunnel release and a trigger finger correction and both of these independent procedures have 90-day follow-up periods (under the Medicare program), the postsurgical visit follow-up care for both procedures involve dressing changes, staff time (e.g., scheduling the patient, bringing the patient into and out of the examination room, cleaning the room and preparing it for the next patient, etc.), the doctor's time to grossly examine the surgical sites, supplies, and so forth. This sharing of work and practice expense during a single global period obviously reduces the overall value of the procedures, compared to a hypothetical situation separating their performance by 1 year.

Two examples of commonly used multiple-fee rules are

- 100% for the first procedure, 50% for all subsequent procedures.
- 100% for the first procedure, 50% for the next five procedures, 25% for all subsequent procedures.

Actual multiple-fee rule discounts vary from third-party payer to third-party payer—and sometimes from insurance policy to insurance policy. When submitting claims, physicians are often confused as to what the particular third-party payer requires of them, what the ultimate reimbursement may be, or in the case of an indemnity plan, exactly what the patient's eventual financial responsibility is. Consequently, health care providers are left to their own design in determining how to value and bill fees for multiple services and procedures.

The use of CPT modifiers is essential to avoid misunderstandings about billed fee amounts between the doctor and the patient or between the doctor and the third-party payer. Once the provider determines which procedure is the primary or most highly valued procedure, it is recommended that the modifier "-51" be attached to the end of the five-digit CPT procedure code, signifying that the procedure is a separate procedure from others performed and billed and a secondary or lesser procedure in terms of value to the primary procedure. It also signifies that regardless of the billed amount for that procedure, the provider is aware that the procedure will be subject to the payer's multiple-fee rule and that the third-party payer is to apply its unique multiple-fee rule to the billed amount for that procedure code.

To optimize legitimate reimbursement, it is suggested that each service and/ or procedure be billed at 100% of its value. The 100% value when coupled with the procedure code modified with "-51" lets the third-party payer know that the provider, while understanding that an allowance reduction may occur under the payer's multiple-fee rule, is unwilling to second-guess the third-party payer regarding the amount of that reduction. Simply put, it is impractical for health care providers to have complete knowledge of every third-party payer's internal multiple-fee rule, and since each third-party payer reimburses according to its own set rules and fee schedules, the payer will automatically apply its multiple-fee rule reduction and pay at a reduced rate. If the doctor, fearful of being perceived as an abusive biller, reduces on billing the value of the secondary or lesser procedure, that provider may find (1) that the procedure he or she thought was the secondary procedure (and reduced in value) was actually valued by a particular payer as the primary procedure—but now at a lesser amount thanks to the inappropriate value reduction by the provider—and (2) that the payer may, without giving it a second thought, automatically reduce what in reality is the already provider-reduced secondary procedure fee. These errors in billing and adjudication are not uncommon and can significantly affect a practice's financial position.

The global surgical services are defining components inherent to each procedure. Ultimately, procedure value is based on these components. Generally, they include the following:

1. *Preoperative component*, made up of the immediate preoperative visit (usually within 24 hours of the procedure), performance and documentation of the elective surgical history and physical, reviewing ordered test or diagnostic findings, discussions with relevant health care professionals (nursing, anesthesia, primary or specialty care, etc.), and consent preparation along with its discussion with the patient.

2. *Intraoperative component*, made up of the surgical examination of the patient, performance of the integral parts of the surgical procedure itself, procedure-related flushes and injections—antibiotic, local anesthetic, and dressing applications.

3. *Postoperative component*, made up of preparing the postsurgical medical record, discussing and dispensing patient instructions, discharge of the elective patient from the facility, and follow-up visits and uncomplicated care of the patient (including the consumption of basic usual and customary postoperative supplies such as gauze, dressings, etc.) for a specified period of time (i.e., the global follow-up period).

BILLING PROCEDURES WITH EVALUATION AND MANAGEMENT SERVICES

Unlike coding and billing for multiple procedures, when an evaluation and management service is performed during the same patient encounter in which a procedure is performed, several factors must be considered. First, if this is an initial office visit, a significant weight is given to the initial evaluation, decision, and considerations to manage the problems encountered as well as prepare the patient record—from scratch. It is usual and customary, therefore, to bill and be reimbursed for the initial evaluation and management service. If a minor procedure is also performed during the initial patient encounter, assuming it is both a policy benefit and medically necessary, it too should be reimbursed. No modifier is generally required as an attachment to the five-digit initial evaluation and management code. Obviously, the medical record must be complete and sufficient to validate the level of evaluation and management as well as the medical necessity and performance of the procedure billed.

Second, if this is an initial patient encounter, such as a consultation, requiring an immediate or same-day major surgical procedure, the appropriate evaluation and management service would be billed with a modifier "-57" attached to indicate that a decision to perform major surgery (defined under Medicare as a procedure assigned a 90-day global follow-up period) was made. The "-57" modifier is an indicator to the third-party payer that a major procedure should be expected for adjudication bearing the same date of service as the evaluation and management service.

Third, if this is an established patient encounter for follow-up procedure outside a global follow-up period—for example, a second cortisone injection in the left knee joint for an acute flare-up of arthritic symptoms—and the patient asks the doctor about a red swollen right hand, the evaluation workup and initiation of management for the right-hand problem deserves reimbursement separate from the injection of the left knee, which is a known condition having follow-up treatment. To properly communicate to the third-party payer that the evaluation and management service and procedures should be independently reimbursed, the health care provider must attach to the five-digit evaluation and management CPT code the modifier "-25." Modifier "-25" indicates that the service and procedures were separately identifiable services. In a recent clarification, modifier "-25" was also approved for use if the diagnosis was established but the evaluation and management service was a significant medically necessary reevaluation of a known condition also receiving procedural treatment. It is very important that the documentation clearly support the independence and medical necessity of the condition(s) and the procedure(s). It is also important that the HCFA claim form or electronic submission specify which diagnosis code is linked to which procedure or evaluation and management code.

Fourth, if an established patient is returning the office for an appointed procedural treatment, whether a new treatment or a follow-up treatment, and the service rendered is primarily procedural, no evaluation and management allowance is independently reimbursed—only the procedure allowance is reimbursed. The point generally made is that every procedure, by global definition, has "some level" of evaluation and management in it. Unfortunately, no one has sufficiently clarified the "some level" consideration, so the rules of "usual and customary" and "reasonableness" hold.

STANDARDS OF MEDICAL BILLING

No one will argue that health care providers deserve a fair reimbursement for the time, effort, and service they render their patients. The classic problem results when what health care providers feel is fair and what third-party payers feel is fair are in conflict. The provider must realize that insurers (1) are obligated to the beneficiary and (2) reimburse based on the limits of the policy and internal guidelines. Third-party payers must keep in mind that a lack of written guidelines, little to no peer review, and consistently ignoring standards of billing and review practices open them to charges of "bad faith" and litigation. Both providers and payers must be fully aware of and speak the same language of reimbursement.

Standards of billing practice have developed over the years to cover appropriate treatment and care rendered to patients. These standards are determined by third-party payers, physician organizations, and specialty associations. As third-party medicine evolved, it was necessary to develop a universal set of guidelines and systems to ensure that the health care provider and third-party payer had similar understandings of the protocols necessary for claim reimbursement.

In the 1950s, the California Relative Value Scale (CRVS) was published, containing a universal coding nomenclature and definition for specific medical services and procedures as well as assigning values to those services. As the CRVS was revised in 1964, 1969, and 1974, services and procedures were added and the guidelines expanded and refined. The code values were maintained, upgraded, or downgraded with each subsequent CRVS revision.

The CPT manual developed parallel to the CRVS and was its ultimate successor. The CPT is universally accepted, willingly or reluctantly, as the preeminent guide to reimbursement management by health care providers and third-party payers. While practitioners establish medical service and procedure fees by using the code descriptors and their respective guidelines within CPT, third-party payers likewise use similar protocols and definitions to assign values and allowances to the same service and procedure codes.

BILLING GUIDELINES

The following suggested guidelines are important for physicians treating patients and submitting claims to third-party payers.

Terminology

The New Patient

The new patient is defined as not receiving professional treatment or care by an individual provider within a 3-year period. This definition is extended to include any similar specialty provider within a single group. A new patient would require the practice to establish both medical and administrative records.

The Established Patient

The established patient is defined as having received professional treatment or care by an individual provider within a 3-year period. This definition is extended to include any similar specialty provider within a single group. An established patient would have existing medical and administrative records.

Referral

A referral is an actual or suggested transfer of partial or total independent patient care from one health care provider to another—generally of a different specialty. Because a referral involves the active treatment of the patient, it does not constitute a consultation.

Consultation

A consultation is a requested evaluation service wherein one provider seeks the opinion or advice of another regarding the evaluation and management of a patient's specific medical problem(s). A consultation report containing the findings should be sent to the referring doctor and copied for the consulting provider's record. The consultation is advisory by nature and does not, in and of itself, involve active treatment by the consultant. The consultant may, if medically necessary, perform services such as a minor or major surgical procedure, but these are considered independent of the consultation definition, coding, and allowance. If a consultant assumes responsibility for ongoing care of the patient, any subsequent evaluation and management service or procedure rendered would be as an attending/specialist rather than as a consultant.

Provider self-initiated conferences, discussions, admissions, or presurgical workups of established patients would not fall within the definition of a consultation.

Second Opinions

Second opinions are confirmatory consultations soliciting only another opinion or advice from another health care provider. A consultation report containing the second opinion findings should be sent to the requesting doctor. Treatment or ongoing care is not part of the second opinion evaluation and management service.

Patients are prudent to seek a second opinion when they are concerned about current or future medical treatment and/or existing, persistent, or suspected medical conditions. If the second opinion is requested by the patient, the consultant provider has a primary responsibility to relate his or her findings back to the patient. The patient may request in writing that the second opinion be transmitted to a previous health care provider or other person.

On occasion, a second opinion is requested by a third-party payer. After examination, the consultant is expected to render an opinion regarding the presenting current and future medical condition and an opinion regarding the medical necessity of the current or proposed treatment. Upon conclusion of the evaluation, a consultation report should be sent to the requesting third-party payer. When billing for second opinion mandated by a third-party payer, the consultant should qualify the five-digit confirmatory consultation CPT code with a "-32" modifier.

It is unethical for the consultant to solicit patients seeking a second opinion. If the patient insists on the consultant taking over his or her care, the health care provider, if he or she feels comfortable with that request, may do so without breaching medical ethics. The provider would be wise to note the circumstances of the patient request to take over his or her care.

Postoperative Complications

Postoperative complications involve conditions that are not usual and customary, expected, or normal considerations within a postsurgical follow-up period. Immediate postoperative pain, edema, joint stiffness, local superficial infection, minor wound dehiscence, and skin discoloration are some of the more common and expected findings following the performance of surgical procedures. Cellulitis, total wound dehiscence, severe prolonged pain or edema, joint stiffness months postsurgery are some of the unexpected significant complications that would warrant independent reimbursement for evaluation and treatment inside a global surgical follow-up period. Each instance of complication should be thoroughly documented in the medical record to substantiate the severity of the problem. When a significant postsurgical complication occurs, the five-digit evaluation and management CPT code should be qualified with a "-24" modifier. If surgical management of a complication is required, the five-digit procedure CPT code is qualified with a "-78" modifier. Both of these modifiers communicate to the third-party payer that a service or procedure was independently performed during an existing global surgical follow-up period.

Evaluation and Management Services

The level of evaluation and management service performed should be commensurate with (1) the complaint, history, examination, diagnosis, treatment consideration, and medical decision made and (2) supporting documentation contained within the medical record. Each evaluation and management service level has established sets of criteria that must be documented as having been met in order to qualify the service for reimbursement.

The levels of service are established through the documentation of key evaluation and management components: history, examination, and medical decision making. Other contributing but not key components include counseling, coordination of care, nature of presenting problem, and time.

Same-Day Surgery

With exception of emergent, urgent, or very minor surgical procedures, it is considered the standard of care to allow a patient a reasonable time to reflect on surgical information and possibly discuss the information with family and friends prior to committing to the procedure. It would be unreasonable to think that a patient could fully comprehend all the ramifications and treatment options available for moderate or major elective surgery when there is a push to perform that surgery on the same day it is initially recommended. Some examples of relatively minor surgical procedures that could be performed on the same day are small-site superficial biopsies, destruction of benign skin lesions, or injection therapies.

The Assistant Surgeon

The ultimate medical necessity to utilize the services of an assistant surgeon is based on the surgeon's judgment. This decision should not be linked to whether the third-party payer will reimburse the assistant surgeon for services performed. Each third-party payer has an internal guideline that defines its determination of medical necessity and its contractual obligation to pay for that necessity. Certain procedures fail to meet the test of medical necessity and consequently are routinely denied reimbursement by third-party payers. The site of service, whether inpatient hospital, ambulatory surgical center, or office operating room, should not alter the assistant surgeon medical necessity; neither should performing multiple minor procedures versus a single minor procedure.

The assistant surgeon should be reimbursed for all surgical procedures performed during the surgical session if at least one of the procedures is assistant surgeon–qualified for reimbursement. It is unreasonable to think that the assistant surgeon should step back and not assist the surgeon during the nonapproved assistant surgeon codes, then step back to the surgical field to resume assisting on the remaining approved procedures. Medicare is the only payer of significance that pays the assistant surgeon only for the qualified Medicare procedures.

Operative Reports

An operative report is a detailed record of the events surrounding and describing the surgical procedure(s) performed. The operative report must include the date of the surgery, the patient's name, the surgeon's name, the name of any assistant surgeon present, the anesthesiologist/anesthetist's name, the type of anesthesia administered (if a local anesthetic is used, the name, dosage, and location of administration should be noted), the preoperative diagnoses, the postoperative diagnoses, a detailed narrative of the procedure(s) actually performed, any unusual findings, and the surgeon's signature attesting to the validity of the record.

Operative reports are medical-legal documents that should be both exact and complete. Preprinted operative reports are held to the same standards as any other type of operative report. Operative reports should be typed or legibly handwritten. A description of incision length, suture type, fixation devices utilized, and injectables administered is essential for reporting accuracy.

Once an operative report is completed and returned to the surgeon, it should be carefully read. If no errors are noted, the report should be signed by the surgeon.

Surgical Follow-up

As previously discussed, the global surgical service definition includes a bundled payment—prepaid, if you will—for postoperative care for uncomplicated usual and customarily seen findings or conditions. The global follow-up period is predetermined by the third-party payer based on the type of surgery performed. This is a very important point. The surgeon should never assume that a non-Medicare payer uses Medicare guidelines for the length of the global follow-up period. In a significant number of cases, if the office insurance staff contacts the third-party payer just prior to or following the performance of the procedures, they may be surprised to find that what Medicare lists as having a 90-day follow-up period has, for example, a 45- or 30-day follow-up period. This difference allows the surgeon to begin billing medically necessary services, in the example, after the 45th or 30th day. And that can mean a better overall reimbursement.

There are several guidelines governing the surgical follow-up period: (1) multiple surgical procedures are not cumulative but based on the procedure with the greatest number of follow-up days; (2) certain services, procedures, and diagnostic evaluations are not included in the global surgical follow-up period (e.g., radiology services, cast application, fiberglass casting material, and unrelated evaluation and management services and unrelated procedures); and (3) only when there is clearly identified and significant complications—not usual or customarily expected in the global surgical follow-up period—is the surgeon permitted to bill for independent services or procedures related to the previous surgery.

Significant complications can include but are not be limited to postsurgical cellulitis, total wound dehiscence, severe prolonged pain or edema, and joint stiffness months after surgery. When they do occur, the surgeon may bill for the following:

- The evaluation and management services, using modified "-24" signifying that the service was performed during a global postoperative period, and/or
- The surgical procedures necessary to resolve the complication using modifier "-78," signifying that there was a medical necessity to perform another procedure on the same or related surgical site in order to resolve the problem; the value of a surgical procedure modified with "-78" is subject to the multiple-fee rule of the original operation.

Complications should not be a routine occurrence for any practice.

Office Surgical Suites

The high costs of hospital-based operating facilities and freestanding outpatient ambulatory surgical centers have prompted a number of surgeons to develop surgical suites within their office settings. An in-office surgical suite is convenient for both the patient and the surgeon; it reduces the overall direct and indirect costs of surgery and has a historically low rate of infection and complication.

Although there is a substantial cost associated with developing, equipping, and maintaining a quality surgical suite, the profitability of such a facility is also substantial in an age of reduced surgeon's allowances. While reimbursements from office-based surgical suites can vary considerably, depending on the certification or lack of certification that the facility has, it is safe to say that third-party payers do not recognize noncertified in-office surgical suites for reimbursement at the same levels as certified facilities. Certifications from the Joint Commission on Accreditation of Healthcare Organizations (JCAHO) and the American Association of Accreditation of Ambulatory Surgical Facilities (AAAASF) are recognized.

Avoiding the expense of accreditation, many surgeons elect to perform their procedures in their office operating rooms. Many times the only reimbursement—other than that negotiated on a managed care contract by managed care contract basis—is a single bulk payment for the facility, sterile trays, equipment, instrumentation, personnel, and supplies used. The HCPCS supply code number used generally is A4550 ("sterile tray") with the HCFA 1500 claim form description reading "Surgical Facility/Supplies/Tray." While an itemized listing of the items used may be included, the actual allowance will be determined by the third-party payer according to (1) a maximum rate based on the overall classification of the procedures performed (e.g., minor, soft tissue; major, bone; major, bone with power equipment, etc.), (2) a percentage of the total surgeon's allowance, or (3) an item rate schedule. Medicare does not reimburse noncertified in-office surgical suites but will reimburse an embarrassingly low allowance for supplies for a handful of procedures.

It is the responsibility of the surgeon using an in-office surgical suite to ensure the quality of care, health and safety of the patient. The surgical suite should be used for no other purpose than surgery. The assistants should be trained not only in sterile technique and assisting but in emergency procedures should a medical problem arise. The surgical suite should be equipped with the appropriate resuscitation equipment and emergency supplies. Performing surgery in an office setting does not exempt the physician from the maintaining the standards of care. Prior to each case, any medically necessary workups, examinations, laboratory tests, consultations, and the like should be performed to help ensure that the highest quality of care is delivered.

Requests for Medical Records and Reports

The physician is the guardian of the original patient medical record. As such, he or she will from time to time receive requests to release all or portions of the record. This release can be requested by other health care providers, third-party payers, or the patient. All requests must be in writing, with the patient's signature clearly evident. Under no circumstances should the original copy of the medical record be released. The physician must assume that once the medical record leaves the office it will never return. When a request for medical records is received, either a photocopy is made and released or a written summary is provided, depending on the nature of the request. Most third-party payers will not accept summaries of events or services for reimbursement purposes.

If the records are unusually long and detailed, a reasonable administrative charge may be charged to cover transcription, copying, and mailing costs. When a third-party payer requests that the specific date of service by copied from the medical record and submitted for review, the issue is generally the health care provider's reimbursement. Prior to demanding a set fee for the release of records to the third-party payer—some will pay a reasonable fee; others will not pay any fee—it is in the best interest of the provider's office to check to see if the third-party payer's policies allow for the payment of any clerical fees. If the answer is no, and the physician refuses to send the requested records, the third-party payer will simply not reimburse the provider's medical claim based on a lack of supporting medical records.

A request for x-rays is not unusual, but it is more controversial because once they are lost, they cannot be reproduced. Patients requesting x-rays often demand them on the basis that they own them because they paid for them. Patients do not, in fact, own their x-rays. They are entitled to a copy of the x-ray findings. Only copies of radiographs should leave the office. If an office has x-ray copying equipment, that can be done on the spot. If an office does not have the capability to copy x-rays, the local hospital radiology department can, for a fee. The expenses for copied radiographs should be borne by the party requesting the films.

When a third-party payer requests a complete copy of the medical records covering a certain interval of time, the provider should be careful to include *all* relevant material that is part of the record—progress notes, laboratory findings, radiology reports, consultation letters, studies, and tests—to support the reimbursement claimed. Sending partial medical records only increases the chances of inappropriately lower reimbursement. All submitted material should not only be complete but also clear and concise. In some cases, prospective submission of certain studies or reports (e.g., pathology findings, operative reports, laboratory test results) with the claim can expedite reimbursement.

Telephone Calls to Patients

If you telephone a patient (rather than a family member) to discuss results of diagnostic testing, coordinate medical management, evaluate and discuss new information, or initiate a treatment plan; the call may be coded with one of the following three CPT codes:

99371: Telephone call by physician to patient or for medical management or consultation or for coordinating with other health professional (simple or brief).

99372: same as above (intermediate).

99393: same as above (complex or lengthy).

Compliance Issues

The Office of Inspector General (016) lists several "hot buttons" for home health care agency compliance. While not specific to group medical practices, the OIG's philosophical insight may be ascertained from the following list.

- Duplicate billing; billing for nonrendered, substandard, or unnecessary services by qualified or nonqualified personnel.
- Fraudulent or nonallowed cost reports.
- Certain physician self-referrals, joint ventures or Stark antikickback violations.
- Withholding credit balances or compensation incentive plans.
- Underutilization, overutilization, or false care plans.
- Misuse-use of certification code numbers.
- Improper patient solicitation.

CONCLUSION

This chapter presented a broad overview of coding and billing definitions, guidelines, and rules. Within the chapter content were a number of "pearls" designed to help the health care provider better understand effective insurance billing while improving the chances of getting paid appropriately and fairly for his or her services.

Note: One reference source for determining which medical/surgical procedure has the highest value is the *Federal Register*. The issue containing HCFA rule changes for 2000 has CPT tables and each code's relative unit value.

READINGS AND REFERENCES

EM Check™ and E & M Software: Evaluation and management documentation tools for Windows 95/98/2000 and NT. (281) 491-9789.

Goldsmith, H. Advanced procedure and service coding practices. In Marcinko, D. E. (Ed.): *Profit maximization and reimbursement*. Columbus, OH: Anadem Publications, 1998.

Goldsmith, H. Effective CPT coding and billing guidelines. In Marcinko, D. E. (Ed.): *Profit maximization and reimbursement*. Columbus, OH: Anadem Publications, 1998.

Physician practice compliance report. MGMA and Opus Communications. *JMGMA*, Vol. 1, No. 7, 1998. (800) 650-6787.

## CHAPTER 6

Basic Capitation Economics for Internists and Other Specialists

A Primer for Evaluating Managed Care Contracts

Jeanne Hogan, Allan Gordon, and Angela Herron

Take all the [capitation] risk you can get, as soon as you can get it. Strive for capitation; not risk pools. The reason: "potential growth is phenomenal."

—Albert Hills, MD, Friendly Hills Healthcare Network

This chapter identifies the key questions that physicians should ask about capitated contracts and provides a methodology for evaluating the potential impact of the contracts on practice economics. The model demonstrates the impact on a solo family practice, internal medical, or other small group practice. However, the method is applicable to any specialty and to small group practices.

CAPITATED CONTRACTS

For physicians in solo practice or in small group practices, the common path to capitated contracting comes through membership in an independent practice association (IPA) or similar affiliation that has the legal authority to secure health plan contracts on behalf of its members. Even though the individual members of the IPA may not be involved in negotiations with the health plans, it is important for any physician to understand the terms of each contract. The key areas of concern are (1) patient mix, (2) capitation rate and contract terms, (3) service responsibility, and (4) stop loss.

Patient Mix

Health plan contracts are marketed to specific population groups, and the demographic characteristics of the patient populations will vary accordingly. Typically, the target population is identified in terms of the health plan's "product"—commercial plan, Medicare plan, or Medicaid plan. It is important for the physician to know about the population that is covered by the contract, in anticipation of the types of services that those patients will require. Physicians should inquire about the age, sex, and health status characteristics of the population the health plan expects to enroll and compare them to the current profile of the practice.

Capitation Rate and Contract Terms

The most important considerations are the actual capitation rate and the factors that can affect that rate, either up or down. It is also important to have a sense of market comparison on the capitation rate provided under the contract. Here is a list of specific questions physicians should ask.

- What is the monthly capitation rate paid to the physician? What is the IPA keeping from the health plan's payments to cover the cost of its services?
- Is the capitation rate a fixed amount per member per month, or will it be age- and sex-adjusted according to the actual blend of patients who are assigned to the physician?
- On what day of the month will the capitation payment be paid? Does the contract stipulate that the IPA must pay interest charges for late payments?
- Are there any low-enrollment guarantees built into the contract to provide for minimum payment amounts in the early stages of contract enrollments? Some contracts provide for fee-for-service payments until enrollments reach an effective level for capitation, such as 500 members.
- Are there provisions for retroactive changes in the enrollment assigned to the practice, and are there specific time limits on those provisions, such as 30 or 60 days? Failure to include time limits on retroactive enrollment adjustments may result in disruptions to cash flow and increased administrative paperwork.
- How are bonuses, if any, earned and paid? What are the specific measures if bonuses are based on performance?
- What penalties and deductions from the capitation payment can be imposed for actions such as inappropriate referrals or for referrals to noncontracted providers?
- How often can the capitation rates be re-negotiated?
- What are the physician's financial obligations on termination of the contract? Does the contract convert to a fee-for-service agreement, or is continuing care for the patient covered under the existing capitation rate? If so, what is the contract time limit for providing continuing care?

Service Responsibilities

Physicians should ask for a copy of the list of the services that are included in the capitation payment. All services should be defined by CPT or a similar billing code. Physicians who take primary care contracts and who also practice in specialty fields, such as allergy, cardiology, gastroenterology, or pulmonology, should have a clear understanding of how these services are managed under the contract— whether they are included or excluded in the capitation payment and whether these services can be billed separately. Other key questions about services include the following:

- What are the restrictions or limitations on billing patients for services that are not covered by the responsibility matrix? If it is permissible to bill for these services, are there restrictions on the billing rates?
- How is the physician reimbursed for nonphysician services, such as supplies, lab tests, and injections? This is particularly important if the practice has a high number of pediatric patients or provides allergy shots.
- What are the financial responsibilities of the practice for call coverage? Does the contract require that the physician pay for call coverage out of the capitation payment? If so, how is this payment handled—physician to physician or as a deduction from the capitation payment?

Stop Loss

Another critical factor is reinsurance for high-cost cases—stop-loss coverage. Physicians should know if the contract has stop-loss provisions, what the costs are for coverage, and what the effect on the capitation rate is once the stop-loss level has been reached. In some cases, the contract may convert to a new capitation rate. In others, payment may be on a predetermined fee-for-service arrangement. It is also important to know who is responsible for identifying cases that reach the stop-loss limit and whether there is a time limitation when filing a stop-loss case.

In addition to these key points in capitation contracts, physicians should also anticipate that there will be administrative burdens related to new contracts. In most situations, the IPA or other physician organization will take responsibility for credentialing for the provider network, for utilization management and quality management programs required by the health plans, and for claims administration. Each physician, however, will be required to submit encounter data and respond to various queries and requests for information. In some cases, health plans or IPAs may stipulate financial penalties for failure to comply, for poor timeliness, or for administrative errors.

BASIC CAPITATION ECONOMICS

To determine the impact that a capitated contract might have on a physician's practice, it is necessary to analyze the economics of that practice. The key economic components for a practice that has no capitated contracts are

1. Net revenue (collection) and net revenue per patient visit.
2. Office expenses—those that vary with patient visits and those that are fixed regardless of volume—and average expenses per patient visit.
3. Net income—the balance remaining from net revenue after all office expenses have been paid. This net income is available for physician compensation or investment in the practice.

To evaluate the impact of capitated contracts, two additional factors must be considered:

- The capitation rate (per member per month).
- Estimated number of visits for each patient covered under the capitated contract (pro forma utilization rate).

The following examples demonstrate the effect of changes in volume and payment mix on a solo physician's practice. The numbers used in the example are generalized from industry experience and do not represent the actual experience of any one practice. The steps in the analysis can serve for any practice, even though the specific numbers will vary from practice to practice, depending on specialty and the size of the practice.

Baseline

The baseline example is a internal medicine physician in solo practice with a part time midlevel professional assistant. The practice is reasonably busy, with room for growth. Payment for services is from traditional fee-for-service sources, including Medicare, some discounted rate plans, indemnity insurance, and cash. In the most recent year, the average net revenue per visit was $100.

To set the baseline for analyzing the potential impact of accepting capitated contracts, it is necessary to compile practice statistics for a previous 12-month period. From the baseline statistics, key components of net revenue, and total operating expenses can be easily identified. The next step is to identify "fixed" expenses, that is, those items that generally do not change within a defined range of service capacity, such as space, staff salaries and benefits, utilities, and educational seminars. Subtracting these fixed expenses from the total operating expenses provides the total cost for "variable" expenses, or those items such as medical supplies that are related directly to the patient visit. The average variable expense per visit is calculated by dividing the total variable expense by the total number of visits. The baseline practice profile is shown in Table 6.1.

Net income in the baseline is $144,250, and on average, each patient visit contributes $37.96 to this net income. The difference between net revenue and variable expenses is $81.38 per patient visit. Net revenue exceeds fixed costs at this level of visits. Each additional visit contributes enough to cover its variable costs of $18.62 and adds $81.38 to practice net income.

TABLE 6.1 Baseline Practice Profile

Baseline	Annual Total	Avg. per Visit
Patient visits	3,800	
Total net revenue	$380,000	$100.00
Total office expenses	$235,750	$62.04
Fixed expenses	$165,000	
Variable expenses	$70,750	$18.62
Net income	$144,250	$37.96

Growth Scenarios

A series of scenarios can now be developed to test the impact of growth for fee-for-service and capitated patients. For demonstration purposes in these scenarios, certain key components are assumed to remain constant. First, it is assumed that the practice has capacity to add 1,000 visits without any increase in fixed expenses. Second, it is assumed that variable expenses per patient visit also do not change.

Growth Scenario 1

Growth Scenario 1 tests the economic impact of increasing the number of fee-for-service visits by 1,000 visits at the current payment rate of $100 per visit. It is assumed that there is market opportunity to add these visits and that the growth can be accommodated with no increases in total fixed expenses or in average variable expense per visit. With the additional visits, total office expenses are estimated by using $165,000 for fixed costs, as determined above, and the average variable expense of $18.62 per visit. In the profile shown in Table 6.2, factors that change from the baseline are presented in bold type; factors that are held constant are in lightface.

It is evident that this growth scenario would be highly successful for the practice. The improvement in overall practice profitability comes from the fact that average expenses per visit are lower than in the baseline, with a corresponding increase in net income per visit.

TABLE 6.2 Growth Scenario 1: Fee-for-Service

	Annual Total	Avg. per Visit
Patient visits	**4,800**	
Total net revenue	**$480,000**	$100.00
Fixed expenses	$165,000	
Variable expenses	**$89,368**	$18.62
Total office expenses	**$254,368**	**$52.99**
Net income	**$225,632**	**$47.01**

Testing the Impact of Capitated Contracts

The next two growth scenarios also add 1,000 visits to the baseline practice. In Scenario 2, half of these visits are fee-for-service and half are paid under a capitated contract. In Scenario 3, all of the 1,000 visits are for patients enrolled in a new commercial contract. In both scenarios it is assumed that the contract capitation rate paid to the physician is $12 per member per month and that enrolled members average three visits per year. The formula below shows how to convert capitation payment per member to a per visit basis for easy comparison with fee-for-service visits:

Capitation payment per member per month: $12

Total annual revenue per capitated patient: $144

Average number of visits per patient per year: 3

Average revenue per visit (capitated patient): $48

Average revenue per visit (F/S patient): $100

Growth Scenario 2

This case demonstrates the impact of adding 1,000 visits, with 500 paid under traditional fee-for-service rates and 500 covered under the capitated contract. It is assumed that the practice has 167 enrolled members who average three visits per person per year. In Table 6.3, changes from Growth Scenario 1 are shown in bold type.

This scenario also yields a positive impact over the baseline, with increases of $55,000 in total net income and $3.64 in net income per visit over the baseline. However, the increases falls short of Growth Scenario 1 because of the much lower average payment rate for the visits covered under the capitated contract.

Growth Scenario 3

Growth Scenario 3 demonstrates the impact of adding 1,000 patient visits for 335 patients covered under a capitated contract, with no increase in the number of

TABLE 6.3 Growth Scenario 2: Additional 500 Fee-for-Service Visits and 500 Capitated Visits

	Annual Total	Avg. per visit
Patient visits	4,800	
Net revenue, fee for service	**$430,000**	$100.00
Capitation payments	**$24,048**	$48.10
Total net revenue	**$454,048**	**$94.59**
Fixed expenses	$165,000	
Variable expenses	$89,368	$18.62
Total office expenses	$254,368	$52.99
Net income	**$199,680**	**$41.60**

fee-for-service visits (Table 6.4). Even though many physicians find that capitated contracts impose administrative burdens that result in additional administrative costs, fixed expenses are held constant for demonstration purposes in this scenario. Factors in the practice profile that change from Growth Scenario 1 are shown in boldface.

On the surface, measured only in terms of average payment per visit, the capitated contract would be unattractive, paying less than half the prevailing rate for fee-for-service visits. However, on top of the existing base of fee-for-service business, the capitated contract adds directly to net income. The practice has already covered its fixed costs, and the average revenue per capitated visit, though lower than fee-for-service revenue, exceeds the incremental variable cost of $18.62 per visit. In essence, the practice is working harder, on a per visit basis, to realize this increase in net income.

Considerations for Payer Shift

As managed care expands, physicians enter into capitated contracts expecting that the patients acquired through the contract will be "new" patients, only to find that many are existing practice patients with a new form of insurance. The effect of this "payer shift" can be described from these factors demonstrated in the scenarios above.

- Average net revenue for a fee-for-service patient visit is $100.
- Average net revenue for a capitated patient visit is $48.10.

If the contract patient is a new patient, then $48.10 is added to practice revenue for each visit. If, however, the patient is an existing patient who converted to managed care, then the practice will have a differential of $51.90 on each patient visit. This phenomenon is particularly important if the contract is a senior plan, which converts patients paid at traditional Medicare rates to lower capitated rates. It is important for the practice to track not only the number of patients who are assigned to the practice under the capitated contract but to compare that list to current patient records to determine if these patients are truly patients new to the practice.

TABLE 6.4   Growth Scenario 3: Adding 1,000 Capitated Visits

	Annual Total	Avg. per Visit
Patient visits	4,800	
Net revenue, fee for service	**$380,000**	$100.00
Capitation payments	$48,096	$48.10
Total net revenue	**$428,096**	**$89.19**
Fixed expenses	$165,000	
Variable expenses	$89,368	$18.62
Total office expenses	$254,368	$52.99
Net income	**$173,728**	**$36.19**

The effect of payer shift is also seen in the change in net income in the three growth scenarios. Net income per visit in the practice with all fee-for-service visits, at $47.01 per visit, is over $10 higher than net income of $36.19 per visit when 1,000 capitated visits are added to the practice.

Practice Operating Expenses

One of the most frequently used rules of thumb for assessing practice perfor-mance is the relationship of practice operating expenses to net revenue, expressed as a percentage. In general (although it varies by specialty), practices with op-erating expenses at or below 60% of net revenue are regarded as strong perform-ers, and higher percentages are regarded as danger signs. Typically, the perspective is that expenses must be controlled to improve performance. How-ever, the introduction of capitated contracts can have a marked effect on the operating expense percentage, attributable to changes in revenues rather than expenses. Consider the changes in operating expenses as a percentage of net revenue between the baseline and the three growth scenarios described above (Table 6.5).

The downward pressure of capitated contract rates on net revenue can be compensated to some degree by even modest adjustments in operating expenses. Table 6.6 shows the effect of reducing fixed expenses by 10% and variable expenses by 5%. First-stage reductions of this magnitude might be achieved by

TABLE 6.5

	Net Revenue	Operating Expenses	Operating Expenses Net Revenue
Baseline	$380,000	$235,750	62%
Growth Scenario 1	$480,000	$254,368	53%
Growth Scenario 2	$454,048	$254,368	56%
Growth Scenario 3	$428,096	$254,368	59%

TABLE 6.6   Growth Scenario 3A: Adding 1,000 Capitated Visits, Reducing Fixed Expenses by 10% and Variable Expenses by 5%

	Annual Total	Avg. per Visit
Patient visits	4,800	
Net revenue, fee for service	$380,000	$100.00
Capitation payments	48,240	$48.24
Total net revenue	$428,240	$89.22
Fixed expenses	$148,500	
Variable expenses	$84,900	$17.69
Total office expenses	$233,400	$48.63
Net income	$194,840	$40.59

outsourcing selected expenses, such as billing and collections, to lower cost services, and by shopping for lower cost medical supplies.

Expense reductions at this level improve the operating expense percentage to 55% of net revenue, compared to 59% of net revenues in Growth Scenario 3. The reductions also add $21,000 to net income.

CONCLUSIONS

Accepting capitated contracts has a significant impact on practice economics. It is important that physicians have a clear understanding of the financial, service responsibility, and administrative terms and conditions of the contracts. It is also important to have an appreciation for the underlying factors contributing to overall practice economics. Testing the potential effect of capitated contracts on practice revenues and fixed and variable expenses, using the methodology described in this chapter, allows physicians to anticipate more accurately the changes that are likely to occur.

REFERENCES AND READINGS

Capitation management report, January 1999. 4343 Shallowford Road, Marietta, Ga., 30062
Institutional Digest, Integrated Health Systems Digest and HMO-PPO/Medicare-Medicaid Digest, 1998. Hoechst Marion Roussel.
Managed Care Digest, 1997 and 1998. Hoechst Marion Roussel.
Managing capitated contracts: Living with managed care—a view from the front. *Proceedings of the Managed Care Sessions* of the MGMAs 69th, 70th, 71st, and 72nd annual conferences (1995–98).

## CHAPTER 7

Contracting and Negotiation Skills for the Physician

Getting on the Best Insurance/Managed Care Plans— and Leaving the Rest

David Edward Marcinko

> You can't always get what you want; you can't always get what you need; but if you try real hard, you just might get what you negotiate for.
>
> —Eugene Schmuckler, PhD, Atlanta

One of the most highly embraced topics for increased managed care profitability is the need for improved negotiating proficiency within the medical community. For example, few practitioners negotiate directly with managed care organizations (MCOs) to acquire medical contracts. Rather, they allow medical networks or independent practice associations (IPAs) to negotiate for them. Unfortunately, this usually results in a lump sum monthly payment to the network, which is then divided among the participating physicians on a pro rata basis. Even more unfavorable is the fact that this mechanism merely accentuates the concept of "managed competition," as the practitioners work feverishly in true competitive American fashion to acquire a larger share of the pie. As a result, the per unit revenue for each procedure performed is actually reduced, using this "capitated risk pool" methodology.

OBJECTIVES OF THE MEDICAL NEGOTIATING PROCESS

Objectives of the medical reimbursement negotiating process are threefold: (1) acquiring and maintaining a long-term relationship with your MCO, HMO, or insurance payer; (2) exerting some control over the manner in which a contract is performed; and (3) persuading the payer to give maximum cooperation to you at a fair price for services rendered.

Although the concept of price is the emotional trigger point for almost all medical contract negotiation sessions, sophisticated physicians realize that price is merely one component of the entire payer-provider relationship. For example, physicians should know the answer to important questions before entering into any MCO contract negotiations. These include, but are certainly not limited to the following:

Subjective Impressions

- How does the plan relate to other plans in which you participate?
- Do you understand operative definitions of care and treatments (e.g., inclusions and exclusions, urgent vs. emergent care, medical necessity and enrollee, service vs. out-of-service area; pharmacy and risk pools)?
- How much control over business decisions will you retain?
- How do employees and other doctors feel about the plan?
- How do patients feel about the plan?
- What is the role of the MD/DO/DDS/DPM physician, PhD, PA, CRNA, or DC chiropractor in the plan?

Clinical Concerns

- Is there independence in the decision-making process?
- Is precertification necessary (oral or written)? Is it worthwhile or tied to payment?
- Can you refer to a specialist? What is the availability of medical records?
- Does the PCP control the specialist? How about retroactive referrals?
- What are the rules on generic drug usage or trade drugs? Laboratories?
- Is there a graduated appeals process in place?

Objective Impressions

- What is expected from the provider? Are there quality improvement reports?
- What is expected from the MCO or the patient?
- Is the contract exclusive or inclusive to other MCOs or providers?
- Are there state insurance commissioner filings and AM Best or other credit ratings?

Economic and Financial Matters

- What are the "carve-outs," "withholds," or bonus structures?
- Are doctors penalized economically for treating patients?
- How quickly are providers paid (turn-around time)?

- Does the number of patients promised offset reductions in payment? Is there a guaranteed number, such as 3,000 members (250 month × 12 months) if a lower number may not economically justify the extra administrative costs to service the plan?
- Is there a *fail-safe* floor, such as 85% fee-for-service equivalent rate if the minimum number of patients is not delivered?
- Medicare risk enrollee rates are usually 3–5 times more than commercial rates.
- How much total capital is available? Is it enough?
- What relative value system is used, and what are the conversion factors?
- What is the impact on return on investment, operating costs, revenues, and profit?
- What are the annual utilization (frequency) and actuarial rates and claims history for the past 3 years? (New demographic groups are more risky than known groups.) As an example, Table 7.1 gives actual rates for gastroenterologists.
- What are the individual or cumulative stop-loss provisions of the risk contract? (i.e., $5,000–$10,000 per patient, individually or collectively)? Recall that 92% of all commercial HMO patients have less than $3,000 in medical claims per year, and about 97% have claims of less than $10,000 per year.

Administrative and Management Concerns

- Do you spend more time with patients or case managers?
- How does the plan's paperwork compare to other plans?
- How often are the "rules" changed and are you informed?
- What are the administrative costs (range: 8%–20%)?

Negotiation Preparation: "Due Diligence"

Obviously, the above concepts suggest that over 90% of the time involved in a successful negotiation must be invested in preparing for the actual deliberation.

TABLE 7.1 Gastroenterology Utilization Rates

CPT Code	Description	Annual Frequency
# 45330	Sigmoidoscopy (diagnostic)	45
# 45331	Sigmoidoscopy (biopsy)	12
# 45333	Sigmoidoscopy (removal lesion)	16
# 45378	Colonoscopy	85
# 45380	Colonoscopy (biopsy)	45
# 45385	Colonoscopy (removal lesion)	75
# 46600	Anoscopy	02

For example, the physician seller must (a) have a technical understanding of all anticipated provided medical services, (b) conduct a cost analysis of these services by using managerial accounting principles, and (c) analyze the payer's relative bargaining position by means of a classic marketing concept known as SWOT evaluation. In this technique, the opponent's (S)trengths, (W)eakness, (O)pportunities, and (T)hreats are objectively considered in relation to the physician's own.

The often contentious dilemma of carve-outs from a capitated managed care contract is another consideration currently involved in much negotiation. Under this scenario, medical services or products such as surgery, traumatology, physical therapy, immunizations, certain tests, wound care, or prosthetic devices may be excluded from a managed care contract in favor of another, often subcapitated provider.

For example, an orthopedic group noted that foot surgery was listed in a new capitation contract that it was considering. Since the members were not comfortable with such surgery, they asked that these services be excluded. The plan would not do so; therefore, the orthopedists either had to accept it and perform unfamiliar surgery or reject it. They decided on the latter course of action.

In another case, a certain primary care group noted that allergy testing, and related services were included in their contract proposal. Since these services were not in their area of expertise, they had them deleted, reducing the capitation rate accordingly.

The following list represents some conditions considered important for subcapitated risk contracts.

1. Equivalent risk for the primary MD and subcapitated specialist.
2. Known fixed expenses for the subcapitated specialist.
3. Predictable and low cost of care, per specialty episode.
4. High episodes of specialty care (not unusual or unpredictable events).
5. Definable and well-understood responsibilities of the specialist.
6. Profit and cost savings potential for both the referring MD and the specialty MD.
7. Reinsurance.

MCO MEDICAL CONTRACTING CONSIDERATIONS

Most physicians and many patients believe that the risks and burdens of managed care far outweigh the proposed benefits, and they consider the following items most onerous. They are dutifully cautioned to consider carefully the following ramifications when deciding to become affiliated with any managed care plan:

1. Credentialing (board certification).
2. Patient stream. Do the numbers justify the discount? Are there referrals? By whom?

3. Dispute resolution mechanism. What is the MD input? Carve-outs and exclusions?
4. Medical records and confidentiality. Security of information systems.
5. Restrictive covenants, gag orders, restrictions, and termination clauses.
6. Arbitration or negotiation clauses. Are there audit rights? Noncompliant patients?
7. Medical standards, guidelines, and indemnification clauses.
8. Rules, rules and more rules?

PITFALLS TO EVALUATING ADULT MCO CONTRACTS

There are seven key pitfalls to watch out for when evaluating an MCO contract, referencing a recent Arthur Andersen Consulting, LLP, survey, as listed below:

1. *Profitability:* Less than 52% of all senior physician executives know whether their managed care contracts are profitable. "Many simply sign up and hope for the best."
2. *Financial data:* 90% of all executives said the ability to obtain financial information was valuable, "yet only 50% could obtain the needed data."
3. *Information technology:* MIS hardware and sophisticated software is needed to gather, evaluate and interpret clinical and financial data; yet it is typically "unavailable to the solo or small group practice."
4. *Underpayments:* This rate is typically between 3% and 10% and is usually "left on the table."
5. *Cash flow forecasting:* MCO contracting will soon begin yearly (or longer) compensation disbursements, "causing significant cash flow problems to many physicians and practitioners."
6. *Stop-loss minimums:* SLMs are one-time upfront premium charges for stop-loss insurance. However, if the contract is prematurely terminated; you may not receive a pro rata refund unless you ask for it!
7. *Automatic contract renewals:* ACRs, or "evergreen" contracts, automatically renew unless one party objects. This is convenient for both the payer and payee but may result in overlapping renewal and renegotiation deadlines. Hence, a contract may be continued on a suboptimal basis, to the detriment of the provide.

CAPITATION DISCOUNT PAYMENT AND FINANCIAL LOGIC

Older Fee-for-Service System

Consider how the MD was compensated in the traditional fee-for-service, indemnity insurance, system:

- Payment per patient visit, per procedure, and per treatment.
- Payment per hospital visit, per surgical and diagnostic intervention.

- A la carte medical menu.
- Patients as assets, not liabilities, and MDs as their advocates.
- *Costs were increased!*

Newer Capitated Payment System

Now compare and contrast how the MD is compensated under the newer, capitated payment, or discounted, managed care system. Financial danger and opportunity are joined, for both doctor and hospital alike.

- Per member, per month, per year, per contract, per life.
- Fixed-price medical menu.
- Patients as liabilities, and MDs may become adversaries, not advocates.
- *Costs were reduced!*

Example: Hospital Contracts and Managed Discounts

St. Joseph's Hospital is a 500-bed facility that was operating at 55% capacity. To increase its occupancy rate, it instituted a direct medical contracting program with Mighty-Soft (MS) Corporation, a major employer in the area. In order to receive the business, St. Joe's agreed to offer a 15% discount on all charges. It also agreed to hold its price increases to 5% per year, for 3 contract years.

Prior to the contract, the hospital had served about 15% of MS's employees, a total of 765 admissions per year, with total charges of $3.2 million. After the contract was executed, the hospital admitted 25% of MS's employees, or about 1,275. These admissions were responsible for $5.3 million of charges. In the second and third year, the hospital received 37% of the employees or 1,887 admissions, which accounted for $8.3 million of charges.

USEFUL PATTERN AND TREND INFORMATION FOR THE PHYSICIAN

As can be seen, homework, due diligence, and information gathering is the key to any successful negotiation process. According to the Hoechst Marion Roussel Managed Care Digest series (*Medical Group Practice Digest* for 1998), the following pattern and trend comparative information has been empirically determined and may provide a basic starting point for the process.

Note that a group practice is defined as a formal and legally recognized organization of three or more practitioners, sharing business management, facilities, personnel, and records.

Procedural Utilization Trends

- Among all physicians in a single specialty group practice, invasive cardiologists averaged the most encounters with total hospital inpatient admissions, down from the prior year. On the other hand, encounters rose for cardiologists in multispecialty group practices.

- Echocardiography was the most commonly performed procedure on HMO seniors, followed by coronary artery bypass graft surgery. Group practices performed cardiovascular stress tests for circulatory problems most often.
- CT studies of the brain and chest were the most common studies for HMO seniors; MRI head studies were the most common diagnostic test for commercial HMO members.
- Colonoscopy was the most common digestive system procedure on senior HMO members; barium enemas were more common among commercial members.
- Hospital admission volume decreased for allergists, family practitioners, internists, OB/GYNs, pediatricians, and general surgeons.
- Internists ordered more in-hospital laboratory procedures than did other physicians in single specialty groups.
- Non-hospitalist MD/DOs used in-hospital radiology services most frequently, continuing a 3-year upward trend.
- Pediatricians averaged the most ambulatory encounters, down from the prior year.
- Non-hospitalist internists ordered a higher number of in-hospital laboratory procedures than any other single medical specialty group, but allergists and immunologists increased their laboratory usage.
- The number of ambulatory encounters increased for general surgeons, whereas group surgeons had the most cases. Capitated surgeons of all types had a lower mean number of surgical cases than did surgeons in groups without capitation. Surgeons in internal medical groups also had more cases than those in multispecialty groups.
- The average number of total office visits per commercial and senior HMO visits fell, along with the number of institutional visits for both commercial and senior HMO members.
- The average length of hospital stay (ALOS) for all commercial HMO members increased to 3.6 days but decreased to 6 days for all HMO members.
- The total number of births increased for commercial HMO members served by medical group practices and decreased for solo practitioners.

Treatment Protocol, Quality, and Satisfaction Trends

- More than one-third of all medical groups use treatment protocols, rising from the year before. Multispecialty groups were more likely to use them than single-specialty groups, which often develop their own protocols. The use of industry benchmarks to judge the quality of health care delivery also increased.
- Outcomes studies are most common at larger medical groups, and multispecialty groups pursue quality assurance activities more often than do single-specialty groups.

- Provider interaction during office visits is increasingly coming under scrutiny. Patients approve of cardiologists more frequently than of allergists and ophthalmologists.

Midlevel Provider and Staffing Trends

- Midlevel provider (MLP) use increased among multispeciality groups, especially in those with more than half of their revenue from capitated contracts. Use also rose with the size of the practice and was highest with OB/GYN groups.
- Medical support staff for all multispeciality groups fell and was lowest in medical groups with fewer than 10 full-time equivalent (FTE) physicians. However, groups with a large amount of capitated revenue actually added support staff. Smaller groups limited support staff.
- Compensation costs of support staff increased, and the percentages of total operating costs associated with laboratories, professional liability insurance, information technology (IT) services, and imaging also increased. Support staff costs increase with capitation levels, and more than half of all operating costs are tied to support staff endeavors.

Managed Care Activity and Contracting Trends

- More medical group practices are likely to own interests in PPOs than in HMOs, and the percentage of groups with managed care revenue continues to rise. Multispecialty and large groups also derive more revenue from MCOs than do single-specialty or smaller groups.
- Managed care has little effect on physician payment methods, which are still predominantly based on productivity. Physicians were paid differently for at-risk managed care contracts in only a small percentages of cases.
- Most medical groups (75%) participating in managed care medicine have PPO contracts. Group practices contract with network HMOs more often than do solo practices. Single-specialty groups more often have PPO contracts.
- Capitated lives often raise capitation revenues in large group practices. Group practices are more highly capitated than are smaller groups or solo practices. Almost 30% of highly capitated medical groups have more than 15 contracts, and 22% have globally capitated contracts.
- Higher capitation is linked with increased risk contracting. Larger groups have more risk contracting than do smaller groups.

Financial Profiles and Trends

- Medicare fee-for-service reimbursement is decreasing. Highly capitated groups incur high consulting fees.

- The share of total gross charges for OB/GYN groups associated with managed care at-risk charges is rising whereas non-managed-care, not-at-risk service charges, are declining.
- Capitated contracts have little effect on the amount of on-site office nonsurgical work. Off-site surgeries are most common for surgery groups, not medical groups. Half of all charges are for on-site nonsurgical procedures.
- Highly capitated medical groups have higher operating costs and lower net profits. Groups without capitation have higher laboratory expenses than those with capitation.
- Physician costs are highest in orthopedic surgery group practices. Generally, median costs at most specialty levels are rising and profits shrinking.

Obviously, the above information is only a gauge since regional differences and certain medical subspecialty practices and carve-outs do exist (see Figures 7.1 and 7.2).

For example, after a period of time on any specific MCO contract, you may wish to perform your own annual utilization summary, as in Table 7.2.

Thoughtful and even professional assistance is often required. However, for the uninitiated, it is a very reasonable starting point from which to play the capitation game. Then, the managed care plan can be tracked.

TRACKING MANAGED CARE PLANS

Simple Fee-for-Service Methodology

1. Record patient payment charges at the usual (UCR) office rate.
2. Post patient and plan payments to the specific client ledger account.
3. Post withhold amounts, which represent adjustments to the account, and a credit (if any) to an account for the specific plan.
4. Post the remaining amount as a contractual adjustment from the patient account.
5. Zero-out the patient account balance, as the plan account is increased by the amount of any withhold.
6. Calculate collection percentages for the plan and benchmark them with other financial classes.

Examples

Patient Account

	Charges	Payments	Adjustments	Balance
	$50	$10		$40
Payment		$23	$2 withhold	$15
			$15 disallowed	

Plan Account

	Charges	Payments	Adjustments	Balance
			<$2>	$2

PERCENTAGE OF PRIMARY CARE PHYSICIANS, BY COMPENSATION METHOD

SIZE (# of FTE physicians)	Productivity			50%–99% Guaranteed Salary	Straight Salary	Equal Shares	Other*
	100%	75%–99%	50%–74%				
10 or fewer	20.1%	5.5%	7.1%	45.3%	17.0%	2.5%	2.5%
11–25	30.2	18.6	10.9	26.4	10.9	0.8	1.6
26–50	27.7	22.3	7.4	27.7	6.4	—	8.5
51–75	36.7	23.3	6.7	26.7	3.3	—	3.3
76–150	34.0	29.8	8.5	19.1	4.3	—	4.3
151 or more	30.0	15.0	10.0	25.0	10.0	—	10.0
ALL MULTISPEC. GRPS.	**25.0%**	**13.0%**	**8.0%**	**36.1%**	**12.7%**	**1.5%**	**3.5%**
SAMPLE SIZE: 19,235 providers/684 groups							

PERCENTAGE OF SPECIALISTS, BY COMPENSATION METHOD

SINGLE SPECIALTY	Productivity			50%–99% Guaranteed Salary	Straight Salary	Equal Shares	Other*
	100%	75%–99%	50%–74%				
Allergy/Immunology	—	—	—	—	—	—	—
Anesthesiology	25.5%	7.3%	3.6%	23.6%	10.9%	16.4%	12.7%
Cardiology	16.3	8.1	9.3	36.0	3.5	14.0	12.8
General Surgery	13.0	4.3	10.9	30.4	13.0	19.6	8.7
Hematology/Oncology	23.8	4.8	19.0	28.6	—	14.3	9.5
Obstetrics/Gynecology	29.5	3.3	13.1	21.3	14.8	11.5	6.6
Ophthalmology	43.2	—	22.7	25.0	4.5	2.3	2.3
Orthopedic Surgery	41.9	10.9	17.1	17.1	2.3	4.7	6.2
Radiology/Diagnostics	3.4	—	—	34.5	6.9	34.5	20.7
ALL SINGLE SPEC. GRPS.	**26.5%**	**6.5%**	**11.5%**	**26.3%**	**6.9%**	**12.8%**	**9.4%**
SAMPLE SIZE: 5,711 providers/710 groups							

DIFFERENTIATION OF MC
COMPENSATION AMONG GROUPS

COMPENSATION FOR MC PATIENTS
AMONG GROUPS DIFFERENTIATING MC

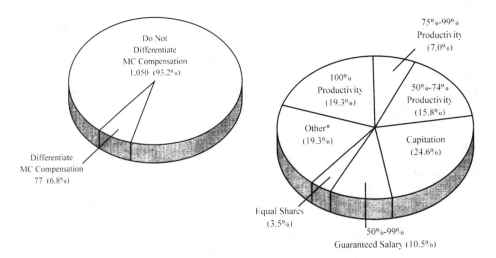

FIGURE 7.1   **Percentage of primary care physicians by compensation method.**

Data source: Medical Group Management Association Physician Compensation and Production Survey: 1997 Report Based on 1996 Data ©1997.

From *1998 Hoechst Marion Roussel Managed Care Digest Series.* Reprinted by permission of the publisher, Hoechst Marion Roussel, Inc.

SALARY AND BENEFITS OF GROUP PRACTICE STAFF

SPECIALTY	Physicians		Allied Professionals		Support Staff	
	Average Salary	Average Benefits	Average Salary	Average Benefits	Average Salary	Average Benefits
Allergy/Immunology	$193,939	$27,251	$25,972	$5,502	$109,206	$15,885
Cardiology	325,352	41,388	38,227	6,826	101,460	21,669
Family Practice	137,190	20,734	16,427	3,625	63,813	13,170
Internal Medicine	176,264	25,604	16,259	4,014	57,097	11,815
Pediatrics	154,631	22,034	16,986	4,003	56,206	13,096
Psychiatry	137,822	18,156	104,761	18,959	49,017	9,984
General Surgery	257,161	33,658	28,279	4,716	76,663	17,341
Neurological Surgery	536,728	36,948	33,223	7,815	45,215	10,531
Orthopedic Surgery	290,215	34,800	32,617	7,222	76,816	17,504
ALL GROUPS	**$205,178**	**$30,482**	**$25,026**	**$6,092**	**$100,862**	**$22,863**

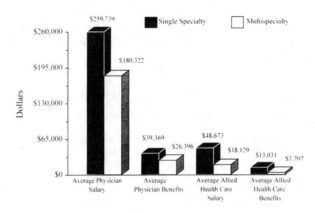

SALARY AND BENEFITS OF GROUP PRACTICE STAFF

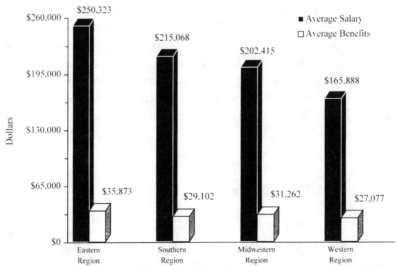

SALARY AND BENEFITS OF GROUP PRACTICE PHYSICIANS

FIGURE 7.2   Salary and benefits of group practice staff.

Data source: American Medical Group Association Practice Survey of Key Medical Management Information ©1997.

From *1998 Hoechst Marion Roussel Managed Care Digest Series.* Reprinted by permission of the publisher, Hoechst Marion Roussel, Inc.

TABLE 7.2   Fill-in-the-Blank Annual Utilization Summary Spreadsheet

Patient visits/net revenue	$$ Amount estimated	$$ Amount received
Current patients	?	?
New patients	?	?
Old patients	?	?
Total visits or procedures	?	?
Visits/current patients	?	?
Total net revenue	?	?
Net revenue/current patient	???	???

The Negotiation Process

Once the numbers are crunched, the formal negotiation process with the MCO consists of a five-step sequence, according to Professors Bruce Patton and William Ury of the Harvard Business School.

1. Don't bargain over positions. Taking them only makes matters worse since egos often become identified with positions. Is it harder to rob a friend or a stranger?
2. Separate the people from the process before considering the substantive problem. Figuratively, if not literally, both parties should come to see each other as working side by side, attacking the problem, not each other.
3. Invent options for mutual gain since having a lot at stake narrows your vision and inhibits creativity. Brainstorm possible solution options that advance shared interests and creatively reconcile differences.
4. Insist on using objective criteria rather than discussing what the parties are willing or not willing to accept. These standards can be a matter of custom, law, informed opinion, or market value.
5. Know your bottom line limit, and recognize that you do not have to come to an agreement in each and every situation. Therefore, you must know your BANTA (Best Alternative to a Negotiated Agreement) and be prepared to say no and walk away.

Negotiating with Office Vendors

1. Ask for a request for proposal (RFP) in writing.
2. Inform vendors that price is your crucial trigger point.
3. Evaluate samples to compare quality and construction.
4. Use well-known suppliers, not "mom and pop" outfits.
5. Understand conditions, terms, and warranties.

KEY STEPS TO SUCCESSFULLY NEGOTIATING CAPITATED MEDICAL CONTRACTS

1. *Develop an accurate pricing model:* There are a number of methods that MCOs use to pay capitated medical contracts. These include (a) per member/per month (PM/PM), the best-known, if not most popular, method, (b) the percent (net) of premium method, (c) single/family coverage, and (d) average blended HMO population. The computer spreadsheet in Table 7.3 illustrates how different capitation rates may be determined.

The Advisory Board Company reported the results of a survey of 60% commercial PM/PM HMO rates in 1994. Compare them with current rates today (5 years later) and then project them into the near future for your specialty (Table 7.4).

TABLE 7.3 Determining Capitation Rates

A Utilization Rate	B Charge/ Service	C Cost/1000 Members (A × B)	D Cost/Member annual (C / 1000)	E PM/PM (D / 12)
20	32	$640	$.64	.053
50	88	$4,400	$4.40	.366
90	88	$7,920	$7.92	.666

TABLE 7.4 Average PM/PM Erosion: Fill-in-the Blank for Your Specialty

SPECIALTY	AVG. PM/PM (1994)	AVG. PM/PM TODAY
Anesthesiology	$1.40–1.77	?
Dentistry		?
Cardiology	.65–.85	?
Cardiology (invasive)	.36	?
Chiropractic		?
ENT	1.38	?
Internal medicine	1.00	?
Surgery (general)	1.10–2.55	?
Neurology	.26	?
OB/GYN	2.30–5.50	?
Oncology	.27	?
Ophthalmology	.60–.70	?
Orthopedics	1.16–1.50	?
Podiatry	.35–1.25	?
Psychology/psychiatry	1.67	?
Radiology	1.91	?
Urology	.35–.50	?
Others	6.00	?

For full-risk capitated care, the following comprehensive health care PM/PM of $120/month for the average commercial HMO plan breaks down into costs divided into components something like this:

- $10–20 for office and administration expenses
- $8–12 for carve-outs and stop-loss insurance
- $5–10 for drugs and pharmaceuticals.
- $80–90 for medical care:
  primary physicians and/or specialists: $20–40
  surgery centers and hospitals: $35–50

Obviously, payments to all of the above cost drivers are decreasing over time.

Percent (net) of premium method: Medical service payment is directly proportional to the MCO insurance premium and indexed for inflation or deflation. This is analogous to a Social Security (SS) cost of living allowance (COLA) for the MD provider, whose compensation will increase or decrease in proportion to the medical coverage premium charged to the insureds (i.e., a form of risk sharing with the MCO).

Single/family coverage. Family size, medical acuity, and other assumptions are compared to the entire MCO contract and prorated accordingly.

Average blended HMO population. A subset of small group assumptions within the larger MCO entity, prorated accordingly.

2. *Use effective negotiation skills.* Review the section on "trick" negotiation tactics, below, and general negotiation skills, above.

3. *Incorporate protective ("safe harbor") contract clauses.* These include termination, renegotiation, catastrophic, solicitation, nondisclosure, non-compete, "gag," and solicitation clauses. Other important clauses to consider include indemnification clauses, procedural carve-outs, low enrollment guarantees, utilization rate "kick-outs," drug or formulary clauses, risk pool limitation clauses, MD/member ratio requirements, "all or none" group clauses, and stop-loss reinsurance, as well as arbitration and mediation clauses in your home state.

4. *Monitor, implement, and renegotiate the deal.* Ongoing TQI evaluation, payment schedules, medical and economic credentialing, and financial ratio analysis should be done quarterly with MCO administrators to ensure that the contract you originally signed is meeting the expectations of all concerned.

For example, Table 7.5 may be used to assess your contract(s) utilization and net revenue(s).

Contemporaneously, as HMOs are themselves increasingly coming under their own cost pressures, many are willing to negotiate complementary care as part of a benefits program, as listed in Table 7.6.

Again, therefore, if you do not inquire about it, you can't negotiate for it.

PITFALLS TO EVALUATING PEDIATRIC MCO CONTRACTS

According to John D. Meerschaert, an associate actuary from Milliman & Robertson, the following four hidden risks are incumbent in evaluating any pediatric managed care contract:

TABLE 7.5   Projected Utilization and Net Revenue

First step: Calculate potential available patients

	(Example)
Total patients covered	30,000
Total patients in service perimeter	12,000
Potential available patients	12,000

Second step: Determine (MD) provider competition

Total panel of MD providers	6
Total MDs in service perimeter	2
Potential MD options (competition)	2

Third step: Determine estimated patient volume

Visits/1000 patients/year	50
× Potential available	12
= total visits/patients	600
Total visits/potential patients	600
Divided by potential MD options	2
= Potential patient volume (visits/year)	300

Fourth step: Calculate projected net $$ revenue

Potential utilization (visits/year)	300
× Projected net revenue/visit	$50
= Projected net revenue/year	$15,000

Modified from Rehnwall, P., Strategies for Effective Managed Care Relations. Healthcare Business Development, 454 Prospect Ave., Suite # 119, West Orange, New Jersey.

TABLE 7.6   Negotiable HMO Complementary Care Benefits

38%	Weight management
33%	Stress management
30%	Nutritional service
27%	Acupuncture
24%	Biofeedback
14%	Massage therapy
8%	Naturopathy
7%	Hypnotherapy
6%	Yoga
5%	Homeopathy
5%	Herbal medicines
3%	Meditation
3%	Guided imagery
2%	Reflexology
2%	Dream therapy

Source: InterStudy: *Modern Physician,* January 1999.

1.   Realize that due to the Balanced Budget Act of 1997, which created a new children's health insurance program (CHIP) under Title XXI of the Social Security Act, antiselection is inevitable. Families with children in need of medical care have a greater incentive to join than do parents of healthy children. Risk-sharing arrangements and reimbursement must account for this increased risk.

2.   Acquire outreach information to enroll a large enough portion of the population to reduce the impact of the smaller percentage of enrollees with higher than average medical costs. Combined CHIP/Medicaid outreach programs are ideal since many families are not aware of their Medicaid eligibility due to the separation of cash benefits and Medicaid that resulted from welfare reform.

3.   Recognize that price controls are likely and that fees will spiral downward. However, if your are already providing free care to this population, *low pay is much better than no pay.*

4.   Understand that MCOs, as well as physician providers, do not yet know how to understand and manage the CHIP population. Financial risk should be shared by the MCO as well as the physician, and all parties should understand that unknown contingent liabilities abound under this new system for the impoverished child.

TEN TIPS FOR MORE EFFECTIVE NEGOTIATED MEDICAL PAYMENT AGREEMENTS

1.   *Do not get emotional, upset or angry. . . Stay cool!*

Although financial negotiations are a vitally important matter to you, it is probably just another job to your MCO opponent. He or she will likely negotiate with many more doctors this day, and you are not important enough for him or her to get upset about. Do the same: stay cool.

2.   *Do not get personal or lose your dignity.*

No one will respect an angry, loud, or abusive doctor. This type of behavior will not only *not* get you a raise, but you may get delisted from the plan because one can reasonably infer that your patients might get treated in the same impolite manner as your MCO opponent.

3.   *Do not share your information.*

If you have good results or outcomes with a particular treatment protocol, do not share it with the MCO unless they sign a nondisclosure, non-compete, or no-sale agreement with you. Get information before you give information that might later be used against you.

4.   *The first offer should not be the last offer.*

Even if you "split the price difference," you might not receive a better financial deal. On the other hand, the initial offer was likely so low that even a split would benefit the MCO, so be careful. Splitting the difference is not negotiation.

5.   *Stand firm and await counteroffers.*

Once you have performed the calculations to determine your bottom line, don't settle for less. You will only be offered less the next time. Be aware of your best alternatives.

6.   *Leave something on the table.*

If you give something in return for getting something, you will foster a continuing relationship with your MCO plan. For example, you might accept a slightly lower PP/PM rate in exchange for a "diabetic carve-out." In a older geographic neighborhood, this might be a better deal for you since wound or ulcer care is expensive. Then your opponent can go back to his or her supervisor and brag about "putting one over on you" by getting a lower capitation rate. In other words, you both get "bragging rights."

7.   *Do not be afraid of calculated risks.*

Partial- or full-risk, fixed-base medical capitation is the wave of the future. So is the corporate practice of medicine seen in professional practice management organizations (PPMOs). Do not be foolhardy, but those who take calculated and informed risks will prosper while conservative types do not.

8.   *Do not give your MCO opponent too much credit.*

Your opponent may know nothing about your medical specialty, so do not give him or her information about your practice or profession to use against colleagues. You might just know more about managed care than your opponent does.

9.   *Take your time—it is usually on your side.*

Unless you have no practice accounts receivable reserve, are a new practitioner, cannot get a line of credit, or are really destitute, you probably have time on your side to negotiate a deal in your favor. Often, simple procrastination will increase your capitation or fee rates.

10.   *Use a professional negotiator if you are uncomfortable.*

Although professional negotiators and business specialists may be expensive in the short run, you may gain much more by using them in the long run, especially if they are knowledgeable. If you have been unhappy with your own results to date, by all means get professional assistance.

WHAT ARE MCOS LOOKING FOR IN MD/DO CONTRACTS?

The conversion to managed health care and capitation financing is a significant marketing force, not merely a temporary business trend. More than 60% of all physicians (MD/DO) in the country are now employees of an MCO, and more the 5% are members of a PPMO. The latter is growing more rapidly than the former, despite the recent financial debacle, according to the Cain Brothers Index of PPMC's valuations. MDs that embrace these forces will thrive, while those oppose the marketplace will not.

After you have evaluated the HMOs in your geographic area, you must then make your practice more attractive to them, since there are far too many physicians in most regions today. The following issues are considered by most MCO financial managers and business experts, as they decide whether or not to include you in their network.

General Standards

1.   Is there a local or community need for your practice, with a sound patient base that is not too small or large? Remember, practices that already have a significant number of patients have some form of leverage since MCOs know that patients do not like switching their primary care doctors or pediatricians,

and women do not want to be forced to change their OB/GYN specialist. If the group leaves the plan, members may complain to their employers and give a negative impression of the plan.

2.   A positive return on investment (ROI) from your economically sound practice is important to MCOs because they wish to continue their relationship with you. Often this means it is difficult for younger practitioners to enter a plan, since plan actuaries realize that there is a high attrition rate among new practitioners. On the other hand, they also realize that more established practices have high overhead costs and may tend to enter into less lucrative contract offerings just to pay the bills.

3.   A merger or acquisition is a strategy for the MCO internal business plan that affords a seamless union should a practice decide to sell out or consolidate at a later date. Therefore, such a strategy should include strong managerial and cost accounting principles, a group identity rather than an individual mindset, profitability, transferable systems and processes, a corporatized form of business, and a vertically integrated organization if a multispeciality group.

4.   Human resources, capital, and IT service for synergism with existing MIS framework: This is often difficult for the solo or small group practice and may portend the need to consolidate with similar groups to achieve needed economies of scale and capital, especially in areas of high MCO penetration.

5.   Consolidated financial statements conforming to GAAP (generally accepted accounting principles), IRC (Internal Revenue Code), OIG (Office of the Inspector General), and other appraisal standards.

6.   Strong and respected MD leadership in the medical and business community: MCOs prefer to deal with physician executives with advanced degrees. You may not need an MBA or CPA, but you should be familiar with basic business, managerial, and financial principles. This includes a conceptual understanding of horizontal and vertical integration, cost principles, cost volume analysis, financial ratio analysis, and cost behavior.

7.   Be willing to treat all conditions and types of patients. The adage "more risk equates to more reward" is still applicable, and most groups should take all the full-risk contracting they can handle, providing they are not pooled contracts.

8.   Are you a team player or solo act? The former personality type might do better in a group or MCO-driven practice, whereas a fee-for-service market is still possible and may be better suited to the latter personality type.

9.   Valid license, DEA narcotics license, CME, adequate malpractice insurance, board qualification/certification, hospital privileges, agreement with the managed care philosophy, and partners in a group practice that meet all these participation criteria. Be available for periodic MCO review by a company representative.

Specific Office Standards

1.   Clean, presentable with a professional appearance.
2.   Readily accessible with barrier-free design (OSHA).

3. Appropriate medical emergency and rescusitation equipment.
4. Waiting room that accommodates 5–7 patients, with private changing areas.
5. Adequate capacity (i.e., 5,000–10,000 member minimum), business plan, and office assistants for the plan.
6. Office hour minimum of 20 hours/week.
7. 24/7 on-call coverage with electronic tracking.
8. MCO-approved subcontractors.

MCO PHYSICIAN AND MEMBER RIGHTS AND RESPONSIBILITIES

MCO physicians and patients have certain rights and responsibilities, implicitly and explicitly expressed in their at-will contracts. Here is a general reminder:
As a doctor, you have the right to

- Receive payments and collect co-payments and co-insurance for covered services and also collect for noncovered services, with disclosure.
- Obtain necessary information to treat patients.
- Be treated with respect and courtesy.
- Request reassignment of a patient with whom an acceptable doctor-patient relationship cannot be established.

As a doctor, you have the responsibility to

- Treat patients with respect and courtesy.
- Ensure medical record confidentiality.
- Provide plan benefits according to plan polices and guidelines.
- Discuss a patient's health status with him or her or a legal representative.

Members have the right to

- Choose a doctor, receive quality care, and change doctors when necessary.
- Receive all benefits to which they are entitled.
- Review all their medical information and maintain confidentiality.
- Express complaints through appropriate channels.

Members have the responsibility to

- Have their medical needs provided or authorized by their doctor.
- Know, understand, and abide by the plan's rules and regulations.
- Keep or cancel appointments, appropriately.
- Furnish medical and health care information to appropriate sources.
- Treat physicians with dignity and respect.

"TRICK" NEGOTIATING TACTICS OFTEN USED BY MCOS AGAINST THE PHYSICIAN

The following trick negotiating tactics can be used to gain an advantage over your opponent, or they can be used against you to your disadvantage. The key is to recognize them immediately.

1.   Deliberate deception with phony facts about contracts, providers, patients, venues, demographics, prices, utilization rates, or services. Some MCOs may even offer a fee-for-service fee schedule as enticement into the plan. Then fees are dramatically reduced once the initial enrollment period has elapsed.

2.   Ambiguous authority regarding negotiating intentions or power. Once the deal is done and a firm agreement has been made, the other side announces that it must take the agenda to a higher authority for final approval and another shot at your resistance.

3.   Avoid stressful personal situations before beginning the negotiating process. Don't negotiate when you are sick, your personal life is in a shambles, your children or spouse is sick, or when you feel too mentally exhausted or "psyched out."

4.   Personal attacks can be in the form of verbal abuse or simply loud talking, avoidance of eye contact, or asking you to repeat yourself, endlessly. Extremely offensive to most physicians and increasingly used today is the phrase "Remember, Doctor, you are an oversupplied commodity." Now ask yourself, do you really want to be on a plan that doesn't respect your profession?

5.   The "good guy–bad guy" routine is a psychological tactic in which one partner appears to be hard-nosed and the other appears more yielding. Small concessions result, which, upon repetition, become larger in aggregate.

6.   The "take it or leave it" tactic can be easily avoided by knowing your best alternative to a negotiated agreement (BANTA). More formally, this is known as a *unilateral contract of adhesion.*

7.   Escalating or increasing demands occur when the opponent increases demands or reopens old demands. Call your opponent's bluff on this by pointing it out and replying that you are aware of its use.

APPEALING DISENROLLMENT DECISIONS

The decision by an HMO to not include you in its plan or network or to disenroll you if you are already included is not irrevocable. You may not have been included or rejected for a number of reasons, including clinical or economic recredentialing, malpractice history, unfavorable patient survey, certification, or a host of other tangible or intangible reasons. Therefore, in order for you to appeal the decision, the following guidelines are suggested in any request for a reconsideration process.

1. Get a letter of explanation from the medical or clinical executive director.
2. Ensure that your initial application went through the proper channels of consideration.
3. Contact your local plan representative, in person if possible.
4. Make sure your state and national medical afflictions are current, as well as hospital and surgical center staffing applications and credentials.
5. Write a letter to the medical director and request a return receipt (US mail) or send it by private carrier. Inform the director of the actions you

are taking to become more attractive to the plan or what you have done to correct the deficiencies that caused your noninclusion initially.

A sample letter appears below, with some of the items that might be included. Be honest and do not lie, but do try to cast your practice in a favorable light. Adjust for your practice specialty.

Dear Medical Director:

As a current nonmember of your managed car plan, I would like to take this opportunity to inform you of the activities we have pursued during this past year in order to gain acceptance into your plan:

I have received ____ hours of clinical continuing education, which is ____ more than the state requires. Topics included recently developed techniques for pain control, nonhospital and nonsurgical based therapy, more effective drug utilization, and a host of other methods of practice to reduce costs and increase patient welfare and mobility.

I have received ____ hours of medical business management training aimed at reducing office overhead expenses, increasing office efficiency and capacity, and improving patient flow and communications. For example, our computerized call-back system is designed to ensure the continuity of patient care.

We have completed a patient survey demonstrating that the average patient can receive a regular appointment within ____ days and urgent appointment within ____ days. Of course, we are fully staffed for immediate care of the emergent patients. Our patient satisfaction rating is high. Most patients spend less than ____ minutes in the waiting room and are discharged in a timely fashion, with appropriate instructions for returning them to work efficiently and comfortably.

We have expanded our office hours to improve access and enhanced the barrier-free design of our office infrastructure. We are OSHA- and Y2K-compliant.

Since we believe in preventive care, our diabetic patients are continually screened and evaluated to reduce the potential for infections and other complications. This includes the liberal use of random accu-check blood sugar readings, with neurologic and circulatory assessment and prompt reporting of aberrant values and findings to their primary care physicians or endocrinologists.

I will be taking my specialty board certification examination, administered by ____, on ____, 2000. Of course, my results will be forwarded to you immediately.

I will become ABQAUR (American Board of Quality Assurance and Utilization Review) certified and/or a Certified Physician in Healthcare Quality (CPHQ) this year, after successful completion of all educational requirements and examinations.

Although I realize that this is a challenging time for all concerned, we strive to make every patient's visit to our office a medically and socially positive one. More specific suggestions regarding our practice would be appreciated.

Therefore, I hope you will consider the probationary inclusion of our practice into your managed care plan for the coming enrollment period.

Fraternally,
Joseph A. Smith, MD/DO

6. Keep current if you have an "any willing provider law" in your state.
7. Remember, once dropped by one plan, it will be easier to be dropped again by another. Fight hard to prevent this from happening. Hire a professional consultant or negotiator to champion your cause.

CONCLUSION

Physicians must realize that managed care contracting and negotiation skills represent free market enterprise in its purest form. These financial and managerial techniques match the skills of determined payers against usually unskilled practitioners. All explore ways to achieve objectives that tend to optimize the self-interest of their respective positions. By rewarding efficiency and penalizing inefficiency, MCOs can and often do determine the medical reimbursement structure for the entire medical health care industrial complex. The reviewed techniques will help equalize the struggle.

REFERENCES AND READINGS

Advisory Board Company, Governance Committee. *Capitation strategy.* Washington, DC: Author, 1995.

Bader, B., & Matheny, M. Understanding capitation and at-risk contracting. *Health Systems Leader,* March 4–16, 1994.

Baum, N. Putting "managed" into managed care. In *Take care of your medical practice.* Gaithersburg, MD: Aspen Publishing, 1996.

Grab, E. L., & Caesar, N. B. Negotiating profitable managed care contracts for your group. *Group Practice Journal,* 42(5):28–30, 1993.

Hultman, J. *Here's how, Doctor.* Los Angeles: Medical Business Advisors, 1995.

Marcinko, D. E., & Hetico, H. R. Managed care contracting and financial negotiation skills. In D. E. Marcinko (Ed.): *Profit maximization and reimbursement.* Columbus, OH: Anadem Publishing, 1998.

Medical Management Institute. *Negotiating managed care contracts.* New York: McGraw-Hill, 1994.

Living with managed care: A view from the front. Medical Group Management Association, 104 Inverness Terrace, East, Englewood, CO, 80112 (1995).

Managed Care Digest series. Hoechst Marion Roussell, PO Box 9627, Kansas City, MO, 1998.

Meerschaert, J. D. Children's health insurance programs: Beware of hidden risks. *MGMA Journal,* February 1999.

Spiro, G. W. *The legal environment of business.* New York: Prentice-Hall, 1993.

Tinsely, R. Negotiating, or re-negotiating managed care contracts. *MGM Journal,* October 1998, p. 66.

Ury, W. *Getting past no: Negotiating your way from confrontation to cooperation.* New York: Bantam Books, 1993.

Ury, W., Fisher, R., & Patton, B. *Getting to yes.* New York: Bantam Books, 1991.

Youngberg, B. A. *Managing the risks of managed care.* Gaithersburg, MD: Aspen Publishing, 1996.

## CHAPTER 8

Essentials of Risk Management

It's NOT About Medical Malpractice Anymore!

Charles F. Fenton III

> The essence of social insurance is bringing the magic of averages to the rescue of millions.
>
> —Winston Churchill

There is much controversy about physicians serving as plaintiffs' expert witnesses. Many physicians feel that the plaintiff's expert witness is a "turncoat." However, that controversy is misplaced. A medical malpractice action is mainly about money—in most of the cases, the insurance company's money. The risks attendant in medical practice today are much greater than the risks involved in a medical malpractice action. The risks today are also mostly about money—*your* money.

In today's medico-legal environment the physician faces risks from many directions. Risks come from the federal government (including the Health Care Financing Administration, the Occupational Safety and Health Administration, the Drug Enforcement Agency, and the Environmental Protection Agency), the state government (including state medical boards), insurance companies (including health maintenance organizations [HMOs], preferred provider organizations [PPOs], and even indemnity plans), patients, and even one's own employees and prospective employees. The practicing physician almost needs to have a law degree to keep track of all of the rules and regulations attendant on practicing.

MEDICARE RECOUPMENT RISKS

Historically, the main risk that the practicing physician faced that would place the physician's own assets at risk was the threat of a Medicare recoupment.

Although many practitioners act surprised when receiving the notice of recoupment, this should not be the case. After all, the majority of recoupment requests are preceded by a request for copies of medical records. The practitioner has, therefore, been forewarned of the risk of recoupment. Many practitioners, on receiving a request to forward copies of several patients' medical records, simply assign the task to a clerk and forget about the incident. That is a mistake. Whenever a request for medical records is received, whether from Medicaid, Medicare, or another third-party payer, there is a golden opportunity.

The medical records in question should be thoroughly reviewed prior to their release. The guidelines of the requester, as well as the CPT definitions of the billed CPT codes, should be reviewed, and both of these should be compared to the record to ensure that proper-level codes and proper documentation was used. Often it is prudent to write an accompanying letter that points out to the reviewer why the documentation is proper. It is much easier to make your case at this juncture than to have treatment denied, have a recoupment request, and have to request additional hearings. If you are not sure how to develop such a document justifying your treatment, you should consult with a knowledgeable attorney or a CPT consultant for assistance.

If, having demonstrated the medical necessity of the treatments, a recoupment letter is received, then the practitioner should retain an attorney to preserve all the legal rights. Generally, there is a right to request a *fair hearing* before a *hearing officer*. At the fair hearing the practitioner is given the opportunity to present justification of the treatments to the impartial hearing officer. If the fair hearing results are adverse to the practitioner, there is a right to request a hearing before an administrative law judge. Even if the practitioner is unsuccessful at that level, there may be additional appeal rights.

The above processes are long and drawn out. The amount of time necessary will result in larger and larger attorney's fees. It is simpler, easier, faster, and cheaper to retain an attorney for assistance when the first request for medical records is received. Although retaining an attorney at this juncture is no guarantee of success, it is the best opportunity to "nip it in the bud."

FRAUD RISKS

The greatest risk to the practicing physician's fiscal fitness in the current medico-legal environment is the fraud risk. With the federal and state governments, as well as the private insurance companies, seeking to reduce health care costs, active investigations into health care fraud has increased. It is relatively easy for an administrative billing error to be labeled as fraud. In this manner, an innocent act becomes a criminal act, which the practitioner must now defend.

Medicare Fraud

The federal government has many weapons in its arsenal to investigate and prosecute Medicare and Medicaid fraud. Some of these are the Medicare and

Medicaid Anti-Fraud and Abuse Statute, the RICO statute, the Federal False Claims Act, money-laundering laws, and civil asset forfeiture laws.

Insurance Fraud

The federal government now has the power to investigate and prosecute fraud involving private insurance companies. The new federal crime of health care fraud, authorized in 1996, gives the federal government wide scope of authority. A practitioner being investigated for Medicare fraud may also end up defending against a charge of private health care fraud.

Misrepresentation

The reader may feel that, once the medical practice is sold and the doctor is retired, the chances of being sued for fraud would disappear. However, the very act of selling the medical practice can potentially expose the seller to fraud accusations by the buyer. Consider the following case.

A physician decided to sell his practice and move to another state to practice. The physician sold the practice to another physician in the same specialty. The value of the sale was based, in part, on the yearly gross of the practice. The physician sold his practice, accepted installment payment terms from the buyer, and moved to the new state.

The buyer began to practice medicine at his new office. Although he was busy, his gross never approached the gross of the prior physician. Eventually, the buyer defaulted on the loan. The selling physician sued for the deficit.

The defaulting physician, who still had all of the seller's patient and computer records, began to do an in-depth evaluation of the seller's practice. The buyer noticed some discrepancies in the billing patterns of the seller. Considering these discrepancies to constitute Medicare and insurance billing fraud, the seller countersued the buyer on the grounds of misrepresentation, the seller's theory being that because the seller allegedly committed Medicare and insurance fraud, the gross receipts of the practice and hence the ultimate purchase price of the practice, was grossly inflated. Therefore, the buyer determined, the seller had fraudulently misrepresented the potential of the practice.

But the seller did not stop at simply filing a countersuit. The seller also notified state and federal authorities and filed complaints of insurance fraud against the seller. The seller thought that he would move to the good life in the new state, but his old practice kept him in constant legal trouble.

SELF-REFERRAL RISKS

The federal and state governments have enacted several overlapping laws to deal with the issue of financial inducement in the referral of patients. These laws create a virtual maze of laws and regulations, which can easily snare the unwary.

The extent of the federal regulation of the area of self-referral includes the Medicare Anti-Fraud and Abuse Statute, the Medicare Safe Harbor Regulations, and the Stark Amendment.

Medicare Anti-Fraud and Abuse Statute

The federal government has addressed the issue of physician fraud and abuse in the Medicare Anti-Fraud and Abuse Statute (anti-fraud statute). This statute applies equally to any abuses in the Medicaid system. However, the statute does not apply to abuses involving private patients. The statute provides, in part, that

> Whoever knowingly and willfully offers or pays any remuneration (including any kickback, bribe, or rebate) directly or indirectly, overtly or covertly, in cash or in kind to any person to induce such person to refer an individual to a person for the furnishing or arranging for the furnishing of any item or service for which payment may be made in whole or in part under a Federal health care program, or to purchase, lease, order, or arrange for or recommend purchasing, leasing, or ordering any good, facility, service, or item for which payment may be made in whole or in part under a Federal health care program, shall be guilty of a felony and upon conviction thereof, shall be fined not more than $25,000 or imprisoned for not more than five years, or both. (42 U.S.C. 1320a-7b[2]).

The anti-fraud statute applies only to persons receiving kickbacks for referring Medicare or Medicaid patients. There are many examples of physicians who ran afoul of the law, including several chiropractors that were paid "handling fees" for collection and transmission of lab specimens to a certain laboratory. In another case, cardiologists who received "interpretation fees" for referring patients to a certain cardiac lab were found guilty of violating the statute. Additionally, a hospital administrator was found guilty when he received perks from an ambulance company to whom he had referred patients. Succinctly, any benefit given or received in exchange for referral of a Medicare or Medicaid patient will violate the statute.

Medicare Safe Harbor Regulations

The Medicare Safe Harbor rules were passed in an effort to identify areas of practice that would not lead to a conviction under the anti-fraud statute. The Safe Harbor regulations provide for eleven areas in which providers may practice without violating the anti-fraud statute. Areas of safe practice under these regulations are briefly highlighted below:

1. *Large entity investments.* Investment in entities with assets over $50 million. The entity must be registered and traded on national exchanges.
2. *Small entity investments.* Small entity investments must abide by the 40-40 rule. No more than 40% of the investment interests may be held by investors in a position to make referrals. Additionally, no more than 40% of revenues can come through referrals by these investors.

3. *Space and equipment rentals.* Such lease agreements must be in writing and must be for at least a 1-year term. Furthermore, the terms must be at fair market value.
4. *Personal services and management contracts.* These contracts are allowable as long as certain rules are followed. Like lease agreements, these personal service and management contracts must be in writing for at least a 1-year term, and the services must be valued at fair market value.
5. *Sale of a medical practice.* There are restrictions if the selling practitioner is in a position to refer patients to the purchasing practitioner.
6. *Referral services.* Referral services (such as hospital referral services) are allowed. However, such referral services may not discriminate between practitioners who do or do not refer patients.
7. *Warranties.* There are certain requirements if any item of value is received under a warranty.
8. *Discounts.* Certain requirements must be met if a buyer receives a discount on the purchase of goods or services that are to be paid for by Medicare or Medicaid.
9. *Payments to bona fide employees.* Payments made to bona fide employees do not constitute fraud under the Safe Harbor regulations.
10. *Group purchasing organizations.* Organizations that purchase goods and services for a group of entities or individuals are allowed, provided certain requirements are met.
11. *Waiver of beneficiary coinsurance and deductible.* Routine waiver would not come under the Safe Harbor.

A physician's actions that come under the Safe Harbor regulations will not violate the Medicare Fraud and Abuse Statute. However, the provider must still abide by the Stark Amendment and must also abide by applicable state law.

The Stark Amendment

The Stark Amendment to the Omnibus Budget Reconciliation Act of 1989 was a step by the federal government to prohibit physicians from referring patients to entities in which they have a financial interest. Originally, the Stark Amendment applied only to referral of Medicare patients to clinical laboratories in which the physician had a financial interest.

The Stark Amendment provides that if a physician (or a family member) has a financial interest in a clinical laboratory, then he or she may not make a referral for clinical laboratory services if payment may be made under Medicare. A financial interest is an ownership interest, an investment interest, or a compensation arrangement. There are certain exceptions to the Stark Amendment, for example if a physician personally provides the service or if a physician or employee of a group provides the services.

Like the Safe Harbor regulations, the Stark Amendment permits physician investment in large entities and provides an exception for rural providers. Under the Stark Amendment, large entities are defined as publicly traded entities with assets greater than $100 million.

There are certain other exceptions that are similar to the Safe Harbor regulations. They include items such as provision for rental of office space, employment and service arrangements with hospitals, and certain other service arrangements. These arrangements must be at arm's-length and at fair market value.

Stark II was passed in 1993 to modify and expand the Stark Amendment. In particular, it acts to bring numerous other entities, besides clinical laboratories, within the prohibitions of the Stark Amendment.

Self-referral and over utilization may become less of a problem as managed care makes further inroads into medical practice. Future legislation is likely to address the concerns of the financial incentives toward underutilization of ancillary medical services.

MANAGED CARE CONTRACTUAL RISKS

The purpose of this section is to alert the practitioner to recent trends in the medical malpractice arena. Attorneys are becoming more aggressive in suing HMOs and other managed care companies. Historical bars to such suits are declining simultaneously with recent federal ERISA protection erosion. The upshot is that more litigation against managed care companies, their affiliates, and their health care providers are likely. The health care provider should be aware of these trends, should evaluate his or her own situation, and may have to take certain steps to limit these newly evolving risks and potential liabilities.

For example, the usual method of protection for the practicing physician, the use of the corporate form of business, often is no benefit when signing managed care contracts. Most managed care companies credential the individual physician and hence require that the individual physician, not the professional corporation, sign the contract. *This puts all of the physician's personal assets at risk.*

HISTORIC BARS TO MANAGED CARE SUITS

Historically, managed care companies have been afforded immunity from negligence and malpractice lawsuits. Several state and federal bars, including ERISA (Employee Retirement Income Security Act of 1974), have insulated managed care companies from liability relating to the treatment of patients. Likewise, managed care companies have historically been immune from malpractice committed by a health care member of its panel of providers.

On a state laws basis, the Corporate Practice of Law often insulated managed care companies from such liability. The theory underlying this protection was essentially uncomplicated; since corporations are prohibited under the Corporate Practice of Law Doctrine from practicing medicine, they should not be held liable for medical negligence and malpractice.

However, in recent years it has become apparent that managed care companies do in fact "practice medicine." These companies tell their panel of providers how to practice, whether it is in a generalized or specific field of medicine. They establish a formulary of approved drugs, limiting those medications available to their subscribers. They review and then approve or deny needed medical care. They create economic incentives for patients to be undertreated or treated in a predetermined manner. They effectively minimize referrals to specialists, often at the peril of the patient subscriber and the health care provider seeking that consultation.

In the federal arena, ERISA has been the primary deterrent to suits against managed care companies. Under the theory of federal preemption, even the lowest federal regulation takes precedence over any and all state laws.

ERISA has however been described as possessing "super-preemption." That term was coined to evince the special deference that courts have displayed to potential defendants who allege defensive protection based on ERISA. In the past, most providers ran into the ERISA preemption when a health plan governed by ERISA was contrary to a state law, such as state antidiscrimination law (i.e., a state law prohibiting insurance payment discrimination based on degree).

In the context of this chapter, the reader should understand that liability claims, such as medical malpractice claims, are state law causes of action. Since the federal ERISA law trumps state laws, then bringing a medical malpractice action against an ERISA entity has been almost impossible.

RECENT TRENDS

Recent cases would imply that the days of ERISA preemption applicable to the vast majority of managed care companies might be limited. At first blush, this might sound like good news to the health care provider. After all, everyone (the patient, the public, and the provider) all tend to dislike the depersonalization that has occurred in medicine since the advent of managed care. But a closer look into the facts will show that this change of events is a very bad omen for the health care provider.

It is axiomatic that the actual providers of medical services, even if employed by a managed care organization, can and usually do shoulder the enormous liability for medical malpractice, even if conforming to the directives of the managed care company. State legislatures are becoming more aggressive in making the managed care companies liable for their actions. Likewise, federal courts are increasingly willing to permit claims against managed care companies. Yet most employment contracts between the health care provider and the managed care entity allow for subrogation of the managed care entity's potential liability, including defense counsel costs, to that of the individual provider.

In one case the court found that ERISA does not preempt the patient's negligence claim against an HMO-employed physician. A US district court held that preemption is inapplicable to a patient's negligence claim against a physician who was employed by an HMO (*Edelen v. Osterman*, 943 F. Supp. 75 (D.D.C., 1996)).

In one federal case (*Dukes v. US Healthcare, Inc.*, 57 F.3rd 350 [3d Cir.] [1995]), the court implied that medical malpractice cases against health care plans based on vicarious liability may not be preempted by ERISA. Under this case and its progeny, it appears that the managed care company can be held vicariously liable for the actions of its independent providers. Several courts have tended to follow the Dukes precedent, but this is certainly far from uniform throughout the United States. Again, this may appear to be a favorable turn of events, but it can spell disaster for the provider.

The state of Texas has a statute, which was upheld in 1998, that allows a patient to sue a health plan if the patient was injured due to denial or delay in approval of treatment. Many more states are likely to follow suit.

With the ERISA shield melting away, lawyers are chomping at the bit to sue these managed care companies. A recent legal publication instructed the reader as to several potential theories of liability to pursue in civil litigation as to managed care companies for negligence of its panel of health care providers. The same journal had an additional, shorter article instructing the reader in ways to avoid ERISA when suing managed care companies. It seems apparent that if this current trend portends the future, the likelihood of managed care companies becoming defendants or co-defendants in medical malpractice actions will rapidly escalate. Such a fate heralds certain issues for the individual health care practitioner.

With such acceptance there has been much debate in state legislatures and in Congress concerning reducing the liability protections that many managed care companies have thus far enjoyed. When the shield from medical negligence liability is finally broken, the floodgates will open for plaintiffs and lawyers to sue the managed care company as a specifically named defendant for its own negligence.

Lawyers have several options when suing managed care companies. The lawyer can opt to institute a direct suit against the company, or he/she can bring a derivative suit based on vicarious liability. In a direct suit, the lawyer alleges that the managed care company did something wrong (i.e., negligent) that damaged his or her client. Such claims can take the form of direct negligence, corporate liability, or contract.

In a derivative suit based on vicarious liability, the lawyer contends that the managed care company is liable because the contracted provider was negligent. Causes of action can take the form of nondelegable duty by contract (the patients contract with the managed care company), nondelegable duty under state statute, joint venture (of the managed care company and the provider), or under various agency principles. It is this type of suit that is more likely to cause later problems for the provider.

If an attorney knows that the managed care company is protected through a hold-harmless clause in its provider agreement, the reader may wonder why the attorney would sue the company rather than just the provider. The answer is simple: money. The company is the deep pocket. Even if the provider has malpractice insurance, the limits are usually $1 million per incident. However, a recovery from the managed care company could potentially be larger. If the attorney is successful against the company, then the attorney will not care if the company files an indemnity or subrogation action against the provider. The attorney will already have his or her settlement.

What It Means to the Physician

Participating in managed care is like a double-edged sword. The practitioner has to participate in managed care, but the contract that is signed creates many potential risks for the individual. The main risk is the hold-harmless clause prevalent in most managed care contracts. Although these clauses cannot negotiated out of the contract, they are still binding upon the signer.

In a malpractice action, the plaintiff has several options. The plaintiff can sue the provider or name the HMO as a co-defendant. In some cases, the plaintiff may decide to forgo suing the provider (if the provider does not have insurance) and instead sue the managed care company directly.

If a patient sues the physician and the managed care company and if a hold-harmless clause exists, the individual physician may be liable for any settlement or award made by the managed care company to the patient. Even if the managed care company were to win a defense verdict at trial, under these clauses, the individual physician would be liable for the managed care company's attorneys' fees. This could be tens of thousands of dollars—even though the defense won!

Some examples of hold-harmless clauses will help the reader understand the import of what they are signing. Below are several examples with commentary. These examples have been taken from actual managed care contracts and are incorporated into contracts which we physicians are signing.

> *Example 1:* The Provider further agrees to indemnify and to hold the Company, its officers, directors, shareholders, employees, agents, and representatives harmless from and against any claims or liabilities, from any cause whatsoever, arising under this Agreement or the provisions of rendering of Healthcare Services. Any claims or liabilities which arise out of this Agreement or the provision or rendering of Healthcare Services are the sole responsibility of the Provider.

This clause is very broad and very one-sided. It is obvious that any claims against the company that are related to alleged malpractice by the provider would eventually become the responsibility of the provider. Moreover, since the clause also covers "any claims or liabilities, from any cause whatsoever, arising under this Agreement or the provision or rendering of the Healthcare Services," it is arguable that the provider might also end up liable for acts of the company, such as denial of services or adverse results related to the drug formulary or practice guidelines established by the company.

Since this clause is skewed and is so broad, the provider should not sign this agreement. The provider should either negotiate out the clause or should sign the agreement in the name of the provider's corporation.

> *Example 2:* Specialist shall indemnify Company for any losses, judgments, costs, claims or expenses (including, without limitation, attorney's fees) that Company may incur because of the negligent or intentional actions or omissions of Specialist or any of Specialist's employees or agents or due to any limitation, lack of coverage, revocation or suspension of Specialist's malpractice insurance.

This clause is more specific than the clause in Example 1. However, this clause clearly shifts the burden to the specialist if the company is sued for any alleged malpractice by the specialist. This clause clearly states that the specialist is responsible for "attorney's fees." The reader should realize that even if the company receives a defense verdict, the specialist will be responsible for the company's attorneys' fees. The specialist will be responsible for the attorneys' fees, even though the specialist had no input into the attorneys' selection, hourly rate, or amount of hours dedicated to the case.

> *Example 3:* Provider further agrees to indemnify and to hold harmless the Company against any claims or liabilities arising under this Agreement.

This clause is very succinct. The physician should not be lulled into complacency by its brevity. This clause has the same impact as the clause in Example 2.

> *Example 4:* Neither the Provider nor the Company shall be liable for defending or for the expense of defending the other party, its agents, employees or representatives against any claims, suits, actions, dispute resolutions or administrative or regulatory proceedings arising out of or related to such other party's actions or omissions. Neither party shall be liable for any liability of the other party or its agents, employees or representatives, whether resulting from judgment, settlement, award, fine or otherwise, which arises out of such other party's actions or omissions.

This clause appears to be a mutual clause. Each party indemnifies the other party. Such mutuality often leads the reader into a false sense of security. Remember that the contract was written by the managed care company's attorney for the sole purpose of protecting the company. The purpose of this clause, like the purpose all of the other clauses, is to render the provider responsible for any suits against the company based on any alleged malpractice of the provider.

This clause has a red flag that should jump out at the reader. The clause makes the provider liable for "any liability whether resulting from settlement." Therefore, if the company decides to settle a pending case, then it can seek reimbursement from the provider. The company can seek reimbursement from the provider for the settlement even though the provider had no input whatsoever regarding the terms or the amount of the settlement.

> *Example 5:* Neither the Company nor the Provider nor any of their respective agents or employees shall be liable to any third parties for any act or omission of the other party.

This is another brief clause. It is essentially similar to Example 4.

MANAGED CARE DILEMMA

The dilemma that a provider will have to consider when facing the adverse effects of a hold-harmless clause is the prospective detriment to his or her practice if he or she does not capitulate to the managed care company's demand to provide indemnification for a settled case. The provider has the option to fight the issue in court. In some cases, the provider may prevail, but it is likely to be a futile and expensive effort in most scenarios.

In any event, if providers do not indemnify the managed care company, most likely they will find themselves deselected from the panel. Such a deselection is likely to create a domino effect of deselection from other panels. Such events could destroy a provider's practice.

POSITIVE DEFENSIVE STEPS TO TAKE NOW

The first and most obvious step that every provider should take is the one that is most often skipped. The provider should read every managed care contract. Most providers simply sign and return every contract that comes across their desks. In recent years, with so much of the population participating in some form of managed care, many providers feel that they have no choice but to sign the contract. Remember that even if the terms are not negotiable, you still have a choice of not signing the contract. If you do sign the contract, you should fully understand the risks you are undertaking. It is okay to assume a risk, *but* only if you understand the risk and are willing to assume it.

It is often not reasonable to expect that the provider will fully understand the import of many of the clauses in current managed care contracts. For that reason, it is prudent to have an attorney review every contract that you intend to sign. Although it costs more initially to pay legal fees to review the contract, it could potentially save a lot of problems and money at a later date.

Once you become aware of a risk or a clause in the managed care contract that is contrary to your interests, your first defensive step is to attempt to negotiate the clause out of the contract. Unfortunately, the individual provider has very little leverage in negotiating such contracts, and the clause is likely to remain.

The next defensive step to take is to "just say no!" Many readers will balk at that statement and will declare: "I don't have a choice. If I don't sign the contract, I will not have any patients!" The point is that you do have a choice. If you choose to sign the contract, then what becomes important is what you do after you sign the contract.

If you choose to sign the contract, then you should sign the contract in the name of your professional corporation and as agent of your professional corporation—*do not sign the contract in your personal capacity.* By signing the contract on behalf of your corporation, your liability (in most cases) becomes limited to your equity in the corporation.

Unfortunately, the usual method of protection for the practicing physician, the use of the corporate form of business, is usually no benefit when signing managed care contracts. That is because most managed care companies credential the individual physician and hence require that the individual physician and not the professional corporation sign the contract. This puts all of the physician's personal assets at risk.

Nonetheless, the provider should attempt to sign all such contracts in the name of the corporation. Some contracts are likely to be accepted by the managed care company. When the company requires the provider to sign in his individual capacity, then the provider can make the decision at that time.

It is important to realize that the risks delineated above apply not only to affluent physicians but to any physician who signs a managed care contract. A typical example resonates when the provider requests legal analysis of the contract and is quoted a fee for this professional service. More often than not, the health care provider will reject this as costing too much, yet in reality the fee, when juxtaposed to the fees charged for medical services, is generally fair and equitable. A young physician with an unpaid student debt load that finds himself or herself on the wrong end of a hold-harmless agreement with a managed care company may be forced into bankruptcy.

Practicing Bare

Many providers in practice would not think of "practicing bare." In the past the term meant that the provider did not have malpractice insurance. Current managed care contracts often require that the provider not only have certain limits of malpractice insurance but also that the provider furnish the company with evidence of such insurance. Therefore, many providers are under the impression that they are not practicing bare.

As can be seen from the example clauses above, most providers are in effect practicing bare. Most providers have no protection from adverse results arising out of a hold-harmless clause in an agreement. Most malpractice insurance companies do not provide such coverage. If your malpractice insurance company does not provide coverage for such events, it is incumbent on you and your associations to lobby the malpractice insurance carriers to provide such coverage. An additional rider, at an additional premium, for hold-harmless coverage would help the practitioner sleep better at night.

The first question that the provider should ask is, Would I consider practicing without malpractice insurance? If the answer to that question is no, then the next question that the provider should ask is, Why am I assuming the risk under the hold-harmless clause? If the provider cannot provide a lucent answer to that question (stating "I have no choice" is not a lucent answer), then the provider should not sign the managed care contract.

Nonetheless, if the provider has signed managed care contracts, then the provider should understand that he or she is practicing bare and should take steps to reduce the exposure. In effect, the provider should attempt to become "judgment-proof." Such a step presents its own risks.

Reducing Exposure

Reducing ones' exposure would require a complete review of the provider's asset situation by an attorney, accountant, or financial planner. Some ideas are briefly presented below for the reader's consideration:

1. Assets can be shifted into the names of the provider's children. Choices include setting up a trust for the benefit of the child or setting up a Uniform

Gifts to Minors Act (UGMA) account. Financial planners often cite many reasons why assets should not be placed in a child's name. The lost potential for scholarship moneys or a spendthrift child are two examples. However, setting up a college fund in the child's name will ensure that the funds are available for the child when the time comes, even if the parent has an outstanding judgment against him or her.

2. Depending on the state, the provider may have statutory protection as to certain assets under federal and state law. Some states provide protection under the Homestead Act or in the method of holding title to real property. Some ERISA retirement accounts and some individual retirement accounts (IRAs) may have a certain degree of federal and state law protection. In other cases, all such accounts may be fully available to satisfy judgments.

There are other options available to protect assets. Each will have its benefits and drawbacks according to the individual provider's situation. Some of the other options include the family limited partnership (which has recently been under attack) and certain offshore trusts (subject to foreign political risks).

Ultimately, the first step for every physician who signs a managed care contract with a hold-harmless agreement is to read the contract and then consult an attorney or other professional. Plaintiff attorneys are beginning to make inroads in suing managed care companies. The managed care attorneys foresaw such events and provided protection for the company in the contracts most providers have signed. As plaintiffs become successful in suing and recovering from managed care companies, those companies are going to seek indemnity from the provider. Unless providers protect themselves, they are likely to become collateral casualties of events. The current practice of medicine presents risks to the provider. The provider may not be able to insure against these risks and therefore should take defensive steps to avoid future problems.

EMPLOYEE RISKS

Practice employees have inside information concerning the practice and the physician's patterns of practice. In most cases, the office staff will have been taught by the practitioner. The staff's frame of reference is thereby limited to what they have been taught. However, more credit should be given to the office staff. Staff members deal everyday with insurance companies (including Medicare), and they field a wide array of patient questions and complaints. An astute staff member will soon realize if the physician is miscoding insurance submission.

An informed, irate employee can be your biggest risk. Many medical malpractice lawsuits have been brought by patients because terminated employees have informed the patient that "something was wrong" with their treatment. Likewise, OSHA investigations have been instituted by disgruntled employees. In these cases the employee had nothing to gain but revenge for real or perceived injustices from their former employer. Now, an employee also has a financial incentive to bring health care fraud charges against a former physician-employer.

ENVIRONMENTAL PROTECTION AGENCY RISKS

The practitioner may not think about the Environmental Protection Agency (EPA) when considering the possible risks of practicing. But that agency could be a nightmare for the unsuspecting physician. Disposal of hazardous wastes is governed by the EPA. A practitioner who improperly disposes of developing fluid, silver wastes, bodily fluids, biohazardous materials, and/or other wastes may become a target of the EPA.

BUSINESS PRACTICE LITIGATION RISKS

A recent report stated that 25% of all suits filed in federal district court relate to a growing field of law loosely called business practices litigation. That percentage is only likely to grow in the coming years. Business practices litigation encompasses a wide variety of issues, but they mostly revolve around the relationship between a business and its employees and customers. The issues include, for example, racial and sexual discrimination, sexual harassment, wrongful termination, and violations of the Americans with Disabilities Act. These claims are not confined to big corporations but can affect the sole proprietor physician.

For example, a Georgia physician recently paid $5,000 in settlement of an employment claim. Apparently, the physician would have won the claim but only after paying over $20,000 in legal fees. That $5,000 settlement was not paid by the malpractice insurance carrier but by the individual physician himself.

PATTERN(S) OF PRACTICE RISKS

One of the next big areas of risk that will surface in the near future is the *pattern of practice risk.* Pattern of practice refers to the way that a particular physician practices medicine. With computers, standardized diagnosis, and treatment codes and the budgetary restraints inherent in medical practice, it is becoming easy to analyze a physician's method of practice.

The treatment and diagnosis codes that a physician uses and submits to third-party payers can be quantified and compared to those of colleagues in the same or similar specialties. Statistical *outliers* can be identified. These outliers will then be further audited and required to justify their treatments. If no rational basis exists for the statistical differences, the outlier may find himself or herself the subject of a fraud investigation.

Fortunately, you can find out how many procedures or specific codes you billed in a particular year by writing to your carrier and requesting a *comparative performance review* (CPR). This will give you an idea of where you stand in comparison to other providers. You can also use your computer or billing service to determine statistics about your billing profile.

COLLATERAL CONSEQUENCES

Many risks inherent in medical practice also have collateral consequences. For example, making a payment in response to a medical malpractice claim requires reporting to the National Practitioner Data Bank. Often such a report instigates an investigation by state boards and hospital staffs. The result is that the medical license or staff privileges can be placed in jeopardy.

Medicare 5-Year Exclusion

Medicare rules provide for a mandatory exclusion of a provider who has been convicted of certain crimes. For example, a physician who is convicted of insurance fraud (unrelated to the Medicare program) could also be excluded from Medicare participation during a 5-year period.

State Board Actions

Many of the state medical board actions are "piggy-back" actions, meaning that a disciplined physician may find himself or herself subject to action by an out-of-state board where he or she holds an additional license. The grounds will be that the practitioner had been disciplined by the practitioner's home state, and therefore the foreign state has grounds for action against the medical license in that state. Some states investigate all closed malpractice cases, even cases that have been settled. The investigation in such cases is to determine whether the practitioner is engaging in practice patterns that would be adverse to the public benefit.

It is easy to see how one incident can snowball. The risk is great. Take the example of a physician who settles a malpractice claim. The physician's state board investigates the matter and determines that there is enough evidence for a reprimand. Next, an out-of-state board takes action simply because of the action taken by the home state.

All of these actions are subsequently reported to the National Practitioner Data Bank. When the physician's local hospital appointment is up for renewal, the hospital (as required by law) checks the National Practitioner Data Bank. Seeing the adverse actions taken against the physician, the hospital restricts the physician's privileges. Finally, the managed care companies, of which the physician is a panel member, learn of all these actions and deselect the physician. The physician's ability to earn a living is therefore significantly impaired. The legal risks today are great.

THE MANAGED CARE REVOLUTION

In the past, a physician could afford an adverse ruling in a legal action (e.g., state board, Medicare, hospital) so long as the penalty was not very severe and so long as the physician kept his or her license and malpractice insurance. However, with the advent of the "managed care revolution," every legal action, no matter how small, can pose a threat to the livelihood of the physician.

Managed care companies provide their subscribers with "panels" of physicians from which they can choose their primary care physician and specialists. The managed care companies limit the number of physicians on their panels. If a physician is terminated from the panel, there are plenty of other physicians who would be happy to join. Managed care companies have application and reapplication procedures. During these procedures the companies investigate certain aspects of the physician's background, such as malpractice history, state board or federal agency action, and Medicare suspensions and sanctions.

An adverse legal action can potentially prevent a physician from gaining access to a panel or could cause the physician to be terminated from a panel. Such an action, therefore, would have a detrimental effect on the physician's income. If the physician has been removed from one panel, the effect could snowball, and the physician could find himself or herself locked out of many panels. Such a situation would ultimately lead to the collapse of the physician's practice.

The following are some helpful solutions.

Compliance Audit

A compliance audit will not ensure against an audit or against fraud charges. However, the fact that a compliance audit was conducted is used as evidence to mitigate an intention to defraud. Essentially, an attorney inspects the practitioner's office to discover any areas of potential risk.

A compliance audit consists of many steps, including the following: review to ensure that the office has the proper manuals and that they are up to date, review to ensure that periodic education (e.g., OSHA yearly education) has been completed, review of medical records to ensure proper documentation, review of medical records and insurance claims to ensure proper use of CPT codes, review of employment policies, review of practice business structure to ensure proper foundation and paperwork, and interview of employees by the attorney. The last item is a vital step in a compliance audit. As discussed above, many times investigations are instigated by disgruntled present or former employees. The interview seeks to determine whether the employee is aware of any practice or procedures that may be illegal or questionable. If any such issues are raised, they are either dealt with immediately or else the employee is educated as to why such practices or procedures are acceptable. The interview concludes with the employee signing an affidavit stating that he or she is unaware of any transgression by the practice. Such a statement can later be used, if necessary, to disprove any false allegations by an employee.

Manuals

Manuals are an important part of every modern medical practice. At one time they were wholly unnecessary. Currently, a medical practice should have many manuals, including

- *O.S.H.A. Bloodborne Standard Manual*
- OSHA Hazardous Substance manuals
- Employment manual
- Employee handbook
- Sexual harassment policy manual
- Americans with Disabilities Act manual
- Emergency procedures manual

Forms

Most physicians develop forms for use in their practices. Most patient encounter forms are used to document evaluation and management visits. Usually, the individual physician has developed these forms independently. Only when the physician is audited is it learned that the form is inadequate. Although no form is audit-proof, when properly developed, the forms will be a huge defense for the practicing physician. With a nationwide consortium of physician-attorneys assisting fellow physicians in defending audits, the forms can be fine-tuned with each and every audit. In time, the forms, when properly used, will be as close to audit-proof as possible.

Today companies such as Wal-Mart, McDonalds, and the like all set nationwide standards that their stores follow. It is incumbent on the medical profession, which has in the past been divisive, to adopt standardized forms and practice methods to be able to stand up to giants such as Medicare. Otherwise, they will pick physicians off, one by one. The goal of insurance companies and the government is to standardize and set strict guidelines for each CPT code. Therefore, a cohesive and standardized approach to documentation is needed by the individual.

The Bell Curve

Staying within the bell curve is a prudent defensive step.

Full Court Press

It is incumbent upon the practicing physician to take every step to avoid any adverse legal actions. The practicing physician must develop a "full court press" attitude and build a defense to prevent adverse actions from developing in the first place. Having appropriate written office protocols and conducting compliance audits helps to form the defense. If a legal action appears imminent, the physician should not attempt to handle the case. At the first hint of legal action, an attorney should be retained to help to protect the physician's rights.

CONCLUSION

Risk management is no longer just about medical malpractice. In fact, since most practicing physicians have malpractice insurance, a malpractice suit should be viewed as a mere inconvenience, and the practitioner should realize that the lawsuit is solely about someone else's money.

A shift in the paradigm is needed. The medico-legal landscape has changed. The physician in practice today is faced with many legal challenges that have the potential to destroy the medical practice and the individual's personal assets. Every practice should have a qualified attorney on retainer. The legal risks are only going to increase.

Quantitative Aspects of Medical Practice

## CHAPTER 9

Fundamentals of Cash Flow Analysis in Office Practice

Recognizing the Pitfalls of Growth, Hypergrowth . . . or No Growth!

David Edward Marcinko

Can we ever have too much of a good thing?

—Cervantes

The statement of cash flows (SCF) is the lifeblood of any medical business unit (MBU). It summarizes the effects of cash on medical operating activities during an accounting interval. In periods of rapid growth, as can occur with the acceptance of some managed care contracts, increased revenue actually equates to less cash and potential trouble in terms of practice survival. Therefore, accurate cash flow analysis (CFA) will allow the physician executive to determine the effects of past strategic business decisions in quantitative form. The accurate and proactive nature of this analysis may spell economic success or failure in the competitive health care environment.

STATEMENT OF PURPOSE

The primary purpose of the SCF is to review the cash flow accounting statement in the context of two better-known financial statements; the balance sheet and net income statement. While useful, these two statements do not fully answer the physician executive's questions about his or her practice. Such important questions include the following: How much cash was generated by the doctor's practice? How can the office's cash account be overdrawn when the practice's accountant says its was profitable? How much was spent for new equipment and supplies and where was the cash for the expenditures acquired? Most important, the SCF is then used to review past fiscal decisions and make a predictive leap into the economic future concerning the acceptance of contemporary managed care contract arrangements. The business tool of CFA will allow the physician to evaluate revenues and more effortlessly make the translation to fixed-reimbursement contractual remuneration and corporatized health care.

FINANCIAL ACCOUNTING STATEMENTS

Financial statements report the activity of an MBU for a specific accounting period through horizontal analysis. Showing changes in this fashion forms a perspective for variances that have taken place. The three traditional statements are (1) net income statement (NIS), also known as the Profit and Loss Statement; (2) balance sheet (BS); and (3) the SCF. To fully understand the significance of the SCF and the CFA, it is vital to briefly review the first two statements.

Net Income Statement

The NIS, or profit and loss (P&L) statement, reflects patient revenues and those medical expenses considered general overhead. The NIS may report physician compensation and benefits as an expense category, during an interval period of time. Smaller practices report income and expenses on a "cash accounting" basis, reflecting income actually received and expenses actually paid. The accrual method of accounting, for larger practices, records expenses when they are incurred and income when earned—not when paid or received, as in the cash method. The cash method is easier, but the accrual method is more accurate. Approximately 80% of medical respondents in a recent survey used the accrual method for accounting purposes; more surgically oriented practitioners also use the accrual method. This will likely increase because of the nature of capitated contracts or other fixed-reimbursement arrangements. Moreover, for medical groups wanting to switch from the cash to the accrual method, it is best to make the change after a fiscal calendar quarter. However, accountants may be leery of the shift because they are filing taxes on a cash basis.

Balance Sheet (Statement of Financial Position)

The BS reports the MBU's financial position in terms of its assets, liabilities, and owner's equity in the practice at a specified point in time. Fixed assets are furniture, equipment, and property. Current assets include those that can be converted into cash within a short period of time, such as accounts receivable (AR), checking accounts, and money funds. Intangibles include goodwill. Accounts payable (AP) and current liabilities are short-term debts and notes; long-term liabilities are loans repaid over many years. The latter category reflects ownership in the form of retained earnings or equity and represents the difference between the total assets and total liabilities of the unit.

The SCF

The cash flow statement is the lifeblood of a medical office because it summarizes the effects on cash of the (1) operating, (2) investing, and (3) financial activities of the medical practice. Operating activities include cash inflows (receipts, interest, and dividends) and outflows (inventory, supplies, and loans). Investing activities include the disposal or acquisition of noncurrent assets, such as equipment, loans, or marketable securities. Financing activities generally include the cash inflow or outflow effects of transactions and other events, such as issuing capital stock or notes involving creditors and physician owners. Prior to 1988 the formal SCF was known as a statement of changes in financial position and projected estimated cash flows by month, quarter, and year, along with the anticipated timing of cash receipts and disbursements.

An MBU's bills and obligations are paid out of cash flow, not net income. Therefore, the *direct method* of cash flow evaluation deducts from cash revenues only those overhead operating expenses that consume cash. Under this method, each item on the NIS is directly converted to a cash basis. For example, assume that office revenues are stated at $100,000 on an accrual accounting basis. If the ARs increased by $5,000, cash collections from patients and third-party insurance companies would be $95,000. All remaining items on the income statement are also converted to a cash basis.

As a general rule, an increase in a current asset (other than cash) decreases cash inflow or increases cash outflow. Thus, when ARs increase, professional service revenues on cash basis decrease. When cast materials, splints, or other DME (durable medical equipment) inventories increase, the cost of goods sold on a cash basis increases (increasing cash outflow). When a prepaid expense, such as malpractice liability insurance increases, the related operating expense on a cash basis increases. The effect on cash flows is just the opposite for decreases in these and other current assets.

Similarly, an increase in a current liability increases cash inflow or decreases cash outflow. Thus, when APs increase, the cost of goods sold on a cash basis decreases. When an accrued liability such as salaries payable increases, the related operating expense on a cash basis decreases. Decreases in current liabilities have just the opposite effect.

Alternatively, the *indirect (add-back) method* starts with accrual net income and indirectly adjusts it for items that affect reported net income (accrual) but do not involve cash. For instance, net income is adjusted (rather than adjusting individual items in the income statement) for (1) changes in currents assets (other than cash) and current liabilities and (2) items that were included in net income but did not affect cash. The most common example of an expense that does not affect cash is depreciation.

Table 9.1 can be used to make the adjustments to net income for the changes in current assets and current liabilities:

Notice that in Table 9.1 all changes in current assets are handled in a similar manner. Also, all changes in current liabilities are handled the same way—but in the opposite manner from that of current asset changes. In applying the rules, a decrease in a current asset is added to net income and an increase in a current asset is deducted from net income. For current liabilities, increases are added to net income, and decrease are substrate from net income.

The financial accounting standards board (FASB) encourages the use of the direct method but permits use of the indirect method. Regardless of the method used, the SCF reflects the internal generation of funds available to owners, investors, and creditors to assess the following:

1. The practice's ability to generate positive future net cash flows.
2. The practice's ability to meet its financial obligations.
3. The practice's ability to generate profits and dividends.
4. The practice's need for external financing.
5. Reasons for differences between net income and cash receipts/payments
6. Effects on financial position for both investing and financing transactions.

Cash Flow: Managed Care Example

Given

Suppose that a medical practice was awarded a managed care organization (MCO) contract that increased revenues by $100,000 for the next fiscal year. The practice had a gross margin of 30% that was not expected to change because of the new business. However, $10,000 was added to medical overhead expenses for another assistant and all account's receivable (AR) are be paid a the *end* of the year, upon completion of the contract.

TABLE 9.1 Cash Flow Adjustments

For changes in these current assets and current liabilities:	Make these adjustments to convert accrual basis net income to cash basis net income:	
	ADD	DEDUCT
Accounts receivable	Decrease	Increase
D.M.E. inventory	Decrease	Increase
Prepaid expenses	Decrease	Increase
Accounts payable	Increase	Decrease
Accrued liabilities	Increase	Decrease

Cost of Medical Services Provided

The cost of medical services provided (COMSP) for the MCO business contract represents the amount of money needed to service the patients provided by the contract. Since gross margin is 30% of revenues, the COMSP is 70%, or $70,000. Adding the extra overhead results in $80,000 of new spending money (cash flow) needed to treat the patients.

Next, divide the $80,000 total by the number of days the contract extends (i.e., 365 days) and determine that the new contract costs about $219.18 per day of cash flows.

Assumptions

Financial cash flow forecasting from operating activities allows a reasonable projection of future cash needs and enables the doctor to err on the side of fiscal prudence. It is an inexact science, by definition, and entails the following assumptions:

1. All income tax, salaries, and APs are paid at once.
2. DME inventory and prepaid advertising remain constant.
3. Gains/losses on sale of equipment and depreciation expenses remain stable.
4. Gross margins remain constant.
5. The MBU is efficient, so major new marginal costs will not be incurred.

Physician Reactions

Since many MBU executives are still not entirely comfortable with fixed-price medical payment contracts, practices are loath to turn away business. Physician-executives must then determine other methods to generate the additional cash, which include the following suggestions:

1. *Extend AP remuneration times.* Discuss your cash flow difficulties with vendors and emphasize their short-term nature. A doctor's practice still has considerable cachet, especially in local communities, and many vendors are willing to work with doctors to retain their business.

2. *Reduce AR collection times.* According to the Medical Group Management Association's 1998 cost survey, about 30% of multispecialty groups' ARs are unpaid at 120 days. In addition, multispecialty groups were able to collect on 69% of charges in 1997. The rest was written off as bad debt expenses or as a result of discounted payments from Medicare and other MCOs. In a study by Hales Corners, Wisconsin–based Zimmerman and Associates, the percentages of ARs unpaid at more than 90 days is at an all-time high, 38% in 1998, up from 35% in 1995. Therefore, multispecialty groups should aim to keep the percentage of ARs unpaid for more than 120 days below 20% of the total practice. The safest place to be for a single-specialty physician is in the 30% range; anything over that is just not affordable.

The slowest-paid specialties (ARs greater than 120 days) are multispecialty group practices, family practices, cardiology groups, anesthesiology groups, and gastroenterologists in that order. So work hard to get your money faster.

3. *Borrow with short-term bridge loans.* Obtain a line of credit from your local bank, credit union, or other private sources. Beware the time value of money, personal loan guarantees, and onerous usury rates.

4. *Do not stop paying withholding taxes in favor of cash flow because it may be illegal.*

Hypergrowth Model

Now, let us again suppose that the MBU has attracted nine more similar MCO medical contracts. If we multiple the above example by 10, the serious nature of potential cash flow problems becomes apparent. In other words, the MBU has increased revenues to $1 million, with the same 70% gross margin and $100,000 increase in operating overhead expenses.

Using identical mathematical calculations, we determine that $800,000 divided by 365 days equals $2,191.78 per day of needed new cash flows. Again, where will the money come from until the contract is paid at the end of the year? Hence, indiscriminate growth without careful contract evaluation and CFA, is a prescription for potential financial disaster.

ASSESSMENT

The SCF has been reviewed to underscore its importance and the potential pitfalls of practice growth in a managed care environment. Cash flow analysis, determined by using two different methods (direct and indirect), is an important technique that allows the physician make proactive business decisions regarding the direction and growth of a practice by reviewing changes in past operating, investing, or financial activities. If the medical executive becomes skillful at performing this analysis, much can be ascertained about the operational efficiencies of the medical practice.

CONCLUSION

Cash flow analysis (CFA) is the comparative norm for all business organizations, and the MBU is no exception. Having access to the analytic tools needed to derive such information is vital to practice survival. Furthermore, CFA and related economic research will only add value to the services rendered by the modern physician, much to the benefit of patient, doctor, and payer alike.

REFERENCES AND READINGS

Brigham, E. F., & Gapenski, L. C. *Financial management*. New York: Dryden Press, 1994.

Dunevitz, B. Physician-administrators can remove mystery from financial statements. *MGMA Update*, vol. 37, no. 20, 1998.

Hermanson, R. H., & Edwards, J. D. *Financial accounting*. New York: Irwin, 1996.

Pavlock, E. J. *Financial management for medical groups*. MGMA, no. 4597. 888-608-5602.

Tschida, M. Left hanging: Late third party payments take toll on physician practices. *Modern Physician*, January 1999.

## CHAPTER 10

Practical Medical Office Expense Models

Recognize the Costs of Treating Patients and Doing Business

David Edward Marcinko

> A cost and volume relationship exists in any mature medical office, and emphasizes the point that the goal of an efficient office should be profit optimization, rather than revenue or volume maximization.
>
> —Jon Hultman, MBA, Los Angeles

M edical cost accounting provides information to physicians about directing and controlling profitable office operations. It consists of five goals, which include (1) providing vital costing information for internal office use, (2) developing proactive future office strategic plans, (3) accentuating the relevancy and flexibility of practice data, (4) reviewing real-time individual segments of the office service mix rather than just total operations, and (5) acquiring nonmonetary business data.

In today's competitive marketplace, managerial cost accounting is often used to set office and long-term office business policy. The information is then used to increase profitability by either increasing revenues or decreasing operating assets. More than ever, the following costing methodologies can mean the difference between a successful medical practice and a mediocre one.

Cost accounting is not governed by the Financial Accounting Standards Board (FASB) as is a certified public accountant (CPA); rather, an expert practitioner is known as a certified managerial accountant (CMA). This differs from the more traditional methods of financial accounting which are concerned with providing static historical information to creditors, shareholders, and those outside the private medical practice.

OFFICE COST STRUCTURE AND BEHAVIOR

Medical office costs may be divided into several categories (fixed, variable, mixed, marginal, direct, indirect, differential, etc.), as described below.

Fixed Costs

Fixed costs can be viewed in the aggregate or on a per unit basis, but they always remain constant, period. That is why they are called fixed. For example, your office rent doesn't increase if you expand office hours into Saturday or Sunday. Total fixed costs are not usually affected by changes in activity (i.e., office rent, taxes, insurance, depreciation, salaries of key personnel). Your rent is still due even if you spend 2 weeks diving in Aruba and see no patients. A fixed cost remains constant, over the relevant range, even if the activity changes (i.e., busy summer or winter slowdown). On the other hand, fixed costs decrease per unit as the activity level rises and increase per unit as the activity level falls. Generally, fixed costs are not altered by decisions or changes in the short term (see Figure 10.1).

Example

Assume that a physical therapy practice dispenses custom-made orthotic devices for various biomechanical conditions. The office rent is fixed over the course of its lease at $9,000 per month. Therefore, the total and per unit rent costs at various levels of orthotic activity would be depicted as in Table 10.1.

Table 10.1 shows the effects of volume (cost per month and number of devices) on the cost of rent per item. If office hours are begun on Saturday, the cost of the rent is less per device because there are more items to disperse it across. However, the cost per item does increase with the vacation trip.

Variable Costs

Variable costs can also be discussed in terms of total and per unit behavior (see Figure 10.2). Total variable cost increases and decreases in proportion to activity, whereas per unit variable costs remain constant per unit. Practice costs that are normally variable with respect to volume include durable medical equipment (DME) and indirect labor and indirect materials, such as utilities, air conditioning, clerical costs, and other medical supplies. Generally, variable costs change as a direct result of making a decision or altering a course of action.

Example

The same large physical therapy practice dispenses a custom-made latex elbow splint for $30 per device. The per unit and total costs of the splints at various levels of activity would be depicted as in Table 10.2.

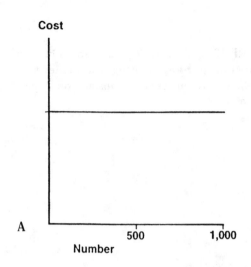

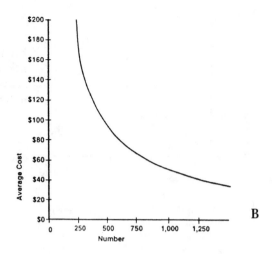

FIGURE 10.1 A: A fixed cost remains constant in total amount throughout a wide range of medical office activity. **B:** A fixed cost varies inversely with activity if expressed on a per-unit basis. **C:** The relevant range is an economic principle that can be defined as the range of office activity within which certain assumptions relative to variable and fixed cost behavior are valid.

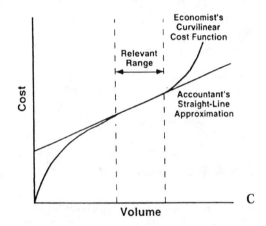

TABLE 10.1   Fixed Cost Behavior

Fixed Rent: Cost per Month	Number of Devices	Rent Cost per Device
$9,000	0	Fixed
9,000	1	$9,000
9,000	10	900
9,000	100	90
9,000	200	45

Generally, the manufacturing community has embraced the trend toward fixed business costs. Conversely, the medical community is trending toward more variable costs because (1) medicine is a personal service industry, and (2) movement is toward locum tenens and hired physician employment (i.e., nonowner physicians).

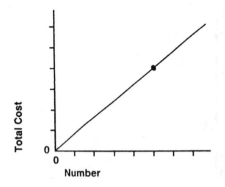

FIGURE 10.2   A variable cost changes in total in direct proportion to changes in the level of activity; a variable cost is constant on a per-unit basis.

TABLE 10.2   Variable Cost Behavior

Cost per Splint	No. of Splints Dispensed	Total Variable Cost per Splint
$30	1	$30
30	10	300
30	100	3,000
30	200	6,000

Simple Cost Calculations

From the above, we intuitively realize that Total costs = Total fixed costs plus total variable costs, or TC = TFC + TVC.

Furthermore, total variable costs, for a physician group practice, can be further equated to Total variable costs = (TVC per visit) × (number of visits). So Total costs = TFC plus {(VC/visit) × (no. of visits)}.

And, if given, Total profit = Revenue (Price × Volume) − Costs, then Total profit = (P × V) − (FC + VC).

Mixed Costs

A mixed (semivariable) cost is one that contains both fixed and variable elements. Although the definition may change from office to office, consistency is important for cost behavioral purposes. For example, an x-ray unit is leased for $2,500 per year, plus $5 per film. In this case, the yearly lease is the fixed element, and the per unit film charge varies depending on use.

Sophisticated physicians also recognize other mixed costing techniques, such as the (a) *high/low method* and the (b) *least squares linear regression technique*.

Direct and Indirect Costs

A direct cost can be obviously traced from its destination and can specifically be traced to the performance of a procedure. The more procedures done, the higher the direct costs. In a medical office, radiographs, surgical supplies, blood panels, DME, and other procedures can be traced to a specific patient, whereas labor is traced to the office staff. An indirect cost must be allocated to general office overhead rather than specifically assigned to the *cost driver* in question. Such expenses as the rent, mortgage, and the office manager's salary are constant. They have no relationship to frequency of use. Of course, some expenses are *mixed costs* and combine both indirect and direct costs. For example, in analyzing your billing department's costs, the purchase expense of the system would be considered the indirect element; the cost of electronic medical claims filing would be considered the direct element, as the more claims filed, the greater the expense.

Differential Costs

Any cost that is present under one alternative but is absent in whole or part under another alternative is known as a *differential cost*.

Example

Dr. Lindsay is a chiropractor with his own solo office, but he has been offered a job in a rural medical center. The differential revenue and costs between the two jobs is depicted in Table 10.3.

Controllable Costs

A *controllable medical cost* occurs at a particular level of the office if the owner-physician has the power to authorize the expenses. There is a risk/benefit and time dimension to controllable costs. For example, costs that are controllable

TABLE 10.3 Differential Cost Behavior

Cost	Office	Medical Center	Differential
Weekly salary	$900	$1,200	$300
Weekly expenses			
Commuting	30	90	60
Lab coat rental	0	50	50
Food	10	0	(10)
Total weekly expenses	40	140	100
Net weekly income	$860	1,060	200

over the long run may not be controllable over the short term. In the very long term however, all costs are variable and controllable.

Opportunity Costs

An *opportunity cost* is the potential advantage or benefit that is either sacrificed or lost when selecting one course of action over another. It is also known as an either-or decision. For example, if Dr. Jones was invited to speak at a local Lion's Club meeting, will the publicity garnered help his reputation enough to compensate for the actual time and revenue lost from the office. Some intangible opportunity costs can not be mathematically calculated.

Sunk Costs

A *sunk cost* is an expense that has already been incurred and cannot be changed by any decision, either now or in the future. It is committed and irreversible. For example, the fancy new treatment chair purchased by Dr. Haley, for cash, is a sunk cost. Nothing can be changed since she owns the chair outright.

Relevant Costs

A *relevant medical office cost* is avoidable as a result of choosing one alternative over another. All costs are considered avoidable, except sunk costs and future costs that do not differ between the alternatives at hand. The physician-owner (office manager) should follow the steps below to identify the costs (and revenues) that are relevant in any costing decision:

1. Assemble all the costs and revenues associated with the alternative.
2. Eliminate sunk costs.
3. Eliminate those costs and revenues that do not differ between alternatives.
4. Decide on the basis of the remaining costs and revenues. These are the costs and revenues that are differential or avoidable and therefore relevant to the medical business decision to be made.

Example

Dr. Hartwell, an orthopedic surgeon, is considering replacing an old x-ray processing machine with a new, more efficient, and automatic one. Data on the machine are listed in Table 10.4.

Dr. Hartwell's office revenues are $200,000 per year, and fixed expenses (other than depreciation) are $70,000 per year. Should the new processing machine be purchased?

TABLE 10.4   Cost Data on Equipment Replacement

New machine	
List price new	$9,000
Annual variable expenses	8,000
Expected life	5 years
Old machine	
Original cost	$7,200
Remaining book value	6,000
Disposal value now	1,500
Annual variable expenses	10,000
Remaining life	5 years

TABLE 10.5

	Five Years Together		
	Keep	Purchase	Differential
Sales	$100,000	$100,000	0
Less variable expenses	50,000 (5 × 10,000)	40,000 (5 × 8,000)	10,000
Less other fixed expenses	35,000	35,000	0
Depreciation (new)	0	(9,000)	(9,000)
Depreciation (old)/book value	(6,000)	(6,000)	0
Disposal value (old)	0	1,500	1,500
Total net income	9,000	11,500	2,500

Erroneous Solution

Some physicians would not purchase the new machine because disposal of the old machine would apparently result in a loss:

Remaining book value: $6,000

Disposal value now: 1,500

Loss from disposal: 4,500

Correct Solution

The remaining book value of the old machine is a sunk cost that can not be avoided by Dr. Hartwell. This can be shown by looking at comparative cost and revenue data for the next 5 years (Table 10.5), taken in the aggregate.

Using only relevant costs, the correct solution is shown in Table 10.6.

Economic Order Quantity Costs

Economic order quantity cost (EOQC) is a standard accounting model for minimizing medical business inventory, such as DME costs. The EOQC makes three key

TABLE 10.6

Sales in variable expenses provided by new machine ($2000 × 5 years)	$10,000[a]
Cost of new machine	9000
Disposal value of old machine	1500
Net advantage, new machine	2500

[a]*Note:* $10,000 − 8000 = $2000.

assumptions: (1) revenues (inventory depletion) are constant, (2) costs per order are stable, and (3) just-in-time delivery allows the placement of orders so that new orders arrive when inventory approaches zero.

The mathematical formula for EOQC is the square root of 2SO/C; where S = annual sales in units; O is the cost per order; and C is the annual carrying cost per unit.

Example

Suppose that a large urban hospital performs a good deal of orthopedic surgery and uses 10,000 special self-absorbing bone screws every year. The cost per screw is $200, and the annual inventory carrying cost per screw is $10. According to the formula, the EOQC is 632, the orders per year is 16, and the time between each order is about 3.3 weeks.

Marginal Costs and Revenue

Marginal cost (MC) is the expense incurred to treat one additional unit (patient); *marginal revenue* (MR) is the revenue received for treating that patient (unit). These two concepts are among the most important in the entire business universe environment of medicine today.

In the office "clinical pathway," or "flow process," we are assuming that time remains on the doctor's schedule to treat an additional patient and that an existing financial base exists to cover all fixed costs. This means that a managed care contract might be considered if the MR received by treating the patient is greater than the MC (i.e., MR > MC) incurred to treat that patient. Profit (total) will continue to increase up to the point where MR = MC, and then it will decrease as additional costs (more office space, equipment or assistants) are incurred to accommodate the increased volume.

In other words, *maximum office efficiency* (MOE) occurs where MR = MC. Since marginal cost can be thought of as the change in total costs associated with any given change in output quantity (Q), MC can be calculated from the following formula(s):

> MC = Change total costs / Change in output quantity, or,
> MC = Change TC / Change Q, or,
> MC = CTC / CQ

TABLE 10.7 Marginal Cost Table

Patient Volume (A)	(Price) Marginal Revenue (B)	(A × B) Total Revenue (C)	Marginal Costs (D)	Total Costs (E)	(C – E) Total Profit (F)
0	20.1	00.00	NA	50	−50.00
1	20.1	20.10	15	65	−44.90
2	20.1	40.20	10	75	−34.80
3	20.1	60.30	8	83	−22.70
4	20.1	80.40	7	90	−9.60
5	20.1	100.50	6	96	4.45
6	20.1	120.60	4	100	20.60
7	20.1	140.70	4	104	36.70
8	20.1	160.80	6	110	50.80
9	20.1	180.90	10	120	60.90
10	20.1	201.00	12	132	69.00
11	20.1	221.10	16	142	73.10
12	20.1	241.20	20	168	73.20
13	20.1	261.30	22	190	71.30
14	20.1	281.40	25	215	66.40
15	20.1	301.50	30	245	56.50

Note: Total costs (column E) are cumulative, derived by adding the marginal cost (D) to the prior total cost figure. This keeps a running total, adding each additional marginal cost to the total cost number.

Now, note that MCs depend only on changes in variable costs. Because fixed costs do not change as output quantity changes, fixed costs don't even influence MCs. MC is influenced only by VC.

The goal of such MC and revenue analysis is to treat the appropriate (optimum) number (quantity) of patients, not necessarily the most (maximum) number of patients. This may be contrary to the norm established heretofore in the fee-for-service medical payment environment, but this mindset must be broken to be most efficient in 2001 and beyond.

Dr. Jon Hultman, MBA, in his book, *Here's How Doctor: You Can Thrive Under Managed Care,* gives the following examples of how, as a new medical office grows, MCs decline. Later, as volume- and capacity-related inefficiencies begin to occur, MCs again increase. Notice that, in Table 10.7, MCs almost always equal MR at a patient volume of 12 units, and total profit is the greatest at this point. When volume increases beyond 12 patients, however, total revenue increases, but total profit declines.

If the practice were to add patients beyond 12 units, the price (fees) would have to be raised to make the addition of these patients profitable. This cost and volume relationship exists in any mature medical office and emphasizes the point that the goal of an efficient office should be profit *optimization*, rather than revenue or volume *maximization*.

Additionally, the point of MOE is where patient volume (V), per patient fee (PP), and cost per patient (C) produces the most profit (P), not necessarily the most revenue (R). "It is a unique equilibrium efficiency point for each medical practice and individual health care provider."

In terms of managed care contracting, understanding the dynamics behind these numbers may provide an insight into making informed volume, fee, and profit decisions. Recall, that fee pricing and profit are "made at the margins" and that an office with 60% overhead, for example, does not produce a marginal profit of 40%. Rather, the *total profit margin* is 40%, but the *marginal profit* might be only 10% or 15% for each *new* patient visit, and expense reduction programs will be more effective in increasing profit than increasing patient volume. Furthermore, consider that if marginal profit for new patient business is 10%, cutting marginal costs by one-third (33%) will produce the same profit as would increasing patient volume by almost 300%.

BREAKEVEN ANALYSIS AND PROFITS

To illustrate the concept of breakeven analysis, relative to profit maximization and the costing concepts just discussed, let's use three more modified examples, again given by Dr. Jon Hultman.

Example 1

The three doctors of ABC practice own a clinic whose fixed operating costs are $200,000. The average variable cost per patient is $22. The breakeven point (BEP) is reached when revenue and total costs intersect at about 2,500 patients. The variable costs (VC) ($22 × 2500 = $55,000), plus the fixed costs (FC) ($200,00), equal the total costs of $255,000, which at the BEP are equal to the total revenues resulting in an economically neutral (breakeven) clinical operation, as seen in Table 10.8.

Furthermore, it can be appreciated that when volume increases, total profit increases at a faster rate than total costs. This is known as *high, or positive, clinic operating leverage.*

Example 2

Now, if the doctors of ABC clinic accept a discounted managed care contract, where the average revenue per patient (REV/PP) declines from $102 to $75,

TABLE 10.8   Breakeven Analysis

FC	VC/PP	REV/PP	Volume	Total Costs	Total Revenue	Profit
$200,000	$22	$102	2,500	$255,000	$255,000	0
200,000	22	102	3,000	266,000	306,000	40,000
200,000	22	102	6,000	332,000	612,000	280,000
200,000	22	102	9,000	398,000	918,000	520,000

TABLE 10.10   Nonleveraged Breakeven Analysis

FC	VC/PP	REV/PP	Volume	Total Costs	Total Revenue	Profit
$250,000	$22	$75	2500	$305,000	$187,000	−$67,500
250,000	22	75	3000	316,000	225,000	−41,000
250,000	22	75	4717	353,774	353,775	1
250,000	22	75	6000	382,000	450,000	68,000
250,000	22	75	9000	448,000	675,000	227,000

the BEP in patient volume is now increased to 3,774 patients. At this volume, profit is at $22, and total revenue and total costs are about equal. At 6,000 patients, profit is $118,000 (77% decline) and at 9,000 patients, profit is at $277,000 (47% decline). To get an appreciation for the leveraging effect of this decline in price, recognize a price decrease of 26% (from $102 to $75), as seen in Table 10.9.

Example 3

The final example for ABC clinic (Table 10.10) is a very likely scenario under many managed care contracts today—that is to say, a decrease in fees (from $102 to $75), combined with an increase in fixed costs ($250,000) involved in servicing the contract.

At a patient volume of 9,000, profit declines by 56%, along with the salaries of each doctor. If volume dropped to 6,000 patients, profit would decline to 87%. To produce the original profit of $520,000, volume would have to increase by 61% (14,528 patients), an unlikely scenario. ABC clinic profit, then, will be determined by its cost position and efficiency in managing a larger volume of patients, along with clinic overhead expenses.*In other words, as long as the revenues received from a medical service is above the variable cost of providing that service, it is said to be making a contribution to fixed costs.*

Additionally, any managed care contract that is below a practice's variable costs will lower its profit and should not be considered. Therefore, an aggressive

TABLE 10.9   Leveraged Breakeven Analysis

FC	VC/PP	REV/PP	Volume	Total Costs	Total Revenue	Profit
200,000	$22	$75	2500	$255,000	$187,500	−67,500
200,000	22	75	3000	266,000	225,000	−41,000
200,000	22	75	3774	283,000	283,050	22
200,000	22	75	6000	332,000	450,000	118,000
200,000	22	75	9000	398,000	675,000	277,000

cost-reduction program, as described in other chapters, along with more modest patient volume increases, might be a prudent strategy for the doctors of ABC clinic to pursue.

EQUIPMENT PAYBACK METHOD OF COST ANALYSIS

The *payback method* (PM) of cost analysis involves making capital budgeting decisions that do not involve discounting cash flows. The *payback period* (PP), expressed in years, is the length of time it takes for the investment to recoup its initial cost out of the cash receipts it generates. The basic premise is that the quicker the cost of an investment can be recovered, the better the investment is. The PM is most often used when considering equipment whose useful life is short and unpredictable. When the same cash flow occurs every year, the formula is as follows:

$$\text{Investment required} / \text{Net annual cash inflow} = \text{Payback period}$$

Example

Dr. Feelgood, a chiropractor, wants to install a new large piece of equipment in place of several smaller modalities in his office. He will have to hire a therapist to administer the larger modality, and he estimates that incremental annual revenues and expenses associated with the equipment would be as shown in Table 10.11.

Parts for the equipment would cost $15,000 and have a 10-year life. The old machines could be sold for a $10,000 salvage value. Dr. Feelgood requires a payback of 5 years or less on all investments. (See Table 10.12.)

CONCLUSION

The cost and managerial accounting techniques presented in this chapter are drastically different from what your financial accountant may tell you, since he

TABLE 10.11   Revenue and Expense

Revenues	$10,000
Less variable expenses	3000
Contribution margin	7000
Less fixed expenses	
Insurance	900
Salaries	2600
Depreciation	1500
	5000
Net income	$2000

TABLE 10.12   Payback Period

Net Income (above)	$2000
Add: Noncash deduction depreciation	1500
New annual cash flow	3500
Investment in the new equipment	15,000
Deduct: Salvage value, old machines	1000
Investment required	14,000
Payback period = $140,000 / $35,000 = 4.0 years	

or she reports only total or average office cost data to you. Although helpful, this general overhead costing information may be the wrong data to use when making managed care contracting decisions in the new millennium. A CMA or financially disciplined MBA might be an additional business expert to work with in this case.

REFERENCES AND READINGS

Brigham, E. F., & Gapenski, L. C. *Financial management: Theory and practice.* New York: Dryden Press, 1994.

Dobler, D. W., Burt, D., & Lee, L. *Purchasing and materials management.* New York: McGraw-Hill, 1990.

Garrison, R. H., & Noreen, E. W. *Managerial accounting.* Boston: Irwin Publishers, 1995.

Garrison, R. H., & Noreen, E. W. *Managerial accounting: Ready notes.* Boston: Irwin Publishers, 1995.

Hultman, J. *Here's how, Doctor.* Los Angeles: Medical Business Advisors Publishing, 1995.

Hermanson, R. H., & Edwards, J. D. *Financial accounting.* Boston, New York: Irwin, 1992.

Muller, S. V. The role of risk adjusters in medical group practice. *MGMA Journal,* December 1998.

## CHAPTER 11

Activity-Based Costing: For Fun and Profit

Learn Your ABCs and Abandon Direct Labor Hour Accounting

David Edward Marcinko

> Activity Based Costing, a managerial discipline, is the accounting method of choice in healthcare today. Traditional methods of financial accounting, based on averages, are passe.
>
> —Herbert Garner, registered investment advisor

S avvy health care providers are becoming aware of the need to demonstrate the cost-effectiveness of their care because this can be an important strategic competitive advantage over other practitioners. When this scenario occurs, hard numerical business information is required and can be obtained by using the managerial accounting tools known as *activity-based costing* (ABC) and the *clinical path method* (CPM). Here's how.

ABC and managerial accounting determines the actual costs of resources that each service consumes, and because internal medicine, for example, requires more service resources than surgery, ABC will assign more costs to the primary care (low volume) of the practice.

In the traditional financial accounting practice system, office costs are assigned to different procedures or services based on average volume (quantity). So if a general surgical service is doing more surgical procedures (high volume) than primary care medical services (low volume), more indirect overhead costs will be allocated to the surgical portion of the practice.

The idea is to get a handle on how much every task costs by factoring in the labor, technology and office space to complete it. In this way, the next time a capitation contract is offered, providers will know instantly whether the pact will make money or lose money.

THE MEDICAL CRITICAL PATH METHOD

An activity is any event or service that is a cost driver. To activity-cost any critical or noncritical medical pathway, five steps are used: (1) identify key transactions, (2) identify the time and resources required for each step, (3) define noneconomically valued activities, (4) note office operational inefficiencies, and (5) determine the cost of each resource.

Examples of several specific medical activities that are cost drivers include the following:

- Surgery setups
- X-ray processing
- Records requests
- Vital sign checks
- Taking radiographs
- Insurance verifications
- Cast changes
- Blood test runs
- Referral orders

ABC improves managerial accounting systems in three ways:

1.   It increases the number of cost pools (expenses) used to accumulate general overhead office costs. Rather than accumulate overhead costs in a single office-wide pool, costs are accumulated by activity, service, or procedure.

2.   It changes the base used to assign general overhead costs to services or patients. Rather than assigning costs on the basis of a measure of volume (employee or doctor hours), costs are assigned on the basis of medical services or activities that generated those costs.

3.   It changes the nature of many overhead costs in that those formerly considered indirect, are now traced to specific activities or services. The office service mix of procedures (CPT codes) may then be adjusted accordingly, for additional profit.

In general, the most important end result of ABC is the shift of general overhead costs from high-volume services to low-volume services.

Example

Dr. Smith works in a large medical group consisting of 25 health care practitioners. In the aggregate, they render 4,000 office visits to the patients from XYZ managed care organization (MCO) and 20,000 visits to patients from the UVW MCO, each year. Each doctor averages 40 hours per week and dispenses various pieces of durable medical equipment (DME) to his or her elderly patient population. The office currently uses doctor hours (DH) to assign general overhead costs to medical services rendered. The predetermined (given) overhead rate is

$$\frac{\text{Office overhead costs}}{\text{Doctor labor hours}} = \frac{\$\ 900,000\ (\text{given})}{50,000^*} = \$18/\text{DH}$$
$$^*(25\ \text{doctors} \times 40\ \text{hr/wk} \times 50\ \text{wk/yr})$$

MCO XYZ requires 2.5 DLH and MCO UVW requires 2.0 DLH. According to a traditional general overhead cost system, the costs to treat one patient in each MCO is determined as shown in Table 11.1.

Now, for simplicity, let's suppose that office overhead costs are actually composed of the five activities listed in Table 11.2.

Also, let's assume that the transactional data in Table 11.3 have been collected by the office manager.

TABLE 11.1 Traditional Cost Method

	XYZ	UVW
Direct materials	$36.00	$30.00
Direct labor	17.50	14.00
General office overhead		
2.5 DLH × 18/DLH	45.00	
2.0 DLH ×18/DLH		36.00
Total cost per patient	$98.50	$80.00

TABLE 11.2 Actual Activity Cost

CPM ACTIVITY	TRACEABLE COST
Cast changes	$255,000
Radiographs	$160,000
Blood panels	$81,000
Dressings	$314,000
DME	$90,000
Total	$900,000

TABLE 11.3 Transactional Activity Cost

	NUMBER OF EVENTS		
ACTIVITY	TOTAL	XYZ	UVW
Cast changes	5,000	3,000	2,000
Radiographs	8,000	5,000	3,000
Blood panels	600	200	400
Dressings	40,000	12,000	28,000
DME	750	150	600

These data can be used to develop general overhead rates for each of the five activities (Table 11.4).

The general office overhead rates developed in Table 11.4 can now be used to assign overhead costs to the respective services, in the manner shown in Table 11.5.

Medical service and product costs using the two different methods can now be contrasted, as shown in Table 11.6.

Again, these spreadsheets demonstrate that the per unit costs of the low-volume services increase, and the per unit costs of the high-volume services decrease. These effects are not symmetrical, as there is a bigger dollar effect on the per unit costs of the low-volume service.

CPM and ABC

ABC is not a new concept; it was born in the 1880s as manufacturers tried to get a handle on unit costs of production. For example, if a company built wagons,

TABLE 11.4   Overhead Rates

ACTIVITY	COSTS	TRANSACTIONS	RATE PER TRANSACTION
Cast changes	$255,000	5,000	$51/change
Radiographs	160,000	8,000	20/x-ray plate
Blood panels	81,000	600	135/panel
Dressings	314,000	40,000	7.85/bandage
DME	90,000	750	120/DME

TABLE 11.5   Assigned Overhead Costs

ACTIVITY	RATE	TRANSACTIONS	AMOUNT
XYZ MCO			
Cast changes	$51	3,000	153,000
Radiographs	20	5,000	100,000
Blood panels	135	200	27,000
Dressings	7.85	12,000	94,200
DME	120	150	18,000
Total overhead (a)			$392,200
Number units (b)			4,000
Overhead per unit (a/b)			$98.05
UVW MCO			
Cast changes	$51	2,000	102,000
Radiographs	20	3,000	60,000
Blood panels	135	400	54,000
Dressings	7.85	28,000	219,800
DME	120	600	72,000
Total overhead (a)			$507,800
Number units (b)			20,000
Overhead per unit (a/b)			$25.39

TABLE 11.6 ABC and Traditional Costs

	XYZ MCO	UVW MCO
Costs using ABC methodology		
Durable equipment	$36.00	$30.00
Doctor hours	17.50	14.00
Office overhead	98.05	69.39
Total cost per unit	151.55	69.39
Costs using tradition accounting methodology		
Durable equipment	$36.00	$30.00
Doctor hours	17.50	14.00
Office overhead	45.00	36.00
Total cost per unit	98.50	80.00

they could divide their total costs by the number of wagons to figure out how much it cost to build each one. But they couldn't use that formula if they built wagons of different sizes. So producers began to use direct labor, materials, and overhead to calculate ABC, as described above. By the 1970s, medicine was heavily skewed toward labor and technology costs, making it more applicable to economic service sectors like medicine.

CPM, on the other hand, is a concept originally developed by the DuPont Corporation as a system of project management, in the late 1950s. Today it is embraced by the health care industrial complex as a way to use deterministic time estimates to control the costs of medical care. In the CPM, medical activities can be *crashed* (expedited) at extra cost, deemed *critical* if unable to be delayed, or *slacked* if a moderate delay would not adversely affect patient care. Since ABC determines the actual costs of resources rendered for each medical activity, it is a de facto measure of CPM profitability.

To activity-cost any medical office activity path, (1) identify the key steps and individuals involved, (2) interview staff and clinicians about the time or resources involved in each step, (3) define nonclinical activities associated with patient care, (4) define and assess possible efficiencies, and (5) ask each caregiver to define the costs of each resource he or she applies to the pathways. Then, "crunch the numbers" as presented above and be surprised at how low-volume medical costs increase and high-volume costs decrease. *In fact, medical practices still using traditional cost accounting systems will be clueless about the financial effectiveness of their care going forward.*

Presently, the Practice Expense Coalition (PEC) has suggested to the Health Care Finance Administration (HCFA) that it produce wide-ranging ABC projects to validate or disprove Medicare practice expense reimbursement fees. Specialties, such as gastroenterology, neurosurgery, thoracic, and cardiac surgery are especially interested. This has occurred because physicians argue that the HCFA uses inaccurate cost information to set practice expense rates under Medicare. Surgeons and procedure-based practitioners are especially worried that greater emphasis on resource-based relative values (RBRVs) reduces their reimbursements. Meanwhile, organizations like the American Society of Cataract and Refractive Surgery (ASCRS) and the American Academy of Orthopedic Surgeons (AAOS) are considering their own costing studies in the near future. DePaul University accounting professor Dr. Gary Siegel is a leader of this new movement.

THE ROLE OF "RISK ADJUSTERS" IN ABC

Traditionally, physician payment risk adjusters focused on variables such as gender, age, and geography to predict an individual's health care cost variability at any given time. Such methods needed only to successfully explain 15%–20% of all variation in order to adequately reflect selection and/or predict 10% of health care claims variability on a prospective basis and/or 33% variability on a retrospective basis to be considered successful 4% of the time. Hence, recent accounting research has focused on ways to segment these variations to enhance the use of ABC in medical practice and augment profitability These newer methods use retrospective ICD-9-CM code utilization rates to indicate prospective health care needs for either an individual or cohort.

Although methods differ as whether a highest-cost or multiple-cost diagnosis should be used as group size increases, costs trend toward the average regardless of the factors selected. Thus, when considering diagnosis-based risk adjusters with any capitated managed care plan, the size of plan, its stop-loss arrangements, and sound medical management are the keys to financial success, since higher-cost patients typically require greater medical skills to manage successfully.

MEDICAL PRACTICE COST ANALYSIS USING ABC, RBRVs, AND RVUs

> RBRVS and now RVUs have become the Holy Grail of medical metrics.
>
> —Ira Isaacson, MD, Egon Zehnder International

In actuality, using ABC as described above is a difficult and cumbersome task at best. Still, you must know your office costs to treat patients and perform medical services and procedures. An excellent way to do this is to perform a *medical practice cost analysis* (MPCA) for your specialty, since it assigns the total costs of operating a practice to the various CPT codes and services you provide. To measure such productivity, the Medicare RBRVs system, which sets benchmarks for various procedures, may be used. This system served as a starting point for RVUs (relative value units), which include (1) a physician's work component for time, intensity, and procedural effort (54%), (2) a practice expense component for equipment, rent, supplies, utilities, and general office overhead (41%), and (3) malpractice insurance expenses (5%). Each component is assigned an RVU adjusted for local cost differences and then multiplied by a conversion factor that translates them into dollars. (The current dollar conversion factor is about

$34.07.) By including practice expenses in the mix, the incentive to perform equipment-oriented procedures is thus reduced.

Under the (old) current charge–based practice expense formula, most primary care providers and internists received lower payments than did their hospital-based peers, which they considered unfair. Primary care doctors argued that surgeons' overhead costs were covered by the hospitals in which they operated, while they paid their own office expenses. Under Medicare's new practice expense HCFA rules of January 1, 1999, most physicians who provide services primarily in the office setting, such as internal medical specialists and family physicians, will receive increased payments from Medicare. Cardiac surgeons, neurosurgeons, pathologists, and gastroenterologists will see the biggest decreases.

According to the HCFA, some selected medical specialties will be affected by the new resource-based practice expense rules, shown as a percentage in allowed charges in Table 11.7.

Additionally, as the system evolved, pay and performance became even more closely linked, with about 10% of projected revenues at risk for so-called *citizenship fees* of administrative duties, cost efficiency, and quality measures. This allows the doctor to determine if the reimbursement for each service is enough to cover the cost of providing it. In other words, it will allow you to decide whether participating in a certain HMO capitated plan or incurring the costs of more labor is justified.

TABLE 11.7   Where Do You Measure Up?

Specialty	Allowed Charges ($ billions)	Impact Per Year (%) (1999)
Anesthesiology	$1.6	0
Cardiac surgery	0.3	−3
Clinics	1.6	−1
Dermatology	1.0	5
Emergency medicine	0.9	−3
Gastroenterology	1.2	−4
Family practice	2.7	2
General surgery	2.0	−2
Hematology/oncology	0.5	2
Internal medicine	6.0	0
Nephrology	0.9	−2
Neurology	0.7	0
Neurosurgery	0.3	−3
OB/GYN	0.4	1
Ophthalmology	3.3	1
Orthopedics	2.0	0
Other physicians	1.1	0
Otolaryngology	0.5	2
Pathology	0.5	−3
Plastic surgery	0.2	1
Psychiatry	1.1	0
Pulmonology	1.0	−1

To conduct an MPCA, according to Berlin and Faber, the following information and equipment are needed:

1. Procedure code (CPT) frequency data for your specialty or office for the prior 12–18 months. A sample spreadsheet (projection of utilization costs for 5,000-member panel) would include the following:

CPT Code	Cost by Component	Projected Utilization	Projected Cost
Totals	Historical Data	Historical Data	$60,000

Per member/per month calculation:
Total costs divided by 5,000 members divided by 12 months = $1 PM/PM

2. Office financial statements for the prior 12–18 months.
3. Medicare fee schedule for medical specialty.
4. Computer spreadsheet, such as Microsoft Excel-TM.
5. Categorization of all office expenses as *direct* or *indirect.*
6. Determine the best standard of measurement to assign costs to each work activity in the office (i.e., time, number of procedures or patients, or assigned RVU). The RVU systems works best for most doctors. Data are available from the US Federal Registry.
7. Separate the RVU of each CPT code into its component parts (physician labor component, practice expense component, and malpractice liability risk).
8. List all CPT codes or the ones used most frequently, as demonstrated in the spreadsheet Table 11.8.

Now, according to the cost accounting techniques of Baum and Schwager, divide total direct and indirect costs by the correct RVU component, as shown in Table 11.9, which will allow you to calculate the cost of one unit of the CPT activity.

Next, unit costs are multiplied by the appropriate work expense and liability component RVUs to arrive at a total unit cost per procedure, as seen in Table 11.10.

Finally, the results in Table 11.10 are added to the cost drivers, other than RVUs, such as the number of patient encounters, as seen in Table 11.11.

The results are then benchmarked to determine reasonableness and compared with the HMO's fee schedule. The contract is then accepted, rejected, or renegotiated based on its fiscal merits. Alternatively, spreadsheet parameters can be changed and various "what if" scenarios can be manipulated in mere seconds. Another example would be the physician allocation of monthly payment using the cost per RVU methodology, according to Berlin and Faber, as given in the following sample spreadsheet:

TABLE 11.8 CPT Utilization Costs

A	B	C	D	E	F	G	H
			(B×C) Total Practice	Practice Exp.	(B×E) Total Practice		(B×G) Total Office
CPT Code	Frequency (Number)	Work RVU[a]	Work RVU	Exp. RVU[a]	Exp. RVU	Liability RVU[a]	Liability RVU
11111	115	0.91	105	0.40	46	0.04	5
22222	44	0.43	19	0.37	16	0.03	1
33333	59	0.32	19	0.32	19	0.03	2
44444	285	0.23	66	0.23	66	0.02	6
55555	528	1.13	597	0.45	238	0.04	21
66666	788	1.66	1,308	2.10	1,655	0.19	150
77777	445	4.39	1,954	4.11	1.829	0.37	165
88888	2,216	4.41	9,773	4.37	9.684	0.39	864
99999	1,103	6.24	6,883	7.05	7,776	0.74	816
12345	1,085	8.69	9,429	8.81	9,559	0.98	1,063
54321	2,764	0.51	1,410	0.30	829	0.03	83
73620	490	0.16	78	0.54	265	0.04	20
73630	373	0.17	63	0.59	220	0.04	15
99203	4,632	1.14	4,973	0.52	2,268	0.06	262
99212	3,753	0.38	1,426	0.28	1,051	0.02	75
99213	1,825	0.55	1,004	0.38	694	0.03	55
Others	2,006						
Totals	32,241		39,104		36,213		3,602

[a]Data available from Federal Registry.

Services Produced Physician A Physician B Physician C Physician D Grand Totals CPT total CPT Cost / CPT Revenue / CPT Revenue / CPT Revenue / CPT Revenue / CPT Revenue

Thus, the financial power of ABC and more specifically, MPCA, is demonstrated.

CONCLUSION

Activity-based costing (ABC) has become the de facto managerial accounting method of choice for the modern medical office. It has replaced the traditional financial accounting methodology of average costs with the more specific methodology of tracing actual resources consumed. The idea is to get a handle on how much every task costs by factoring in every resource used to complete it. Thus, by assigning overhead expense costs to low-volume CPT codes, a better appreciation of each procedure's profit (or loss) can be ascertained and/or adjusted.

In this way, the next time a managed care capitated contract is offered, you will know instantly whether it will make money or lose money.

TABLE 11.9 Cost per CPT Procedure

A	B	C	D	E	F	G	H
Expense	Acct. Mgmt.	MD Labor	MPCA	Staff Labor	Misc.	Insurance	Other
MD salary		1,362,300					
Staff salary	257,635		111,378	42,600	55,000		
Malpractice						58,100	
DME lease					2,388		
Dues/subs							13,850
File fee	9,350						
Laboratory						1,428	
DME					201,366		
Other exp.	30,000				22,000		368,850
Total exp.[a]	296,985	1,362,300	111,378	42,600	227,182	58,100	436,850
Total units[b]	32,241	39,104	39,104	36,213	36,213	3,602	36,213
ABC/unit	9.21	34.84	3.08	1.18	6.27	16.13	12.06

[a]Total expenses for each column divided by total units.
[b]Total units from Table 11.8.
Direct costs = B, C, D, E, F.
Indirect Costs = G, H.

TABLE 11.10 Patient Encounter (Cost Driver)

A	B[a]	C[b]	D	E[a,c]	F[d]	G	H[a]	I[e]	J	K[a]	L[d]	M	N
			(B×C)			(E×F)			(H×I)			(K×L)	(D+G+ J+M)
CPT Code	Unit Cost	RVU	Unit Total	Unit Cost	RVU	Unit Total	Unit Cost	RVU	Unit Total	Unit Cost	RVU	Unit Total	TOTAL
	Physician/MDs			RN Staff/Labor			Insurance/Liability			Other Misc.			
11111	34.84	0.91	31.70	10.53	0.40	4.21	16.13	0.04	0.65	12.06	0.40	4.82	$41.39
22222	34.84	0.43	14.98	10.53	0.37	3.90	16.13	0.03	0.48	12.06	0.37	4.46	23.82
33333	34.84	0.32	11.15	10.53	0.32	3.37	16.13	0.03	0.48	12.06	0.32	3.86	18.86
44444	34.84	0.23	8.01	10.53	0.23	2.42	16.13	0.02	0.32	12.06	0.23	2.77	13.53
55555	34.84	1.13	39.37	10.53	0.45	4.74	16.13	0.04	0.65	12.06	0.45	5.43	50.18
66666	34.84	1.66	57.83	10.53	2.10	22.11	16.13	0.19	3.06	12.06	2.10	25.33	108.34
77777	34.84	4.39	152.95	10.53	4.11	43.28	16.13	0.37	5.97	12.06	4.11	49.57	251.76
88888	34.84	4.41	153.64	10.53	4.37	46.02	16.13	0.39	6.29	12.06	4.37	52.70	258.65
99999	34.84	6.24	217.40	10.53	7.05	74.24	16.13	0.74	11.94	12.06	7.05	85.02	388.60
12345	34.84	8.69	302.76	10.53	8.81	92.77	16.13	0.98	15.81	12.06	8.81	106.2	517.58
54321	34.84	0.51	17.77	10.53	0.30	3.16	16.13	0.03	0.48	12.06	0.30	3.62	25.03
73620	34.84	0.16	5.57	10.53	0.54	5.69	16.13	0.04	0.65	12.06	0.54	6.51	18.42
73630	34.84	0.17	5.92	10.53	0.59	6.21	16.13	0.04	0.65	12.06	0.59	7.12	19.90
99203	34.84	1.14	39.72	10.53	0.52	5.48	16.13	0.06	0.97	12.06	0.52	6.27	52.43
99212	34.84	0.38	13.24	10.53	0.28	2.95	16.13	0.02	0.32	12.06	0.28	3.38	19.89
99213	34.84	0.55	19.16	10.53	0.38	4.00	16.13	0.03	0.48	12.06	0.38	4.58	28.23

[a]Activity cost/unit from Table 11.9
[b]Same RVU from column C, Table 11.8.
[c]Sum of activity cost/unit from columns D, E, and F in Table 11.9.
[d]Same RVU from column E in Table 11.8.
[e]Same RVU from column G in Table 11.8.
Direct costs = Physicians/MDs, RN staff/labor.
Indirect costs = Liability insurance, other, miscellaneous.

TABLE 11.11

A	B[a]	C[b]D	
			(B + C)
			Total
	Account	Patient	Procedure Cost
CPT	Mgmt.	Encounter	
11111	9.21	41.39	50.60
22222	9.21	23.82	33.03
33333	9.21	18.86	28.07
44444	9.21	13.53	22.74
55555	9.21	50.18	59.39
66666	9.21	108.34	117.55
77777	9.21	251.76	260.97
88888	9.21	258.65	267.86
99999	9.21	388.60	397.81
12345	9.21	517.58	526.79
54321	9.21	25.03	34.24
73620	9.21	18.42	27.63
73630	9.21	19.90	29.11
99203	9.21	52.43	61.64
99212	9.21	19.89	29.10
99213	9.21	28.23	37.44

[a]Activity cost/unit from column B, Table 11.9.
[b]From column N, Table 11.10.

REFERENCES AND READING

Baum, N., & Schwager, R. M. Determining costs is the key to success. *Podiatry Today*, January 1997.

Berlin, M., & Faber, B. P. Financial applications using cost per RBRVS methodology. *MGM Journal*, November 1996.

Medical Group Management Association (MGMA). *Cost survey*. Englewood, CO: Author. 1998 (published yearly).

Ramsey, R. H. Activity based costing in hospitals. *Hospitals and Health Services Administration*, 338(3): 39 (1994).

Siegel, G. Institute of Management Accountants' Foundation for Applied Research. October 1998.

## CHAPTER 12

Advanced Office Cost Behavior Techniques

Applying Cost-Volume Profit Analysis to Contribution Margins

David Edward Marcinko

> Healthcare in the US can no longer remain the best if our health care system becomes one of the world's worst. Millions of people are underinsured or uninsured and the number is rising, yet money that could be destined for medical care is funneled off to for-profit HMOs, many of which selectively enroll the healthy and exclude the sick.
>
> —Jerome P. Kassirer, MD, Editor, New England Journal of Medicine

I n the fee-for-service past, a physician would traditionally raise his office fee(s) if more income was desired. Correspondingly, income increased and volume changed very little, if at all. As we have seen previously, this occurred because patients (insurance payers) were willing to pay almost any price and medical fees were considered inelastic, within the relevant price range.

Economists call this relationship *elasticity of demand* and formally define it as a number representing the percentage change in quantity (patient volume) demanded of a service resulting from each 1% change in the price of the service.

Elastic demand prevails if the price if the service exceeds 1 and is deemed inelastic if equal to or greater than 0 but less than 1. In other words, if medical pricing is elastic, revenues can be increased only by lowering the price. Conversely, raising the price will decrease revenues. Currently, medical care has a ratio of about .35. Inelasticity occurs in a growth industry, such as the computer business, where a fee increase will also increase revenues in the relevant range; elasticity occurs in a mature (nongrowth) business, such as medicine, where revenues are increasing but profits are stagnating or decreasing. In other words, the marketplace becomes resistant to price pressure, as it has done with managed care organizations (MCOs) and health maintenance organizations (HMOs).

As we know, medical profit can be defined by the following equation:

Profit = (price × volume) minus costs, or P = (P × V) − C,
where revenue = price × volume, or R = PV.

To increase profit, therefore, we must either increase price (if possible), increase volume (if possible), or decrease costs (if possible) and ideally perform all three maneuvers simultaneously. If we assume that only costs are under our control (a not altogether valid strategy), any long-term planning process that ignores them will not be beneficial.

A more efficient office addresses cost and volume together, but at some point more volume does not equate with more profit. This point is known as the average cost per patient and should be determined and known for each practice. If visually graphed, the curve would be U-shaped, with both arms extending upward and the hump pointed downward at its most efficient point. This tangent is the point of *maximum efficiency* (ME), and it is where you want to be.

In other words, more volume does not translate into more profit, and this is precisely how capitated contracts are determined. Working harder in this scenario will not get you ahead, only farther behind. *Thus, our main goal is profit improvement, not just revenue improvement since office operating overhead costs are so darned high!*

Once the fixed and variable costs of a medical practice are known, the effects of changes in volume on its costs structure can easily be determined. This is known as the *cost-volume relationship*.

For example, the effects of varying volume decreases on an OB-GYN practice is demonstrated in Table 12.1.

If the cost structure remains unchanged in the face of declining volume, the consequences will be higher average costs, reduced profitability, and an overall deterioration in the financial profitability and flexibility of the medical organization. In fact, the increased average cost/visit accelerates faster in the downward capacity direction than it decreases in the upward capacity direction. *This is very bad.*

TABLE 12.1   OB-GYN Practice

Capacity	TFC	VC/ Visit	Visits	TVC	TC	Avg. Cost/ Visit
70%	150,000	$20	3500	70,000	220,000	$62.86
60%	150,000	20	3000	60,000	210,000	70.00
50%	150,000	20	2500	50,000	200,000	80.00
40%	150,000	20	2000	40,000	190,000	95.00
30%	150,000	20	1500	30,000	180,000	120.00
20%	150,000	20	1000	20,000	170,000	170.00

TFC, total fixed cost; VC, variable cost; TVC, total variable cost; TC, total cost.

On the other hand, the effects of a volume increase are quite the opposite and much more pleasing. For example, at 70%, 80%, 90%, and 100% capacity rates the average cost per visit decreases to $62.86, $57.50, $53.33, and $50.00, respectively, when calculated in a similar fashion. Theoretically, at 110% of capacity, for a limited time the average cost per visit decreases to $47.27 but at a slower rate (120% capacity @ $45.00 average cost per visit). Nevertheless, this is an unrealistic expectation in a capitated and/or managed care environment, which encourages a lower utilization rates.

However, if the cost structure described above—$150,000 TFC and $20 VC/Visit—is more realistically transformed to $100,000 TFC and $34.29 (number of visits), the total practice costs at 70% capacity remains at $220,000: (a) $150,000 + ($20) (3,500) = $220,000 and (b) $100,000 + ($34.29) (3,500) = $220,000.

In fact, Table 12.2 demonstrates how the fixed cost decrease responds using the new reduced, fixed-cost formula.

Note that at 60% capacity, in comparison to the old cost structure, the practice has total savings of $7,142 and $2.38 reduction in average costs. For 50% capacity, there are total savings of $14,285, and an average cost drop of $5.71.

MORE ABOUT MARGINAL PROFIT

Recalling the equation Profit = (price × volume) − Total costs, we could rearrange it and say that Total profit = P × V − (FC + VC). However, most HMO contracts are based not on total profit but on additional or marginal profit, since overhead cost always remains and fixed costs are not important in this case. For other pricing decisions, we realize that the equation can be rewritten to emphasize variable costs, as follows: Marginal profit = (P × V) − VC.

Cost-Volume Profit Analysis

Once a basic understanding of medical cost behavior has been achieved, the techniques of cost volume profit analysis (CVPA) can be used to further refine

TABLE 12.2   Reduced Fixed Cost Formulas

Capacity	TFC	VC/ Visit	Visits	TVC	TC	Avg. Cost/ Visit
70%	100,000	$34.29	3500	120,000	220,000	$62.86
60%	100,000	34.29	3000	102,585	202,858	67.62
50%	100,000	34.29	2500	85,715	185,715	74.29
40%	100,000	34.29	2000	68,580	168,572	84.29
30%	100,000	34.29	1500	51,435	151,435	100.96
20%	100,000	34.29	1000	34.290	134,290	134.29

TFC, total fixed cost; VC, variable cost; TVC, total variable cost; TC, total cost.

the managerial cost and profit aspects of the office business unit. They can also help illustrate the important differences between the traditional office net income statement and the more contemporary *contribution margin income statement* (CMIS). CVPA is thus concerned with the relationship among prices of medical services, unit volume, per unit variable costs, total fixed costs, and the mix of services provided.

Traditional Income Statement Approach

In financial accounting, the traditional net income statement (NIS) incorporates office medical costs organized by function.

Example

January revenues: $12,000

Less costs: $6,000 (variable and fixed costs)

Gross margin less operating expenses: $5,000

Net income: $1,000

Contribution Margin Approach

The CMIS approach to managerial accounting, however, is more useful in CVPA. For example, a CMIS for Dr. Smith, a solo MD, for last month is shown in Table 12.3.

Recognize that the revenue amounts (net of variable expenses) contribute toward covering fixed expenses and then toward profits. Also, the per unit contribution margin (CM) remains constant as long as the office visit price and the variable expenses per unit do not change.

Now, to illustrate the powerful affects that change makes in CVPA, a CMIS is presented in Table 12.4 for monthly revenues generated by treating 1, 2, 400, and 401 patients.

At this time, appreciate three important points from the above illustrations:

TABLE 12.3   Contribution Margin Income Statement

	Total	Per (Unit) Patient	Percentage
Revenues (500 patients)	$25,000	50	100
Less variable expenses	15,000	30	60
Contribution margin	10,000	20	40
Less fixed expenses	8,000		
Net income	2,000		

TABLE 12.4 Cost Volume Profit Analysis Using Various Patient (Unit) Visits

	Total	Per (Unit) Patient	Percentage
Revenues (1 patient)	$50	50	100
Less variable expenses	30	30	60
Contribution margin	20	20	40
Less fixed expenses	8,000		
Net income (loss)	($7,980)		
Revenues (2 patients)	$100	50	100
Less variable expenses	60	30	60
Contribution margin	40	20	40
Less fixed expenses	8,000		
Net income (loss)	($7,960)		
Revenues (400 patients)	20,000	50	100
Less variable expenses	12,000	30	60
Contribution margin	8,000	20	40
Less fixed expenses	8,000		
Net income (Breakeven)	0		
Revenues (401 patients)	20,050	50	100
Less variable expenses	12,030	30	60
Contribution margin	8,020	20	40
Less fixed expenses	8,000		
Net income (profit)	$200		

1. If the office treats exactly 400 patients a months, it will *break even* (no profit or loss).
2. The breakeven point can be defined either as (a) the point where total office revenue equals total expenses (variable and fixed) or (b) the point where total CM equals total fixed expenses.
3. Once the breakeven point is reached, net income (profit) is increased by the amount of the unit CM for each additional patient seen.

The point is for the practice to be able to increase its patient volume (V) with little or no corresponding increase in its fixed costs (FC).

Contribution Margin Ratio

The contribution margin ratio (CMR) is the ratio of CM to total revenues, expressed as a percentage (i.e., CM/revenues). The CMR also can be calculated by using per unit figures (patient CM per patient revenue). The CM in our example is 40%, as calculated: $10,000/25,0000 = 40\%$ or $20/50 = 40\%$. Interestingly, the CMR demonstrates how the CM will be affected by a given change in total revenues.

Example

Assume that revenues for Dr. Smith increase by $15,000 next month. We can now inquire what the effects on (1) the CM and (2) the net income for Dr. Smith will be.

   1. *Effect on CM*
      Increased revenues: $15,000
      Multiplied by CM: × 40%
      Increase in CM: $6,000
   2. *Effect on Net Income*
      If fixed expenses do not change, Dr. Smith's net income will again increase by $6,000. (See Table 12.5.)

As can be seen from the above spreadsheet, as long as the revenue received from the practice is above the variable costs of providing the medical service, the CM is positive and contributing to fixed costs. In the "real world" of managed care, any MCO contract that is below a practice's variable costs, will lower its profit and should never even be considered.

Capitation (Cost) Volume Profit Analysis

One factor for determining profitability in CVPA is the accuracy range of estimated utilization rates for each managed care contract. Too much patient utilization of the doctor's resources means little or no profit, whereas less utilization means more profit (at-risk contract).

Example

A primary care medical group has 20,000 patient lives under a pm/pm contract and is offered a capitation rate of $.12 pm/pm. The estimated variable costs for the service is $2.50 per patient. The gross revenue for the 12 cent contract is $2,400 a month (20,000 × $.12). What is the profitability range against different

TABLE 12.5   Revenue Increases and the Contribution Margin Statement

Proof	PRESENT	EXPECTED	CHANGE
Revenue (patients)	50	80	30
Revenues (dollars)	$25,000	40,000	15,000
Less variable expenses	15,000	24,000	9,000
Contribution margin	10,000	16,000	6,000
Less fixed expenses	8,000	8,000	0
Net income	2,000	8,000	6,000

utilization rate (UR) assumptions? (See Table 12.6.) Can the group afford to take the contract?

It can be seen from the spreadsheet (Table 12.6) that this contract is profitable over the entire range of utilization rates (20, 50, 90, and 100). However, the group might determine that it cannot managed the additional lives without more staff, office space, or other resources beyond a UR of, say, 50 (no excess capacity). At this rate, the contract would be rejected because the annual increase in overhead costs would begin to erode the estimated profit of $26,300 (Law of Diminishing Returns). Contract risk is now quantified, and the group can make other what-if scenarios regarding increased variable costs per patient (costlier injections, x-rays, dressings, lab tests, etc.) or other parameters, such as a new capitation rate.

As an example, Table 12.7 demonstrates the same scenario but with a new and increased variable cost rate of $10, rather than the $2.50 rate used above.

Now it can be seen that profits decrease as variable costs increase, by $3,000, $7,500, $13,500, and $15,000, respectively, at the relevant URs 20, 50, 90, and 100. Moreover, at a UR of 150, with the new V/C factor of $10, the group actually looses money (minus $1,200), since profit becomes negative beyond some utilization and/or variable cost point. This breakeven point can be calculated by finding the utilization and/or variable cost rate that produces zero profit.

TABLE 12.6   Utilization Range

A	B	C	D	E	F
		Utilization			
	UR/1,000	(per/	V/C	Total costs	Profit
Annual revenue	(estimate)	20,000)	(patient)	(increased)	contract
2400 × 12		(B × 20)		(C × D)	(A − E)
28,800	20	400	$2.50	1000	$27,800
28,800	50	1000	2.50	2500	26,300
28,800	90	1800	2.50	4500	24,300
28,800	100	2000	2.50	5000	23,800

TABLE 12.7   Profitability Range

A	B	C	D	E	F
		Utilization			
	UR/1,000	(per	V/C	Total costs	Profit
Annual revenue	(estimate)	20,000)	(patient)	(increased)	contract
2400 × 12		(B × 20)		(C × D)	(A − E)
$28,800	20	400	$10.00	4000	$24,800
28,800	50	1000	10.00	10,000	18,800
28,800	90	1800	10.00	18,000	10,800
28,800	100	2000	10.00	20,000	8800
28,800	120	2400	10.00	24,000	4800
28,800	150	3000	10.00	30,000	(−) 1200

Can you determine the breakeven point (BEP) using the above scenario? It is 144 per 1,000, with B being the UR, calculated in the following way: B(20)(10) − 28,800. Therefore, B = 144.

Thus, capitation cost volume analysis seeks to determine at what volume capacity the group maximizes profits but not necessarily revenue. The group wants to see the optimal number of patients for profitability but not the greatest number of patients. In other words, it wants to maximize its profits, not gross revenues. In terms of HMO contract negotiations, the group can now leverage this information by trying to either (1) increase the pm/pm capitation rate, (2) control URs (rationing care?), or (3) "carve out" certain services. Or sacrifice the contract altogether!

On the other hand, gross variances in CVPA might warrant further investigation and/or contract consideration when

1. Actual dollar compensation (profit) exceeds established guidelines.
2. Variance does not exceed an acceptable range of compensation (profit).
3. The anticipated benefits of CVPA are more than expected profits.
4. Past CVPA benchmarks warrant a further review.

MORE ABOUT BREAKEVEN ANALYSIS

Breakeven Analysis (BEA) can be illustrated by using Dr. Smith's office data (Table 12.8).

Mathematics

X = BEP in patients

Revenues = Variable expenses + Fixed expenses + Profits

$\$50X = 30X + 8,000X + O$

$\$20X = 8,000$

$X = 400$ patients or, in terms of revenue dollars, $\$50 \times 40 = \$20,000$

X = BEP in dollars

Revenues = Variable expenses + Fixed expenses + Profits

$X = .6X + \$8,000 + 0$

TABLE 12.8 Contribution Margin for Dr. Smith

	Per patient	Percent
Revenue price	50	100
Variable expenses	30	60
Contribution margin	20	40

.4X = $8,000

X = $20,000

Finally, it must be realized that CVPA depends on the following economic assumptions, which may (in rigidly structured capitated contracts) or may not be true in every case.

1. The behavior of *revenue and cost is linear* (i.e., proportional to volume).
2. Costs can be accurately *divided into fixed and variable elements.*
3. There is a *constant service mix* in multiservice offices.
4. *Office treatments remain the same.* In other words, the number of patients seen equals the number of unit revenues received. This is ideal for a capitated service contract.
5. The value of a dollar today is the *same* as the value of a dollar in the future.

MEDICAL OFFICE TARGET PROFIT ANALYSIS

The above formulas used to compute the BEP can also be used to determine the revenue volume needed to meet net target profit analysis (NTPA) figures.

Example

Assume that Dr. Barry Miller, a dentist, would like to earn a minimum profit of $7,000 per month from his medical office practice. How many intermediate office visit patients must be treated each month, at $50/patient, to reach his net target profit goal?

Equation Method

X = Number of patients to attain the target net profit

Revenues = Variable Expenses + Fixed Expenses + Target Profits

$50X = 30X + $8,000 + $7,000

$20X = 15,000

X = 75 patients, or in terms of total revenue dollars, $50 × 75 = $3,750

Margin of Safety

The *margin of safety* (MS) is the excess of budgeted or actual revenues over the BEP in revenues. It demonstrates the amount by which medical office revenues can drop before losses begin to be incurred. The MS can be expressed in either dollar form or percentage form, as seen in the following two equations:

(1) Total revenues minus breakeven revenues = MS (dollars)
(2) MS (dollars) divided by total revenues = MS (percentage)

Office Operating Leverage

Medical office *operating leverage* (OL) is a measure of the mix of variable and fixed costs in a medical practice. The formula to calculate the degree of OL at a given level of revenues is as follows: Degree of operating leverage (DOL) = CM divided by net income. It is very useful when comparing two or more satellite medical offices (Table 12.9).

Furthermore, the DOL can be used to predict the impact on net income of a given percentage revenue increase. For example, if the DOL is 2.5 and there is a 10% increase in revenues, then net income will increase by 2.5 × 10, or 25%.

Example

Assume that each of the below satellite offices (1 and 2) experience a 10% increase in sales revenue (Table 12.10).

Finally, be aware that the DOL is not constant and changes with the level of revenues. Ordinarily, the DOL declines as revenues increase. When profit, but not necessarily revenue, increases at a faster rate than costs, a high DOL is said to exist.

"PHILOSOPHICAL SANITY CHECK"

The Role of Office Undercapacity and Intangibles

Many so-called business gurus preach the concept of strict financial "number crunching" as described in this chapter. In other words, how much revenue is

TABLE 12.9   Satellite Office Data for Dr. Smith

	SATELLITE OFFICE 1		SATELLITE OFFICE 2	
Revenues	$50,000	100%	$50,000	100%
Less variable expenses	35,000	70%	10,000	20%
Contribution margin	15,000	30%	40,000	80%
Less fixed expenses	9,000		34,000	
Net income	6,000		6,000	
DOL		2.5		6.7

TABLE 12.10   Office Contribution Margin Comparison

	SATELLITE OFFICE 1		SATELLITE OFFICE 2	
Revenues	$55,000	100%	$55,000	100%
Less variable expenses	38,500	70%	11,000	20%
Contribution margin	16,500	30%	44,000	80%
Less fixed expenses	90,000		34,000	
Net income	75,000		100,000	
Increase in net income		25%		67%

derived, from how many patients per month, week, and day, according to some estimated UR? With this method, physicians are reduced to hourly "employees" and patients to "encounters." Actuarial firms may even be hired to legitimize the numbers and suggest standards.

This is especially evident when one realizes that such firms may be thinly disguised benefits consultants, with a built-in bias toward rationed care. Consequently, be aware of the potential negatives of a strict business output mentality and recognize that medicine is an intensely personal experience and other intangible factors must also be considered. Lowering the economic "per unit cost" of a widget may be desirable to a manufacturer, but price is only one aspect of good medical care.

Example (Airplane Model)

Recall the often used but erroneous example of selling airplane seats as a good way to illustrate the concept of office undercapacity and health plan contract intangibles.

Let's assume a plane has a capacity of 100 seats, 90 of which are sold at the normal ticket price of $100, for a total revenue of $90,000 ($100 × 90). If total costs represent a BEP of $80,000, a $10,000 profit is realized. Hence, if any single remaining seat can be sold at a discount, more profit is generated, since the plane will fly anyway. Therefore, doctors should strive to fill every office schedule time slot, right? Well, perhaps not! Why? It's because management consultants have a CVPA manufacturing/merchandising bias that originates in business school as their training is usually not in a service-oriented business sector like medicine.

Now, further appreciate that the less than full airplane in our example may make a return flight at business fare or full fare to recoup lost profits. *Once locked into a managed care contract, however, no similar upward pricing pressure is available to physicians*, and MCOs are demanding longer and longer contract periods of 1, 2, or even 3 years in length! Extending our analogy to the typical medial office, traditional management experts might still argue that a discounted HMO patient is better than no patient at all. But as a human being, suppose your empty room is occupied by a noncompliant capitated diabetic patient or a litigation-prone patient. Economic considerations aside, don't the potential medical, legal, and emotional entanglements of these situations exceed their marginal benefits? Philosophically, one could argue that these possibilities still exist in a fee-for-service environment and be quite correct.

Therefore, rest assured that we are not advocating the wholesale nontreatment or abandonment of patients in need. We are simply noting the capitalistic and very demoralizing human feelings of "why bother." Or shall doctors accept the socialistic epistemology of laborers who "pretend to work while the government pretends to pay"?

Also, understand that *an efficient practice is not necessarily one that makes the most profit but one that produces the greatest profit at the most appropriate level of service.*

Using this definition, of course, entails a different concept of success, because a highly efficient practitioner may still be deemed prosperous if he or she makes only 90% of the prior year's profit yet is in the office only 70% of the time.

CONCLUSION

The reviewed CVPA accounting principles represent powerful techniques for increasing medical practice profits in the competitive health care marketplace. Their use may result in improved profits and patient care, the ultimate successful outcome in any medical practice.

REFERENCES AND READINGS

Berlin, M. F., & Budzynski, M. R. Budget variance analysis using RVUs. *MGMA Journal*, December 1998.

Finkler, S. *Essentials of cost accounting for healthcare organizations.* Gaithersburg, MD: Aspen Publications, 1994.

Hansen, D. *Management accounting.* Boston: Pas-Kent Publishers, 1990.

Mayer, G., & Barnett, A. *Making capitation work.* Gaithersburg, MD: Aspen Publishing, 1995.

Thibadoux, G. M., Scheidt, M., & Jeffords, R. Costs under capitation. *MGM Journal*, September 1998, p. 95.

## CHAPTER 13

Augmenting Return on Your Office Investment

Decomposing ROI and Residual Income

David Edward Marcinko

> Return on Investment, and Residual Income calculations, will be the medical office profitability measure of choice in the next decade.
>
> —Herbert Garner, registered investment advisor

The *return on investment* (ROI) for any medical office is an important managerial accounting concept to understand. It is a key parameter that must be high enough to warrant continued existence of the medical office business unit, or the practice will eventually cease to exist, because capital tends to flow only to profitable business endeavors.

To enhance understanding of this concept, as well as to facilitate its pragmatic use, ROI may be decomposed into three individual component parts, as demonstrated below:

$$\frac{\text{Net operating income}}{\text{Practice revenues}} \times \frac{\text{Practice revenues}}{\text{Avg. operating assets}} = \text{ROI}$$

Example: New practitioner Dr. Morgan reports the following office data:

Practices revenues: $500,000

Avg. operating assets: $200,000

Net operating income: $30,000

ROI = $30,000 / 500,0000 × 500,000 / 200,000 = (6%) × (2.5) = 15%

Using the above example, it is intuitive that there are three ways in which Dr. Morgan can improve her ROI: (1) reduce expenses, (2) increase revenues, or (3) reduce operating assets.

Approach 1: Reduce Expenses

Assume that Dr. Morgan is able to reduce expenses by $10,000 per year so that net operating income increases from $30,000 to $40,000. Practice revenues and operating assets remain unchanged.

$$(\$40,000/500,000) \times (500,000/200,000) = (8\%) \times (2.5) = 20\% \text{ ROI}$$

Expense reduction is the simplest and fastest parameter of office ROI to adjust, and the recent downsizing of corporate America is an example of the social tumult it can produce. Many believe that in a mature market or health maintenance organization (HMO) environment there is more leverage for increasing profits by cutting costs than by increasing revenues (revenues = price × volume). In fact, the smaller the HMO contract's profit margin, the greater the leverage achieved through cost reduction in the short term (the inverse also applies).

For example, at 12.1% and 25.2%, respectively, anesthesiology and surgical cardiology groups have the lowest percentage of overhead among selected specialists, and neurosurgeons are among the highest ($275,000), as listed in Table 13.1.

Moreover, in a reduced or discounted fee environment there is far more leverage for increasing profit by reducing expenses (costs) than by increasing revenue.

There are many items whose costs can be reduced through innovative purchasing and volume buying. These include printed material, superbills, and stationery; telephone, travel, car rental, and airline reservation costs; computer and copier equipment, maintenance, and supplies; durable medical equipment (DME) and laboratory fees; staff salary, benefits, and overtime pay; and bulk purchases (economies of scale) by pooling with other groups to obtain discounts.

Contemporaneously, www.MedicalShopper.com purports to save 15%–50% when ordering medical products over the Internet (800) 246-8353, and may prove a fertile source for low-cost office supplies in the future.

TABLE 13.1   Medical Office Overhead Operating Expense Cost Percentages (Total Net Revenues) According to Specialty

12.1%	Anesthesiology
25.2%	Surgical cardiology
26.4%	Radiology
32.9%	Nephrology
37.0%	Gastroenterology
37.2%	General surgery
42.8%	Cardiology
48.7%	Urology
54.6%	Ophthalmology
55.3%	Internal medicine
59.5%	Family practice
67.0%	Hematology/oncology

Modified from *MGM Update*, December 1998.

Another pertinent example in medicine is the increasingly popular permanent employee leasing (PEL) or professional employee organization (PEO) option, or outsourcing strategy, as pioneered by such companies as National Employer Solutions, Inc. (NES), of Atlanta. In this physician cost-reduction business model, PEL or PEO is an industry that is transforming the way small and medium-size businesses and medical offices are run, giving them many advantages previously available only to very large group practices, medical service organizations (MSOs), independent practice associations (IPAs), or physician practice management corporations (PPMCs). This innovative approach helps doctors to concentrate more time and economic resources on treating patients and less time and money running and/or growing their practices. According to Mr. George Bennington of NES, advantages include the cost reductions associated with no longer having to deal with administrative services such as payroll processing (2%), tax administration (2%), employee benefits (1.5%), claims and audits (1%), and insurance and human resource management (2%). In fact, it has been estimated by Professor Nathan Jones, PhD, MBA, superintendent of the Professional Medical Management Academy, that these services are the equivalent of about 8.5% of the typical gross office payroll.

Still, some of the cost reduction strategies noted above may be merely a "temporary fix" since some baseline costs of business will always remain. Such a "slash and burn" costing mentality also does not foster future growth, expansion, innovation, research, or business development. Remember, you can be cost-conscious without being too neurotic.

Approach 2: Increase Revenues

Again assume the Dr. Morgan is able to increase revenues to $600,000 because she is in a growing market. Net operating income increases to $42,000 and the operating assets remain unchanged.

$$(\$42,000/600,000) \times (600,000/200,000) = (7\%) \times (3.0) = 21\% \text{ ROI}$$

An increase in office revenue is a bit more difficult to engineer than simple cost-cutting efforts, but the results are also more worthwhile. Growth is again emphasized in this model, with corresponding profit increases (i.e., 21% > 20% ROI).

Approach 3: Reduce Assets

Finally, assume that Dr. Morgan is able to reduce her average operating assets from $200,000 to $125,000. Revenues and net operating expenses remain unchanged.

$$(\$30,000/500,000) \times (500,000/125,000) = (6\%) \times (4.0) = 24\% \text{ ROI}$$

Now it can be seen that asset reduction is the most profitable economic course to pursue in search of increasing practice ROI (24% > 21% > 20%). Growth takes precedence over continued downsizing and is augmented by asset reduction; as variable or virtual costs are increased only on an as needed basis.

Criticism of the ROI Approach

Although physicians are just beginning to use the ROI approach in evaluating medical office performance, it is far from being a perfect profitability analysis tool. The ROI method is subject to the following criticisms:

1. ROI tends to emphasize short-term performance rather than long-term profitability. In an attempt to protect or increase ROI, a physician may become motivated to accept or reject an otherwise wise investment opportunity.
2. ROI is controllable only by physician owners and not employed practitioners, associates, or HMO physician employees. This inability to control ROI not only leads to personal frustration but can make it difficult to distinguish between performance of the practice and performance of the physician. Thus, professional and/or independent business consultation may be helpful in this regard.

RESIDUAL PRACTICE INCOME

Residual income (RI) is the net operating income that a medical office is able to earn above the minimum ROI. In fact, some physicians believe that residual income is a better measure of performance than ROI. The RI approach encourages office managers to make profitable investments that would be rejected under the ROI approach.

Example

Dr. Ridley, a medical entrepreneur, owns two large office complexes, A and B. Complex A has $1,000,000 in operating assets, and Complex B has $3,000,000 in operating assets (Table 13.2). Each complex is required to earn a minimum of 12% on its investment in operating assets.

TABLE 13.2 Office Data for Dr. Ridley		
	Complex A	Complex B
Avg. operating assets	$1,000,000	$3,000,000
Net operating income	200,000	450,000
Required return		
(12% × avg. operating assets)	120,000	360,000
Residual Income	$80,000	$90,000

Dr. Ridley's Medical Complex A has an opportunity to make an investment of $250,000 that would generate a return of 16% on invested assets (i.e., $40,000/year) (see Table 13.3). This investment would be in his best interest, since the 16% rate of return exceeds the minimum required rate of return. However, the investment would reduce the complex's ROI.

On the other hand, the investment would increase the complex's RI (Table 13.4). Thus, informed physicians realize that extraordinary profits are made by pursuing the financial triad of decreased costs, increased revenues, and decreased operating assets.

Criticism of the Residual Income Approach

The major disadvantages of the RI approach to practice profitability analysis is that it cannot easily be used to compare the performance of different sizes of offices, as appreciated above. Economies of scale and other efficiencies are not considered, nor are the intangible goodwill attributes of the personal patient-physician relationship. This last objection is increasingly less important as medicine becomes commoditized by producing a standardized HMO medical service product.

CONCLUSION

Although bewildering to the uninitiated, a careful analysis of the ROI and RI methodologies presented in this chapter will assist the physician to develop the most economically profitable service, financial, and operational flow process. This will result in improved profits, decreased personal stress, and improved patient care, the ultimate successful outcome in any medical office.

TABLE 13.3   Reduced ROI

	Present	New Project	Overall
Avg. operating assets (a)	$1,000,000	$250,000	$1,250,000
Net operating income (b)	200,000	40,000	240,000
ROI: (b) / (a)	20.00%	16.00%	19.20%

TABLE 13.4   Increased Residual Income

	Present	New Project	Overall
Avg. operating assets	$1,000,000	$250,000	$1,250,000
Net operating income	200,000	40,000	240,000
Rate return			
(12% × avg. operating assets)	120,000	30,000	150,000
Residual Income	80,000	10,000	90,000

REFERENCES AND READINGS

Garrison, R. H., & Noreen, E. W. *Managerial accounting.* Boston: Irwin, 1997.

Garrison, R. H., & Noreen, E. W. *Managerial accounting: Ready notes.* Boston: Irwin, 1997.

Jones, N. Professor of Management and Business Policy, University of Texas and the US Chamber of Commerce, 1999.

Marcinko, D. E. *Profit maximization and reimbursement.* Columbus, OH: Anadem Publishing, 1998.

Meredith, J. R., & Mantel, S. J. *Project management.* New York: John Wiley & Sons, 1995.

Muller, S. V. The role of risk adjusters in medical group practices. *MGMA Journal,* December 1998.

Physician's Advisory. PO Box 97113, Washington, DC, 20090.

Piturro, M. Carrots and sticks: MCOs tie physician compensation to productivity. *Managed Healthcare News,* vol. 14, no. 10, 1998.

Premier management prepaid medicine (PMPM). 1425 River Park Drive, Suite 230, Sacramento, CA, 95815; (916) 565-6130.

Tschida, M. Shifting gears: Specialists take a hit under new practice-expense rule. *Modern Physician,* January 1999.

## CHAPTER 14

An Economic "Report Card" for Physicians

Taking the Financial Pulse of Your Practice Through Trend Analysis

Gary L. Bode

> I advise you to go on living solely to enrage those who are paying your annuities.
>
> —Voltaire

This chapter discusses the techniques and tools required to evaluate and monitor your practice. It makes a strong case for active practice management and illustrates some of the tools needed to do so. It starts with the external point of view, as in the case of a banker considering making you a loan. Financial statements are briefly discussed, with emphasis on their translation from financialese to English. Some of the more common and useful financial ratios are then explained at a specific point in time and as successive values over time for internal managerial purposes. Then the internal office financial perspective gets examined, with emphasis on creation of an intuitively obvious managerial report, using financial parameters, practice statistics, and trend graph analysis to help guide the practice to increased profitability.

YOUR PRACTICE AS AN ASSET

Your practice is a valuable asset in two respects. First, it provides the work environment that generates your personal income. Second, it has inherent value. Some of this inherent value lies in the current market value of medical equipment, minus any money owed. The other aspect of inherent value is goodwill, or the worth of the practice as an ongoing concern that allows you to sell it to another practitioner.

Despite the importance of the practice to the practitioner, some essentially run without a manager. This is like an orchestra without a conductor in that the individual facets of talent have no common pathway to make music.

Many other practices evolve over time reactively, and are not what the practitioner would have proactively defined as ideal.

ECONOMIC REWARDS OF A WELL-RUN PRACTICE

Most medical practitioners are not well trained in business. Lack of time beyond clinical duties also limits the practitioner as a "hands on" manager. However, your services are provided in an underlying business environment. Let's consider the financial rewards since they are the most tangible. Table 14.1 shows the financial benefit of improving practice performance 1%, in three key parameters. This example uses a practice with $500,000 per year of gross fees, a 20% contractual write-off rate, 3% of bad debt and 70% of overhead. The money available for pre-tax practitioner salary is $116,400:

1. 80% (100% minus the 20% of contractual write off) of 500,000 in gross fees is $400,000.
2. 97% (100% minus the 3% of bad debt) of 400,000 is $388,000.
3. 30% (100% minus the 70% of over head) of 388,000 is $116,400.

TABLE 14.1   Financial Benefits of a Well-Run Practice

	Additional Pre-tax Practitioner Salary
One parameter	
Decrease overhead	3880
Decrease bad debt	1200
Increase gross fees	1164
Two parameters	
Decrease overhead	
Decrease bad debt	5120
Increase gross fees	
Decrease overhead	5083
Increase gross fees	
Decrease bad debt	2376
Three parameters	
Decrease overhead	
Decrease bad debt	
Increase gross fees	6335

The financial leverage inherent in a practice makes even small improvements in performance yield dramatic bottomline or "in pocket" results. Table 14.1 shows that cutting overhead 1% nets the practitioner an extra annual $3,880 of potential salary. Likewise, decreasing bad debt 1% yields $1,200. A simultaneous 1% improvement in both parameters yields $5,120, all for the same amount of patient care with no additional malpractice liability. Notice that increasing gross fees, the area most practitioners think of when discussing practice management, has the least impact of the three key parameters. Conversely, many practitioners complain that managed care erodes and limits their traditional patient bases. While outside the scope of this chapter, good services marketing can improve any practice's gross fees, even in today's environment. The key to this is superb patient service, of which the clinical result is only a component. Making the patient's total perceptions exceed their prior expectations ensures a full appointment book.

The rewards of a well-run practice transcend financial considerations. Other benefits include

1. A better, more consistent clinical result.
2. Improved patient perception, which increases referrals and decreases liability.
3. Less employee turnover.
4. Less stress.
5. More free time for the practitioner.

EXTERNAL EVALUATION: FINANCIAL STATEMENTS

Financial statements are usually provided by an independent accountant. External parties, like banks, often use these tools for evaluation of the practice. Financial ratios, examined later in this chapter, are the cornerstone of utilizing these statements. Interpretation of these documents is discussed later. Financial statements have potential problems and are often suspect for several reasons:

1. They rely on unverified information from the practitioner. A practice's internal bookkeeping, even with the highest of intentions, is often sloppier than an accountant might hope. Professional liability with the IRS and time constraints keep the average accountant from doing anything but merely compiling the figures given them. The standard disclaimer on their financial statements loudly proclaims this fact.

2. Most accountants are generalists in that they service other industries, like hog farms and flower shops, besides health care. Specialization in health care developed for a good reason: it became too complex for a single person to have a comprehensive grasp of all of it. The accounting industry has not followed suit. Thus, they often have little direct experience in the health care profession and certainly not enough to differentiate between the subtleties of the various sub-specialties.

3. Accountants generally limit their scope of service to merely interfacing with the government for you on tax issues. Thus, their statements reflect tax position, which is only one component of the practice's total financial condition. Although important, this is hardly all your accountant is capable of. The common result of this is that financial statements, though accurate for tax compliance, are less than optimal for managerial purposes. Unfortunately, many practitioners never even look at their financial statements or ever learn how to interpret them. The accounting expense is viewed as a necessary evil for tax compliance. This is a shame because such information, properly derived and presented, can be an important managerial tool. The following is a concise presentation of what each type of statement is, along with the common problems encountered in interpreting them.

The *income statement* (profit and loss statement) reports what income came in, what expenses occurred, and the difference between them within a specific time period. The most common use for this statement is the "bottom line," or net profit, for tax purposes. Sometimes multiple time periods are presented for comparison. Sometimes the percentages of each category are presented.

While obviously important, such a limited goal of tax compliance can diminish the income statement's use for internal managerial evaluation. Since this is the most important accounting statement to the average practitioner, it deserves more discussion than the other two reports. The most common significant limitation of the accountant-rendered income statement, even with trained interpretation, is poor classification and categorization. For tax purposes, many types of expenses can be grouped together and still render a correct figure. It is common to see income statements that categorize expenses into illogical groups. This may occur because the accountant (1) does not understand your practice, (2) cannot or will not customize the accounts, or (3) has encountered a lack of proactive input from the practitioner. Furthermore, if you have the accountant enter your checks into a software program, additional blending of categories can occur as low-level employees incorrectly key in your information. Such blending of categories negates an opportunity to see objectively where all the money goes.

Over time, an income statement, set up with intuitively obvious expense categories, yields an aggregate, bird's-eye view of cash flow. Gradually, spending patterns emerge. Commonly, if the only attempt to control expense has been on a check-by-check, best-effort basis, significant savings can be achieved, without being overly anal, after an appropriate data base is built. This is often not a single dramatic thing, but more likely $10 a month here, $200 a year there. These figures add up. Even a 1% savings on a $300,000 per year practice puts an extra $3,000 back in your pocket with no additional work or liability. Remember, if your expenses (exclusive of physician salary) run 33% of the gross money taken in, every $1 of expense saved has about the same effect on the practice as generating $3 of income. With contractual write off (the amount a third-party payer forces you to deduct from your gross fees), each dollar saved in expenses can easily have the same effect on the practice as $4 of services rendered.

The best way to build yourself such a tool is by doing the accounts payable yourself, using an electronic check register program, like Quicken® or

Quickbooks®. Once this accounts payable program is operational, a properly trained staff member can generate most of the checks in house and maintain proper categorization. You produce a true cash flow statement, which can be easily modified by your accountant into tax format. Such programs allow for customized categorization of expenses, which can be a powerful managerial tool. The trick is to think of how you will ultimately use these categories. Who else is better qualified to determine that than the practitioner? In some practices income classifications can also be useful, although the specialized accounts receivable programs generally do a good job on this.

The *balance sheet* gives a "snapshot" of the practice at a specific point in time. This timing is different from that of the income statement, which uses a period, not a point, of time. The balance sheet uses tne formula: Assets (what you own) equal liabilities (what you owe) plus owner's equity (what you have left).

The third type of financial statement is the *statement of cash flows*. This statement reconciles the change in financial position between two balance sheets. Opinions vary, but it is the least useful to the average practitioner.

TURNING FINANCIALESE INTO ENGLISH

Even with great accounting, financial statements can be difficult to interpret. Let's start with the *net income statement.* The main interpretation issue here is depreciation and its relative, amortization. Depreciation merely takes the cost of a tangible asset like equipment and divides this expense into the successive time periods over which the asset is expected to help produce income. Logically, if you're trying to figure up true practice costs, a piece of durable equipment often helps produce income long after it was purchased. There are several methods of depreciation. Generally, practice financial statements use the deprecation methods and time frames allowed by the IRS. These have no relationship to the true life span and productivity of the item. For internal managerial purposes you can assign your own type and duration of depreciation. The dual bookkeeping is often worthwhile. The actual cost of the equipment is reflected on the balance sheet.

Let's say you bought a piece of equipment 3 years ago for $10,000. For tax purposes, the government forces you to deduct this expense equally over 5 years. Thus, for the past 3 years you depreciated (wrote off, deducted) $2,000 on your taxes each year ($10,000/5) despite the fact that you paid the whole $10,000 long ago. In the next 2 years you also can take a $2,000 deduction a year to obtain, belatedly, the entire deduction for the initial expense. The original $10,000 is entered and accounted for in the balance sheet. The government does allow a certain amount of depreciation expense to be deducted in the current year, under Section 179, if desired by the taxpayer. Thus, if other assets purchased during the year do not exceed the limit ($19,000), the practice could deduct the entire $10,000 expense of the equipment in a single year.

Amortization is the same concept as depreciation but applied to intangible assets, like goodwill. Many a practitioner has wondered where all that net income his accountant says he made actually is. Most times a true "cash" net profit never existed; it was only an accounting artifice for tax purposes. Depreciation often causes discrepancies between "checkbook profit," which is how much cash you actually have left over after paying the bills, and taxable income. Initial financing of the asset also confuses matters. A standard installment loan payment, like a mortgage, has two components: principal, the amount actually put toward the face value of the loan, and interest, the expense of borrowing the money. Initially, the percentage of each payment constituting interest is high, and this decreases during the course of the loan. Conversely, the percentage of principal repaid with each payment increases. An extreme example of this cash flow profit and taxable interest discrepancy is buying equipment with a loan but depreciating it completely through the use of Section 179 in a single year—wonderful for that first year. However, in the following years, only the interest component of the loan is deductible, and your taxable income exceeds your true cash flow because the principal, though paid that year, is unavailable to reduce it. This discrepancy is greatest in the last year of the loan, where the bulk of loan payment is principal.

Other income statement translation problems include different accounting methods:

1.   Cash method, in which money is counted only as you deposit it and spent only as you write a check. Simplistic but intuitively obvious, this resembles your check register. Unfortunately, the true cash flow method is seldom seen. Most accountants use a tax-modified version of the cash flow method, as required by the IRS for tax reporting purposes.

2.   Accrual method, in which income is counted as you earn it, so your accounts receivable are counted as income when you treat patients, despite receiving no cash as yet. Expenses get entered as you incur them (i.e., you enter a supply order as an expense as its placed, not just when you pay for it). This method affords logical treatment of a wider variety of accounting issues than does the cash method, and the IRS requires it once certain criteria are met.

3.   Modified cash (tax) method, which is the cash method modified by depreciation and amortization as required by the IRS.

The following balance sheet problems sometimes arise:

1.   Asset valuation. Commonly, balance sheets reflect *book*, or tax, value of assets. This is the historical value (what you paid) minus what you wrote off (depreciated or amortized) for tax purposes. Let's use the same piece of equipment used in a previous example, bought 3 years ago for $10,000. Again, for tax purposes, the government forces you to deduct this expense over 5 years. Thus, for the last three years you depreciated (wrote off, deducted) $2,000 on your taxes ($10,000/5), for a total of $6,000 ([$10,000/5] × 3). The current book or tax value reflected on the balance sheet is $4,000 ($10,000 − $6,000). Note that this probably does not match the current market value of the equipment.

2.   Assets are usually combined into groups, so a single asset can be evaluated only by examining the accountant's work papers. Second, these groupings origi-

nate to suit the accountant's software, which results in categorization different from the way the practitioner thinks of the assets.

3. The book value is not immediately apparent because the historical price is listed in the asset section, followed by an entry labeled "accumulated depreciation." Sometimes the math is a little harder to follow than just the $10,000 – $6,000 of our example. The book value and historical value may have no relation to the true current market value of the asset. A piece of land you paid $100,000 for stays on the books as $100,000 despite the fact the neighborhood has eroded it to $75,000 or, conversely, escalated it to $125,000. The resulting $25,000 gain or loss is never reflected in the balance sheet. A 20-year-old building may have a book value of $49,000 ($100,000 purchase price minus accumulated depreciation of $51,000) but is really worth $110,000 in the current market. With buildings, improvements are not listed in the value of the building, making interpretation even more difficult.

4. Some assets are intangible. Let's consider goodwill, for example. Goodwill is basically the value of the practice as a going concern minus the book value of the assets. In a mature practice, where accumulated depreciation has decreased the book value of the assets below true market value and the reputation of the clinic allows selling it for a premium price, goodwill can be considerable but not reflected in the balance sheet.

COMMON FINANCIAL RATIOS USED FOR EVALUATING YOUR PRACTICE

Financial ratios are figures or percentages derived from components of the financial statements. Even with the inherent limitations, financial ratios are the cornerstone of interpreting financial statements. They are being increasingly used by external sources to value and evaluate practices; thus, it behooves you to understand them. Some financial ratios are valuable in the managerial report; a time series of certain practice financial ratios helps reveal its trends, strengths, and weaknesses. All practice information, including financial ratios, should be integrated into the "big picture," and undue emphasis on a single facet may skew interpretation.

These financial ratio values are benchmarked to values obtained by surveys that become "industry standard." As described above, the average practice's financial statements have some inherent problems, making the derived financial ratios suspect. The government regulates and the accounting industry strongly guides the accounting principles used to generate a publicly held company's financial statements. This makes them more uniform and accurate than the average financial statements of a health care practice. Note that benchmark figures in publicly held companies are based on published financial statements. Surveys add another level of unreliability in using financial ratios for health care practices.

Financial ratios fall into four main classifications: (1) liquidity and solvency, (2) asset management, (3) debt management, and (4) profitability ratios.

LIQUIDITY AND SOLVENCY FINANCIAL RATIOS

The two most useful are the *current ratio* and the *current liabilities to net worth*.

Current Ratio

$$\frac{\text{Current assets}}{\text{Current liabilities}} = \text{Current ratio}$$

The current ratio measures short-term solvency. Unfortunately, practice financial statements often do not segregate current and long-term assets and liabilities accurately. Current assets include cash on hand, the percentage of accounts receivable you can reasonably expect to collect, and short-term investments, like a 3-month CD. Current liabilities are notes payable and loans due within 1 year. This ratio should be at least 1, preferably higher. A banker or venture capitalist probably wants this in the range of about 1.3 to 1.5.

Short-term solvency has an impact on the ability to pay current obligations, which dramatically affects credit, an essential tool to controlling practice expenses. Thus, it is an important figure to track internally over time. Establishing your definitions allows consistent calculation of the current ratio. For example, if you enter gross fees into accounts receivable and then adjust for contractual write-off and bad debt, use the past 6 months' figures of these adjustments to establish the true eventual cash value of your accounts receivable.

Current Liabilities to Net Worth

$$\frac{\text{Current liabilities}}{\text{Net worth}} = \text{Current liabilities to net worth}$$

This should be low, probably beneath 0.5, but not 0. Net worth, or owner's equity, is often distorted on the financial statements, as most practitioners take out all the money "left over" as salary or distributions. This can be especially true if the practitioner holds major assets personally, like the building (a common scenario), and leases them to the practice. Bankers circumvent this by evaluating the practitioner and practice simultaneously.

Asset Management Financial Ratios

The four most important asset management financial ratios are the (1) average collection period, (2) fixed assets utilization, (3) fixed assets to net worth, and (4) total assets utilization ratio.

Average Collection Period

$$\frac{\text{Total accounts receivable}}{\text{Average daily charges (those not collected on the day of service)}} = \text{Average collection period}$$

The acceptable figure depends on the type of practice. A practice that handles a lot of personal injury cases has a higher number than one that deals mostly in cash. Note that the total accounts receivable is inherently overvalued if it includes eventual contractual write-offs and bad debt. Average daily charges would vary on the time period sampled and can be difficult to obtain. This is a vital practice parameter, however, and it is well worth setting up the process to obtain and track the required figures. Tracked over time (see "Trend Graph Analysis," below), it provides essential monitoring of the entire collections and billing process. For internal managerial purposes, the top dollar, third-party payer components should be tracked individually, as the aggregate figure may not immediately detect a rapid change in a single insurance company.

Each extra day of this parameter means that someone else is enjoying the float, or interest, on your money for an additional day. Ten extra days of $50,000 in accounts receivable means at least an additional expense to you of $120 a year if you could have banked this at 8% annual percentage rate (APR). Since a practice with protracted collections usually has cash flow problems, this probably translates to $270 if you're borrowing money at 18% APR.

Fixed Assets Utilization

$$\frac{\text{Net revenue}}{\text{Net fixed assets}} = \text{Fixed assets utilization}$$

Fixed assets utilization shows how productively a practice utilizes its assets. Obviously, you would like any asset you invest in to render as much as possible in additional revenue. Asset evaluation issues (like accumulated depreciation described above) and true practice assets being held by the practitioner for tax purposes make the managerial use of this figure marginal.

Fixed Assets to Net Worth

$$\frac{\text{Fixed assets}}{\text{Net worth (doctor-owner's equity)}} = \text{Fixed assets to net worth}$$

A higher ratio indicates a greater investment in fixed assets which, conversely, may indicate low working capital. This is a great concept in publicly held companies with strict accounting but less useful to the average practitioner. See the potential problems of fixed asset evaluation (and ownership) and net worth described above.

Total Assets Utilization

$$\frac{\text{Net revenue}}{\text{Total assets}} = \text{Total assets utilization}$$

Total assets utilization is similar to the fixed assets to net worth ratio described above, but it eliminates some of the asset evaluation problems. If the proper definitions are consistently employed, this is a good figure to track internally over time. An example of an appropriate definition might be any asset originally costing over $250 that is in current use, including any held "artificially" by the practitioner for tax purposes. Although a "soft" figure, it has value as an indicator of productivity.

Debt Management Ratios

The two most common debt management ratios are (1) total debt to total assets and (2) total liabilities to net worth.

Total Debt to Total Assets

$$\frac{\text{Total debt}}{\text{Total assets}} = \text{Total debt to total assets}$$

Obviously, less debt is generally preferable, so this ratio should be low. Remember, debt can be a useful managerial tool if used wisely, and a total debt to total assets figure of 0 might have negative implications. Bankers look for low figures because they are being asked to provide more debt and want to ensure their investment.

Total Liabilities to Net Worth

$$\frac{\text{Total liabilities}}{\text{Net worth}} = \text{Total liabilities to net worth}$$

This can be a useful figure if appropriate definitions are used, and some practitioners track this internally. Generally, lower is better.

Profitability Ratios

These include (1) profit margin and (2) return on investment ratios

Profit Margin

$$\frac{\text{Net income}}{\text{Net revenue}} = \text{Profit margin}$$

Generally expressed as a percentage, this figure reflects how much profit the practice makes on each dollar of revenue, usually gross fees. When the practitioner's salary encompasses what's left over, this is zero. For internal purposes it can be considered as potential practitioner salary over gross fees. Obviously, higher is better.

Return on Investment

$$\frac{\text{Net income}}{\text{Total assets}} = \text{Return on investment}$$

This reflects how well assets are used to generate net income. Again, one would strive to make the most money with a given asset, making this figure as high as possible. This concept appears in a breakeven analysis where the expected return on investment on an individual asset is calculated before buying it. Sometimes it makes sense to refer potential gross fees to outside sources, despite inherent clinical expertise, because of the equipment cost involved. Other times, traditionally outsourced services now performed in house help the practice.

INTERNAL MONITORING

A prudent practice manager keeps close, regular tabs on the business, especially in today's dynamic health care environment. Failure to do so results in a practice that loses opportunities for income, pays out too much in expenses, and endures unnecessary stress. How much personal responsibility will you take for the care and growth of your most valuable asset?

A good tool used in many other types of businesses is a *managerial report*. This helps you work smarter, not harder. Such a report gathers all the data important to the manager in one place, on a regular basis, in a format that is intuitively obvious. Once formulated, the staff can update virtually all of the information for you, making the ongoing time requirement minimal.

Different aspects of the practice may require different time frames. Usually this falls into weekly, monthly, and quarterly categories. Accounts receivable logs and reports, the check register, and cash flow planning are good candidates for weekly review. The *trend graph analysis* report described in the following section is generally a monthly category. Your accountant's financial statements may get quarterly review.

Remember the 90/10 rule, which states that 90% of progress is made in the first 10% of time expended. The law of diminishing returns sets in quickly after that. Setting limits of time and energy for practice management, both high and low, is appropriate. Proactive prevention of "brush fires" is generally more time- and resource-efficient than putting them out.

Trend Graph Analysis

Your practice's history can help you predict its future performance. Trend graph analysis charts practice statistics and/or financial parameters and/or derived figures thereof (ratios) over time. This makes practice trends visually emerge from an otherwise nebulous collection of data before they might otherwise become apparent and aids in strategic planning. Practitioners, either by nature or training, intuitively understand a graph. Newer practice accounts receivable software offer various graphing capabilities, and these should be checked out for usefulness. However, the ability to highly customize your data presentation is usually worth the extra effort of using a separate spreadsheet program. Graphs constitute the bulk of a managerial report.

Trend graph analysis is also useful for marketing and collections parameters. It can be used to track retail trends too if this is a significant aspect of the practice. Expense monitoring and control is more efficient through a properly categorized accounts payable program (electronic check register).

Required Spreadsheet Skills

Only basic spreadsheet skills are required, and trend graph analysis is a good project to learn these with. Windows®-based programs generally have excellent intrinsic tutors, wizards, assistants, and the like to help with the basics. Other market programs are available to help you learn. Try your local university's business school for a personal tutor to help show you the basics. Spreadsheets are versatile and, once learned, have many other professional and personal uses. You should be able to do the following:

- Point, click, and drag with a mouse.
- Enter data.
- Format numbers.
- Delete.
- Copy.
- Lock and unlock cells.
- Create a data table.
- Create a graph.
- Format graphs.
- Create a trend line.

Trend graph analysis requires four steps. Setting it up properly is the key, and this requires some time and thought. The first phase is to determine what information might be managerially useful. The staff can generally gather the data for you. Usually this involves obtaining data such as how many new patients were seen each calendar month during the past 2 years. If figures are not readily available, establish a process that makes them so at least from now on.

Next, the figures are entered into a spreadsheet table. Other derived relationships (e.g., the ratio of new patients to established patients seen per time period) are calculated within the spreadsheet and appended to the table. Graphs are then created and formatted. The spreadsheet table and graphs become a template that requires only a minute to update in the next time period. All the internally derived ratios and graphs then automatically update, as well.

Interpretation requires integrating the information presented into the practice's big picture. Isolated parameters can be misleading. For example, just keeping track of the number of new patients seen doesn't tell everything you need to know by itself. If that number goes up, one might assume the practice is doing great, and it may well be. However, managed care may be paying less collections on these patients while simultaneously restricting follow-up care. A proper analysis would include the number of existing patient visits, average gross fees generated per new and existing patient visit, average collections per patient visit, absolute collections, percentage of contractual write-off, and percentage of bad debt write-off. Fortunately, the doctor is in an excellent position to integrate multiple factors into the big picture. Of course, any analysis without appropriate follow-up action is futile. Obtained information helps you guide the practice by implementing reinforcement strategies to stressing strategies to help prevent negative outcomes from occurring.

Although trend graph analysis yields useful information, it has some inherent limitations, and soft data may result from some calculations. For example, all components of the accounts receivable cycle for a single patient seldom occur within a given time evaluation frame. Say you perform $100 of services for a patient in June. She pays $10 in cash, and you file her insurance. In July the insurance company forces you to write off $9, per your contract with them, and pays $74 on the claim. You bill the patient for the remaining co-payment. However, in September you decide the remaining $7 ($100 − $10 − $9 − $74 = $7) is uncollectible and write it off the books. June's report would show the gross fees and $10 of collections but would not compare this with the same patient's contractual write-off, insurance payment, or bad debt.

Note that if the practice handles billing and collections in a consistent manner, valid trends still appear despite the lack of any "hard" figures. Also ratios, like the percentage of collection, while not absolutely correct for a given time period (because of the inherent delay in insurance payments), still have managerial use. Aggregate payments, such as a batch insurance check for multiple patients or claims, and practitioner down time, like an annual two-week dive trip in June, will skew figures.

Determining What Information Is Managerially Useful

"Backing" into a managerially useful report is perfectly appropriate. It can be hard to anticipate all of the information you will need or use. Trial and error eventually renders the best format and content of a managerial report. There is always a way to present information so that it is intuitively obvious to a particular practitioner. Therefore, "overproduce" the first report by graphing more data and in multiple ways. Then, see what makes the most sense to you in the least amount of time (i.e., graph absolute dollar change in collections from January this year compared to January last year and the percentage of change in those same figures). These take only seconds to produce. As you become more adroit at interpretation, some of these charts may clarify analysis. If not, they're easy to delete.

What Kind of Information to Collect

First, decide on a time period that is useful to you, the practicing physician. Monthly figures are appropriate for most parameters in a health care practice. Weekly figures can create more detailed information without much more effort, and the increased number of data points helps smooth the curve. Remember, once you set up the templates, the staff can track the data as far back as you want to collect information. Usually, 2 years of monthly figures yields decent results. Diminishing returns occur as you go farther back and get more detailed. Associated usefulness really depends on the practitioner's interest and managerial style.

On the clinical side of the practice, we can suggest collecting the following data:

1.   The number of new patients seen per time period. Further subcategorizing these by type of patient or insurance may be appropriate in some cases. Remember, you would have to segregate the billing and collections in the same manner. Most accounts receivable programs can easily provide such information, and the actual trend graphing goes quickly once you know how.

2.   The number of previously established patients seen per time period. Again, this could be further differentiated if useful to the practitioner.

3.   Gross fees generated per time period. Remember that this subcategorization has to match the way you classified patients above.

4.   Collections actually taken in per time period. Some practitioners segregate cash payments collected for the service on the day of service. This helps enforce a policy of collecting more up front from the patient.

5.   Amount of contractual write-off per time period. These are gross fees generated that a third party forbids you to collect. If you can match this to the type of patient, as above, and/or the gross fees associated, you can track the amount of contractual write-off in more detail. Otherwise a major dip in just one third-party payer could get buried in the aggregate figure.

6.   Amount of bad debt per time period. This is the amount of gross fees you are legally entitled to but cannot collect from a patient secondary to noncontractual issues. Note the difference in bad debt and contractual write-off.

7.   Amount of accounts receivable present at the end of each period.

The retail side is trickier, and the clinical aspects above are a better place to start. Much of retail data can be tracked via your accounting or accounts payable program. This could be used to eventually maximize your retail profit. It pays to be familiar with your accounting software if the practice has a significant retail component.

Although outside the scope of this chapter, other useful items can be correlated to help show practice efficiency. For example, staff gross salary as a ratio of gross fees and/or collections helps to monitor the amount of revenue produced by each dollar of staff salary. This is analogous to the asset utilization financial ratios explained above. The current ratio, explained above, can generally be derived without the financial statements. Tracking this with a trend graph may help keep the important topic of short-term liquidity in mind.

Constructing the Spreadsheet Table

Table 14.2(a) and 14.2(b) are abbreviated tables that can be used to produce graphs like the one in Figure 14.1. The primary figures you enter render other, derived figures. Simple formulas entered in these cells calculate the desired values. Such figures automatically recalculate if you change the associated primary figures. Some of these underlying formulas have been left visible in Table 14.3(a), 14.3(b), and 14.3(c) to demonstrate their use. These cells should be locked to prevent accidentally changing or deleting the formulas. Some of these secondary figures include the following:

1.   Absolute change between this year's time period and last year's time period. Consider generating change figures whenever different time periods are being compared. On graphs with a compressed axis (large changes between major tick points on the axis), calculating the change between consecutive time periods clarifies the picture. These changes form another data series, which get graphed with the original but on a secondary Y-axis because of their lower range and scale. Figure 14.1 uses the actual figures as data labels adjacent to the plot points.

2.   Percent change. Very similar to paragraph 1 above. Remember to correlate absolute change and percent change back to each other since a 1% change may not sound like much but can mean thousands of dollars annually. Conversely, a large percentage of change in some parameters may be misleading (like the percent change in the new patient section of Table 14.2b) if the base you derive them from is small.

3.   Correlation of two parameters. For example, tracking the percentage of new patients (from the total number of patients seen per time period) helps to integrate these two classifications of patients. This could corroborate your concerns that the new managed care program limits the gateway for new patients into your practice.

4.   Ratios (i.e., the amount of average gross fees generated per new patient).

5.   Indicators (i.e., the average amount of total collections per new patient, established patient and total (combined) patients seen). While not absolutely accurate (see the above explanation of soft data), these can help predict trends, aid in strategic planning, and visually present changes in reimbursement rates.

The chart created in a spreadsheet stays linked to those cells the data is in. Your chart will automatically update if you change these figures, a desirable feature. Therefore, care must be taken not to break this link when it comes time to get rid of the oldest month's figures and add the newest month's figures. Deleting an entire row at the bottom and inserting a new row at the top, although logical, destroys the table-chart linkage by changing the cell "addresses." To keep the cell references intact, you must clear the contents of the row of cells at the bottom (not delete the row itself) with the old information, cut and paste the remainder of the table down an entire row and then add the new data in the top row. Sophisticated analysis would show time-extracted data from a true database program—elegant but not really necessary.

TABLE 14.2a Spreadsheet Table for Producing Graph

	No. New Patients				No. Established Patients				Total No. Patients				
	96/97	97/98	CH	% CH	96/97	97/98	CH	% CH	+B4	+C4	+D4	+E4	96/97
AUG.	18	22	4	18.2	251	314	63	20.1	269	336	67	19.9	10518
SEP.	22	19	-3	-15.8	311	267	-44	-16.5	333	286	-47	-16.4	13020
OCT.	21	24	3	12.5	321	361	40	11.1	342	385	43	11.2	13335
NOV.	23	25	2	8.0	317	349	32	9.2	340	374	34	9.1	13294
DEC.	31	34	3	8.8	433	464	31	6.7	464	498	34	6.8	18142
JAN.	19	21	2	9.5	266	294	28	9.5	285	315	30	9.5	11144
FEB.	15	17	2	11.8	221	235	14	6.0	236	252	16	6.3	9228
MAR.	21	18	-3	-16.7	288	251	-37	-14.7	309	269	-40	-14.9	12082
APR.	24	26	2	7.7	333	338	5	1.5	357	364	7	1.9	13959
MAY	27	22	-5	-22.7	379	311	-68	-21.9	406	333	-73	-21.9	15875
JUNE	17	13	-4	-30.8	239	188	-51	-27.1	256	201	-55	-27.4	10010
JULY	21	22	+C15 -B15	+ (D15/ +C15)* 100	294	308	+G15 -F15	+(H15/ +G15)* 100	+B15 +F15	+C15 +G15	+K15 -J15	+(L15/ +K15)* 100	11034

234

TABLE 14.2b Spreadsheet Table for Producing Graph

Collections			% of New Patients of Total				
97/98	CH	% CH	96/97	97/98	CH	% CH	
13373	2855	21.3	6.7	6.5	-0.1	XXXX	1
11383	-1638	-14.4	6.6	6.6	0.0	XXXX	2
13886	551	4.0	6.1	6.2	0.1	XXXX	3
14885	1591	10.7	6.8	6.7	-0.1	XXXX	4
19820	1678	8.5	6.7	6.8	0.1	XXXX	5
12537	1394	11.1	6.7	6.7	0.0	XXXX	6
10030	802	8.0	6.4	6.7	0.4	XXXX	7
10706	-1376	-12.8	6.8	6.7	-0.1	XXXX	8
14487	528	3.6	6.7	7.1	0.4	XXXX	9
13253	-2621	-19.8	+(B13/J13)* 100	+(C13/K13)* 100	+V13 -U13	XXXX	10
8000	-2010	-25.1	6.6	6.5	-0.2	XXXX	11
13163	+015 -N15	+(P15/ +015)* 100	6.7	6.7	0.0	XXXX	12

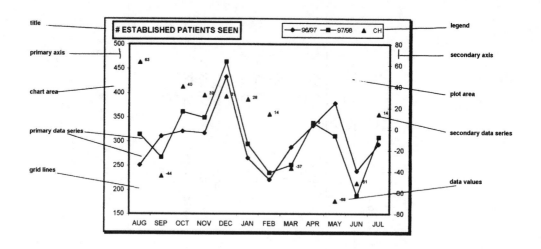

FIGURE 14.1
Prior time period
Maximum value: 433 December ("lookup" function)
Minimum value: 221 February
Average value: 304

Current time period
Maximum value: = MAXIMUM (G5:G19)
Minimum value: = MINIMUM (G5:G19)
Average value: = AVERAGE (G5:G19)

Combined time periods
Maximum value: 433 December (96/97)
Minimum value: 188 June (97/98)
Average value = AVERAGE (F5:G16)

Greatest positive change: 63 August
Percent change: 20.1%

Greatest negative change: −68 May
Percent change: −21.9%

With your underlying table and subsequent charts, consistent formatting is essential. Initially there are a lot of data and a myriad of charts, which can easily confuse someone. Consistent formatting eventually saves you stress and time when you actually utilize your work to manage your practice.

Examination of Table 14.2a and b shows the basic data organization necessary for graphing. Remember: the staff may eventually work with your template, so make it understandable. With clients, we use sets of 12 consecutive calendar months exclusively as the time period. So all data are in one, very wide table. If you decide to chart different time periods (weeks are very appropriate) or different

TABLE 14.3a   Recalculated Spreadsheet Table for Producing Graph

Month	96/97	97/98	CH
Sept.	21345	20883	−462
Oct.	19378	20227	849
Nov.	19920	19887	−33
Dec.	21400	20778	−622
Jan.	21111	20336	−775
Feb.	21466	19996	−1470
Mar.	19854	20005	151
Apr.	20789	21445	656
May	21345	20355	−990
June	18800	19004	204
July	21233	19722	−1511
Aug.	20922	19455	−1467
Total	247563	242093	−5470

TABLE 14.3b   Refunds, Bad Debt and Contractual Write-Offs

Month	Refunds	Bad debt	CWO
Sept.	34	0	0
Oct.	0	155	1265
Nov.	0	0	1436
Dec.	52	312	1488
Jan.	26	107	0
Feb.	0	86	2778
Mar.	72	94	1698
Apr.	54	111	1444
May	21	0	0
June	93	398	2998
July	0	122	1945
Aug.	41	81	2076
Total	393	1466	17128

numbers of the same time period, a separate table must be constructed for each style.

Note the underlying formulas, displayed in bold as examples, instead of the actual derived figure. Copying and pasting these formulas makes filling in all the derived data series a snap. For example, the absolute change columns were filled first by entering the simple subtraction formula only once in the new patient section, copying it in the remainder of that column, and then copying that entire column to the absolute change columns in the other sections. This also ensures—assuming that you entered the original formula properly—that they are all correct. Once these are in place, merely changing the primary data automatically updates the entire table. Remember to protect these cells from accidental deletion or erroneous data placement.

TABLE 14.3c   New Patients, Established Patients, and Fees

	EST PT	TOT PT	NP	NP/ EST PT	EST PT/NP	Fees/NP	Fees/ EST PT	Retail Sales/PT
Sept.	188	206	18	9.6	10.4	90.23	84.78	19.22
Oct.	182	201	19	10.4	9.6	90.21	84.91	19.21
Nov.	201	219	18	9.0	11.2	90.32	84.65	19.17
Dec.	196	215	19	9.7	10.3	90.3	84.61	19.16
Jan.	188	206	18	9.6	10.4	90.25	84.88	19.14
Feb.	191	209	18	9.4	10.6	90.22	84.91	19.12
Mar.	196	216	20	10.2	9.8	90.4	84.75	19.09
Apr.	199	218	19	9.5	10.5	90.27	84.41	19.11
May	171	191	20	11.7	8.6	90.33	84.96	19.07
June	202	224	22	10.9	9.2	90.31	84.89	19.04
July	191	211	20	10.5	9.6	90.34	84.86	19.01
Aug.	188	209	21	11.2	9.0	90.37	84.91	18.96

References

References automatically duplicate the contents of another cell. Thus, you can just change the item once and the information appears everywhere you referenced it without transcription error

1.   As demonstrated in cells J4 to M4 of Table 14.2(a), the references of B4, C4, D4, and E4 would display 96/97, 97/98, CH, and % CH respectively. When you change B4 to 97/98, 97/98 would automatically appear in J4 too.

2.   Other uses of references include duplicating data as a convenience when used in other calculations (even though you can graph nonadjacent data series) and repeating the months as row labels for ease of reading in wide tables.

Notice that the labels are kept short (and consistent) to conserve space on the subsequent graph's axis and legend. The headers refer to the related graph and help to organize the table. Similar columns are colored to differentiate them and to act as spacers between the related series for each graph. The numbers at the right-hand side merely convert time periods into data that the spreadsheet uses for calculations—see the figures beneath Figure 14.2.

Create excess data on the off chance that it might come in handy when interpreting the overall picture. Any distractions or delays during actual interpretation of the graphs is frustrating. When a column is determined to be worthless, still keep it filled with markers to remind you that it is an invalid parameter. You can set your monitor's display (a view function) to always show the left-hand (months) column regardless of where you are in the table and eliminate needless horizontal scrolling.

Graph Creation

Graph creation is a snap with most spreadsheet programs. First, simply highlight the columns (data series) you want graphed, including both the month names

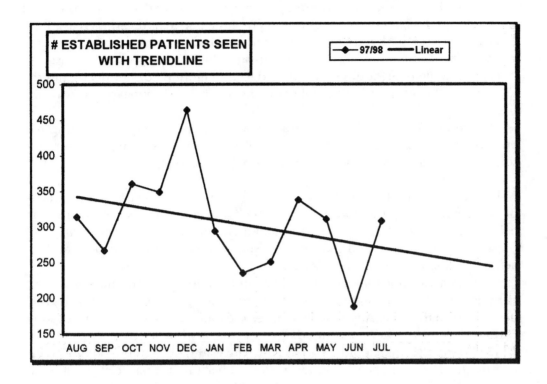

FIGURE 14.2   Extrapolated values:
AUG. 264
SEPT. 257
OCT. = FORECAST (15,G6:G17,Y6:17)
NOV. 244

for the X-axis labels and the labels in the legend. Then select the type of graph you want. Next, select an area where you want the chart placed. Finally, you format it.

We find multiple data series, horizontal line graphs to be the most intuitive. The most common type, which, in addition to plotting the two primary time data series, also graphs the change between them, using a secondary Y-axis on the right-hand side. Try creating different types of charts or even combinations with the same data. Then pick the one or two that make the most intuitive sense. Generally, simpler is better. Fancy and exotic charts look good, but quick and intuitive interpretation is the main objective. Don't put appearance before function.

Organize chart placement in any logical manner. Charts that fall into more than one category can be duplicated if that eases interpretation. Place graphs of no immediate interest on a separate spreadsheet work page for instant reference if and when required for clarification of the primary report.

Individual components of the graphs can be formatted to your tastes and needs. Again, formatting goes beyond mere appearance and can increase (and certainly decrease) functionality of the charts. Once you create one graph the way you like it, the graphs produce a consistent-looking project that is easier to interpret. Remember, your chart is linked to the figure placed or derived in the spreadsheet table: update the table and the same graph appears but with the new data.

The implications of formatting transcend visual pleasantry. Formatting can and should be customized to best enable you to quickly spot trends. Here are some of the graph components to play with (Figure 14.3).

1.   Appearance of each data set. This includes (a) the shape color and size of data markers; (b) the appearance of the connecting line (solid, dashed), its color and thickness; (c) what axis its plotted on primary or secondary; (d) presence of data labels and the typeface, size, and color of such labels; and (e) actual chart type (i.e., a bar series can be overlaid with a line series).

2.   Plot area appearance: (a) background—solid, pattern, and color—and (b) grid lines. Use thin, light gray, dashed horizontal grid lines. Anything heavier detracts from the data. Anything less makes the data values less obvious. In some cases vertical gridlines are required.

3.   Chart title: this should be brief, descriptive, and obvious but not too space-consuming. Remember, you'll have a series of charts that superficially look alike.

4.   Legend: we always include one, but with consistent formatting it becomes superfluous. You might try no legend per se but have a page wide standard that appears as a reference. I make mine small, which keeps it from subtracting space in the plot area.

5.   Axis: scale is the important point here. Your spreadsheet will automatically set this, but the lower limit of zero may be inappropriate and require manual resetting. You can use different scales on different graphs, but keep these consistent from report to report. If your collections have never dropped below $20,000 per month, consider raising the minimal value on the axis to $15,000 or $20,000.

Where the data crosses the axis, offset the intersection from the plot area borders to ensure readability of first and last data points, especially if using data labels.

Size, typeface, color, and placement of axis labels: consistency, space, and readability are the key requirements.

Graphs visually display trends well, but the underlying value of the data points can be lost. Sometimes this deficiency can be adequately addressed by showing the data values. Often, it is helpful to display the value and time period of the greatest and/or least figure in a data series. This offsets the tendency to lose actual values in trend graphing The average value of a data set can be useful. See these values in Figure 14.2. Spreadsheets can extract such information from any group of numbers by the use of functions. Functions are merely prepackaged equations and procedures that you plug values (or the range of cells in which the data series resides) into. Note the examples of underlying functions displayed.

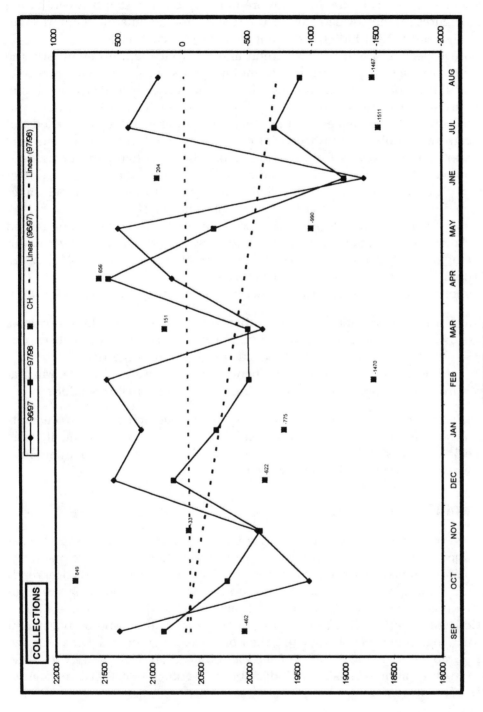

FIGURE 14.3

Eventually, you would pare down what information is displayed. For example, the figures of the combined periods are not helpful. As a step between having these figures present (which clutters the report) and eliminating them, you can have the spreadsheet hide the content of those particular cells.

Spreadsheets can also produce trend lines on your graph to emphasize the direction a data series is going. In fact, multiple types of trend lines are available. Linear regression produces straight lines that are easier to understand. Trend lines are statistical analysis techniques, but the computer does all the work and merely presents the requested line. Again, the desired values are called out beneath the graph. Spreadsheets can calculate trends from a data series and extrapolate the values for future periods. Since the exact figure can be used for planning, calculate these using another function. Note that the spreadsheet doesn't use the months per se to calculate this value. It uses the number values assigned to the rows as seen at the far end of Table 14.3(c).

How you define the underlying data series obviously affects the resulting trend line. Smoothing techniques can produce too many scenarios. If multiple scenarios are employed, keep the type of trend line constant and use the last 24 months, 12 months, and 6 months as your data series.

Simultaneously, your data can be used to model "what if" scenarios:

1.   If I improved patient service so that the number of established patients rises 10% over the next year, what will that mean in terms of actual collections? These are easy to generate but are outside the scope of this article.

2.   If I decrease the average length between routine exams 5%, what will that mean in terms of patient flow (for staffing issues) and actual collections?

These scenarios are great motivators, as very small, easily achieved improvements can mean thousands of dollars available for practitioner salary annually. The large financial base of your practice leverages the financial rewards of these small improvements dramatically in your favor.

How to Use Trend Graphs

Here's an example of how to use trend graphs. The discussion here is reactive, as most new clients do not see an accountant until conditions deteriorate markedly. Regular use of managerial reports by the practitioner often detect practice trends earlier, allowing proactive institution of preventive and/or stabilizing strategies to be implemented. Earlier prevention is always better than later correction.

Collections are the first thing practitioners, at least those who do not have a regular, logical method of evaluating their practice, see going bad. Let's examine the possible underlying etiology of such an observation. Note that by the time such an observation is made, clear indications of eventual collection deterioration have been present a for a long time.

Verify the Problem (Figure 14.3)

The trend analysis graph of collections shows a decrease this year compared to last year. Adding trend lines to the two primary data series shows a stable, albeit erratic, collection trend during the 12 months in the 96/97 period. The trend line for 97/98 has a negative slope. The change in November and February of this year's time periods bucks the historical trend by dropping instead of rising. Absolute collections have decreased in 8 months of the 12 during 97/98. A valid problem exists and warrants investigation and action.

Quantify the Problem

Collections are down $5,470 (2.21%) in the past 12 months, compared to the prior 12 months. Two percent is about the usual level at which a financial constraint is felt in the checkbook. If this negative trend continues, collections will be about $10,000 in 98/99 over 97/98. Since many practice expenses are fixed, the money left over for practitioner salary or perks, after expenses, is even more adversely affected than collections themselves.

Check the Parameters That Monitor the Collection Process (Figure 14.4)

The collection graph itself shows large rises and drops between months, probably more than mere seasonality would account for. The amount of patient/insurance refunds is consistently low, often literally zero, implying not enough money is being collected up front. It is better is to use a stamp to send back money you already have than to expend resources chasing money you may never get. Also note that bad debt and contractual write-off is erratic, implying inconsistent collections administration.

   Conclusions: billing and accounts receivable administration is not consistent or optimal.

Number of Patients Seen (Figures 14.5 and 14.6)

Gross fees or retail sales must occur before any collections take place. Gross fees arise from charges or sales from providing services or goods to new and existing patients. In this case:

   1.   The trend line superimposed on the graph of new patients seen during this 12-month period shows a modest improvement.
   2.   The trend line superimposed on the graph of established patients shows almost no change.
   3.   The graph of the total number of patients seen shows results similar to the new patient graph previously discussed. The graph concerning the mix of new patients and established patients, shows an increase in the ratio of new patients seen compared to established patients, and conversely, a decrease in the percentage of established patients seen compared to new patients.

   Conclusions: collections are down despite more total patients being seen. The retention rate of new patients is slipping and the attrition rate of new patients is increasing.

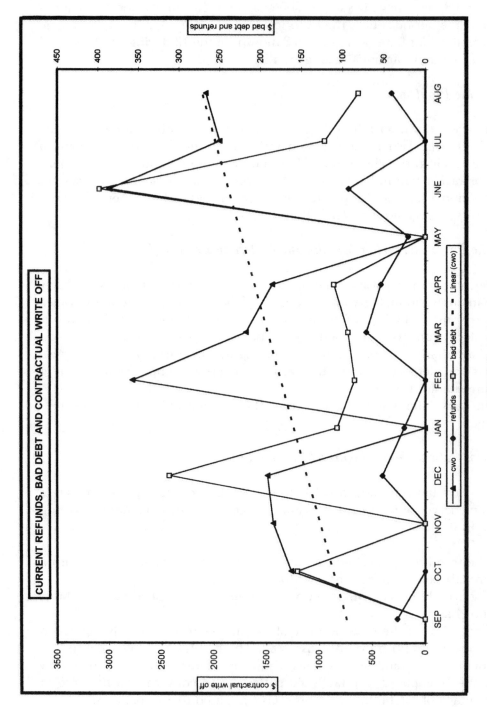

FIGURE 14.4

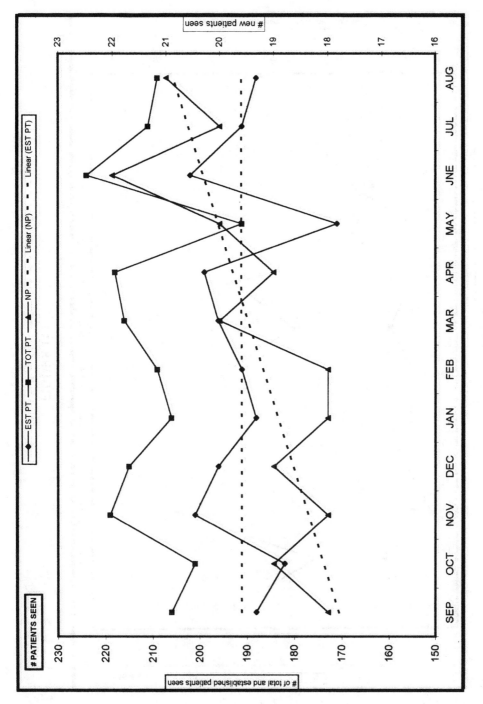

FIGURE 14.5

245

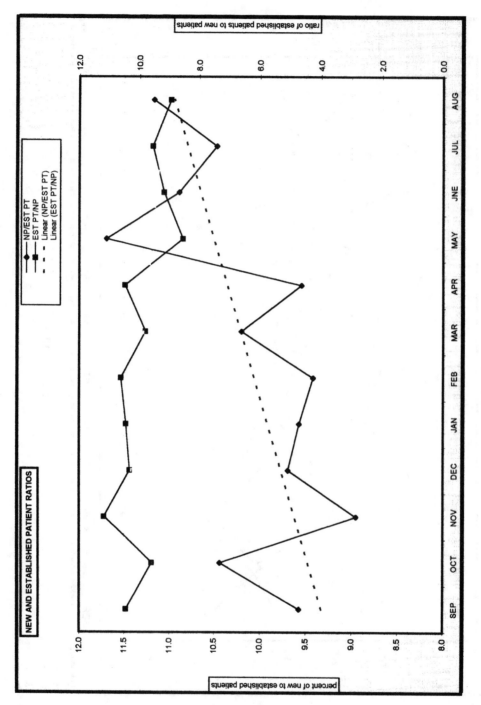

FIGURE 14.6

Gross Fees and Sales Generated per Patient (Figure 14.7)

Gross fees generated per new patient and established patient appear stable, with a very modest upward trend despite no internal fee schedule increases. Gross retail sales per anything are down somewhat. This alone accounts for about 20% of the collections drop. Retail sales must be revitalized, or money from sales is being pocketed.

1. Are all legitimate fees making it to the billing department?

Currently, no way to know for sure. Since gross fees are stable and even improved, this does not seem to be a problem. Check for internal controls on this when the billing and collection processes are reviewed. Back office staff should routinely check that all services they observe being rendered are recorded.

2. Are all fees at the front desk being accounted for?

Are some claims being misplaced before submitting? Currently, there is no way to know for sure. However, superbills are not sequentially numbered and are not reconciled to the appointment book.

3. What is the contractual write-off doing?

The contractual write-off graph (Figure 14.4) has a progressively positive trend. In addition, it appears jagged and irregular. This appears to account for over half of the noted collections drop.

4. How is the accounts receivable turnaround time doing?

This is not currently being tracked. A quick before-and-after calculation shows an increase of about 4 days over the past 12 months. Either insurance companies are paying more slowly or the practice is filing on a less timely basis.

5. How is the bad debt doing?

This is clearly erratic but absolutely is historically appropriate. In the aggregate, this was $1,466 in the past 12 months. Not too bad, but a little proactive effort and organization should recoup much of this. Why not collect more of what you earned?

6. Are the collections making it to the bank?

Probably, but this currently relies on the honesty of staff members.

Four problem areas were detected in the investigation:

1. Increased contractual write-off
2. Decreased retail sales
3. Erratic billing and collection procedures
4. Decreased patient retention

Increased Contractual Write-off

The largest detriment in this practice is the increased contractual write-off with probable limitation on scope or frequency of reimbursable services. Today you must often see more patients in less time to keep your income stable. True but a bit pessimistic. Good data help to predict what you need to keep your practice lucrative. Streamlined patient flow and additional marketing will keep you "even."

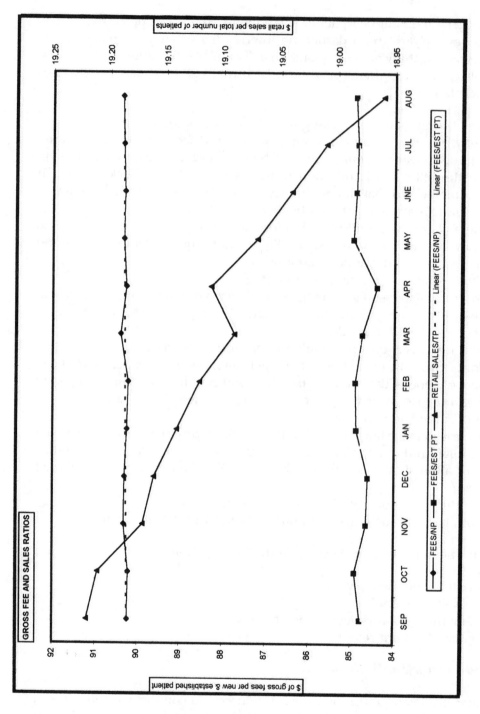

FIGURE 14.7

Investigate which providers are the most restrictive. Usually it is just a few third parties. Sometimes these can be shamed into changing policy with a concerted effort of multiple patients and practitioners. Another alternative is to expand your patient base in other areas and avoid these companies. In any geographic area, one provider overcomes all these barriers and becomes the practice of choice. It might as well be you.

Decreased Retail Sales

Check out you competitors. Are you offering everything you can to your clientele? Are your sales people knowledgeable? Is there a marketing niche you can fill? Is there a sales course offered at the local university's business or graduate school? Even if your competitors do have the same high-tech items, you're still on the cutting edge in the patient's perception if they hear or see it from you first.

Does the clinical side of the practice help promote retail sales or is it a "touchy" subject? There is no reason your retail department cannot compete with major chains, especially with the clinical gateway to it. Price is not the only benchmark consumers base purchasing decisions on.

Erratic Billing and Collection Procedures

Further examination of the collections and billing process shows no clear practice guideline for this vital function. Many other practices evolve over time reactively and are not what the practitioner would have proactively defined as ideal. Fair and consistent written internal policies make life easier for everyone.

Read the last sentence again. Subsequent random checks verify compliance. In this case, the doctor often doesn't write the superbill. This information is sometimes hard to reconstruct secondary to the elapsed time. Greater cooperation of the doctor in filling out the superbills, greater cooperation of the doctor in allowing the staff time to clarify such matters, and better fee training of the back office staff, with instruction and training to verify that each observed service is on the superbill, will eliminate most of those problems.

If superbills are sequentially numbered, the billing software can report any missing ones. A sequential stamper is a cheap, cost-effective investment. Checking the superbills against the appointment book on a daily basis would help accomplish the same thing.

A receptionist well trained in billing often makes his or her salary by catching fees he or she suspects should be on the chart. This is a good thing to institute as a check point. Good interstaff communication allows the receptionist to verify any suspicions without disturbing the doctor. The front desk rarely collects money from clinical patients in the belief it will be received after the insurance pays. Establish a fair co-payment policy by knowing what each insurance company will likely pay and collect the balance up front. Done properly, within fair limits, patients accept this as a sound business practice.

Office personnel sequester charts pending additional documentation before submitting them to billing. Solution: the entire chart is not always needed for billing, or a list of expected documentation is kept instead of making notes on each chart. Claims submission now occurs every other Thursday for claims through Wednesday morning. A better procedure is a written guideline for submitting all of last week's claims the following Tuesday (or on your day off). Simultaneously, staff meetings point out how and where claims get waylaid and subsequently can then be instituted. This may be as simple as making the staff aware of how their actions affect each other.

Incoming payments are posted sporadically. Establish a fair plan and stick to it. Daily is best. Insurance write-offs are posted appropriately, but patient billing occurs every other Thursday, so some patient bills go out 2 weeks late. Received payment erodes parabolically with elapsed time.

Collection reminders are done once a month, and then with a 2-week grace period. Thus, some patients are not reminded until 6 weeks after they receive a bill and perhaps 10 weeks after service has been rendered. Once a week is better.

No collection policy on bad debt exists. It is better to proactively establish a fair collection policy than deal with each case independently when emotions may run hot. Timing and number of written or phone contacts is established with guidelines on when to write off, go to small claims court, get a writ of execution, and so on. A check of associated retail sale expenses reveals that no major embezzlement is occurring. It's said that opportunity is the greatest promoter of dishonesty. Would you walk by an unguarded, open bank vault day after day if your child needed expensive medical treatment you could not otherwise afford? A proactive system that assures the staff that they will not be suspected of stealing.

Decreasing Patient Retention

The decrease in the percentage of returning patients is critical. Some of this may be secondary to third-party payment allowances. If such constraints are detrimental to the patient's well-being, they can be educated and encouraged to return at their own expense. Even one additional established patient visit per week means an extra 50, times whatever your average fee is per visit, dollars per year.

Even where there is excessive intra- and interprofessional competition, third-party restriction on payments, a less than optimal location, and the like, a practice can retain patients by providing service where patient perceptions exceed their expectations. This is internal marketing, the most cost-effective and dignified way to promote the practice. In most cases internal marketing, positive or detrimental, affects the patient's perceptions despite equal clinical results. Kindness, empathy, improved staff training, and responsiveness can make your practice seem like the best choice to a certain percentage of patients. These patients provide more income, actively market for you, and create a more pleasant, positive environment. Remember, internal marketing goes on constantly whether you're aware of it or not. Just structure the environment so that positively perceived outcomes occur regularly and place safeguards to prevent negative perceptions from occurring, at least most of the time.

Your practice needs hands-on management. A managerial report is a good tool for managing your practice in a time-efficient manner. Trend graph analysis is a valuable component of a practice's managerial report. It can help spot both negative and positive trends earlier than they would otherwise become apparent. Trend graph analysis helps with the differential diagnosis of the underlying etiology behind such trends so that preventive or supportive strategies can be implemented.

HOW TO WASTE MONEY

1. Have no consistent billing policy. Design appropriate controls and implement monitoring so that all services get billed, bills are accurate, bills are sent in a timely fashion, and accounts receivable gets checked for potential problems regularly.

2. Have no consistent collections policy. Your chances of getting paid erode progressively with time. Collect more cash up front. Don't be afraid to institute phone reminders of past due balances. Become familiar with your county's small claims process, especially the techniques available (e.g., writ of execution, to have the sheriff seize property for you).

3. Have no internal controls. Proper controls help ensure that good things happen consistently and minimize chances of bad things, like embezzlement, happening.

4. Bounce checks. Each incident can cost up to $50 in bank and vendor fees along with time and stress to remedy the situation, more if attorneys get involved. Criminal charges against you are also possible. Use an electronic check program like Quicken, get on-line service that helps you calculate the checking balance daily, and arrange with the bank to set up overdraft protection at a reasonable cost.

5. Run up a lot of employee overtime. Have a reasonable schedule that prevents you from paying time and a half whenever possible.

6. Fail to claim all legitimate deductions for tax purposes. Let's say you spend $1,000 a year out of your own pocket on legitimate business meal expenses instead of running these through the clinic. Remember, meal expenses are only 50% deductible, making this a dramatic example. Maybe you think the relatively small amount of each meal is too trivial to track, or the hassle of tracking meals is too cumbersome. At your marginal tax rate, plus payroll taxes, the clinic has to pay more than $1,500 up front for you to net the $1,000. It gets this extra $500 back in tax savings eventually. If the practice pays directly, it only costs $1,000 up front and produces a $500 deduction (half the cost of the meals), making the eventual cost around $750. Let Uncle Sam pick up the tab occasionally.

7. Don't have the most advantageous business entity for the practice. This decision depends on the state you practice in, the goals of the clinic, and your own personal tax position. For example, if the practice needs to save up money for a down payment on a building, it may make more sense to be a C corporation than an S corporation. Although the C corporation pays "double taxes," it proba-

bly does so at a lower rate than the marginal tax rate of the practitioner to whom this money would flow with an S corporation.

    8.   Don't make timely payroll and unemployment tax deposits. Cascading penalties on late 941 payments start a vicious cycle with the IRS, often increasing eventual cost 15% or more, excluding additional accounting fees. The government feels you are holding employees' money in trust and that not depositing it is criminal embezzlement. Imagine that.

    9.   Don't pay off the practice's credit card bills in full each month. This starts an expensive cycle of paying expensive interest on expensive interest. Credit cards are a great tool, but abuse of them costs big money.

    10.   Pay vendors late. Most vendors charge 18% interest on unpaid balances. A habit of late payments inevitably makes itself known in your Dunn and Bradstreet report and erodes credit.

    11.   Don't take advantage of vendors "early pay" discounts. A 2% discount, even at 30-day net terms, is a substantial reward for having adequate cash flow and paying responsibly.

    12.   Don't do retirement planning, estate planning, or overall general tax planning. Proactive planning often nets significant legal tax savings.

WHAT YOUR ACCOUNTANT CAN DO FOR YOU

Your financial accountant can do more than just compile your bookkeeping into a tax format. For someone who works to live, instead of living to work, health care practitioners have more power to control their own destiny than most of America. Many people work as hard as they can and adjust their lifestyle accordingly: life happens to them. Instead, try imagining what you want life to be like at a certain point in the future. I want a house in X neighborhood, with a full recording studio and indoor/outdoor pool, vacation three weeks a year, etc. If you can't dream it, it probably won't happen. Proactive planning sometimes makes such dreams more affordable too. Have your accountant help you "back in" to what your practice has to be doing to support that lifestyle. This will probably result in a spreadsheet that you can play "what if" scenarios with. Also consider asking about the following:

    1.   Your current business entity, S or C corporation, for the practice and the state you live in. C corporation, for example, is the most advantageous for your practice. The answer depends or your long-range plans.

    2.   Taking all the legal deductions allowable, professional and personal. It is surprisingly common for people to underclaim deductions. Remember, most accountants only look for "red flags," expenses that are present but shouldn't be. They may not think about the converse: what is not there but should be.

    3.   Proactive tax planning. This is not the same as retroactive restructuring in March.

    4.   Performing a breakeven analysis before completing a major purchase.

    5.   Different ways to finance major purposes. Issues include cash flow, immediate tax ramifications, and long-term tax implications.

6.   Setting up a cash flow projection system that you can perform yourself on a regular basis.

BANKERS VERSUS MEDICAL PRACTITIONERS: A CASE OF PERSPECTIVE

Consider a banker evaluating you and your practice for a loan. Bankers sometimes get a bad reputation. Aphorisms like, "banks won't loan money unless you don't need it," typify this perception. Bankers are different from practitioners in the following ways:

1.   Bankers are well trained financially; practitioners usually are not. In fact, medical professionals have earned the stigma of being poor businesspeople by historically overpaying for products and services. Some of us are even disdainful about the business aspects of the practice. Anticipate this perception by the banker. A bit of homework on the practitioner's part, along with prudent use of an accountant or business manager, can ameliorate this potential disadvantage.

2.   Bankers tolerate risk less than the average practitioner does. This stems from the practitioner's belief in his own intangible strengths, like skill and dedication, along with the inherent risk in entrepreneurship.

3.   Bankers want to cover their assets, of course, but don't really want a loan going bad. Conversely, a practitioner may feel that it is no concern of the banker's how a loan is handled, since the underlying collateral more than covers the loan should adverse conditions ensue. A bad loan signifies poor judgment and makes the banker look bad to his or her superiors. Second, bankers are generally not in the business of seizing collateral, like medical equipment, and trying to resell it. Red tape makes this a hassle while limiting their profit. They much prefer that you live up to the loan agreement.

4.   Bankers generally do not understand the current trends and dynamics of your profession. Bankers have to justify their decisions to superiors. Educating them on what it is you do and the business environment you do it in helps them "sell" a loan to the bank.

Now, consider your banker's reaction after you improve practice performance by 1% through trend analysis, in three key parameters; gross fees, contractual write-offs, and overhead expenses. This example uses a practice with $500,000 per year of gross fees, a 20% contractual write-off rate, 3% of bad debt, and 70% of overhead. The money available for pretax practitioner salary is $116,400:

80% (100% minus the 20% of contractual write-off) of 500,000 in gross fees is $400,000.

97% (100% minus the 3% of bad debt) of 400,000 is $388,000.

30% (100% minus the 70% of overhead) of 388,000 is $116,400.

The financial leverage inherent in a practice makes even small improvements in performance yield dramatic bottom-line or "in pocket" results. Table 14.1

shows that cutting overhead 1% nets the practitioner an extra annual $3,880 of potential salary. Likewise, decreasing bad debt 1% yields $1,200. A simultaneous 1% improvement in both parameters yields $5,120, all for the same amount of patient care with no additional malpractice liability.

CONCLUSION

The appropriate use of the financial ratios and managerial accounting techniques outlined in this chapter are not familiar to most medical practitioners today. They will become more important in the future, as physician-executives or physician-owners seek to achieve maximum profits and economic efficiencies from their ongoing medical practice operations.

READINGS AND REFERENCES

Bernstein, L. A. *Financial statement analysis theory: Applications and interpretations.* Homewood, IL: Dow-Jones-Irwin, 1988.

Foster, G. *Financial statements.* Cincinnati: Southwestern Publishing Co., 1986.

Gibson, C. *Financial statement analysis.* Cincinnati: Southwestern Publishing Co., 1992.

Marcinko, D. E. Financial analysis in the medical practice. In Marcinko, D. E. (Ed.): *Profit maximization and reimbursement.* Columbus, OH: Anadem Publications, 1998.

Renshaw, E. *The practical forecaster's almanac.* Homewood, IL: Business One, 1992.

## CHAPTER 15

Creating Equity Value in Your Practice

Effective Strategies in the Era of Mergers and Acquisitions

David Edward Marcinko

> Numbers, numbers, numbers; soon most medical practices will be acquired, merged, organized and consolidated by the financial numbers.
>
> —Barry K. Smith, health care consultant

While most physicians have been helping their patients achieve physical health, many have ignored their own financial health. Even if you are practicing good medicine and making money, you may not be building equity into your practice's *strategic business unit* (SBU).

There are many medical practitioners out there (800,000 domestic MD/DOs), about 30% too many on an absolute basis, or mal-distributed on a relative basis; which means hyper-competition. The surprising fact is how a minority of small group practices, control the vast majority of assets, as well as the majority of medical managed care contracts. This trend will undoubtedly continue as the process of consolidation takes place in the profession. The clear message is that you are going to have to build value into the business unit of your practice, just to compete.

The good news is that there is an almost geometric growth potential possible for doctors in the new millennium, but competition is going to come from a variety of known, and unknown, fronts. As a consequence, doctors are going to need (1) executive management skills, (2) information systems technology (IST) with regional partners, and a (3) significant amount of capital resources in order to succeed.

IS YOUR PRACTICE WORTH ACQUIRING OR MERGING?

How do you recapture your youthful dreams of practice success and build value into your business? It is not going to come from just adding more managed care patients, shifting your markets or demographics, or specializing in surgery or sports medicine. You may already be doing that, and that's very good. The real paradigm shift however, will come from creating value inside your SBU. You do that by making your business worth buying to someone else. In other words, a group "brand" identity, rather than individual identify, is the hallmark of increased practice value in the future.

In fact, most authorities opine that in today's medical marketplace, bigger is better and size matters. We are now in an environment of large group practices, where cache' value matters, not individual MD or practitioner accomplishment. Hot medical groups; not individual doctors will flourish going forward. Even if you are a young practitioner and not interested in merging your practice, you still want to build it up as if you were going to sell it at some point in the future, because this strategy will maximize your SBU's value. The secret is to create the best medical systems around. Systems not only make your practice profitable and build value but also do right by your personal, corporate, or private investors.

In the past, most doctors only worried about the patient since the idea was to stay focused on their needs, and success was sure to follow. But to remain competitive today, you are going to have to think of both your bankers, and yourself. Absent a business degree and/or gobs of money, what is needed is a quick and easy template to follow. Moreover, if you wanted to sell your SBU today, could you? Do you know how much it is worth in today's market? Do you have transferable systems in place?

Obviously, there is risk when a corporate merger acquires a practice. Still, there is a strong parallel between the corporate and private side of medical practice. Both sides are patient-oriented, revenue-focused, and entrepreneurial in nature, but they do have significant differences in valuing their business models.

WHAT DETERMINES PRACTICE EQUITY?

There is no magic rule of thumb to build equity into your practice; its just not that simple. However, the following helpful suggestions, are offered regardless of the practitioner's specialty or degree designation.

1. *Maintain good financial records,* including all three consolidated financial statements, according to FASB (Financial Accounting Standard Board) rules: (1) balance sheet, (2) statement of cash flows, and (3) net income statement (profit and loss statement). Keep them for at least 3 years. There is nothing that will kill the sales of a practice quicker than not having these important documents. Consultants are often amazed if 1 in 10 doctors can produce even simple monthly reports of what they've budgeted, what was actually spent, or what was at variance. CPA intervention is vital in this regard.

2. *Monitor key financial ratios,* such as profitability ratios, creditor ratios, and long-term debt management ratios:

Profitability ratios include profit margin, return on assets ratio (net income + [interest expense × 1 (1-tax rate)], fixed/total assets utilization ratio (gross charges/net fixed practice assets), and fixed assets/net worth ratio.

Creditor (solvency) ratios include working capital ratio (excess of current assets over current liabilities), current ratio (current assets/current liabilities), acid test ("quick") ratio (current ratio net of inventory), accounts receivable (AR) turnover ratio (noncash revenue/average AR balance), and the current liabilities to net worth ratio (current liabilities/equity).

Long-term debt management ratios include total debt to total assets ratio, total liability to net worth ratio, times interest earned ratio (net operating income/ interest expense) and the debt to equity ratio (assets provided by creditors per owner assets). Other considerations include managed care organization (MCO) contracts under management and free cash flow. Try to benchmark them with other comparable practices and monitor them at least quarterly. Intervene immediately when necessary.

3. *Be profitable:* you are in practice not only to help your patients but also to make money. No one is going to buy a dying practice for more than a few pennies on the dollar, and you can't help anyone if you are not in business. Charity work is fine as long as you realize that it is pro bono. Think long-term profits versus short-term transactions. Also remember that if you sell your practice to a physician practice management corporation (PPMC), for example, you are still going to be expected to work hard, perhaps as hard as though you never sold it in the first place. Be prepared for this eventuality. A practice sale, merger, or acquisition is simply not retirement.

Additionally, large medical groups have certain advantages over solo or independent group practices. These include access to capital, avoidance of "vendor" status, elimination of redundancy, control, and potential physician ownership in an organization larger than the sum of its individual practices. Financial managers and other corporate health care professionals possess the business acumen lacked by most physicians. Philosophically, the larger groups often separate the "individual current income" approach to wealth building, from the "organizational future growth" approach by focusing on maximizing equity value, by retaining capital and generating a return. This *value differential* is illustrated in Table 15.1.

4. *Have a buy/sell agreement* because it spells out the manner in which a physician can buy into the practice and how the practice will buy out an owner. Every group practice should have it reviewed once every 1–2 years since the advent of health care reform. Medicare cuts and the resource-based relative value scale (RBRVS) payment system are just a few of the changes that have had an impact on these agreements. Typically, buy/sell agreements will cover such topics as appraisal and valuation methods, accounts receivable equalization, excess earnings (profits) distribution, buy in/out time span, interest rate ranges, goodwill rates, tax deductibility of buyout payments, and a host of other issues important to the involved principals.

TABLE 15.1   Value Differential

End of Year 5	OBJECTIVE	
	Individual Wealth	Group Wealth
Present value compensation (1)	$500	$500
Present value group equity	1000 (1,2)	6200 (1,3)
Total value	$1500	$6700
Differential value	$1500	$5200

Assumptions: (1) 10% discount rate, (2) Net book value, (3) 1X revenues.

5.   As we have seen, the *corporation status* of a medical practice is a legal entity and is important for liability reduction purposes. It is not available to the physician sole proprietor or general partnership, as defined below:

Sole proprietor: This business form eliminates corporate taxes, as income is taxed only at the shareholder level. The sole proprietor physician, however, is personally responsible for all debts and liabilities of the medical practice. Capital may be difficult to raise.

General partnership: Enjoy the advantages of establishment ease, management flexibility, and "pass through" tax treatment. On the other hand, partnerships have the disadvantage that each partner has unlimited personal liability for the other partners' liabilities, debts, and malpractice obligations.

S Corporation: Recent tax law changes have made some S corporations eligible for employee stock ownership plans, which is a change from past policies. Certain restrictions, however, limit the eligibility of this corporation to 35 shareholders. Liability avoidance is available in this corporate entity.

Professional corporation: This business entity has limited liability that is not transferable to nonprofessional entities. It may be either an S or C corporation.

C corporation: A publicly traded company, such as a PPMC, has to be a C corporation and will have too many shareholders (> 35 doctors) to qualify as an S corporation. The four characteristics that define a corporation are (1) centralized management (less than all doctor owners have decision-making authority), (2) transferability of ownership (substitution through assignment, gift, or sale), (3) limited liability (no personal responsibility), and (4) continuity of life (notwithstanding certain "trigger events" such as retirement, bankruptcy, and/or death of the owner). Capital is easier to raise under this business structure.

Limited liability corporation/partnership: LLCs, LLPs, and limited partnerships are cousins of the S corporation that combine the corporate and partnership forms of business, limit partner liability, are size neutral, and as flow-through entities avoid the burden of double corporate taxation. Moreover, if they are properly structured to have two or fewer of the four corporate characteristics, they will be taxed like a partnership and avoid corporate taxation. Cautious physicians recognize the relative scarcity of case law to help doctors judge how the law will be applied through established legal principles to these new business entities.

Tax consequences are important considerations because there are many creative strategies doctors can use to minimize state and local taxes. For example, a C corporation is its own taxpaying entity, as opposed to an elected S corporation, in which net earnings are passed directly to the owner shareholder(s) (conduit). When an owner dies, the C practice corporation may have to pay an unexpected AMT (alternative minimum tax). As a way to avoid the AMT, the practice may wish to alter its officer's life insurance into the form of a cross-purchase agreement. In this case, the owners have life insurance on each other, and the agreement provides that, should an owner die, the other owners have the right to acquire his or her shares.

6. *Develop a forward-thinking valuation business plan:* all MDs should plan to sell their practices at some point in the future, whether to retire or to merge with or acquire another practice. By understanding how practices are valued and designing sales value into your SBU, you can create tremendous value for yourself. For example, according to IRS guidelines, the three most common methods of practice valuation are (a) discounted cash flow analysis (DCFA), (b) the multiplier (comparable sales) method, and (c) the replacement cost method (RCM).

Discounted cash flow analysis: The DCFA, or income method, is where a dollar's present value today is discounted by some factor to estimate its future value. DCFA is used to establish the present value of these future practice cash flows, using mutually agreed upon financial assumptions, such as time frame, interest rates (discount rate), lump sums, periodicity (annuitization), and equality or inequality of actual funds received.

The discount rate depends on prevailing interest rates and risk factors (more risk means a larger discount). For a physician thinking about a capital partner, sale, or merger, the appropriate rate in 1999 might be between 10% and 18%, as calculated in Table 15.2.

To compute the present value of future cash flows, the net income (profit-and-loss sheet normalization) statement must be analyzed to recast it, if necessary, to eliminate expenses not related to running the practice (i.e., payroll salary expense for absent wife-secretary), project future after-tax cash flow, and develop a rate of return, as indicated above.

The second part of this economic model is to calculate the present value of future net income without merging with the capital partner (large group, hospital,

TABLE 15.2 Family Practice Discount Rate

Risk Factors	Rate Impact
Risk free rate (treasuries/CDs)	6.00%
Business risk rate (specialty)	3.00%
Competition risk	3.00%
Medicare/Medicaid risk	2.00%
Management risk	2.00%
Commercial managed care risk	1.00%
Capitalization rate	17.00%

venture capitalist, PPMC, etc.) and remaining independent. In some cases, staying independent requires the application of a higher rate because it may be a more risky endeavor. Therefore, the discount rate might even be higher, likely in the range of 15%–25%. The difference between the present value of the baseline scenario and what can be expected from taking a capital partner is the best measure of economic consequences to physicians and medical groups.

Replacement cost method: The RCM seeks to replace tangible assets or certain intangible assets (workforce and patient records) at current or fair market value prices. It assumes that a prudent buyer will pay no more for an existing practice than the cost of creating a similar new practice. It merely represents the actual cash value (ACV) of the practice, less its liabilities, plus the depreciated value of those assets; expressed mathematically by the equation RCM = ACV + depreciation. In other words, it is the cost to reproduce or replace appraised property less allowances for deterioration or functional or economic obsolescence. This method is most applicable in cases of land ownership and improvements (i.e., physician medical building ownership), special-purpose buildings (i.e., ambulatory surgery centers), and other special instruments. The approach is static and provides only a snapshot of the value of a practice as of a certain date. It does not take into account attributed *goodwill* and ignores your practice's past and future ability to generate income.

Alternatively, the cost method for the "ongoing concern" practice may be the cost avoided by not having to start a practice from scratch and grow its operation to a breakeven point. For example, the going concern value is inclusive of all practice assets as shown in Table 15.3.

Thus, this fair market value cost approach is simply the estimated amount at which the practice might be expected to be exchanged between a willing buyer and a willing seller, neither being under a compulsion to buy or sell and each having reasonable knowledge of all relevant facts. Often, both the cost and income methods are used to appraise a practice and serve as a cross-reference to develop a valuation range rather than specific price.

Example: A family practice was evaluated by using the two methods just discussed, and the results are given below: At what price should the practice sell?

DCFA method: valuated @ $500,000

Replacement cost method: valuated @ $350,000

TABLE 15.3   Practice Going Concern Value

	$$$$
Working capital (current assets less current liabilities)	W
Tangible assets	X
Intangible assets	Y
Goodwill	Z
Total (going concern value)	WXYZ

Using the cost method of appraisal, one would expect that a book value of $350,000 is at the bottom of the market price range for this medical practice since goodwill and ongoing concern estimates were not considered. On the other hand, the DCFA method of analysis did consider these factors. Therefore, the price range of the practice would be $350,000–500,000, but $450,000 or so might be a more reasonable number to consider in a sales situation.

Multiplier (comparable) sales: Although DCFA is probably the most precise method of practice valuation today, the comparable sales method, where gross revenues, net earnings before income tax, depreciation, and amortization (EBITDA) or net profits are multiplied by some established industrial norm, may occasionally be used.

The gross revenue multiplier is most appropriate for a market share gaining strategy, while an EBITDA multiplier might be generally more reliable if earnings are an important concern. A net profit multiplier is probably most unreliable since many income tax machinations are possible to alter this number.

Unfortunately, this multiplier market approach is also difficult to use because of the limitation of data relative to similar practice sales and the lack of full transparency in private business transactions. Key information that might drive valuations and market price include fee schedules, payer mix, cost structures, physician compensation, collection rates, productivity, and prospects for future practice growth. Thus, the use of the comparable method is limited by the constraint of information on practices sold.

Above all, realize that according to Dr. Carl M. Caplan, MBA, "the value of a medical practice today is not a function of its gross revenues, but of net income; and that net income applies more to the purchaser's ability to perform rather than the seller's." In addition, it is not unusual for a practice sold on the open market to experience some attrition of patients and managed care plans upon the change of ownership.

7. *Build a transferable patient base.* This is increasingly more difficult with all of the managed care contracting today, but it still can be done. If you build a system that revolves around either a single or a few MCO contract(s) or even yourself or another key person, it is difficult to transfer the business to someone else. Also, if you project yourself as the medical guru for your area, patients will have a hard time accepting a new doctor, MSO, or PPMC business organization. By focusing on something larger than yourself, such as group practice, you will begin to develop a business that others can operate easily.

8. *Use proper management information systems* (computer hardware, software, and peripherals) without spending too much money on information technology gadgetry. You do not necessarily have to become an early adopter of the newest or untested information technology systems, but do become an adopter of mature products nevertheless.

9. Absent a covenant not to compete, if a physician leaves the practice and immediately competes against it, the departing physician will probably take revenue away from the original practice and potentially decrease its value significantly and abruptly. Therefore, such a covenant should specify the procedures to follow should a departure occur. For example, the covenant may provide there be either

a time bomb, distance bomb, or buyout discount in the case of a departing partner, precluding the new practice or practitioner from achieving a monetary gain. Although covenants may have many different inclusions, such contracts depend on the laws of the state in which the practice is located. Moreover, many believe that the covenant is not worth the time and money necessary to enforce it and that its existence will add equity value to the existing practice, to the benefit of the remaining practitioners.

10. *Maintain services, responsiveness, and consistency with your patients, referring doctors, fellow MDs, and supply vendors.* This is critical; if you do not build strong relationships with these local players, premium value just isn't there because a new doctor will not be able to rely on those established relationships going forward.

11. *Identify the right buyer,* be it another MD, a larger group practice, or a PPMC. Make sure that the buyer has the necessary capital and that you are not taking all of the risks in the transaction. You want to risk financial share with the buyer and have faith that he or she can pull off the sale. You also want a good, intangible, heuristic match, since your life blood probably went into building the practice and you should want it to flourish going forward.

12. In addition to selling or buying a practice, it is often important to know its value—during your lifetime or at death—when making a gift ($10,000 individual annual exclusion and $20,000 tax free with spouse) of your practice interest, planning your estate, or for other practice succession needs, whether to physician offspring or to practice outsiders. If you don't know its value, and the IRS determines its fair market value to be higher than the value set under your buy/ sell agreement, for example, your estate could be required to pay estate taxes (37%–55%) on an amount of money never received, leaving much less to your perhaps disgruntled heirs. Gifting is usually advantageous for practices that are not yet highly appreciated but could grow in value over time. For example, if you make a gift of your entire $1 million in practice interest in 1998, you owe a gift tax of $375,000, the amount over your lifetime combined gift/estate tax exemption. If you procrastinate a decade, until the practice has grown to $2 million, you will face gift taxes on $1 million (the amount over the lifetime exemption in the year 2006).

Furthermore, minority stake discounts in a practice may be possible. Suppose your practice is worth $1 million with 100 shares of stock. A pro rata value of each share would be $10,000. But by applying a 30% minority discount, you and your spouse might be able to give each of your four children 2.86 shares valued at $7,000 without triggering gift taxes, rather than two shares valued at $10,000 per share. In this case, although the dollar value of the gift is $20,000 in each case, your children would receive a greater ownership interest if the share values are discounted. Beware of restrictive covenants that mandate transfer only to physician offspring.

13. *Assist the transfer,* but don't think you can sell your practice in a couple of months. The average time is about 1–2 years. So if you become sick or disabled, you may lose your practice or have to sell it for a fraction of its value. Make sure you have an ample capital surplus during the sales period, with contingency plan and timetable if you can't sell. If you provide owner financing to the buyer, make

sure that you purchase an insurance policy on his or her life. After retirement, you probably won't want to suddenly return to practice if your income stream abruptly stops upon the premature death of the buyer.

14. *Finally, get professional assistance* if you can't or do not want to go it alone. Align yourself with a trusted MBA, CPA, CFP, JD, MHA, CMA, investment advisor, or practice management (specialty-specific) firm or consider selling out to a larger group in order to create an exit strategy or to continue practicing as a corporate employee.

Fortunately, the Medical Group Management Association's (MGMA) "Top Ten Super Search Packets" offer the following informational compendiums for about $55 (members and affiliates), plus shipping and handling charges; (800) 608-5602 or (303) 397-7888. All can help you add value to your practice in an era of mergers an acquisitions.

Medicare Corporate Compliance Plans (No. 5060).

Income Distribution (No. 1007).

Everything You Wanted to Know about RBRVS (No. 4999).

Physician Incentive Plans (No. 4893).

Physician Productivity (No. 2101).

Cost Accounting (No. 4996).

Nurse Practitioners and Physician Assistants (No. 2685).

Buying, Selling and Valuing a Practice (No. 1018).

Management Service Organizations: MSOs (No. 4874).

Starting a Telephone Triage Program (No. 4992).

CONCLUSION

Contemporary physicians have a huge opportunity to build equity value into their medical practice—for sale, merger, or consolidation. Whether or not this becomes a reality, by focusing on creating maximum value as if a transaction were possible, physicians can design and modify their SBUs to enhance their value and achieve everything dreamed about when the practice was first begun, many years ago.

REFERENCES AND READINGS

American Appraisal Associates. *Valuation Issues in Healthcare.* New York: Author, 1996.

Bowen, J. J. Jr. Creating equity. *Financial Planning*, March 1997.

Caplan, C. M. The five big mistakes doctors make when contemplating retirement. *APMA News*, January 1999.

Friedman, S. E. Consider operating your medical practice as an LLC or LLP. *MGM Journal*, September 1996.

Hagan, J. S. Value management: Decision making using the value paradigm. *MGM Journal*, November 1996.

Hitti, M. Mind your C's and S's. *Business to Business*, October 1998.

Marcinko, D. E. Creating equity value in your medical practice in an era of mergers and acquisitions. *Podiatry Today*, January 1999.

Marcinko, D. E. Creating medical practice equity. *Foot and Ankle Quarterly*, vol. 12, no. 1 (1999).

Reece, R. L. Looking ahead, experts see large organizations struggling. *Practice Options*, December 1998.

Richards, R. Know what your business is worth. *Business to Business*, November 1998.

Schryver, D. L. How to determine fair market value. *MGM Journal*, December 1998.

Thomas, S. How much is your medical practice worth? *Podiatry Today*, January 1997.

## CHAPTER 16

Medical Practice Valuation and Appraisal Techniques

How Much Is Your Business Really Worth?

Bridget Bourgeois

> In almost every other walk of life, people buy more at lower prices; in the stock market and bond markets, they seem to buy more at higher prices.
>
> —James Grant, *Minding Mr. Market,* 1993

The health care industry continues to undergo major renovations in its structure of health care delivery. The market evolution has been described at times as industry revolution, fraught with continual organizational changes and merger and acquisition frenzies in many health care sectors. Recent years have been marked by significant, highly visible, and increasing politically sensitive industry consolidations.

The major industry segments grabbing most of the headlines are the physician, hospital, and payer consolidations. Other industry segments, such as long-term care, medical devices, pharmaceutical and supply distribution, outsourcing and staffing are also setting record levels in terms of volume and dollar value of business combinations. Health care merger and acquisition fervor will continue to be robust well into the new millennium. Why this urge to merge? Industry consolidation is being fueled by the rapid growth of managed care and the continuing squeeze on the health care dollar.

The health care market is over $1 trillion, with physicians controlling 85% of total health care spending. According to the Health Care Financing Administration (HCFA), the government agency that administers the Medicare and Medicaid programs, direct spending on physicians has grown from $5.3 billion in 1960 to over $201 billion in 1995. HCFA estimates that physician spending will reach almost \$500 billion by 2005. Figure 16.1 illustrates this explosive growth trend in physician spending.

FORCES DRIVING CONSOLIDATION

The federal government is the largest single payer in the United States, accounting for approximately one-third of all of health care expenditures. With the aging population, legislative efforts to control health care spending can only escalate. Further accelerating the urge to merge, many insurers are increasingly basing provider payments on some level of Medicare reimbursements. Health care organizations are continually attempting to offset declining revenues by controlling costs and offering broader services. With market forces squeezing the health care dollar, continual change and industry consolidation is imminent and is the reason for many public debates.

PUBLIC CONCERN

This fast-paced, market-driven transformation is causing growing concern in the public sector over access and quality of care. Central questions focus on how well managed care will perform as it enrolls sicker, more vulnerable populations, the consequences for the uninsured, the risks to access and quality, and the capability to monitor and measure access and quality.

In recent years, a Washington, DC–based coalition was formed to examine the trend of for-profit hospital acquisitions of not-for-profit community hospitals and to shape policies regarding these takeovers. The swift movement and changes occurring in the health care industry continue to fuel public concern and increase regulatory oversight.

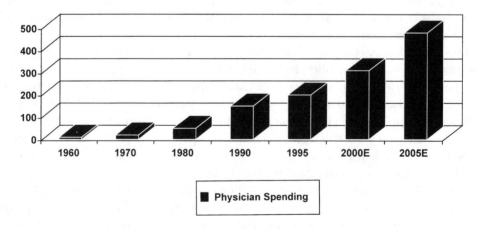

FIGURE 16.1   Growth trend in physician spending.

Source: Health Care Financing Administration, 1998.

REGULATORY CLIMATE

Federal and state fraud and abuse laws, self-referral laws, tax-exempt entities, prohibitions on inurement and private benefit, and a host of other federal and state laws and regulations have significant impact on which health care entities can acquire and how those acquisitions are structured. The IRS and the Office of the Inspector General (OIG), Department of Health and Human Services, are scrutinizing the formation of integrated delivery systems (IDS), with major focus on physician transactions. The impact on the health care industry has been:

- Increased scrutiny by regulators.
- Need for greater understanding of regulations and their impact on determining value.
- Need for greater documentation in rationale and support of underlying value conclusions.

Current health care policy issues are likely to address four broad areas: Medicare, Medicaid, access to care, and managed care. With Medicare and Medicaid taking up significant portions of the federal budget, efforts to bring revenues in line with spending will require painful reductions of provider payments. Under recently enacted Medicare reform legislation, provider-sponsored organizations (PSOs), which are groups of hospitals, physicians, and other providers, are allowed to contract directly for Medicare capitation. This recent legislation also has significant negative impact on physician payments, particularly specialty practices. Medicare, Medicaid, access to care, and anti-managed-care legislation will continue to be hotly debated topics.

URGE TO MERGE: PHYSICIAN MOTIVATION

There are approximately 600,000–800,000 physician practitioners in the United States, and according to the American Medical Association, slightly over 200,000 are organized in groups of three or more. This huge fragmentation of physicians has allowed for the proliferation of managed care organizations commanding significant reductions in provider payments. Declining incomes and increasing administrative challenges have motivated a significant number of physicians to sell their practice assets and join hospital systems, align with corporate partners, or decide to merge with larger medical groups to form even larger regional groups. There are countless acquisition and physician management models, some successful and many unsuccessful. Undoubtedly, more models will evolve as there will always be organizations that think they have built a better mousetrap. And the truth is that these affiliations must be flexible and evolving to adapt to an ever changing health care market.

Medical group acquisitions continue at a steady clip despite the retreat by major players such as MedPartners, PhyCor, and FPA Medical Management. Investors have become increasingly wary of the industry since MedPartners and PhyCor called off merger plans in January 1998. Concerns accelerated in July

1998 when FPA Medical Management filed for Chapter 11 bankruptcy protection and after recently publicized financial difficulties of many physician practice management companies (PPMCs).

Since January 1998, the industry has lost substantial value in public equity markets. PPMCs that have not met earnings expectations are taking a beating from Wall Street. Initial public offerings have slowed down to almost nil. A few companies that proceeded with public offerings despite the sour market are taking a beating on price.

Why all this market uncertainty? No one knows precisely the best formula for physician integration. The move from a traditional fee-for-service environment to capitation and other fixed-fee reimbursements is shifting financial risks from payers to providers. Additionally, physicians are faced with ever increasing needs for negotiating clout, capital for expansion, and administrative and management burdens in a time of declining incomes. All the market forces continue to exist that motivate physician consolidation.

NEED FOR VALUATION: WHAT'S THE PURPOSE?

Physicians are entrepreneurial by nature and take great pride in the creation of their businesses. Market pressures are motivating physicians to be proactive and to make informed decisions concerning the future of their businesses. The decision to sell, while often financially driven, is inherently an emotional one. Therefore, it is critical that physicians fully understand the purpose of their valuation, and how their assets will be valued. Estimates of value can be markedly different, depending on the purpose of the appraisal. Some of the many reasons to value a medical practice include the following:

- What is the value of the operating business of a medical practice for purchase or sale?
- What is the value of a medical practice for merger with other medical groups?
- What is the value of medical practice assets for joint venture with a health system or corporate partner?
- What is the practice value to establish the buy-in or buyout arrangements for partners?
- What is the value of certain medical practice assets for purchase or sale apart from the ongoing business operations?

To arrive at an appropriate estimate of value, qualified appraisers will ask the following questions:

1. What is the purpose of the valuation?
2. What assets require valuation?

The answers to these questions will guide the appraiser to select the appropriate definition of value and appraisal methods to value your practice.

UNDERSTANDING VALUATION DEFINITIONS

Most practice valuations for mergers and acquisitions use *fair market value* as the standard to derive a reasonable value for the medical practice. This key definition of value is important, as it guides the appraiser's choice of methods to apply in determining the appropriate value. Fair market value means that the appraiser will value your medical practice assuming an arm's-length transaction of "any willing buyer and any willing seller" scenario and without the synergies of a specific buyer. Synergies common among the most likely hypothetical (any willing) buyers, however, are appropriately considered in valuing medical practices.

If you are selling your medical practice as a going-concern business, inclusive of all the medical practice's underlying assets, then you should understand the term *business enterprise*. The business enterprise of a medical practice equals the combined values of all practice assets (tangible and intangible) and the working capital of a continuing business. Stated another way, the business enterprise value is equal to the combined values of owner's equity and long-term debt, also referred to as the invested capital of the operating business.

The value of the *owner's equity* of a medical practice equals the combined values of all practice assets (tangible and intangible), less all practice liabilities (booked and contingent). In essence, the equity value is the net worth of the business (after deducting debt). The business enterprise value is the total sum for the business, including the owner's net worth plus the long-term debt.

The business enterprise value and the owner's equity value definitions are relevant when you are contemplating sale of your ongoing medical practice, inclusive of all medical practice assets. In transactions involving the sale of medical assets separate and apart from the ongoing business operations, other value definitions and methodologies will apply.

Many medical practices are acquired without *working capital*. The working capital of a medical practice equals the excess of current assets (cash, accounts receivable, supplies, inventory, prepaid expenses, etc.) over current liabilities (accounts payable, accrued liabilities, etc.). When working capital is not a part of the transaction, the business enterprise value is adjusted for the buyer's postacquisition buildup of practice receivables and the associated delay from the collection of those receivables.

WHAT HAS VALUE?

The medical practice's tangible and intangible assets can be grouped into four broad asset categories. Medical practice assets typically valued for merger and acquisition include tangible (physical) assets:

• Real estate or leasehold improvements
• Medical equipment and furnishings
• Accounts receivable

and intangible assets: goodwill.

The tangible assets of the medical practice include medical office building furnishings, medical equipment, and practice receivables. Depending on the facts and circumstances, intangible assets include professional goodwill and may also include favorable leasehold improvements, location, patient relationships, a trained and assembled work force, and restrictive covenants, among others. The combination of all the intangible assets of a medical practice is collectively referred to as goodwill.

Medical practices can be valued in their entirety as an operating business, often referred to as the business enterprise. The business enterprise value includes all of the underlying assets employed in the medical practice's business operations. The business enterprise analysis is the more cost-effective way of estimating practice value. Practice assets can also be valued apart from the operating business or in addition to the operating business. What assets can be acquired and the deal structure will determine whether there is a need to separately value the practice assets only or in addition to the business operations.

Medical practices are dependent on the highly specialized skills of the physician providers. With the exception of practices that own real estate, typically the majority of practice value lies in intangible assets, or goodwill.

HEALTH CARE REGULATION: WHAT YOU NEED TO KNOW

Federal and state regulatory oversight is increasing. The trend of not-for-profit community hospital conversions into for-profit is generating business for appraisers to perform fairness opinions to calm community benefit fears. A number of industry regulations must be considered, regardless of the buyer's tax status, when organizations acquire or affiliate with physicians:

- Medicare fraud and abuse legislation makes it a criminal offense to offer, pay, solicit, or receive payment for patient referrals for business covered by a federal health care program
- Anti-self-referral legislation (Stark I and II) makes it illegal for physicians to refer Medicare patients for certain identified services if the physician holds an ownership interest in the business of the service provider. The legislation identifies health services such as lab work, radiology, magnetic resonance imaging, ultrasound, home health services, durable medical equipment, computerized axial tomography, and hospital services.
- Section 501c(3) of the Internal Revenue Code makes it illegal for not-for-profit organizations to pay more than *or* receive less than fair market value in physician and other transactions.
- Intermediate sanctions allow the IRS to impose tax penalties on individuals in tax-exempt organizations as well as those physicians who benefit from excessive compensation.
- Antitrust laws protect against combinations that may preclude market competition.

REGULATION WILL AFFECT YOUR VALUE

Both the buyer and seller must understand how industry regulation affects practice value and also must have an appreciation for accepted appraisal definitions and methodologies used by qualified appraisers to estimate value. *The Uniform Standards of Professional Appraisal Practice (USPAP)* are promulgated standards that provide the minimum requirements to which all professional appraisals must conform. *USPAP* requires that the three recognized approaches to value (the income, market, and cost approaches) be considered to estimate value.

In the fall of 1994 and 1995, the IRS issued training guidelines pertaining to the valuation of physician practices. These guidelines suggest that appraisers consider all three of the general approaches to valuation as required by the *USPAP*. Specifically in transactions involving physician organizations, the IRS implied:

1. The discounted cash flow (DCF) analysis is the most relevant income approach.
2. The DCF analysis must be done on an after-tax basis regardless of the tax status of the prospective buyer.
3. Practice collections must be projected for the DCF based on reasonable and proper assumptions for the practice, market, and industry.
4. Physician compensation must be based on market rates consistent with age, experience, and productivity.

THE VALUATION PROCESS: WHAT TO EXPECT

Valuing your medical practice will require consideration of many factors that influence value. A thorough valuation analysis will include a study of the economics of the health care industry, reimbursement trends, competitive market conditions, and historical earnings trends, as well as management experience. These factors, collectively considered, influence the future prospects of your medical practice and, ultimately, its estimate of value as a going concern.

The appraiser will want to gain an understanding of the history of your practice and its operations, local competition, and payer contracting issues. The business and management fundamentals studied are patient retention and potential for new patient growth, providing services efficiently and cost-effectively, timely collections for services, and maintaining competitive equipment and facilities.

After the need for an independent valuation is determined, here is what you can expect:

- Who pays the bill? An independent valuation appraiser is engaged sometimes by the buyer, sometimes by the seller, or in some cases jointly by both buyer and seller.
- Make sure the appraiser understands the health care industry and, most important, educates both the buyer and seller in the conduct of an appraisal.

All too often, values are misunderstood and may result in deals unnecessarily falling apart.

- The appraiser will request financial information, operating statistics, and other information in advance of a site visit.
- The appraiser should visit your medical practice to conduct key interviews and review the physical condition of the facilities and medical equipment.
- The appraiser will review historical practice patterns and financial and operating performance as a basis for forecasting future operations.
- The appraiser will adjust historical financial data to eliminate one-time, nonrecurring expenses, adjust for excessive or below-normal expenses, and eliminate expenses not expected to be a part of future practice costs. The rationale for adjusting practice costs is to estimate the fair market value price of the business that is transferable.
- The appraiser should work with you to assist with the development of key assumptions concerning future reimbursement trends, physician productivity, practice cost structure, and physician compensation for use in financial projections.
- The appraiser should review valuation assumptions and forecasts with you.

APPROACHES TO MEDICAL PRACTICE VALUE

As discussed earlier, industry regulations will govern how a deal will be structured and what medical practice assets can be acquired, which in turn will determine what assets require appraisal and what appraisal methods should be applied.

In most cases, a significant amount of practice value lies in the business operations as opposed to the physical assets. The value of a going-concern medical practice is directly linked to the value of the practice's ability to generate economic benefits to its owners, as measured by future cash flows. As a result, the development of a reasonable forecast of future operations is crucial to determining a meaningful practice value.

INCOME APPROACH

Since medical practice value correlates directly with the measurement of economic benefits to owners, earnings or cash flow methods are the best tools for estimating practice value.

Capitalization of (Excess) Earnings Method

The *excess earnings method* estimates value by dividing normalized historical or current earnings by an appropriate rate of return for the buyer. This method can provide a reasonable estimate of practice value in situations where limited information is available, or when the practice is likely to maintain stable cash flows. The main advantage of this method is that it does not require assumptions regarding future forecasted operations for the medical practice.

Discounted Cash Flow Method

The DCF method is favored by the IRS and is considered more relevant given the changing nature of the health care. The DCF is a sophisticated analysis requiring assumptions of forecasted practice operations regarding future reimbursements and physician productivity, practice efficiencies, and competitive market conditions. An estimate of practice value is developed by discounting future net cash flows to their present worth based on market rates of return required by an investor.

The value of your medical practice is primarily dependent on future practice earnings that will provide an adequate return on an investment for the buyer. An informed buyer will not pay more than the present value of all anticipated future economic benefits of ownership. Supportable practice values are entirely dependent on realistic financial and operating assumptions about future practice operations.

Key DCF Assumptions

A DCF analysis includes a financial forecast projecting net cash flows for the business operations, usually for a period of 3–5 years or until the practice achieves stable operations. In estimating practice value, key variables and assumptions used can have a significant impact on your value. The following are key DCF elements

1. Reasonable supportable projections of future practice revenues based on historical practice patterns and with consideration of future physician productivity, reimbursement trends, and shifts in payer mix.
2. Reasonable supportable projections of future practice cost structure based on expected normal levels of practice expenses.
3. Projected physician compensation based on market rates for physicians with comparable age, experience, and productivity.
4. DCF model calculates after-tax cash flows regardless of the tax status of the buyer. The tax rate is based on a blend of federal and state rates.
5. Reinvestments in the business are necessary for funding working capital needs and capital expenditure requirements to replace and acquire new equipment or other medical assets.
6. Terminal value represents the going-concern value at the end of the projection period. Stated another way, it is a residual value for the expected remaining practice value at the end of the forecast period.
7. Discount rate is applied to the future net cash flows to arrive at the present (cash equivalent) value for the medical practice. The discount rate must be based on the industry's weighted average cost of capital that takes into consideration the specific risks for the practice.

The DCF analysis consistently produces higher values than other methods of estimating practice value because there may be supportable reasons to forecast improvements in future practice performance. Understanding the key DCF variables and assumptions used in the income method will assist in producing a meaningful estimate of practice value.

MARKET TRANSACTION APPROACH

The market transaction method is a useful gauge in setting a valuation bottom and top range for comparison with the income approach. Market multiples are ratios developed by correlating market sale prices of guideline practices to key practice performance measurements. Common physician practice market multiples include comparisons of sale price to revenues, sale price to earnings before interest and taxes (EBIT), sale price to earnings before interest, taxes, and depreciation (EBITDA), and sale price to number of physicians.

Market transaction multiples are typically limited to serving as benchmarks for testing the reasonableness of the income approach. To apply the market approach, information on guideline practices, such as size of practice, specialty, number of physicians, growth potential, cost structure, payer mix, and profitability, are necessary for determining comparability to the medical practice being valued. Often, information concerning transaction specifics and practice particulars are either insufficient or not available for direct comparison with the practice being valued.

COST APPROACH

The cost approach to estimating value calls for the identification and separate valuation of all the practice assets, including goodwill. Also referred to as *sum of the assets*, this approach is more labor-intensive and costly than using the business enterprise analysis to estimate practice value. Generally, this approach is not very useful for estimating-going concern value.

Although rarely used to estimate going-concern value, another cost approach method may be used to estimate the costs that would be incurred to start up a medical practice and develop to the current level of practice operations. The costs of establishing a new medical practice typically include the expenses involved in the recruitment of physicians; acquisition of space, office furnishings, patient treatment equipment, computer software, and medical records; advertising for staff; and losses incurred during the start-up period.

This estimate of *replacement cost or cost avoidance* value represents an upper limit (or ceiling) of value. It has a limited use, as no prudent buyer would pay for an existing medical practice a price equivalent to what it would cost to build and develop a new medical practice.

The most appropriate application of the cost approach involves the valuation of medical practice tangible assets. However, valuing only the tangible assets used in a profitable, medical practice is not representative of the business value of the company. Since the intangible assets typically represent a significant portion of practice value, the cost approach is generally not considered useful in estimating the value of a going-concern medical practice.

UNDERSTANDING DEAL STRUCTURE

Many buyers are hospitals and health systems. The most common deal structure has been to acquire substantially all of the medical practice assets, excluding the working capital, and to enter into employment agreements with the physicians. In this scenario, the selling physician is left with the accounts receivable, cash, and the practice liabilities. Most of these asset purchases are cash deals. When the sale price is based on an enterprise value, this usually provides the physician with the ability to settle the practice debt.

Stock Purchase Versus Asset Purchase

There will be some variation in appraisal methods depending on whether the transaction is structured as a stock purchase or an asset purchase. Due to corporate practice of medicine laws in some states and the desires of buyers not to assume practice liabilities, most practice acquisitions are structured as asset purchases. In an asset transaction, the buyer will receive a tax amortization benefit associated with the intangible value of the business. This tax amortization represents a noncash expense benefiting the buyer. In this case, the present value of those future tax benefits is additive to the business enterprise value.

Corporate Partner Transactions

PPMCs historically have acquired the medical practice assets, excluding real estate, and have entered into a *management service agreement* (MSA) with the physician. There are a myriad of MSAs involving fees based on a percentage of revenue, compensation based on a percentage of practice profits, and some fee arrangements that vary with managed care enrollment levels. The negotiated MSA fee depends on the scope and level of services provided, such as practice management, administrative services, contract negotiations, and marketing. The current market has seen fees drop to 8%–20% of relevant revenues, depending on the level and menu of services provided.

Practice management agreements with physician organizations are coming under closer scrutiny, particularly when the agreements are fee-based revenue arrangements for management services. The OIG is concerned when compensation arrangements for management services based on a percentage of net revenues include business from managed care contracts arranged by the PPMC. The OIG may imply such activities implicate an antikickback statute because the compensation will, in part, be for marketing services.

Market uncertainties in 1998 have resulted in downward pressure on prices paid for physician groups by PPMCs. It has been estimated that prices for multispecialty groups fell by as much as 25% in 1998.

In 1997 some PPMCs paid as high as 8 to 10 times EBIT to secure a strategic practice. Since the industry fallout in 1998, however, those sale prices have fallen to a range of 4 to 6 times EBIT. The deals usually involve a combination of cash, common stock, notes receivable, and possibly assumption of liabilities. When common stock is used as payment, considerable premiums are included in the sale price to compensate for the risk of receiving stock instead of cash. The use of equity adds a premium of as much as 50% or more to the sale price.

Restrictive Covenant Value Is Goodwill

Restrictive covenants for physicians usually involve covenants not to compete related to the sale of a medical practice or other assets. The value of a covenant not to compete lies in the protection it affords the buyer from potential loss of income due to competition from the selling physicians.

To estimate the value of a covenant not to compete, the income approach is considered to be the most appropriate method. The cost to secure the agreement is irrelevant to the value of the protection afforded the buyer. The sales comparison approach requires sales of similar or like assets; because each medical practice is unique and public data are unavailable for transactions of physician's non-compete agreements, the sales comparison approach is not useful. Generally, an income approach includes the value associated with a non-compete agreement as part of the intangible asset value. As such, the non-compete agreement value is not additive to your business enterprise practice value. Instead, it is a component of practice goodwill, which can be separately valued if desired.

Buyer Blunders

Significant federal funding has been provided targeting physician transactions, with penalties potentially imposed on both the physician and individuals in the acquiring organizations. In 1998 there were several federal investigations of for-profit hospital systems alleging that those systems deliberately overpaid for physician practices as inducement to receive patient referrals (a violation of the antikickback statute). When selling your practice, beware of the following buyer blunders:

- *No Outside Appraisal Performed:* If the buyer is a tax-exempt entity *or* participates in federal health care programs, get an independent third-party valuation from a qualified appraiser. There are too many stories of hospitals and health systems that bought practices with no appraisal. *Big mistake!*
- *Overpaying Physician Practice Value:* Some buyers obtain a business enterprise value and also obtain separate values for the medical equipment and non-compete agreements. These values can be useful in allocating the overall

purchase price. The business enterprise value, however, represents an estimate for a 100% ownership interest in the medical practice. The separate values for the assets are not additive to the business enterprise value but rather are components of the total value of the business. Some buyers have overpaid for physician practices by adding these separate asset values to the overall business enterprise value to determine the sale price. *Big mistake!* Not understanding values can be misconstrued as overpaying in exchange for patient referrals.

- *Overpaying Physician Compensation:* Industry surveys have reported that more than 70% of practices acquired fall short of projected productivity used in the valuation. This fact coupled with exposure to IRS audit and intermediate sanctions has increased the need to value practices based on reasonable appropriate projections of practice collections and market rates for physician compensation.

- *Not Buying Insurance on the Physician:* Much of the value to an investor rests with the physician's skill and talent to remain with the practice after acquisition. The buyer expects to achieve a return on the investment in the medical practice based on future cash flows and to eventually recoup the purchase price. Since most practice acquisitions are cash deals, the buyer is at significant financial risk due to a business interruption associated with an unexpected loss of life or permanent disability.

HOW MUCH IS YOUR BUSINESS REALLY WORTH?

Now that you have a background of what factors influence value, needs for valuation, a general understanding of appraisal theory and how industry regulations affect value, the valuation process and methodologies employed, we get to the heart of the matter.

Understanding Your Value

Understanding value is crucial to a successful negotiation. Both buyers and sellers too often misinterpret the value conclusions of appraisers, straining buyer/seller relationships and unnecessarily jeopardizing deals.

How to Maximize Your Practice Value

There a few critical areas you can review for opportunities to maximize your practice value.

- Use the DCF method to estimate practice value. This method consistently produces higher values than others.

Practice Revenue:

- Can the practice and local market support additional providers such as physicians or midlevel providers? Providers usually take 2 to 3 years to ramp up their practice before they begin to significantly contribute to the bottom line. Generally, adding a midlevel provider will produce a greater value, as their compensation levels are lower than that of physicians.
- What future provider productivity is expected?
- Does the practice plan to offer new services?
- Is the current practice fee schedule at market rates? Is there an opportunity for fee increases?
- Is there an opportunity to improve payer mix?

Review Practice Costs:
- Eliminate any unnecessary practice expenses. Identify any unusual, nonrecurring costs.
- Eliminate any physician-related costs not likely to be paid by a buyer.
- Eliminate any special perks of business ownership.
- Adjust for any overinflated salaries of relatives and eliminate any unnecessary salaries.

Physician Compensation Inverse Relationship to Value:
- Although physician compensation must be based on market rates, fair market value is a range. Practice value correlates directly with the net cash flows available after all practice expenses, including physician compensation. As a consequence the higher the compensation, the lower the practice value; and conversely, the lower the compensation, the higher the practice value. As little as a $10,000 swing in salary can have significant impact on value. As Figure 16.2 illustrates, as physician compensation rises practice value falls.

LET'S MAKE A DEAL

Depending on whether the likely buyer is a health system or a corporate partner, the deal structures will vary. From the physician's perspective, deal negotiations

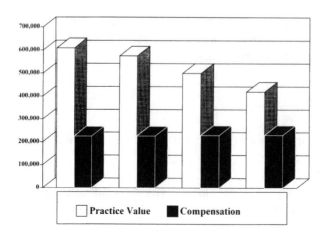

FIGURE 16.2 As physician compensation rises practice value falls.

are based on consideration of personal and financial planning goals. Some of the key negotiations considered include the following

1. *Working capital—in or out.* Including working capital in the transaction will increase the sale price.
2. *Stock versus asset transaction.* Structuring the deal as an asset purchase will increase practice value due to the tax amortization benefits received by the buyer for intangible assets of the practice.
3. *Common stock premium.* The sale price can be as high as 50% more than a cash equivalent price for accepting the risk of common stock as part of the payment (see Figure 16.3).
4. *Physician compensation.* If your personal financing planning goals are to maximize practice value, negotiating a lower salary within a range you feel comfortable with will increase the sale price.

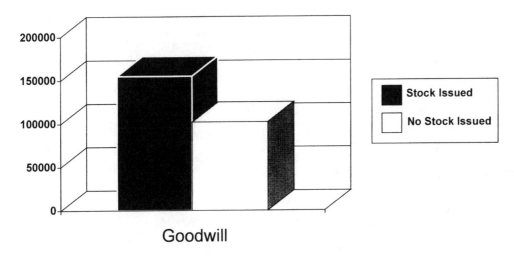

FIGURE 16.3   Consideration premium.
Source: Adapted from CHIPS.

CONCLUSION

The above discussion solidly presents the reasons for and methodology behind acquiring a professional appraisal when contemplating the sale, purchase, or merger of any medical practice.

Contemporary Aspects of Medical Practice

## CHAPTER 17

Medical Support Services: Assistance or Hindrance?

Accept Utilization Review and Case Management . . . or Perish

---

David Edward Marcinko and Hope Rachel Hetico

> Good is not good, where better is expected.
>
> —Thomas Fuller

The costs associated with traditional indemnity or fee-for-service medical care, along with the growth of managed care to curtail those costs, have given rise to several new infrastructural delivery medical management support services. While seemingly intrusive to MDs, the most common type of managed care organization (MCO)–insurance support services include (1) medical utilization review and (2) medical case management. They have been developed in an attempt to answer important questions, such as (a) how can physicians determine whether they are using economic and human resources efficiently? (b) how can payers, insurance companies, and MCOs control physicians? and (c) how is medical quality measured so that cost controls do not compromise care? The need for proper understanding of these concepts, relative to provider reimbursement, is obvious.

UTILIZATION REVIEW

Medical utilization review (MUR) refers to all the ways insurance companies, MCOs, or health maintenance organizations (HMOs) attempt to assure that their contracted physicians are used in the most appropriate, efficient, and cost-effective ways. MUR techniques, developed and refined in the late 1970s, involve the review of services, either before, during, or after they are provided. Within any payer organization, MUR usually includes the following *prospective*, *concurrent*, and *retrospective* components.

Prospective MUR

Prospective MUR involves evaluation prior to the initiation of patient care, and usually is composed of the following component parts:

1.   *Second opinions* for elective expensive procedures, nonemergent surgery, or so-called experimental procedures such as bone marrow transplants may be required from an unaffiliated physician, confirming the necessity of the procedure. The need for a second opinion relative to elective surgery reached its zenith in the late 1980s and has waned ever since because it was not demonstrated to be cost-effective. Not surprisingly, surgeons tended to give colleagues and patients the benefit of the doubt and approved more than 90% of second opinions rendered. The gatekeeper model has since proved more restrictive and cost-effective in reducing unneeded care.

2.   *Precertification* must be obtained from the payer before being covered for certain medical procedures. Typically, it is required before surgical procedures, nonemergent hospitalizations, physical therapy, or certain diagnostic tests (MRI, CAT scans, x-rays, and even physical therapy). It may also be used prior to the utilization of home health care benefits, such as I.V. therapy, nursing, or wound care.

Concurrent MUR

Concurrent MUR (CMUR), on the other hand, represents a formal evaluation of a patient's office, hospital, or surgical treatment record. CMUR not only documents appropriateness of care but the necessity of care and results of the rendered care. It may also be known as *discharge planning* (DP) and involves arranging for a patient to be discharged from the hospital, surgical center, nursing home, or extended care facility and coordinating services that will be required after discharge. Many payers begin DP even before the patient enters the facility. Effective DP can help shorten the length of stay, and many MCOs work closely with the institution to ensure timely discharge without compromising patient care. Unfortunately, it can be exaggerated to the detriment of the patient. Typically, the attending physician is always responsible for the patient's care; not the planner.

The role of the case manager (CM) is similar to that of a discharge planner (DP); however, there are significant differences between the two roles:

1.   The DP has limited and short-term responsibility once the patient leaves the medical facility. The CM, on the other hand, has the patient's long-term care in mind, regardless of venue.

2.   The DP is on site and may actually work for the facility, whereas the CM is a remote manager usually working for the MCO.

3.   The DP is responsible and takes authority from a specific acute care facility. CMs are generally authorized to arrange care that is ordered by the patient's physician. As can be seen, the CM's role is much larger in the overall management of patient care (Figure 17.1).

Retrospective MUR

Finally, retrospective MUR includes the following three component parts:

1.   *Peer review* is the process of having one's contemporaries or colleagues evaluate compliance with practice protocols, guidelines, or standards. Suggestions for improvement are then made as needed. Peer review is not considered chastisement but should rightly be seen as an opportunity to improve care and decrease costs.

Example Scenario:

Dr. Sadowski is concerned when asked to appear before the peer review committee of his MCO. The physician reviewers tell him that his patients have a longer length of stay (LOS) than those of his peers. As their primary care physician, he is expected to round on patients in the hospital and continue to *monitor* their care. The committee reviewed all of Dr. Sadowski's recent cases. They point out one case where a patient who developed an infection following bladder surgery was kept in the hospital for almost 2 weeks. How sick was the patient? Was he in the hospital primarily for I.V. antibiotics? Could he have been discharged earlier and received the needed drugs from the MCO home health care provider?

Dr. Sadowski agreed that the patient could probably have done well at home. He agrees to examine the MCO's guidelines and review their material on home health care services. The atmosphere is cordial, but Dr. Sadowski realizes that the next step after peer review could be formal sanctions against him. He realizes that he must monitor his patients more carefully and shudders to think of the consequences.

2.   *Pattern reviews* involve examining how physicians utilize resources, such as specialty referrals, diagnostic tests, therapeutic procedures, or other economic consumables. These rates are then compared to industry standards to create a practitioner profile. The profiles are used to provide feedback to physicians and insurance plans. Information may also be used to determine which physicians may require sanction or dismissal from the plan, insurance company, or network. Reviews are increasingly becoming the industry norm as *outliers* are being purged from the insurance system. *Economic credentialing* is thus becoming almost as important as medical credentialing.

3.   *Medical claims review* specialists scrutinize medical claims for improprieties, overcharges, surcharges, or mistakes. No longer the domain of the CPAs or those similarity trained, these quasi-professionals ensure that the patient was eligible for the claimed benefits, that the patient actually received the treatment billed

AVERAGE LENGTH OF STAY (DAYS) FOR PREPAID HMO MEMBERS*

TYPE OF STAY	Commercial HMO Members			Senior HMO Members		
	1994	1995	1996	1994	1995	1996
Acute-care Facility	3.12	3.30	3.07	4.42	4.45	4.00
Skilled Nursing Facility	10.10	12.03	10.91	16.10	14.16	12.85
Psychiatric Facility	6.75	6.10	5.48	7.34	7.65	7.95
TOTAL	**3.31**	**3.56**	**3.33**	**6.01**	**6.31**	**5.89**
MEMBER MONTHS	**19,263,275**	**18,406,920**	**14,084,476**	**2,168,893**	**2,292,067**	**1,553,143**

AVERAGE LENGTH OF STAY FOR PREPAID HMO MEMBERS (ACUTE)*

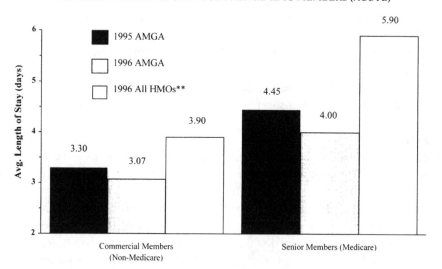

AVERAGE LENGTH OF STAY FOR PREPAID HMO MEMBERS*

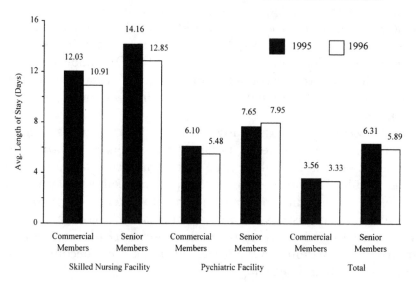

FIGURE 17.1   **Average length of stay (days) for pre-paid HMO members.**

Data source: American Medical Group Association Statistical Database, 1996 © 1997.
From *1998 Hoechst Marion Roussel Managed Care Digest Series.* Reprinted by permission of the publisher, Hoechst
Marion Roussel, Inc.

for, and that all paperwork was properly prepared. Miscreants are often adjusted without human consideration, as insurance constricts are becoming literally interpreted in favor of the MCO.

MEDICAL STAFF UTILIZATION REVIEW

Medical staff utilization review usually involves the following four medical professionals or committees:

1. *Medical directors* usually intervene when there is a disagreement between two parties, such as a primary care physician and a CM or MUR specialist. Otherwise, the medical director acts more as a manager than as a direct mediator of medical care. Many directors possess advanced management degrees, such as the MBA or MHA, and are trained in leadership skills, negotiation tactics, and other aspects of the corporate medical structure.

2. *Primary care physicians* are *gatekeepers* who triage patients and perform a type of prospective or concurrent medical review. In some MCOs, hospitals, or large clinics, physicians perform their own hospital-based MUR by discussing difficult cases with hospital staff and other medical specialists. Retrospective reviews may also be performed when serious quality issues were missed or unaddressed on a real-time basis.

3. *Utilization review committees* usually develop protocols or algorithms for either populations, communities, medical risk classes, or specific cohorts. Most important, they administer committee suggestions and continuously monitor and track trends based on individual input as well as industry-wide accommodations. Epidemiological statistics and mathematical medical outcomes databases of hospitals, clinics, group practices, and even independent physicians are being formulated to resolve appropriateness of care issues.

4. *Utilization review specialists* were originally registered nurses whose primary function was to review bills, claims, and medical records and evaluate pattern trend analyses. Over time the UR specialists lost the RN degree and ceased being a medical clinician of any sort. Often, they were merely LPNs, clerks, or other nonprofessional personnel. In an effort to improve care, raise wages, and increase professionalism, a body of knowledge leading to the designation certified case manager (CCM) has been developed, along with the publication of an educational periodical, the *Case Manager.* Many have earned the designation of certified disability consultant, and standards have improved for this growing field.

MEDICAL PROTOCOLS

Medical protocols are being developed and used to reduce the caregiver level to the lowest common denominator while saving precious human and economic resources for more serious cases (Figure 17.2).

In 1999, about 40% of all Medical Group Management Association members reported using treatment protocols. Usually, the percentage of group protocols

GROUP PRACTICES THAT USE TREATMENT PROTOCOLS

SIZE (# of FTE phsicians)	Percentage Using Treatment Proctocols	Treatment Protocols Apply to:*		
		Primary Care	Specialty Care	Other**
10 or fewer	38.0%	26.2%	77.4%	2.8%
11–25	37.9	43.7	69.9	3.9
26–50	40.2	46.7	68.9	0.0
51–100	34.0	77.8	55.6	0.0
101 or more	55.9	78.9	84.2	10.5
SPECIALTY COMPOSITION				
Single Specialty	40.3%	17.3%	87.3%	0.0%
Multispecialty	37.8	71.2	62.6	2.2
ALL GROUPS	**38.5%**	**43.3%**	**75.4%**	**1.2%**

DEVELOPMENT OF TREATMENT PROTOCOLS

SIZE (# of FTE physicians)	Treatment Protocols Developed by:*			
	Medical Group Practice	HMO/PPO/ Insurance Company	Hospital	Medical Specialty Organization
10 or fewer	77.2%	9.6%	12.3%	21.1%
11–25	91.7	14.6	20.8	8.3
26–50	95.7	13.0	13.0	8.7
51–100	90.0	10.0	20.0	0.0
101 or more	88.9	16.7	11.1	5.6
SPECIALTY COMPOSITION				
Single Specialty	86.7%	9.3%	14.7%	18.7%
Multispecialty	82.0	13.7	18.7	8.6
ALL GROUPS	**84.4%**	**11.4%**	**16.6%**	**13.8%**

DEVELOPMENT OF TREATMENT PROTOCOLS

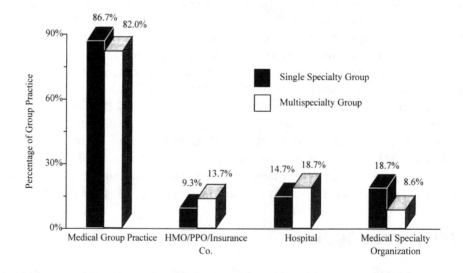

FIGURE 17.2   Group practices that use treatment protocols.

Data source: Medical Group Management Association Member Database, 1997 © 1998.
From *1998 Hoechst Marion Roussel Managed Care Digest Series*. Reprinted by permission of the publisher, Hoechst Marion Roussel, Inc.

rise with group size, and multispecialty groups are more likely to use protocols than are single-specialty groups. For example, more than half of groups with 51 to 100 full-time equivalent (FTE) physicians and groups with more than 100 FTEs used protocols.

1. *Medical guidelines* are used for interventions or treatments where the outcome of therapy is considered certain or occurs more than 80% of the time. Guidelines are used for the more mundane, ordinary, or usual medical problems. Sample conditions include hypertension and diabetes management, asthma management, prostatitis and carcinoma, or other forms of practice considered within the normal scope of care.

About a third of group practices use self-developed treatment guidelines, and a much lower percentage of group practices follow guidelines developed by HMOs/PPOs, insurance companies, or medical specialty organizations. About 45% of large groups, with more than 50 FTE physicians, use treatment guidelines developed internally.

The federal government, through the Agency for Healthcare Policy and Research (AHPR), has released practice guidelines on the following subjects, among others:

- Angina (unstable)
- Alzheimer's disease screening
- Bedsore prevention in adults
- Benign prostatic hyperplasia
- Cataracts in adults
- Congestive heart failure
- Cardiac rehabilitation
- Depression, anxiety, and panic disorders
- HIV (AIDS)
- Mammography quality determinants
- Otitis media in children
- Pain control after surgery and cancer
- Poststroke rehabilitation
- Sickle cell disease in newborns
- Smoking prevention and cessation
- Urinary incontinence in adults.

Example Scenario:
Honeywell, Inc., in Minneapolis, now requires that the health care providers with whom it contracts, develop and implement protocols and practice guidelines. The employers who pay the health care bills want their providers to be able to demonstrate that medical interventions are necessary. They will contract only with organizations that are able to establish standards and parameters of care.
Source: Cordero and Christensen/*Practice Guidelines.*

2. *Medical standards* are used for interventions or treatments where the outcome of care is considered uncertain and a favorable outcome occurs less than

20% of the time. Serious, unique, and/or catastrophic illnesses or diseases are encountered with this standard. Conditions include certain cancers, massive trauma, AIDS, birth defects, pediatric neonatology, or the more esoteric aspects of medical practice.

3.   *Medical (clinical) trials* are controlled studies, typically done in a single- or double-blind fashion, to study the effects of some new drug, surgical procedure, or medical intervention on a human sample. Some believe, however, that the term *trial* may be nothing more than a pseudonym for wholesale, nonspecific, and nonindividualized treatment of a given disease entity or process. Sometimes this may be masked by using the popular term *disease management* protocol.

Examining the Shibboleths of Medical Guidelines

The Institute for Clinical Systems Integration (ICSI), a collaboration of 17 health care providers, is a strong proponent of the value of medical guidelines and cites the following shibboleths that plague their implementation and acceptance:

1.   *Guidelines are a legal hazard.* Good guidelines specify good medicine because they are evidence-based, not opinion-based, drivers of care.
2.   *Guidelines are cookbook medicine.* Evidence-based clinical guidelines are text-book medicine, not cookbook care, and are far removed from the rote concept of mindless algorithms.
3.   *Guidelines don't work.* This may be true when used on a solo basis. However, when incorporated into an organized and systematic total quality improvement (TQI) approach, they do improve care by reducing variation in practice patterns.
4.   *Guidelines are available now.* True guidelines are developed on a national as well as a local basis but have not yet been developed for regional use in most cases.
5.   *Physicians will not use guidelines.* Doctors should realize that guidelines are only one part of the total treatment picture, since a team approach to patient care is becoming the norm, as solo practice disintegrates.
6.   *Guidelines should be validated by outcomes data.* This is not true if outcomes are based on individual events but is quite correct when based on a TQI process.

Example Scenario:
An HMO in Minnesota requires specialists to consult computerized guidelines before surgery is recommended. Each surgeon must input clinical indicators to standard criteria for that particular surgery. If the guidelines indicate that surgery is appropriate, it is automatically approved. If not, the case is sent to peer review. A negative response may evoke an appeal or alternative care. If the appeal fails, the surgery is not covered for insurance purposes.
   A similar system for primary care has recently begun operations. Initial procedures included ear tube insertion, tonsillectomies, and adenoidectomies, among others.
   Source: Cordero and Christensen/Practice Guidelines.

Health Plan Employer Data Information Set

A team of health care providers, health plans, and employers developed HEDIS as a tool for collecting information on the quality of care delivered by MCOs and HMOs. HEDIS is grouped into five categories:

1. Membership satisfaction surveys
2. Physician and provider networks
3. Medical quality and member access
4. Utilization and review
5. Membership and financial issues

CASE MANAGEMENT

Medical case management is defined as a collaborative process that assesses, plans, implements, coordinates, monitors, and evaluates options and services to meet the individual's health care needs. The case management concept was developed as a partial response to soaring medical costs incurred by a small number of chronically ill patients. For example, it has been estimated that 1% of the American population is responsible for 29% of all medical costs, and 5% is responsible for half of all costs. However, CMs have been around a lot longer than MCOs. The United States first used them to handle wounded veterans returning from World War II.

The ranks of CMs surged in the late 1970s, when a renewed national focus on workers' compensation laws changed the relationship between patients and insurers. And still more intermediaries were needed in the 1980s, when managed health care created greater demands for accountability in medical spending. Today, about 18,000 CMs have been certified since a national program to do so, the Commission for Case Management Certification, was created in 1993, according to the Rolling Meadows, Illinois, case management agency. More than half are nurses.

Most recently, Chi Systems, Inc., of Ann Arbor, Michigan, has been instrumental in assembling experts to produce a position paper and a series of three case management publications that summarize the group's major 1998 research study. According to Sara Atwell, a Chi Systems principal, two new case management models are currently under consideration: (1) a model that focuses on incorporating multiple providers, including physicians, employers groups, and health plans, into a broad integrated cohort, and (2) a more narrowly focused model that can work within a specific integrated health care delivery system.

Regardless of the future, the current process takes place in five stages:

1. *Appropriate identification:* The ideal patients for case management are those who will require extensive medical services and will respond well to existing cost-effective options. The cases might include diabetes complications, AIDS treatment, chronic osteomyelitis, trauma, and extensive reconstructive surgery.

Besides the diagnosis, others signs in the medical record that may signal the need for case management include hospital readmission, multiple emergency room visits, repeated surgery, high medical claims for the same disease, and treatment by multiple physicians.

2. *Needs assessment:* This stage of case management is performed to determine if the patient's medical needs can be addressed in a less acute setting or with less intensive or invasive methods. In all cases, CMs attempt to ensure that cost savings will not affect care quality. For example, should carpal tunnel surgery be performed initially or should orthotic brace control be first attempted in the newly diagnosed patient. Obviously, this appears to be a debatable point.

3. *Benefits coverage:* In the majority of cases, if certain medical benefits are not included in the insured's health care policy, they will not be rendered unless the CM can demonstrate the cost-effectiveness of such care. In most cases, exceptions are made only if this avoids or shortens a hospital stay, negates the need for surgery, or prevents hospital readmission. For example, if certain benefits such as home care are not covered for parenteral antibiotics, the CM may recommend that the insurer make an exception because of the cost-effectiveness of such therapy. The CM acts as the patient's advocate in this role, yet is paid by the insurance carrier. An intrinsic conflict of interest is apparent.

4. *Intervention:* CMs work with physicians to coordinate hospice care, home care, and long-term care. They may contact equipment or supply vendors, compare prices, and select physicians on the basis of factors such as expertise, timeliness, and quality parameters. CMs also may negotiate with physicians to decrease their charges. The difference is usually, but not always, placed back into the financial risk pool for continued patient care.

5. *Evaluation:* After disposition of the case, the CM must assess the effectiveness of intervention. The manager evaluates the quality of vendor services and prepares reports for others involved in the case. Then the CM calculates savings by adding up the costs of the requested services and subtracting the costs of the actual services. Some experts claim that CMs save between $5 and $10 for every dollar spent on their services.

Case Management and Economic Compensation

Case management services may be compensated in several of the following ways:

1. *Hourly rate:* The manager or management company may charge the insurer on an hourly basis, per case hours worked, or in a relevant range of $12–$18 per hour or 3–5 hours per case.

2. *Case fee:* The management company may charge a flat rate per case, typically about $3,000–$5,000 per catastrophic general medical case managed, or $250–$500 per acute case.

3. *Capitated rate:* The management may accept a per member per month (PM/PM) rate for its services. Typically, this rate appears generous, compared to typical medical capitation reimbursement rates, until one realizes that case

management requires a 100% utilization rate, rather than the normal 3%–10% range for elective MURs. Unlike physicians, capitated CMs or case management companies do not get paid for *not* managing a case, since virtually all are reviewed.

4.   *Time and materials:* In this instance, the case management company may charge for all the time and materials expended on the case. This represents an older, retroactive payment system that is being superseded by the fixed reimbursement schedules encountered in all of medicine.

5.   *Salary:* Many CMs are salaried employees of the insurance company, HMO, or MCO. Annual compensation levels reach about $30,000–$35,000 per year for a full-time manager.

Cost-Effectiveness

Case management is an expensive service, yet it is effective in reducing medical care costs. According to most studies, good case management can reduce a plan's overall costs by 2%–5%. Unlike utilization review specialists, a standard for credentialing CMs was established in 1992, and credentialing examinations were given for the first time in 1993.

Most recently, even CMs have been evaluated for appropriateness of care concerns and cost-effective issues, and are under increasing pressure to prove their impact. For example, according to one anonymous CM, "A decade ago, an insurance company would hire a case manager and say, 'Just go figure out what's going on.' But now there is more sophistication on the part of the payers. A case manager will actually keep track of every dollar they save the insurance company." It seems that in this climate, cost pressure is on anyone involved in patient care.

Example Scenario:

After Fred Black was sent home from the hospital, his CM, Flora McKay, began evaluating his case. She called him daily after he was released, monitored his progress, and prepared her cost savings report.

She started with the projected costs for Fred's treatment if she had not intervened. Fred would probably had stayed in the hospital for the 3 weeks that he was on I.V. medication. At about $1,000 per day, his care would have cost $21,000.

Flora deducted the costs of the treatment plan, infusion supplies, nursing care, and supplies. After negotiating a good rate with a local vendor, she received a daily rate of $400, or a total of $8,400. Her own CM services cost a flat rate of $2,500, which demonstrated a total savings of $10,100. She saved her MCO about $4 for every dollar it spent on case management services.

CONCLUSION

Remember, if the patient truly needs a medical test or procedure, it is still incumbent on the practitioner to provide the service. MDs are responsible for the patient's welfare, not the MCO or insurance company. Lack of prior approval or authorization is not a valid malpractice defense strategy. Get the medical director's, reviewer's, or CM's name or social security number and tell him or her that you will hold him or her and the MCO personally responsible for the patient. Chart all telephone conversations and denials, using their direct quotes. Ask for a written facsimile report to prove your case and build your own solid evidence against them. Remember, they might even accidentally forget that you were denied a certain test, treatment regimen, drug, or medical intervention and put the blame for poor outcomes on your shoulders. Do whatever it takes to honestly care for patients. Doctors practice medicine; CMs, DPs, and utilization reviewers do not.

REFERENCES AND READINGS

Agency for Healthcare Policy and Research: http://www.ahcpr.gov/
Health Quality, Inc.: voice (617) 587-4200.
Hetico, H. R., & Marcinko, D. E. Reimbursement support services in medicine. In Marcinko, D. E. (Ed.): *Profit maximization and reimbursement for the physician.* Columbus, OH: Anadem Publishers, 1998.
Medical Case Management: voice (800) 999-3123.
Medical Management Network: voice (800) 564-2177.
The Pace Group: voice (800) 422-5611.

## CHAPTER 18

Outcomes Management and Performance Improvement

Evaluating and Tracking the Results of Your Care

David Edward Marcinko and Hope Rachel Hetico

> What gets measured, gets improved.
>
> —Unknown

In medicine, outcomes management (OM) may be defined as a processes to measure, track, modify, and achieve the best clinical outcomes (quality) while incurring the fewest costs (economic, intellectual, technical, and time). OM may be initiated by demands from internal forces (i.e., increased costs related to labor, technology, rent, equipment, or complications) or from external forces (commercial, governmental, or state insurance purchaser requirements). Regardless of source, OM involves three steps which usually entail 2–3 years of continuing process improvement efforts in the medical office setting.

OUTCOMES MONITORING

This first stage in medical outcomes management involves identifying the outcome(s) to be measured (e.g., breast cancer treatment, orthopedic complications [e.g., delayed union], or change in functional status [subjective pain or demonstrable limp]). Then, aberrant clinical and utilization information is considered if needed to properly analyze the collected data.

The choice of outcomes measurement varies between what is valued by the health care purchaser (the patient) and what provides sufficient information to the physician to improve future patient care and reduce costs. These outcomes generally fall into four categories.

1.   *Clinical information:* These data include objective, radiographic, parametric, and all other quantifiable parameters that are monitored to assess the effects of treatment.

2.   *Functional status:* These data include subjective parameters judged by the patient's perception of his or her pathology, such as the inability to dance because of a painful nonunion or the inability to achieve an erection because of diabetic neuropathy. Although a variety of scales are available to all practitioners to determine the quality of complete life, parameters of most health concerns have not yet been established.

3.   *Patient satisfaction:* This is a subjective measure of the patient's perception of service quality and care rendered by the physician. While not an effective measure of clinical quality, satisfaction is still considered a valuable assessment of provider quality by many managed care organizations (MCOs). Additionally, many researchers link patient satisfaction to clinical outcomes.

4.   *Financial and economic factors:* These measure of the cost of resources consumed to produce a clinical outcome.

OUTCOMES MEASUREMENT

This tracking OM phase includes the ongoing collection of data related to the outcome measures selected and the analysis of results. The results and descriptions of patients who did and did not achieve the outcomes selected are presented and can be shared with other physicians. There are two goals: (1) to establish a norm (i.e., what is the recurrence norm and what is the cost norm associated with rehospitalization of a condition such as chronic diabetes or asthma?) and (2) to determine what results are considered outside the norm. (i.e., what are the patient "outlier" outcomes and costs associated with the repeated hospitalization?). The identification of outliers highlights not only potentially problematic results but also potentially best demonstrated practices and consumers. Increasingly, these comparisons will become public knowledge as outcomes data is demanded by a variety of health care purchasers

OUTCOMES MANAGEMENT

The final phase of OM includes using data to (1) isolate behaviors (laboratory tests, MRIs or CT scans, surgical procedures, orthotic devices, etc.) that most often produce a predictable outcome and (2) identify opportunities to improve the processes of care and patient outcomes. This means finding more cost-efficient and effective ways to provide care (i.e., which preoperative laboratory tests are not needed, which surgical procedures are not required, or when can a knee pad be substituted for an orthotic device for bursitis?).

Sample Size

OM requires a reasonably large patient experience ($N > 100$), according to the Theory of Large Numbers and Central Limit Theory of statistical analysis. It also requires sophisticated management information systems (MIS) and computer hardware to interpret data. Therefore, effective OM may increasingly be practical only in group practices ($N > 5$) that are linked by wide area networks (WANs) or local area networks (LANs) for the purpose of improving outcomes.

Provider Benefits

OM has several significant benefits for medical providers, specifically, the following items:

- Identify opportunities to improve patient outcomes and cost-effectiveness as well as continuously monitor and demonstrate the effects of the changes initiated.
- Offer a way to meet the demands for proof of performance from consumers and purchasers of health care.
- Increase marketability through outcomes and utilization information valuable to third-party benefits managers as they select providers for their health plans.
- Demonstrate a commitment to providing the purchaser with value and to delivering quality patient care.

Payer Benefits

Provider organizations are under great pressure to establish OM programs. In some cases, they may even be required by state regulations or federal laws. In other cases they are required by health care purchasers. The following is a general summary of who is using OM in today's marketplace, as related to medical care.

Health Care Purchasers

OM is used by health care purchasers to make decisions about benefit selection and payment for particular treatments or interventions. Some organizations are currently conducting cost-benefit analyses (CBAs) and cost-utility analyses (CUAs) to determine the cost associated with achieving a particular outcome.

For example, the cost of an occult blood stool screening program may be compared to the future potential savings of not having to surgically intervene in a patient whose condition has progressed to the point of metastatic colon cancer

Some MCOs are also interested in measuring how treatments change quality of life, how long those changes last, and ultimately, how much those treatments cost. They are using an analysis called Quality Adjusted Life Year (QALY) to assess both the quality and quantity of a patient's life.

For example, to construct a QALY foot analysis for orthopedic foot surgery, or podiatry, a scale may be used to assess a patient's quality of pedal life. This Foot Quality Well-Being (FQWB) scale might be ranked from 0 (amputee) to 1 (perfect foot health). Now, suppose that a group of 60 patients with a painful bunion deformity had a mean foot health index of 0.58 and then were subjected to a treatment intervention (i.e., larger shoes, shields, nonsteroidal anti-inflammatory drugs (NSAIDS), injection, orthotics, or surgery) that increased their index to 0.70 for 1 year. In the aggregate, 7.2 QALYs would be gained in this population of patients. The calculation is as follows: $70 - .58 = .12 \times 60$ patients $= 7.2$ QALYs.

To determine the economic impact of the intervention on the 60 patients, the cost of treatment would be divided by the 7.2 QALYs to yield the cost/QALY. In the very near future, purchasers may decide to pay only for those therapeutic interventions that result in the lowest cost/QALY ratio. The important point is that computerized statistical software tools exist to allow purchasers to compare and contrast the costs of intervention in order to make the most appropriate payment decisions for the interventions given to their patients.

The Federal Government

Currently, the federal government requires hospitals to maintain information on only two outcomes: mortality and morbidity. In 1986 the Health Care Financing Administration (HCFA) collected and published these statistics to much criticism since they were not adjusted for the huge variation in patient populations and acuity needs served by the participating hospitals. Although not directly related to all specialties and branches of the medical arts, national databases are now being constructed that include other parameters to effectively manage Medicare and Medicaid expenditures and to notify the public of medicine's performance.

For example, one well-known national MCO lists the following seven adverse parameters in their specific OM review:

- Patient death.
- OR time twice as long as expected.
- Surgical procedure(s) not listed on consent form.
- Unexpected return to the operating room.
- Surgical procedure resulting in a hospital admission.
- Unscheduled ICU admission.
- Readmission within 2 weeks of any procedure or prior admission.

The National Practitioner Data Base (NPDB) is another good example of OM, although the American health security act (Hillary Clinton's health care reform proposal) was not established after the 1992 election. Nevertheless, the stated intent of publicly comparing providers, plans, and individual states, according to a risk-adjusted system, is going forward in earnest by the private corporate sector. And although it is obvious that private sector MCOs are ahead of the federal government, it may be only a matter of time until corporate and national bodies unite for the common good of protecting the nation's health care.

State Governments

In about 40 states nationwide, outcome databases have been funded to collect medical information, as described above. Pennsylvania and New York are notably ahead in this quest. In these two states, data is made public and compares the costs and outcomes of hospitals and physicians. In several other states, similar data are being gathered to address outpatient and ambulatory surgical center (ASC) care in the coming years. Therefore, if you practice in any of these venues, your medical and economic outcomes data will be gathered, tracked, and monitored.

Accrediting Bodies

The primary accrediting bodies in health care are encouraging and may soon mandate OM programs. These agencies are the Joint Commission on the Accreditation of HealthCare Organizations (JCAHO) for hospitals, health care facilities, long-term and behavioral health care programs; the American Osteopathic Association (AOA) for DOs, the Performance Measurement Coordinating Council [PMCC] (an alliance of the AMAs American Medical Accreditation Program [AMAP], for individual physicians), and the National Committee on Quality Assurance (NCQA). The latter organization is the primary accrediting body of managed care organizations and HMOs. It includes representatives from the business community, employers, and major health and insurance plans, along with a host of other technical consultants.

For example, the following is a condensed summary of NCQA guidelines that may be used when reviewing medical office records:

- Legibility of progress notes.
- Dated entries with author's signature and patients name and ID number.
- Biographical and personal information.
- Medical problem list with allergies.
- Past medical and surgical history.
- History and physical examination results with appropriate objective and subjective information.
- Social history and substance abuse recordings (patients > 14 years).
- Laboratory, imaging, and consultation results.
- Working diagnosis.
- Treatment plan.
- Unresolved problems and previous office visits.
- Medical risk tolerance and immunization record (if applicable).
- Appropriate availability of screening services.

On the other hand, during the more intense NCQA accreditation process, health plans may be reviewed against more than 60 standards (with percentage weights) in the following areas:

- TQI/TQM = 40%
- UR/CM = 17.5%
- Rights and responsibilities = 17.5%
- Credentialing = 10%

- Preventive health services = 10%
- Medical and surgical records = 5%

Interestingly, the Health Plan Employer Data and Information Set (HEDIS 2.0-2.5-3.0) database was developed in conjunction with NCQA and has generated interest in the following quality measures.

Preventive service: cervical cancer screening, childhood immunizations, cholesterol screening and mammography.

Prenatal care: first-trimester care and low-birth-weight infants.

Acute and chronic illness: asthma inpatient admission rates and diabetic retinal examinations.

Mental health issues: ambulatory follow-up care after hospitalization for major psychiatric affective disorders.

In a newer version, HEDIS was directed toward developing indicators relating to the treatment of diabetes and coronary artery/peripheral vascular disease. Other, more recent aspects of HEDIS include compliance audits, NCQA quality compass informational database information, and consumer research, along with other various assessments.

According to the director of Scientific, Professional and Section Affairs of the American Public Health Association (APHA), interested physicians and APHA members are invited to submit comments and new item contributions for the HEDIS 3.5 and 4.0 projects by fax (202) 789-5661 or E-mail (rebecca.parkin @ msmail.apha.org).

RANKING HEALTH CARE PLANS

> If a health plan doesn't have NCQA accreditation, then, on a marketing standpoint, it can lose some big accounts.
>
> —Alan L. Schocket, health care consultant, Denver

Every year NCQA requests that the nation's 650 or so managed care plans submit information about themselves. Many do not participate because some feel that HEDIS standards are imperfect. What to submit and how to submit it are defined in 310 pages of technical specifications. These HEDIS results are blended with other data, such as accreditation, board certification, and participating physician specialist ratios. The final product is called the *Quality Compass*, which is sold to medical plans, employers, and various other health care consultants (Table 18.1).

The following managed care plans earned the four-star (top 25) rating in the 1998 *US News & World Report* ranking of 271 pans in the United States. Scores demonstrate performance on a scale of 0 to 100 in 28 measures of quality (Table 18.1). The magazine generates this unique ranking based on the data. NCQA

TABLE 18.1 Managed Care Plan Quality Ratings

MANAGED CARE PLAN (Type and Region)	POINT SCORE (Quality Indicators)
1. Fallon Community Health Plan HMO (MA)	100
2. Finger Lakes—Blue Choice HMO (NY)	99
3. Tufts Health Plan HMO (MA, ME, NH, RI)	99
4. Harvard Pilgrim Health Care HMO (MA, ME, NH, RI)	99
5. Welborn Health Plans HMO (IN)	97
6. HealthSource CIGNA (HMO (MA)	97
7. BC/BS HMO Choice ME POS	96
8. ConnectiCare HMO (CT)	95
9. Capital District Physician's Health Plan HMO (NY)	94
10. BC/BS MA HMO Blue	94
11. Kaiser Foundation, So. CA HMO	94
12. Preferred Care HMO (NY.)	93
13. Group Health Co-operative So. Central WI HMO	93
14. Health New England HMO (CT, MA)	92
15. HealthSource-CIGNA HMO (ME)	91
16. Matthew Thornton Health Plan HMO (MA, ME, NH, VT)	90
17. BC/BS ME HMO	90
18. Health America PA HMO (Pittsburgh)	90
19. Blue Care Health Plan HMO (CT)	89
20. Kaiser Foundation—Northeast HMO (CT, MA, NY, VT)	89
21. Finger Lakes—Blue Choice POS (NY)	88
22. Health Care Plan—New York HMO	87
23. HMO—CNY HMO (NY)	87
24. Blue Care Health Plan POS (CT)	87
25. HealthSource—CIGNA HMO (MA, NH)	87

provides numbers on how well plans perform in individual measures, but it does not rank the plans itself.

Insurance Companies, MCOs, and other Payers

Insurance companies, HMOs, PPOs, and MCOs are increasingly using and requiring OM from providers in order to differentiate among them. For example, United HealthCare, Cigna, US Healthcare, some Blue Cross/Blue Shield (BC/BS) plans, and many others sell benefits to employers that require that minor surgery be performed at designated hospitals or ambulatory surgery centers (ASCs) that can demonstrate expected outcomes and provide the service for a defined or reduced fee. Physicians not associated with these organizations are at a competitive disadvantage to those that are affiliated with them.

PERFORMANCE IMPROVEMENT

Performance improvement (PI) is defined as a systematic approach to the measurement, evaluation, and improvement in the quality of a medical office's services and patient care, through disciplined inquiry and teamwork. PI is a global undertaking that involves a practice's entire operations. It is based on the concept that high-quality health is the lowest-cost solution to the current health care dilemma (Figure 18.1).

Benefits

PI incorporates the concepts of OM just described above. PI uses information and feedback from the provider and patient to assess and improve the value of its medical services. PI advocates build in quality as care is provided, on a prospective real-time basis, in contrast to the less effective and dated method of inspection or random sampling through retrospective review. The benefits of PI to a medical practice are listed below:

- Allowing MDs to continually monitor the care delivery process.
- Cost control and efficiency utilization, initially achieved through charge reductions but then maintained and increased through revenue enhancement processes.
- Development of practice guidelines for the creation of a clinical (critical) path method (CPM) by incorporating OM results.

Case Example

The MMI Companies, Inc., of Deerfield, Illinois, recognized the increasing role of nonphysician health care providers and the movement away from hospital

QUALITY ASSURANCE ACTIVITIES OF GROUP PRACTICES

SIZE (# of FTE Physicians)	Patient Satisfaction Studies	Drug Formulary	Outcomes Studies	Benchmarking	Accreditation
10 or fewer	72.6%	34.1%	28.0%	21.0%	15.9%
11–25	76.9	29.7	31.2	30.6	8.1
26–50	91.5	42.0	39.7	50.0	18.8
51–100	94.6	48.6	47.2	50.0	18.2
101 or more	88.0	48.0	58.3	58.3	39.1
SPECIALTY COMPOSITION					
Single Specialty	66.3%	29.8%	31.1%	19.8%	13.6%
Multispecialty	82.7	38.3	33.5	35.4	16.4
ALL GROUPS	**75.6%**	**34.2%**	**32.3%**	**28.3%**	**16.0%**

QUALITY ASSURANCE ACTIVITIES OF GROUP PRACTICES

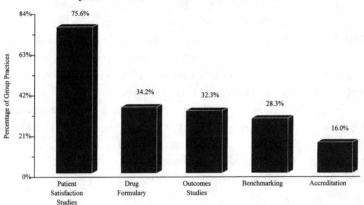

QUALITY ASSURANCE ACTIVITIES OF GROUP PRACTICES

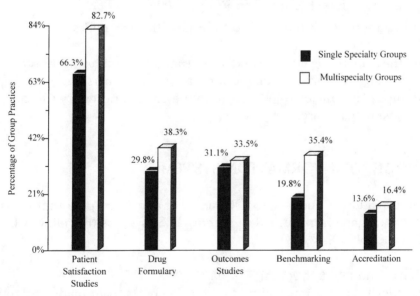

FIGURE 18.1   Quality assurance activities of group practices.

Data sources: CRAHCA Performance Efficiency Evaluation Reports: 1996 Annual Report © 1997, 1995 Annual Report © 1996 and 1994 Annual Report © 1995.
From *1998 Hoechst Marion Roussel Managed Care Digest Series.* Reprinted by permission of the publisher, Hoechst Marion Roussel, Inc.

care into the ambulatory, home, or physician office setting over a decade ago. Consequently, emerging patient risks occur when

- new medical procedures are performed by underskilled medical personnel without appropriate training or credentialing;
- patients complaints are nonspecific, delayed specialist referrals;
- patients are sicker and management communications system failures result in more serious and/or acute or chronic complications;
- health maintenance or prevention services are reduced.

Therefore, MMI's Clinical Risk Modification Triad-SM program was instituted to enhance patient care, improve provider performance, and mitigate professional liability. Three medical services were studied: (1) perinatal, (2) emergency, and (3) anesthesia services. After 5 years of evaluation, linear regression analysis demonstrated a statistically significant inverse relationship between participation and the number of liability claims. In other words, as PI participation increased, the number of claims considered an inverse surrogate for care quality decreased. Actual results are presented below, and it was demonstrated that central to a change in provider behavior is a reduction in liability losses with implementation of a PI and/or other clinical risk modification program.

MMI's liability claims reduction over a 5-year period:

Perinatal services: From $24 to $20 per birth

Emergency services: From $47 to $35 per 100 visits

Anesthesia services: From $172 to $118 per 100 anesthetics

Using these methods, MMI also demonstrated that achieving substantial and sustained change in PI behavior required at least 2–3 years and that long-term relationships play a major role in creating the change necessary to manage risk and improve patient care.

MANAGEMENT INFORMATION SYSTEMS

Good information is the key to OM and PI, and both philosophies require powerful management information system (MIS) systems that allow MDs to accomplish the following:

- Collect and tabulate volumes of data.
- Statistically collate internal and external reports from many different perspectives, most commonly cost and clinical success.
- Keep internal reports confidential through password protection or encryption mechanisms.
- Produce and manipulate reports on a regular basis, with minimal cost and input time.

Since computer-generated reports are only as accurate as the data used to produce them, such comparisons must do the following:

- Be valid and accurately reflect costs and patient care. Correct coding units, such as current procedural terminology (CPT), relative service value (RSV), capitation rates, and patient encounters must be properly used.
- Be reliable, with risk adjustments to consider differences in patient populations or physician subspecialties.
- Be tabulated over an adequate time frame, since short-term reports skew and limit data. They also fail to provide consistency of results.

THE MANAGED CARE AUDIT

MCOs usually screen for provider credentials, premium costs, and scope of benefits. The often nebulous concept of quality is now the fourth component that auditors are evaluating when, not if, they review your office. The following list represents some key aspects of the medical office review process. Remember, forewarned is forearmed.

- Safety precautions, lighting, fire extinguishers, and annual inspection devices Occupational Safety and Health Administration (OSHA) and Clinical Laboratory Improvement Act (CLIA).
- Office appearance, cleanliness, rest rooms, parking, and accessibility.
- Staffing (front and back office) needs.
- Appointment waiting lists for office care (< 30 days), nonurgent care (< 7 days), urgent care (< 24 hours), and emergent situations (immediately).
- Medical and surgical records review.
- After-hours, on-call, and emergency call schedules.
- X-ray equipment inspections, CPR training, and resuscitation equipment.
- Equipment, inventory, medications, and samples, inspection and material safety and data sheet (MSDS) stickers, expiration dates, and supplies.
- Continuing education for you and your staff.

PHYSICIAN ECONOMIC PROFILING

Just as managed care plans have their performance evaluated by the National Committee on Quality Assurance (NCQA) though HEDIS, individual physicians are also subject to clinical and economic profiling by the plans, insurance companies, and other consumer groups. This information includes medical school, internship; residency and fellowship educational background; board eligibility and certification; office location(s) and hours of operation; languages spoken; affiliated hospitals, surgery centers, and areas of subspecialization; policies on credit card payments and a list of the managed care plans with which they affiliate.

To excel on a personal *practice and patterns* basis, the following should be examined to enhance any practitioner's clinical and economic profile:

- Consulting, specialty, and subspecialty referral practices, etc.
- Prescription habits, sample dispensation, and generic equivalents, especially for NSAIDs, antibiotics, antihypertensives, and other chronic agents.
- Use of invasive tests, such as angiograms, IVPs, bone scans, and biopsies.
- Use of noninvasive procedures and tests, such as MRIs, stress tests, ultrasounds, and CT and PET scans.
- Average length of hospital stay (ALS), surgical operating times, etc.

Remember, most medical quality management experts are of the opinion that if the results of a test will not change or alter a patient's treatment plan (decision point), it probably should not be done.

Utilization rates also can be controlled and reduced to some extent through the prudent use of the following techniques:

- Appropriate use of telemedicine and/or telephone triage systems, usually staffed by nurses or other ancillary medical personnel.
- Upfront co-payment collection systems.
- Appropriate preventive care, patient education, and use of emergency or urgent care facilities.

Finally, doctors are using physician assistants (PAs) more frequently as the expanded role of the nation's 38,000 PAs (61% female, 39% male) penetrates the marketplace through expanded Medicare payment rules, enacted in 1998 and partially listed in Table 18.2.

According to the Academy of Physician Assistants, the typical PA-accredited training program lasts 24 months and requires at least 2 years of college and some health care experience prior to admission. Certainly, the use of PAs can enhance patient satisfaction levels, an important measure of quality, since they usually are able to spend more time with patients than are their employer physicians. The use of PAs is geographically represented as follows: Northeast, 24%; Midwest, 18%; South, 33%; and West, 25%. Additionally, consideration must be made of a $25,000 payment differential between PAs and MDs; according to

TABLE 18.2   Expanded Medicare Payment Rules for PAs

Payment for PA medical services in hospitals for assisting in surgery
   Old: 75% and 65% respectively of physician fee schedule
   New: 85% for both
Payment for PA services in a health professional shortage area
   Old: reimbursed only when a physician is nearby
   New: 85% of physician fee schedule and absent on-site requirement
PA payment for facility venue
   Old: restricted to hospitals, nursing homes, and rural locations
   New: no restrictions regarding location
PA payment for practice ownership
   Old: reimbursement only through a physician
   New: may own rural clinics and receive payment for services provided

Modern Physician Magazine, PAs may earn $65,000, whereas MDs coming out of residency earn about $90,000.

MEDICARE OUTCOMES AND PERFORMANCE COMPLIANCE TOOLS

The Center for Healthcare Industry Performance Studies (CHIPS) has developed three compliance tools used by hospitals and physicians to identify possible areas that the Office of Inspector General (OIG) may view as violating Medicare fraud and abuse standards [(800) 859-2447]. These have met initial acceptance in the Joint Commission on American Health Care Organizations (JCAHO, ORYX) program and include the following:

1. The *Electronic Compliance Audit—Ambulatory Surgery* provides information outlining CPT-4 code combinations submitted to Medicare by a facility, which are contrary to guidelines outlined in the *National Correct Coding Initiative Manual.* These code combinations are considered to be examples of unbundling or overcoding of surgical procedures and represent potential exposure to fines and fraud and abuse charges if investigated by the OIG.
2. The *Electronic Compliance Audit—Comprehensive* is based on UB-92 data from the most recently submitted Medicare claims. Advantages include more current information, linkage of code combination violations specific to patient claims, and identification of potential problems in areas other than the ambulatory surgery setting (i.e., laboratory).
3. The *Inpatient Compliance Assessment* is designed to help financial officers find compliance exposure issues related to incorrect diagnosis-related group (DRG) assignments.

Other miscellaneous services available from CHIPS include the *Clinical Assessment Profile (CAP)* series, the departmental *Facility & Activity Center Tracking (FACT) Service*, the pricing and utilization service, and the facility comparison benchmark service (www.chipsonline.com).

THE FUTURE OF OM AND PI

The demand for individual physician practice and economic data to reduce costs and improve medical quality and performance is so great that Wisconsin became the first state to require physicians to turn over medical and financial quality data to a government agency, something it and 37 other states already require hospitals to do. The state of Indiana also required a similar law in its 1999 legislative session, even though such a disclosure effort failed in 1998. Thus, the use of OM and PI in medicine will increase because of the following:

• MCOs will continue to seek value in health care and comparison-shop between plans and providers.

- Physicians constrained by cost controls will find OM and PI useful in their own internal efforts to improve cost-effectiveness without sacrificing quality.
- The development and improvement of practice guidelines through feedback loops. Guidelines will be based on OM data and modified through PI techniques and clinical experience.
- Enhanced marketability of care by using data to trumpet the performance of particular practice organizations (i.e., your private practice, group or network).
- Consumers *(Health Pages)* and buyers of health care services will be allowed to hold integrated service networks (ISNs), MCOs, and other providers accountable by using data generated through the OM and PI process.
- Reimbursement will be linked to standard practices that achieve appropriate outcomes. High-quality providers, defined by outcomes, will earn more than mediocre ones.
- Health care organizations will offer performance-based records to purchasers, who will use them to differentiate medical services.

Employers may even contract with physicians and specify what outcome measures they wish to purchase. For example, if an insured population has a large average rate of diabetes mellitus, they might desire data on foot care, neuropathy rates, amputation rates, infection ranges, or trauma prevention programs.

SUMMATION

MCOs are asking physicians and health care organizations to demonstrate the value and improve the quality of their services. Two important business tools to accomplish this goal are OM and PI. Both concepts involve constantly monitoring and comparing treatment results to improve the quality and cost-effectiveness of care.

According to the Performance Measurement Coordinating Council (PMCC), these methods of establishing performance standards will grow and become more important in the coming years. The PMCC strives to ensures that measurement processes are efficient, consistent, and useful for consumers, purchasers, providers, the government, or others who rely on them to make health care decisions by developing and implementing the following:

- Universal measures to assess performance of physicians, facilities, and health plans.
- Standardized data requirements for varying measurement systems.
- Guidelines for the appropriate use of data.

It is hoped that all will assist the physician to improve patient care and augment professional success.

ACKNOWLEDGMENTS

This chapter was modified with permission from D. E. Marcinko, outcomes management and performance improvement. *Medical Products*, May 1996.

REFERENCES AND READINGS

Balestracci, D., & Barlow, J. L. *Quality improvement: Practical applications for medical group practices.* MGMA, no. 4949.

Cook, R. Laying down the law: Wisconsin legislates collection of physician practice data. *Modern Physician*, October 1998.

DeMattia, R. F. Team players: New Medicare rules expand physician assistant roles. *Modern Physician*, October, p. 66, 1998.

Dunevitz, B. Clinical data crucial to establishing quality controls. *MGMA Update*, January 1999.

Dunevitz, B. NCQA watchdog tactics assess health plan's performance. *MGMA Update*, January 1999.

Monitoring quality, enhancing safety and managing healthcare risks in a time of change. Deerfield, IL: MMI Companies, 1999. (800) 222-4774.

Moore, P. L. Compliance must be done. *MGMA Update*, January 1999.

Moretz, S. Common ground: Accreditors team up to set industry performance measures. *Modern Physician*, November 1998.

Novak, A. *Governing policies manual for medical practices.* MGMA, no. 4929.

US News and World Report, October 1998.

Warn, B. A., & Woodcock, E. *Operating policies and procedures for medical practices.* MGMA, no. 5052 (1999).

## CHAPTER 19

Antitrust Issues in Modern Medicine

It's All about Health Care Fraud and Abuse

Charles F. Fenton III

> For a small minority of physicians, even the possibility of treble monetary damages and jail time is not a disincentive to health-care chicanery.
>
> —Hope Rachel Hetico, health care consultant

Increasingly, the medical practitioner is under scrutiny and under fire. By far the most potent arsenal of weapons against the medical practitioner is held by the federal government. The two areas in which medical professionals may find themselves at odds with the federal government are (1) antitrust and (2) health care fraud. This chapter is dedicated to these two issues.

ANTITRUST CONSIDERATIONS

Medical business entities, such as a Group Practice Without Walls (GPWW) and Professional Practice Management Cooperation (PPMC), have been developed because medicine has shifted from a *retail* mentality to a *wholesale* business model. In the past, physicians would gain or lose patient volume one patient at a time. In the current environment, physicians are at risk of losing 10%, 20%, 30%, or more of their patients at once, as a result of having been deselected, or barred, from an Independent Physicians Association (IPA) panel or group network. Therefore, the intentional or unintentional temptation to commit insurance fraud, zealously collect accounts receivable, or breach antitrust issues, has increased.

Fortunately, current integrated business models have been developed to thwart this loss. Such measures are entirely legal and ethical in nature. However, agreements among competitors, insurance companies, medical associations, and the government, don't always come easily. For example, a collegial discussion of pricing, insurance fraud, or collection issues may be construed as a violation of antitrust legislation.

Typically, the judicial system will use the "rule of reason" to examine whether such agreements may actually enhance cost-efficient care, to the benefit of the patient and payer; or attempt to develop a monopoly in order to enhance the gains of providers and their associated group networks. It is easy for the medical practitioner to run afoul of various antitrust laws, Internal Revenue Service (IRS), Federal Trade Commission (FTC), Internal Revenue Code (IRC), insurance, or medical fraud penalties; therefore, the following compliance issues are presented.

Compliance Issues

1. *Monopolistic risks* are reduced when more than a few networks or contracts are available in the local area for excluded providers to join.
2. Fee-schedule managed care organization (MCO) contracts per se are not generally considered price fixing if the providers have not conspired with one another to set those prices. Moreover, such a network pricing schedule should not spill over to the nonnetwork patients.
3. Individual providers may be excluded from a network if there is a rational reason to do so. It is much more difficult to exclude a *class* of providers than it is to exclude an *individual* provider.
4. A *safety zone* can be created if networks or other contractual plans require a substantial amount of financial risk sharing among plan participants since Stark II laws have been relaxed. Such zones have been created by the Department of Justice (DOJ) and the FTC in recent policy statements.
5. The FTC and DOJ are not likely to challenge an exclusive provider IPA that includes no more than 20%–25% of the doctors within the panel, who share financial risk. Such panels are likely to fall within a *safe harbor*.
6. *Tying arrangements* (e.g., the requirement to buy one item or service in order to buy another item or service) are suspect if not reasonably justified. For example, a patient should not be required to obtain a brace prescription from a specific provider in order to purchase the device from a laboratory that the doctor owns.
7. *Nonexclusive provider panels* will not usually be challenged if no more than 30% of the providers are included (another safe harbor provision).
8. *Physician networks* are often analyzed according to four criteria: (1) anticompetitive effects, (2) relevant local markets, (3) pro-competitive effects, and (4) collateral agreements.
9. Antitrust considerations consist of analyzing *market power*. This consists of two factors: (1) geographic power and (2) product power.

Geographic power is difficult to define in today's environment. In the past, the geography that was analyzed when medical practices merged was the immediate neighborhood. Currently, the geographical area could consist of an entire metro-politan area. In the past, individual patients would often seek a physician whose office was close to work or home. Now they seek a physician based on inclusion in a health plan, and health plans choose physicians based on needs within an entire metropolitan area.

Product power relates to the specific service being performed. There are two products in today's environment: (1) primary care and (2) specialty care. Since there are so many primary care physicians in practice, it would be difficult for all but the largest group to acquire product power.

It is easier for specialists to develop product power. However, certain specialists may never be able to obtain product power. For example, foot care is provided by many types of physicians. Primary care physicians, emergency physicians, chiropractors, physical therapists, orthopedic surgeons, nurse practitioners, and podiatrists all provide foot care. Therefore, it would be difficult, even for a large group of podiatrists, to obtain significant product power.

GPWW and PPMC Rules and Regulations

A PPMC or GPWW may be formed in order to gain marketing clout in the managed care arena. However, physicians must ensure that they meet the defini-tion of a legal group practice. To incur reduced liability from antitrust laws, the following requirements should be considered:

1. A formal and legal partnership, corporation, or limited liability company should be created, with centrally administered management services.
2. There should be a single tax ID number and an integrated delivery system in which each member provider should be able to perform essentially all the same services.
3. Salary and provider compensation packages should not be determined by the number of referrals to other members of the group or to ancillary group services, such as lab or radiology. Such arrangements often trigger Stark violations.

Safe Medical Group Risk-Sharing Considerations

Some states have prohibitions against IPAs and other physician groups from accepting *full-risk* medical capitation contracts as part of their business strategy. The reason is that by accepting such full-risk contracts, the physician or group becomes a de facto insurance company and hence becomes subject to all the laws governing insurance companies in that state. Consequently, consideration must be given to becoming part of a larger organization such as a physician hospital organization (PHO) or physician practice management corporation (PPMC). Occasionally, group practices can consider accepting the concept of *shared risk*, which can be characterized by the following points:

- Vertical integration of medical services.
- Data and information collection, mining, collation, and sharing.
- Defined fiscal accountability and partnership philosophy.

Additionally, providers must be willing to share financial risk with payers on the basis of actual experience, not just on some utilization rate estimate.

For example, if actual medical costs (based on utilization and standard fee schedules) come in between the proposed rates, the difference is shared equally between the physician group and MCO payer. If cost comes in above the highest rate, then the groups absorbs the excess costs. Alternatively, if costs come in below the lowest rate, the physician group enjoys all of the surplus.

PROVIDER HEALTH CARE FRAUD CONSIDERATIONS

Fraud in the health care arena has become a high priority for the U.S. DOJ Health care fraud ranks second behind drug crimes, as the DOJ's top priority. Because physicians are engaged in delivering health care services and because a high percentage of those services are delivered to patients covered by federal plans (e.g., Medicare, Medicaid, CHAMPUS), many physicians may soon find themselves subject to a federal investigation. As the investigators seek to uncover health care fraud, many innocent or unsuspecting physicians may find themselves the subject of investigation.

During the 1980s, physicians dealt with fears from the "malpractice crisis." During the 1990s, physicians saw their practices and income shrink due to the "managed care crisis." The new millennium may become the time of the 'health care fraud crisis." Whereas a claim of malpractice involves only money—in most cases, the insurance company's money—a charge of health care fraud will involve not only your personal assets but may very well involve your very liberty! During the late 1990s, many physicians will find their professional and personal lives devastated by charges of health care fraud.

In the past, practitioners feared an audit because it meant the possibility of paying back prior reimbursements. Often this repayment placed a financial burden on the practitioner. Now, with the increased emphasis on fraud, the repayment of such amounts will seem insignificant compared with the burden of paying back those amounts, paying civil penalty fines, paying lawyer fees, being subject to forfeiture, and being placed in jeopardy of going to jail.

The government has always had an arsenal of laws to deal with health care fraud. These included the Medicare and Medicaid Anti-Fraud and Abuse Statute, the Stark Amendments, the Federal False Claims Act, and mail and wire fraud laws. Recently, the federal government's arsenal has been significantly augmented.

The Kennedy–Kassebaum Bill

The Health Insurance Portability and Accountability Act of 1996, known as the Kennedy–Kassebaum health care bill, enacted last year, provides a whole section to fight health care fraud. In particular, the bill authorizes a new crime of "health care fraud." It changes the intent requirement to include "reckless disregard of the truth" or "deliberate ignorance" of the truth. This intent definition is important because it will probably eliminate the provider's defense that the billings in question were "clerical errors" or the defense that "the E/M codes are too difficult to understand, so I never bothered to learn them." In fact, the report *Documentation Guideline for Evaluation and Management Services* (AMA-HCFA, May 1997) is most helpful in this regard.

The bill increases the civil money penalties from $2,000 per line item to $10,000 per line item! Even *one* erroneous item can be devastating for the provider. Add 20 or 30 such items, and many physicians will see their net worth drop to near zero! The bill also makes it easier for money laundering charges and civil asset forfeiture to be brought against health care professionals. Furthermore, unlike the past, when the federal government concerned itself with fraud in federal programs, the law extends the federal government's power to include *all* health plans, public and private. The practitioner could potentially face civil asset forfeiture for alleged claims of fraud involving a health maintenance organization (HMO) or an MCO.

The bill also authorizes the use of "bounty hunters" in the pursuit of health care fraud. If an individual provides information to the government that results in a recovery of only $100, then the whistle-blower will share in the recovery. The frightening fact is that now your own patients (or their relatives) or employees may become bounty hunters against you. Additionally, the bill authorizes the Health Care Financing Administration (HCFA) to contract with private entities to pursue health care fraud on a wide scale. Private entities will now have financial incentives to investigate health care providers in an attempt to uncover health care fraud. The practitioner will find their activities under scrutiny from different sides.

Balanced Budget Act of 1997

The Balanced Budget Act of 1997 provides some additional tools that the federal government can use in their fight against health care fraud. In particular, physicians convicted of three heath care–related crimes can be permanently prohibited from Medicare.

Federal False Claims Act

A Civil War–era law, titled the False Claims Act (*qui tam* [in the name of the king]), is increasingly popular with prosecutors who pursue inappropriate billing mishaps by physicians. This is due to the fact that, in 1990, the health care industry accounted for about 10% of all false claims penalties recovered the federal government. By 1998 the health care share was almost 40%.

This act allows a private citizen, such as your patient, your employee, or a competing physician to bring a health care fraud claim against you on behalf of and in the name of the United States of America. The "relator" who initiates the claim is rewarded by sharing in a percentage of the recovery from the health care provider. Essentially, this act allows informers to receive up to 30% of any judgment recovered against government contractors (Medicare, Medicaid, CHAMPUS, prison systems, American Indian reservations, or the Veterans Administration (VA) systems). With a low burden of proof, triple damages, and penalties up to $10,000 for each wrongful claim submission, these suits are the enforcement tools of choice for zealous prosecutors pursuing health care fraud. All that must be proved is that improper claims were submitted with a reckless disregard of the truth. Intentional fraud is irrelevant to these cases, even if submitted by a third party, such as a billing company.

Therefore, it is imperative that the attending physicians review all bills before they are submitted to any state of federal agency. The Federal False Claims Act is a federal law that has been on the books since the days of the Civil War and that recently has become a tool to battle health care fraud.

Money Laundering

Charges of money laundering may seem foreign to the practice of medicine. The term evokes visions of a suitcase of drug cash being brought into a legitimate business, being transformed into that business's receipts, and later funneled through legal channels. In medicine the route begins with receipt of a claim payment check (i.e., a check as opposed to the drug dealer's cash). The check is then deposited into the professional corporation's checking account. The funds are then paid to the physician in the form of wages. Those wages are then deposited into the physician's personal checking account. Those funds and other similarly situated funds are then accumulated until a check is written to pay for a sports utility vehicle. The money received from the alleged fraudulent insurance claim has successfully been "laundered" into a hard asset.

Civil Asset Forfeiture

We have all heard stories of civil asset forfeiture run amok and out of control. The family that lost its home because a child had marijuana in his bedroom, the man who lost his boat because a friend who (unknown to the owner) borrowed it and used it to smuggle drugs. These cases will pale in comparison to what can happen if civil asset forfeiture is applied to health care professions. Just like the drug dealer who has his Cessna plane seized because it was used to smuggle drugs, a health care provider may find his entire office and practice seized by the federal government because the office was the conduit for committing the crime.

Furthermore, the practitioner's house, furnishings, car, bank account, and retirement assets could likewise be seized because they constitute "fruit" of the illegal activities.

Civil asset forfeiture is a seize now, ask questions later activity. This appears on the surface to constitute punishment without due process. However, in civil asset forfeiture there is due process, it just comes *after* the seizure. Civil asset forfeiture is to property like an arrest is to the person. A warrant is issued stating in essence that the property did something wrong. The property is "arrested" (i.e., seized), and a hearing or trial will follow at some later date to determine the facts.

Examples of Vicarious Physician Medical Risk

In certain situations the doctor may be at risk of a fraud charge even if he or she never submitted a questionable claim. The two classes of practitioners that may have such risk involve physicians who are members of a group practice and employed (or contracted) physicians.

Employed Physician

You may think that simply because you are an employed physician that you are not at risk. However, in some cases, your risk could be greater. For example, if you work for a physician who employs you to see patients at a contracted nursing home and you either get paid per patient or per day, realize that Medicare is being billed under your name as the provider of services. Although you may never receive the money, if there is a question of fraud, you would be the one liable because the billing was done under your name. The point is that whether you are self-employed, a member of a group, or an employed physician, you should personally ensure that the billing being conducted under your name and signature is proper.

Group Practice

If you are a member of a group and your income is at all dependent on the income of another member of a group (e.g., expense sharing or production-based income), then you may be liable for the fraud of another member of your group. The rationale is that every member of the group benefits financially from the money received secondary to the fraudulent activity. This can put a practitioner in a very difficult position. One must choose whether to continue in practice with a practitioner employing questionable billing techniques or whether to dissolve the group.

Certificates of Medical Necessity

Physicians are asked daily to sign certificates of medical necessity (CMN). Under the new law, you may be liable if you sign a CMN and the product or service is later found to be not medically necessary. In most cases, a physician should have no problem with this rule. The practitioner should be careful in signing CMNs that come into your office unsolicited. For example, you may be asked to sign a CMN for transportation of a Medicaid patient to your office. But was that transportation or the particular level of transportation medically necessary? Extreme caution should be employed when signing a CMN for transportation. In most cases, transportation to your office will be nonemergency transportation of an ambulatory patient. Unscrupulous transportation companies have been known to bill for stretcher transportation of ambulatory patients. Do not allow yourself to be swept into another's fraudulent scheme. Be careful what you certify as medically necessary!

Avoiding Accusations of Medical Fraud

"Will the defendant please rise." These words should strike terror in all who read them. By taking certain measures *now,* one can hope to avoid hearing them. There are actions that can be taken by the practitioner now in an attempt to limit charges of fraud. They include an awareness of the statistics that third-party payers have about billing patterns, changing certain outlying patterns, and changing questionable documentation.

Statistical Analysis and Fraud Investigations

To determine where an audit is likely to take place, one need only study this report to find out "where the money is" to quote noted bank robber Willie Sutton. Luckily, the federal government has provided adequate statistics so that the provider can determine risk, at least to a certain extent. Whether you are charged with health care fraud first depends on whether you are audited and on the results of that audit.

The HCFA compiles data concerning fee charges and payments by all physicians. These data are broken down into various categories, such as by CPT code, physician specialty, and state. Each and every physician should obtain a copy of this report and review it thoroughly. These data are available through HFCA or can be downloaded from its Internet web site (http://www.hcfa.gov). The report contains valuable yearly statistical information concerning the rendering of services to Medicare beneficiaries. By comparing the statistics of this report with the statistics of your office, you can determine your risk of an audit.

Since the likelihood of an audit is dependent on where the money is, the nationwide average and the placement of your state in the table can indicate the likelihood of your being audited. Therefore, the risks are that many physicians in high-reimbursement states will be audited, and few physicians in low-reimbursement states will be audited. This is not as arbitrary as it may seem. There must be a reason that the average physician's Medicare charge in one state is higher than that of the national average. Unfortunately, only an audit will determine the reason—whether it is due to valid treatments or health care fraud.

These statistics are available to Medicare. Since "knowledge is power," you should familiarize yourself with the data that Medicare will use in targeting audit candidates. By knowing where a likely audit will take place, the practitioner can alter procedures and documentation to ensure that they have the ability to withstand an audit.

Standard Deviation or the Bell Shaped Curve

Although a bell curve will not ensure that you will not be audited, it can go a long way to disprove any intent to defraud a third-party payer. Understanding your options is the first step in visualizing the bell curve.

There are five new patient evaluation and management (E&M) codes (99201, 99202, 99203, 99204, 99205) and five established patient E&M codes (99211, 99212, 99213, 99214, 99215). A normal bell curve for most physicians would probably see most of the visits spread fairly evenly over the different levels of codes of each group, with a smaller amount in the level 1 and 5 codes.

You can use your computer to evaluate whether your CPT codes, especially the E&M codes, and the other codes all fall within a bell curve. If these codes do not fall within a bell curve, then you should consider whether you should adjust you coding patterns to bring them into a bell curve.

Proper Medical Documentation

Documentation is the key to surviving an audit and preventing charges of health care fraud being brought. Often, the practitioner is simply guilty of poor record keeping. Most practitioners have developed a "form" they use when evaluating their patients, especially their E&M patients. However, most of these self-made forms are inadequate. The problem is that the individual practitioner is unaware of such inadequacies until it is too late (i.e., after the audit is complete).

In today's computerized and interconnected society, it should be easy to share information concerning what type of documentation is needed to provide proof of the services rendered *and* the medical necessity for those services. McDonalds, Wal-Mart, Subway, and the like all provide nationwide standards that are followed by all of its establishments. With the establishment of PPMCs, perhaps this leadership will help streamline and standardize the record keeping of its members. Such standardization can help to provide a measure of assurance to the practitioner that their records are "audit-proof." Nationwide standards also can be easily disseminated to members when forms need updating or when a particular portion of a form proves inadequate.

Until that time, individual practitioners must fend for themselves. If you are unfamiliar with the exact definitions of the E/M codes, then you should consider attending a coding seminar. If you feel that you still may not understand the subject matter, even by attending a seminar, then you should employ a CPT consultant to evaluate your practice and your patterns of practice. The role of a CPT consultant is to evaluate your current coding patterns, evaluate any areas of risk that may be present, and provide you with instruction as to which usage to change or eliminate. Such consultants, however, do not enjoy the attorney-client confidentiality privilege but often work with lawyers on specific issues.

The practitioner also should consider revamping the charting and documentation system. Your documentation system should be the best that is available. Your documentation of your patient encounters is like the stonewall of a fortress. If a reviewer or auditor is unable to penetrate your documentation, then you will be able to successfully fend off any attack against your finances and your integrity. Several physician groups have developed sets of "encounter" sheets to allow the physician to document fully each encounter. Such encounter sheets have been tested and retested in several Medicare audits. When an audit signals that a change in the form is necessary, the change is made. Until some entity takes the lead in establishing a nationwide standard, the practitioner should seriously consider adopting such forms.

The Medical Compliance Audit

The importance of regular *compliance audits* cannot be overstressed. Such audits uncover areas of potential liability. By unearthing these sources of potential liability, remedial action can be taken to limit risk. Furthermore, such regular compliance audits serve to undermine any accusations of criminal intent.

CONCLUSION

In times like this it is important that the practitioner ensure that his or her medical records adequately document the services provides *and* the medical necessity for those services. The risks are simply too great to ignore.

During a health care fraud investigation or trial, it is you, the doctor, who will be labeled the "greedy physician." The fact that you actually did the work and deserve to get paid for providing the service gets lost in the hyperbole. The fact is that the patient received the service. The real question boils down to who pays for the service, the patient or the insurance company, or you! If the third-party payer pays for the service, then you are bound by all of its terms and requirements, including the right to audit your records and recoup any inappropriate amounts previously paid.

In a malpractice action it is easy to take sides. It is easy for physicians to argue that the aggrieved patient, the plaintiff attorney, and the plaintiff's expert witness are taking advantage of a defendant physician who is only trying to do his or her best treating patients. *In health care fraud however, it is not so easy to take sides with the accused.* A physician who commits health care fraud denigrates his profession, steals taxpayer or third-party payer dollars, and decreases the amount of the health care "pie" available for honest practitioners. Those few practitioners who actually commit health care fraud will find few allies except their attorneys. Honest practitioners must position themselves so that they do not inadvertently fall victim of the dragnet for health care fraud.

By heeding the warning that the federal government is targeting providers for health care fraud and by changing habits that might be fraught with antitrust, insurance compliance, or medical fraud issues, the astute physician may be able to avoid some of the legal torment described in this chapter.

REFERENCES AND READINGS

Fenton, C. F. Medical fraud and anti-trust compliance: Legal issues in Medicine. In Marcinko, D. E. (Ed.): *Profit maximization and reimbursement.* Columbus, OH: Anadem Publishing, 1998.

## CHAPTER 20

Relinquishing the Leadership Role of Physicians

Change and Stress Management for the Newly Led

Eugene Schmuckler

> For every complex problem there is a simple solution . . . and it's wrong.
>
> —H. L. Mencken

Many of you can remember the day you first went into practice. Idealistic, you subscribed to the philosophy of the need to take care of your patients, your family, and yourself. Economic rewards would surely follow.

To meet these idealistic goals it was necessary for you to remain independent. Most doctors are accustomed to being in charge, making split-second decisions single-handedly, often simply by screaming at somebody.

The practice of medicine is undergoing radical changes. Over the past 5 years, managed health care has transformed American medicine. One of the major consequences has been the loss of the doctor's independence.

In 1998, according to the American Medical Association (AMA), at least 92% of the nation's physicians had some type of managed care contract. "Capitated" contracts, those that pay a set fee for each patient, accounted for one-third of the average doctor's salary.

As doctors are rapidly discovering, barking orders does not work when bargaining with insurers and hospitals. Doctors, now more than ever, must learn to work in groups. As such there is a shift in responsibility. The primary responsibility of a doctor has been to perform specific technical (albeit at a high level) skills. The doctor's contribution had been individual in nature. Now the doctor is of necessity forced to become a generalist. Doctors must learn to cope with burdensome paperwork, discounted fees, and insurance company restrictions on the specialists to whom they may refer and the drugs they may prescribe. Many doctors are finding that they need a better understanding of how to talk in business terms and how to get comfortable with accounting spreadsheets.

A major cause of these changes is the number of medical mergers and acquisitions. This results in "doctors selling their practices outright, trading patient charts for cash payments and employee status at hospitals, HMOs, or 'physician practice management' firms." The AMA reports that, in 1997, 43% of the nation's physicians worked for someone else. This is up from 24% in 1983. Barking orders doesn't work when you are an employee and now find that the orders are being barked at you. This may lead to a dysfunctional workplace that in turns leads to an increase in employee turnover. We now speak of health care "systems." These systems have been formed by collecting older businesses—hospitals, doctors' organizations and clinics—that are now looking for new ways of operating. Hospitals once made money by putting people in beds. Doctors traditionally charged fees for services. Now the future lies in what has been termed *clinical integration*. This refers to the establishment of *business units* organized to treat specific medical problems, such as heart disease, mental illness, or cancer. The idea is that a patient will receive full treatment within one of these special centers, including hospitalization.

Although managed health care has its adherents and supporters, especially on Wall Street, it is taking a toll on practitioners. With doctors losing jobs and patients, there is intense competition for work. Collegiality and camaraderie are on their way out.

Many physicians are also finding that their patients are not the most loyal. With the number of employer-funded health plans directing employees to managed health care providers, doctors are realizing that they are losing patients. Given the options of loyalty to a longtime doctor and cheaper medical care, the patient will choose to pay less.

Doctors are seeing their way of practicing undergoing a major transition. This requires a profound psychological adjustment, a transformation. Some transitions are designed to keep an individual on a fixed career track. Others are turning points, shifting the entire balance and direction of one's career. In one MBA program geared to physicians, it has been found that one third of the graduates are trying to enhance their existing practices; a third have sold their practices and gone into management, mainly at managed care companies; and the final third are developing new careers as health care consultants. This latter group has decided that they simply want to get out of medicine. Those who do remain as practitioners will have to learn how to think, feel, and value differently from their predecessors.

Today's doctor is now confronted by ever increasing competition, decreasing job security, decreasing personal income, and increasing patient load. Less time is spent with the patient, who then becomes dissatisfied. Increased patient dissatisfaction leads to increased patient migration. This is turn causes an increase in doctor complaints, with the end result being stress and burnout.

Hans Selye defined stress as "the body's non-specific response to any demand made on it." It is the state of being on "duty." Another way of looking at stress is to say that it represents the complex interaction between each individual and his or her unique life situation. Regardless of the definition, it is accepted that stress is a normal accompaniment of life. As demands increase, the body and mind reorganize continually to cope with them. Eventually, under chronic conditions of overload, the efficiency of the coping process becomes marginal and the quality of work and personal life is threatened.

Doctors usually pay little attention to the demands posed by their career, stage in life, economic situation, professional and political affiliations, and family and friends. Stress is a concept with no "plus" or "minus" implications. It may be just as stressful to adapt to an unexpected family problem that arises quickly as to finding that a long-term office assistant has decided to take employment elsewhere.

Another reason for this diminished awareness of stress comes from cultural stereotypes. Denial is a protective device used all too often. This stems from the notion that doctors have to maintain a certain facade. Doctors tend to hold back from expressing fatigue, uncertainty, diminished recall, temporary depression, and other causes of anxiety. Many doctors have made the determination to no longer show any feelings, as a result becoming psychically numb. This is considered necessary to maintain their image and role.

At home, the constraints on voicing vulnerability may sometimes relax. Over the years, however, many doctors seal off such awareness, even from themselves. Later, when under severe stress, they do not pick up warning signals early enough. This can result in, at a minimum, irritability and inefficiency. Some doctors choose to cope by means of self-medication, resulting in additional consequences of stress.

In our culture there is a commonly shared myth that no matter how heavy the demands on a doctor, he or she will continue to maintain a high volume of work and remain in reasonably good spirits. This comes at the expense of personal and family life. Too many doctors consider this deprivation to be temporary.

Job-related issues are not discussed at home as a means of protecting the family. Discussions with colleagues center on problems confronting the profession. Friends and patients voice complaints to the doctor, who in turn has no one to whom he or she can complain.

Stress is a vital function, necessary for survival. When Selye postulated his concept of stress he spoke of the *general adaptation syndrome*, the automatic reaction triggering the "fight-flight-freeze" response. The stress response occurs when demands (stressors) exceed an individual's ability to control them. These stressors are able to penetrate the wall of denial that individuals establish. Ideally, stressors and the abilities to manage them are balanced. This balance may be actual or perceived. It is important to point out that stressors are personal (unique) to an individual. What is seen as stressful for one person is not necessarily stressful for another. In fact, what is stressful at one moment in time is not necessarily stressful at another.

Thus, we see that there are at least two separate classes of stressor: acute and chronic. *Acute* may be identified as one in which the body is actually threatened; *chronic*, as a long-term stressor with little prospect of resolution. This may include marital problems, physical problems, or an intense dislike of one's professional situation. It has been empirically shown that high levels of job stress are related to lower job satisfaction and negative attitudes toward one's health. High job satisfaction is related to fewer occupational stressors and positive attitudes toward one's health. It has also been found that an individual's anticipation of difficult events can be as stressful or provocative a stimulus as the event itself.

STRESS INHERENT IN A MEDICAL CAREER

There are many stressors built into the medical job, and these can exhaust and paralyze if they are not confronted. To be effective, medical practitioners must learn how to cope with their stressors and the attendant emotions. It becomes necessary to attain "emotional competence." This refers to learning how to absorb the emotional strains of uncertainty, interpersonal conflict, and responsibility. For one who is used to being in charge, this can be quite difficult.

Medical practitioners find that they now have to learn to cope with a variety of stresses: role strain, negativity, isolation, financial pressure, information and topic overload, midlife passage stress, and stresses inherent in the profession.

Role Strain

A number of sources of role strain are built into the medical role: overload, ambiguity, and conflict. There is too much work to do in too little time, with imperfect information and limited resources. The practitioner finds himself or herself responsible for too many things, some of which seem contradictory (such as increasing revenues but holding down costs). And now the practitioner finds that it is necessary to interact with too many people: subordinates, customers, superiors, and peers.

The role of employee is quite different from that of employer. Nowhere in your training after your residency have you been given preparation to assume this new role. The amount of paperwork that is required seems to occupy a major portion of the day. What may occur is that the family takes a back seat to the demands of the job. Indeed, for many it is no longer a profession; it has become just that, a job. The nonmedical spouse assumes the dominant role in caring for the children and other household chores. As one physician's wife told me, "I feel as if I am a single parent."

Negativity

Today's medical practitioner becomes aware of the negativity associated with the role. The management group, patients, and employees all point out something that is wrong. There is a continuous confrontation with those things that are either wrong or less than perfect. Employees may start to complain because they are working long hours but not making any more money. They may complain, look for a scapegoat, and always ask for more money. It now begins to feel as if you are being squeezed from both the bottom and top simultaneously.

Isolation

Most individuals who enter the medical profession are by nature as outgoing and gregarious. There is also the craving for independence and self-reliance. Patient contact and warm relationships with colleagues are important sources of satisfaction. The trend today is for isolation to creep in. A sense of isolation often follows a career transition, and the roots of this isolation run deep. Today's practitioners may feel lost since they find themselves without a clear reference group by which to identify appropriate values and norms. They may find that they have been taken off the top of the heap and put on the bottom of another heap. This creates feelings of alienation, loneliness, and uncertainty about the initial choice of career and the desire to remain in that career. Questions may arise as to what types of decisions they may make now and what decisions will be made for them.

It is rare for today's medical practitioner to own his or her own practice, set his or her own rates, and practice his or her own style of medicine. Doctors are subject to outside management, and most doctors find themselves employees of an organization or being highly managed. This results in a loss of autonomy and control.

To counter this, practitioners may elect to build a wall around themselves as a means to distance themselves from the negativity. This, of course, only serves to add to the negativity. Here again we see the impact of denial: many practitioners are fearful of turning to others lest others find out that they are experiencing anxiety as a result of their new role. These insecurities rob the individual of invaluable support just when it is most needed.

Financial Pressures

Our society tends to equate success and income. Large medical groups are absorbing smaller practices. When a practice turns entrepreneurial, it functions in the same manner as does any other business enterprise. That is, it seeks to cut expenses. This is most quickly accomplished by terminating doctors while keeping their patients. When doctors lose their jobs and their patients, there is intense competition for work. This leads to the reality of having difficulty in paying off existing student loans, a house mortgage, and the other expenses associated with living. Concerns about an ever increasing cost of living are raised combined with how to pay for the education of one's children.

Ironically, the need to increase one's patient load in order to increase the group's profitability causes one's hourly pay to go down. The growing lack of job security, along with downward pressure on income, serves to increase internal family strife.

Information and Topic Overload

With the rapid advances of science, the information processing capacity of the individual is often strained. The amount of data to be absorbed, organized, and weighed is staggering. The advent of the Internet has seen an increase in the amount of data generated as well as the speed with which it is released.

Midlife Passage Stress

Although midlife stress has always existed, the other stressors discussed serve to amplify its impact. Midlife crisis occurs when people compare the expectations of where they would like to be against the realities of where they actually are. This is usually the time when a person begins experiencing physical and emotional awareness of limits and mortality. It is a time of reassessment, interest in new relationships, and new work or specialization. There is the sense that this may be one's last chance. It is at this point that one may be tempted to experience an extramarital relationship. There is a great awareness of how fleeting life is. Time to talk with one's children is precious.

It is easy to see how individuals in the practice of medicine can mistakenly assume that they are disappointed in their work. Doubts about one's marriage can also be distracting and counterproductive. The spouse, if about the same age, is also likely to be experiencing some aspect of the same phenomenon. This increases the likelihood of marital difficulties coinciding with professional ones.

Stresses Inherent in the Job

It is impossible to address all the stressful factors inherent in the medical profession. The emotional impact on the practitioners is the feeling that they are anchored in their offices, having to face whatever and whoever is put before them. With the pressure to produce and the workload continuing to increase, a feeling of dread and helplessness can come over even the most conscientious and hardworking practitioner; one cannot get away. Under a reasonable workload this might not be a problem. But under chronic overload it is probably asking too much to expect a person to maintain high internal standards of objectivity and a dispassionate attitude.

EARLY SIGNS OF BURNOUT

When the stress of the transition from independent practitioner to employee, midlife passage, family life, and the pressures of the job combine, the physician may begin to show signs of what has been referred to as burnout (see Table

20.1). These signs are highly individual and may affect each person in different degrees. In general terms, burnout may be defined as a personal energy crisis that can lead to intellectual, emotional, physical, and interpersonal exhaustion. It results when one has devoted oneself to one's work, often to the exclusion of other interests, and that devotion has failed to produce the expected rewards.

According to Freudenberger, burnout is a state of physical and emotional depletion resulting from conditions at work. It is a syndrome of physical and emotional exhaustion, negative self-concepts, negative attitudes toward work, loss of emotional feelings for co-workers and patients and a sense of failure in the quest for ideals. The victim of burnout is angry, impatient, irritable, inconsiderate, and usually experiencing tension at home. Decreasing productivity and practice revenue are by-products of physician burnout.

Individuals experiencing burnout will use some of the following self-descriptive statements:

"I feel tired most of the time."

"I am not very interested in discussing my work."

"I delay or never answer many of my phone messages."

"I somehow feel uninterested in my colleagues and their concerns."

"My attention wanders a lot, despite my efforts."

"I am reluctant to be identified as a physician."

"I am easily irritated and feel generally impatient."

"When others are emotional, I feel nothing for them."

"I increasingly want to sleep, drink, get away."

"I keep glancing at the time a lot; I cannot wait for the day to end."

"It's been a long time since I've had an interesting discussion with someone."

"I've stopped fighting administrative battles. Let them do it their way. It doesn't matter to me."

"Cancellations give me almost physical relief."

"I sometimes cannot make out my own notes."

TABLE 20.1   Signs and Symptoms of Burnout

Significant decline in enthusiasm for job
Decline in quality and quantity of work
Persistent failure to perform required tasks
Absenteeism; tardiness
"Acting out" behaviors (e.g., silent withdrawal, destructive criticisms)
Quickness to explode
Negativity; blaming organization, co-workers, patients, family
Apathy
Use of substances (alcohol, drugs) on the job
Unwillingness to engage in conflict resolution
Psychosomatic illnesses

As can be seen from the above, there are suggestions of poor memory for recent events, a blunting of sensitivity and empathy for others, an unfounded egocentric self-confidence, a feeling of disconnection from others, general cynicism, and feelings of despondency and hardened pessimism.

There also can be physical symptoms. The more typical ones are chronic fatigue, headaches, insomnia, excessive drinking, lowered resistance to infections, and reduced sexual drive. Physicians who are emotionally, physically, and attitudinally depleted because of the practice of medicine will not experience job satisfaction. If the physician is unable to acknowledge these signs as stress-related and therefore make changes may be at increased risk for a lapse in medical judgment, alcoholism, drug addiction, depression, and suicide.

The new medical paradigm has heightened the interplay between the physician's emotions and behaviors. Feelings of insecurity or defensiveness will lead to regressed forms of behavior. Physicians in this new environment may experience hardship and self-doubt. If not dealt with, such feelings can become debilitating.

SURVIVING IN THE NEW ORDER

It serves no useful purpose to look over our shoulders and long for the good old days. The "golden age" of medicine is gone, and while what we are experiencing today will also change, it will never return to the way it was.

Emotional and psychological survival requires a profound adjustment, in a sense a transformation. It now becomes necessary to learn how to think, feel, and value as a member of a *team* as opposed to being an individual contributor. This entails (1) learning what it means to be a member of a team (organization, group practice, etc.), (2) developing interpersonal judgment, (3) gaining self-knowledge, and (4) coping with stress and emotion.

There are a number of steps that can be taken to accomplish the above, such as the following:

- Discuss your thoughts and feelings about your work with your closest friend and your spouse.
- Read one book in a totally unfamiliar field or topic (something in the classics is a good start).
- Tell several close colleagues that you are going through a period of important reassessment. Do not be apologetic, defensive, or humorous about it. Meditate, pray, or simply relax, with eyes shut, for a brief period each day.
- At home, finish one house repair or gardening project. If there are none to complete, consider starting and completing a project that has been put off.
- Call, visit, and/or chat with three friends you have not seen for a long time.
- Do an alternating tensing and relaxing exercise for 3 minutes, twice each day.
- Cut out all sugar and salt in your diet; limit coffee, tea, and liquor to one drink a day.
- At the end of each day, take 15 minutes to talk over the day with your colleagues and staff and go over plans for the next day. Show an active interest in their jobs and problems.

- Find funds and time for a course or workshop not directly related to your work: a "mini-sabbatical."
- Change unreal, unrealistic, or irrational beliefs about yourself and others.
- Cultivate positive attitudes.

The new order of the practice of medicine may lead physicians and employers to make decisions on the basis of impulse. The consequence of these reactions is the constant crisis mode within the individual and the organization. Management and physician turnover (voluntary as well as involuntary) result, causing high anxiety, stress and paranoia for those who remain, as well as for family members. Efforts by the profession to increase efficiency and improve organization are going on and are, of course, essential. However, an ignored dimension has been the emotional and cognitive effects of stress on the medical practitioner.

Implicit throughout this chapter is the notion that the practice of medicine is usually profoundly satisfying. Unfortunately, the paradigm shift has reduced that satisfaction. Most practitioners have concentrated on logistics and system improvement only. It may now be time to add to that effort the techniques of stress reduction through emotional self-awareness, behavior self-modification, and knowledge of group psychology.

REFERENCES AND READINGS

Barnes, L. B. Managing the paradox of organizational trust. *Harvard Business Review*, March–April, 1981, pp. 107–166.

Champy, J. The starfish school of management. *Forbes*, December 20, 1998.

Freudenberger, H. J. *Burnout: Contemporary issues and trends.* Paper presented at the National Conference on Stress and Burnout, New York, NY, 1981.

Kessler, R. L., Wortman, C. B., & Price, R. H. Social factors in psychopathology: Stress, social support and coping processes. *Annual Review of Psychology*, 26(1985):531–572.

Schein, E. H. Individuals and careers. In J. Lorsch (Ed.): *Handbook of organizational behavior* (pp. 155–171). Englewood Cliffs, NJ: Prentice-Hall, 1987.

Selye, H. *The stress of life* (rev. ed.). New York: McGraw-Hill Book Co., 1978.

Stolberg, S. G. Doctors caught up in rapidly changing health-care system. *New York Times*, August 3, 1998.

## CHAPTER 21

Whither the Physician Practice Management Corporation?

Salvation of the Medical Profession . . . or Ruination?

David Edward Marcinko and Thomas A. Knox

> We are currently undergoing the largest and most significant restructuring of an industry in history.
>
> —Alan Stoll, principal, TWM Associates

HMO, PPO, IPA, PHO, and MCO. These terms were unknown several years ago but are currently on the lips of every physician and patient in the country. Not only are these acronyms part of the everyday vernacular, they are also part of daily medical practice, regardless of degree designation. No American is immune to their effects.

Accordingly, now is a good time to add another abbreviation to the alphabet soup of health care nomenclature. A *PPMC (physician practice management corporation)* is a strategic business unit that may ultimately become the destination of physicians across the country who are willing to aggressively seek control of their professional lives through this new business entity.

THE PPMC DEFINED

A PPMC is a corporate entity that provides administrative and management services to medical practices; such as financial, marketing, human resources, contract negotiations, and information technology solutions, in order to achieve the economies of scale and profits not otherwise attainable by the solo or independent small group practice. The concept involves a local, regional, or nationwide vertically integrated network of medical practices, physical therapy centers, ambulatory surgery centers, prosthetic centers, wound care centers, clinical trials and outcomes centers, or nursing and medical specialists, joint-ventured together as a single corporate entity to provide comprehensive health care needs. Information from each location is electronically shared, integrated, and compiled into a repository, allowing each diagnosis and treatment service to be tracked within the entire continuum of care. The practitioner is thus freed from the management, financial, purchasing, business, and administrative burdens of daily medical practice. He or she is freed to practice the art of medicine and surgery.

EVOLUTION OF A HEALTH CARE BUSINESS MODEL

Historically, PPMCs have evolved over the past decade as physicians have become disenchanted with the practice of medicine for reasons obvious to all. One of the first PPMCs was the Scripps Clinic, founded in San Diego in 1924 and then spun off as an independent for-profit medical group in 1996. Today it is planning a public offering of shares when sufficient revenue and sustainable profits are achieved. Another well known physician multispecialty PPMC is PhyCor, Inc., which was founded in 1988 and become a publicly traded company in 1992.

The corporate rationale for the PPMC business model includes the large and fragmented medical practice marketplace; health care industry trends toward consolidation, cost reductions, and integration; need to accept and manage risk; desire to be proactive and not retroactive to the changing health care climate, and validation of the unique opportunity for niche players, such as physicians, in the medical marketplace.

Advantages

PPMCs have certain advantages over solo or independent group medical practices. These include access to capital, avoidance of "vendor" status, elimination of redundancy, and control and potential physician ownership in an organization larger than the sum of its individual practices. Financial managers and other corporate health care professionals possess the business acumen lacked by most physicians. Most important, PPMCs can revive the philosophy and joy of practice, as physicians take over the clinical aspects of care.

Financially, the PPMC also separates the "individual current income" approach to wealth building, from the "organizational future growth" approach by focusing on maximizing equity value, by retaining capital and generating a return.

Disadvantages

Obviously, the above advantages come at the price of management consulting fees between 10% and 22% of annual net practice revenue, or 20%–35% of annual gross revenues. Consequently, the economic value added by the PPMC must surpass the independent physicians' lost profits This may involve constant pressure to meet monthly, quarterly, and annual earnings forecasts, either publicly or privately. Investment banks, venture capitalists, or equity owners will exert pressure to cut costs, increase revenues, and decrease operating assets to enhance PPMC valuation. The organization also may act as a wedge between existing relationships, such as MSOs or PHOs. In the case of a publicly traded PPMC, stock price volatility may be extreme, with long-term contracts (10–40 years), noncompetition clauses, employee agreements, and restrictive covenants encumbering the practitioner.

Accounting Issues

The accounting structure of some PPMCs may be possible due to various Financial Accounting Standard Board (FASB) rules, which govern arrangements between physician practices and the PPMC when the later seeks to acquire the former. Since legal or business reasons often prevent the PPMC from acquiring outstanding practice equity instruments, the PPMC may acquire some or all of the net assets of the practice, assume some or all contractual responsibilities, and/or execute a management agreement to operate the practice and receive valuable consideration (management fees) in exchange. Additionally, the PPMC may secure the future services of individual doctors employed in the practice, through employment, non-compete, and other agreements, since physicians practice medicine and PPMCs do not. This accounting distinction was more fully explored by the *FASB Task Force* of January 1997, no. 97-2, as summarized below:

1. *FASB Statement No. 94, Consolidation of All Majority-Owned Subsidiaries,* affirms that physician practice consolidation is appropriate when one entity has an "other-than-temporary controlling financial interest" (issue 5[a]) in another entity, as is the case with PPMC contractual relationships. The term *controlling financial interest* was not defined, although the usual condition is ownership of a majority voting interest as an appropriate but not exclusive measurement of subsidiary control.

2. *APB Opinion No. 16, Business Combinations,* addresses the combination of two or more business enterprises, or their net assets, that are brought together into one accounting entity. However, it does not address whether execution of the management agreement can be considered a business combination. This opinion is vital relative to the profit and loss (net income) statement of these organizations and to which ones are allowed to consolidate the gross revenues of its components together, rather than just the aggregate of the management fees each receives from each individual practice. This concept is vital for IPO (initial public offering) valuation purposes, among others, and be can explored in the simplified example below.

Example

Ten solo doctor medical practices each have gross revenues of $100,000/year. All then join a PPMC under a single corporate umbrella and pay a 10% annual management fee to the new corporate entity, with an aggregate total of $100,000/

year ($10,000 × 10 = $100,000). In certain cases, *Opinion No. 16* may allow for a valuation of $1 million ($100,000 × 10) for the PPMC, rather than the $100,000 obtainable only through collection of its management fees. This is a modification of the *roll-up model* of corporatized medicine and is designed to allow larger valuations for private and public investor marketplace, particularly in terms of a possible IPO, for the PPMC. After all, would you rather invest in a smaller or a larger company?

Legal Issues

PPMCs are generally concerned with the same antitrust issues as group practices, PHOs, and MSOs. Additionally, there may be a potential to book full professional revenues that are contingent on FASB booking rules, whereas the enforceability of non-compete and restrictive covenants are contingent on state laws. Interesting enough, attorneys are retained for form, rather than substance, and may spend more time on functional organization than governance or actual legal matters. The situation may drastically change, however, in cases of malfeasance and/or business unit demise.

Publicly Traded PPMCs

In 1996, $3 billion was already consolidated into the public PPMC sector. The potential market was originally estimated to be over $200 billion but has decreased dramatically of late. Strong industry trends toward lower physician reimbursement rates drive this exodus.

Examples of PPMC single-specialty "pure play" public companies:

- American Oncology Resources (AOR)
- FPA Network (FPAN)
- OccuSystems (OTC: OSYS)
- Physician Reliance Network (PPSI)
- PhyCor (PHYC)

Examples of PPMC multispecialty public companies:

- Apogee (OTC: APGG)
- Caremark (CK)
- Coastal (DR)
- EmCare (EMCR)
- InPhyNet (IMMI)
- MedPartners/Mullikan (MED)

Privately Held PPMCs

In 1996 there was approximately $500 million of invested money placed in the private PPMC market, consisting of about 65 transactions and averaging about $7.7 million per transaction. Examples of privately held PPMCs include

- American Ophthalmic
- Avanti
- HealthCap
- HealthSpring
- Preferred Oncology Networks

Currently, there is no pure podiatric medical PPMC in operation, although several have begun to solicit interest in the community. One is Podiatry Services Group, Inc., of Minneapolis, MN, with a presence concentrated in the Midwest.

Dental PPMCs include the recent mergers of Gentle Dental Service Corporation (55%) and Dental Care Alliance, Inc. (45%) to form a new company with locations in California, Oregon, Washington, Idaho, Hawaii, Florida, Georgia, Michigan, and Indiana.

Characteristics that would suggest the ingredients for successful PPMC consolidation, regardless of specialty, include practice size (neither too big nor too small), local or regional industry knowledge, strategic competitive advantage, history of prior corporate experience, potential for synergy; and a host of other tangible and intangible factors, as listed in Table 21.1.

Obviously, some practices will possess several of these features, some will have none, but no practice will have them all. The PPMC selection process is a financial

TABLE 21.1   Decision Factors in Joining a PPMC

	STRATEGIC ↔ ALTERNATIVES	
	Remain Independent	PPMC Affiliation
Medical training	Exceptional	Exceptional–Strong–Moderate
Medical leadership	Strong	Moderate
No. MD/DO partners	> 5	< 5
No. Employees	> 15–20	< 15–20
Gross practice revenues	> 1–2 million	> 350,000, < 1.5 million
Gross profit margin	> 50%	< 50%
Net income	Rising	Static or declining slowly
Ancillary services	Yes	No
Business plan:		
Exists	Yes	Yes/No
On target	Yes	No
Failing	No	Yes, slowly
Chronological age	< 45 yrs	> 45 yrs
Managed care experience	Significant	Strong–Moderate–Weak
Bu siness knowledge	Formal	Good - OJT
Financial acumen	Strong	Moderate
MCO market penetration	Weak	Strong
Future confidence	Negative	Positive
Total All Factors:	Stay solo	Join PPMC
Indifference point	Practice value + Intangibles = PPMC consideration	
Solution	Transactional	Operational

OJT, on the job training.

yet heuristic one. Nevertheless, it is time to evaluate those attributes that seem to comprise a successful start-up PPMC. They include management, capital structure, the acquisition deal, and long-term operations, as discussed below.

THE MANAGEMENT TEAM

As discussed in the chapter on medical business plans, management team experience and education are considered by venture capitalists (VCs) to be the most important component of any start-up company. In PPMCs, as in life, honesty, integrity and credibility count. Still, the econometric aspects of the organization seem to get most intense scrutiny and produce the most emotional reaction from physicians. Conceivably, this is because physicians view their individual practices as only a small part of the corporate picture, whereas PPMC executives view a regional or national perspective. In other words, physicians look at the present negative tumult rather than the positive professional future. If you do not share this vision, consider why every entrepreneur on Wall Street is so interested in medicine today.

Correspondingly, some shortsighted PPMC management teams consist of those "branded" physicians who serve to attract attention to the fledgling enterprise. Some even use paid spokesmen or older physicians seeking to retire from practice.

Many of these so-called physician-executives have no formal business expertise or interest in running daily operations. Others have outstanding management credentials. Therefore, beware of potential "loss leaders," feasting on the fear, uncertainty, and doubt of the current managed care climate. As nationally known health care consultant Hope R. Hetico, MHA, of Atlanta, recently stated, "[A]s in any new business paradigm, there is no guarantee that yesterday's icons will again become tomorrow's luminaries. In fact, corporate history seems to suggest that in times of tumultuous change, new visionaries are spawned from its younger members, not existing or entrenched leadership."

Fortunately, after early capital is raised, the professional management team commences its work. This phase usually begins when short-term or impulsive investors have lost money, and unscrupulous organizers have moved to the next deal; enter the professional managers. Practices are then merged, bought, or sold, and a spirit of strategic planning, integrated structure, and professional governance emerges. The initial modified PPMC model is then surpassed by a true integrated health care delivery system, and revenue losses diminish as they are replaced by growth over time.

CAPITAL STRUCTURE

A PPMC uses either debt or equity to finance its capital structure. Deciding the correct proportion of each is one of the most difficult issues facing the management team. It is virtually impossible to specify a point value for an optimal capital structure, particularly since industry comparables, are scarcely available and notoriously inaccurate. However, the following minimum seed capital requirements for various organizations has been estimated:

PHO: < $1 million

Niche MSO: $1–10 million

Podiatry PPMC: $5–15 million

Dental PPMC: $10–20 million

Large MSO: $10–20 million

General PPMC: $20–30 million

X-Spec PPMC: > $35 million

Nevertheless, the risks and benefits of both financing types should be understood by the individual physician to fully appreciate the PPMC business model.

Debt Financing

Traditional debt instruments of PPMCs include *term loans* with a series of interest and principal payments; *secured bonds,* including first (senior) and second (junior) mortgages with varying maturities; and *unsecured debentures* without liens against specific assets. More recent debt innovations include *zero (low) coupon bonds, floating rate debt,* and high-yield *(junk) bonds* secured for risky PPMC ventures.

Privately, debt can be raised from MD partners in the form of upfront cash or as promissory notes to leverage "units" in the business. This means that not only is the medical practice a member of the PPMC but it may also be an "at-risk" investor due to the debt obligation. Moreover, since many of these models are exempt from regulation by the Securities and Exchange Commission, under Regulation D, the medical investor may have little recourse should the PPMC *private placement* go belly-up. Be aware that Regulation D is the SEC exemption that allows an unlimited number of high-income (> $200,000/year), high-net-worth (> $1,000,000) MDs to invest in unregistered securities by virtue of their "sophisticated" status. The exemption mandates that no more than $5 million be raised in a 12-month period and no more than 35 *unaccredited* or naive investors be involved in the deal.

Regardless of type, the use of debt financing has three important implications: (1) stockholders maintain control, (2) creditors can look to equity for security, and (3) if the PPMC earns more on investments financed with borrowed funds than it pays in interest, the return on equity is magnified, or *leveraged.* Unfortunately, leverage also magnifies loses during times of business hardship. Financial formulations are beyond the scope of this discussion but are useful to evaluate existing PPMC debt.

Equity Financing

PPMCs typically acquire seed capital from VCs, investment bankers, or private investors (*angels*) who believe in the PPMC business model. Well-known VCs interested in the early PPMC start-up phase include Hambrecht & Quest, Accel Partners, Welsh, NEA, Carson, and Matrix Partners. VCs more interested in later-stage *(mezzanine)* financing include Summit Partners, TA Associates, Horsley Bridge Partners, PriceWaterhouseCoopers, and Greylock Capital Partners. This type of financing is often needed because current capital is not readily raised from physicians, commercial banks, or other sources.

PPMCs may have several classes of stockholders in the physician equity model, although three is the usual number. *Class "A" stock* is typically practitioner voting equity, sold to doctors who maintain at least a 51% majority. *Class "B" shares* may consist of voting venture capital stock maintaining 49% of the vote. B shares may also hold *enurement* and *supermajority privileges,* which may have the power to veto new members, certain mergers, and acquisitions, to approve budgets, and to exercise other incidental rights. *Class "C" stock* may be nonvoting, with a dividend accrued annually. Typically, PPMCs have a limited *payout ratio* (no retained earnings) to limit income taxes, decrease further equity and debt flotation costs, and enhance return on investment (ROI) relative to other investments limiting growth and internal capital reserves.

Combination Financing

Pragmatically, the PPMC executive management team should focus more on identifying a prudent debt/equity ratio than on setting a precise level. A prudent ratio should capture the benefits of debt in prosperous times yet not excessively dilute shareholder ownership in lean times. This constant balancing act will keep financial risk at a manageable level and ensure flexibility when opportunity presents, allowing the firm to maintain a desirable rating with its creditors while simultaneously attracting new shareholders as the market value of the company grows.

"Roll-up" Financing

A few PPMC's have initially "rolled up" existing practices based on their aggregate equity and then sold shares to the public in an IPO. If growth and/or operations are successful, market value will rise; if not, it will collapse since there was no real initial history of operations, economies of scale, geographic distribution, or integration of affiliated practices in the first place. Needless to say, this is a speculative venture, best left to entrepreneurs.

For example, on completion of a typical roll-up-equity-based PPMC consolidation, that progresses to a successful IPO, the deal may look something like the following:

Initial practice ↔ Consolidated ↔ Public (post-IPO) value
(Founder's level 1–3×) (3–7× multiple value) (15–25× value)

Comparable data valuation is a commonly used method because of its simplicity. Of course, its difficulty rests in obtaining the correct values to compare.

THE PRACTICE ACQUISITION DEAL

In the development of any PPMC, the incentive for the doctor to participate will be either the capital provided by investors or the purchase of practice assets, as well as the assumption of the daily obligations incurred by the physician. In other cases, a buyout, with cash paid to the practitioner, may promote a closer relationship with the PPMC. Some medical groups may even insist on the sale of practice property, the assumption of practice indebtedness, or the sale of real property to the PPMC partner. Of course, from the PPMC perspective, existing real property is much more affordably leased than purchased in most communities.

The most obvious point of contention, is the practice' assigned value for its work force, existing insurer contracts, ancillary services, and entire ability to generate profit. As physicians become experienced in business matters, it seems risky to seek or pay for these types of increasingly intangible assets, which may actually be created or lost through political fiat.

In fact, in the past few years several large PHOs have collapsed after paying inflated prices for local physician practices, while other more experienced venture capitalists have flourished by purchasing undervalued medical groups from inexperienced physicians. Of course, the purpose of a true physician-organized and professionally managed PPMC is to purchase and eventually maintain many practices that are fairly valued at conception. This results in a "win-win" situation for all concerned and appears to be the fate of medical practices in the future.

Currently, the valuation of a medical practice is governed by standard business valuation techniques and Internal Revenue Service (IRS) guidelines. However, most techniques include some combination of (1) discounted cash flow analysis, (2) replacement cost analysis, and (3) comparable sales analysis.

BUSINESS OPERATIONS

In the long-term operating phase of a successful PPMC, it is reasonable to expect that revenues and earnings will rise as the PPMC matures into a refined entity. It is at this point that the decision to remain private or to go public through an IPO is considered. Nonbusiness economic factors, such as rising interest rates and falling stock prices, as seen in 1992, further complicate the decision.

Advantages of an IPO include access to capital markets and the potential for almost unlimited growth. Disadvantages include public scrutiny, initial flotation costs of 7%–10%, and continued public disclosure costs of 10%–20% annually. Hence, margins must grow at rates proportionally higher than these costs in order to produce profit. Prudence dictates and experience proves that IPOs are more successful when PPMCs have a documented operating history as well as a period of accelerated earnings.

While it is true that PPMCs should theoretically produce profits exceeding the sum of their component practices, it may not be realistic to expect an eclectic group of doctors to instantaneously accept a collectivist mentality. After all, as growth through acquisitions eventually wanes, earnings will eventually have to be produced through the daily toil of physician members. If not, the organization will collapse like a Ponzi scheme.

RECENT DEVELOPMENTS

According to the *Cain Brothers Physician Practice Management Index (CBPPMI)*, of 13 publicly traded PPMCs, share prices took a beating and were down more than 75% in 1998–99, even as the health care industry in aggregate managed slight gains. This was a big change from 1997, when PPMCs stocks were up more than 20%. Indeed, PPMC industry bellwethers MedPartners and FPA Medical Management both experienced considerable financial difficulties in the first half of the year, as did Coastal (DR). On the other hand, Phycor just raised the possibility of a financial partner taking it private in a *leveraged buyout* (LBO) because of depressed stock prices and positive news claiming that the company can meet its capital needs through internal cash flow. Despite Wall Street's antipathy for the physician-practice industry, private investment firms such as Kohlberg, Kravis, Roberts & Company and Welsh, Carson, Anderson & Stowe have found certain deals financially attractive. For example, the firms, both based in New York, joined together this summer to acquire MedCath, Inc., a physician-practice management company specializing in cardiology.

Not all PPMCs fared badly in 1998. For example, Kelson Pediatric Partners, in Hartford, Connecticut, accepts capitated medical contracts only for the professional services it offers. It is composed of 20 practices, with 177 physicians in 7 states. It may float a public offering next year. Another growing concern is Women's Health Partners, an OB-GYN PPMC in Nashville, Tennessee. It is affiliated with 145 physicians in four states. Physicians have a 75% ownership in the company and hold six of eight positions on the board of directors. OrthoLink, an orthopedic PPMC, along with Integrated Orthopedics, has also enjoyed recent growth through its 180 affiliated physicians in six states. Its specialty is ancillary services, and a public offering is planned when its revenue stream is predictable. All totaled, more than 6 other major and 50 regional companies have generated considerable growth for the first 6 months of 1999.

Several dental PPMCs, like Orthodontic Centers of America, Orthoalliance, and Dental Care Alliance, posted strong gains and were another bright spot in the sector last year.

At present, PPMCs are represented by the following specialties: allergy and asthma, dermatology, emergency medicine, ENT, eye care, mental health care, multispecialty medicine, neurosurgery, oncology, orthopedics, osteopathy, pathology, pediatrics, plastic and cosmetic surgery, primary care, radiology, reproductive medicine, elder care, urology, chiropractic and acupuncture, hearing care, and veterinary medicine.

ASSESSMENT

For physicians to compete in the managed care environment, particularly one dominated by prepaid or risk-sharing arrangements, new and different skills will be required. Cooperation must occur between honest business partners who will not only bring management talent to the health care table but much needed capital as well.

In summary, the solo medical practice has been relegated to the past and will not soon return. Given the right PPMC, physicians who are at the core of the health care delivery system have an enormous opportunity to become leaders in the new millennium if a new business structure can be discerned. To achieve this goal and regain professional and economic status, it is essential to remember three points.

1. *Avoid PPMC pitfalls.* Common reasons for PPMC failure include incorrect partnerships, excessive management fees, undervaluing the practice, merging at the wrong time, excessively long management contracts, misunderstanding health care delivery models or financial formulas, integrating too quickly, going public too soon, staying private too long, or holding on for practice autonomy for too long.

In fact, according to Townsend Frew and Co., Durham, North Carolina, we may soon be entering the second generation of PPMC development, with the characteristics, modifications, and changing values, along with enhanced success, shown in Table 21.2.

2. *Understand venture capital mentality.* Venture capitalists do not supply funds if a business is in decline. As income declines, MDs may have little or no understanding of how or why their revenue has fallen. Practitioners erroneously think that capital partners will come to the rescue and provide capital during the difficulties inherent to moving into the managed care arena. This is a wrong assumption.

3. *Perform due diligence.* Avoid problems by reading and understanding the PPMC business plan, appreciating contemporary fixed rate and "risk-retention" medical reimbursement contracts, and considering the PPMC's mission state-

TABLE 21.2 Evolution of the PPMC

First-Generation PPMC (Past)	Second-Generation PPMC (Future)
Growth through acquisition	Growth through operational improvements and economics of scale
Rush to go public via IPO	Successful operating history/profits; remains private
National scope	Local and regionally based diversity, no national scope
Lack of ancillary services	Surgery, wound care, imaging, and other centers
Centralized management (traditional)	Decentralized management (matrix organization)
Charismatic physicians (entrepreneurs)	Physician executives (professionals)
"Exit strategy" mentality	Practice continuation mentality
Greed, hubris, self-centered	Value, dedication, humility, service
Reduces overhead expenses	Reallocates but does not reduce expenses

ment. If you cannot or will not perform these tasks, hire a professional to guide you. Remember, if you do not do it, it will not get done. Inertia is death, and no decision is actually a decision to remain with the past and not contemplate the future.

CONCLUSION

PPMCs may or may not be the next evolutionary rung on the medical practice business model. Fueled by legislative initiatives and purchaser demands to reduce health care costs and improve outcomes, consolidated integrated delivery systems have emerged in this model.

Again, according to Hope R. Hetico, "[L]iquidity, ignorance and greed has been wrung from the first generational PPMC models, and the next generation of PPMCs are no longer imaginary. To provide high quality services, regain professional control and survive economically, today's physicians must vertically integrate their practices into a local geographic distribution network. It may no longer be a matter of IF . . . it may only be a matter of WHEN . . . what MODEL . . . and by WHOM."

Therefore, when a PPMC executive comes to town wanting to buy your practice, you will know how to begin your preparation and realize that reasonable profits in the range of 8%–15% are the goals of a credible PPMC, not the get-rich schemes of economically unsound PPMCs despite the hyperbolic protestations of their organizers to the contrary. Always remember the adage *vendor emptor* and be confident that, with professional help, you can determine if the proposed PPMC will be your professional salvation—or ruination!

READINGS AND REFERENCES

Boylon, R. The equity market for physician practice management companies: Is there really gold in those hills? *MGMJ*, November/December 1996, p. 22.

Cook, R. As bad as it gets: Downtrodden investors wonder if PPMs are still relevant. *Modern Physician*, October 1998, p. 2.

Cook, R. Second quarter slump: Lukewarm PPM earnings elicit cool response from Wall Street. *Modern Physician*. October 1998, p. 86.

Inside PPMCs: (800) 521-4323.

Katz, H. L., & Knight, C. C. Selecting an MSO. *MGMA Journal*, February 1999.

PriceWaterhouse. *Giving structure and balance to PPM transactions* (2nd ed.). New York: Author, 1998.

PriceWaterhouseCoopers. *Focus on PPMCs: Financial issues.* New York: Author, 1999.

The physician practice management industry (PPM): Kicking into high gear. New York: Bear Sterns Publications, 1996.

Sharpe, A. Phycor considers going private as option to address depressed price of its shares. *Wall Street Journal*, October 30, 1998.

Townsend, D. W. L., & Frew, J. S. Private PPMCs continue to prosper. *Practice Options*, December 1998.

## CHAPTER 22

Redefining the Standard of Care

Appreciating Subtle Differences Between Medical and Legal Codes

O. Kent Mercado

> First, do no harm. That is the overriding precept of medical practice. The paramount objective of managed care—profit—is diametrically opposed to this precept.
>
> —Michael DeBakey

> There is no profession from the members of which greater purity of character and a higher standard of moral excellence are required than the medical; and to attain such eminence is a duty every physician owes alike to the profession and to patients. It is due to the patients, as without it their respect and confidence cannot be commanded; and to the profession, because no scientific attainments can compensate for the want of correct moral principles. (*Principles of Medical Ethics of the American Medical Association,* 1903, chap. 2, art. 1, sec. 5)

As a practicing physician and attorney, I am concerned by the lawyer's ability to withdraw from legal care for failure to maintain a contractual obligation with the client (i.e., a client either refuses to pay or is unable to pay the legal fees). I was certain that contemporary medical ethics would never sanction such conduct.

There is, however, no medical ethical consensus on this issue; therefore, the problem with relying on medical principles of ethics as a source of public policy is that the principles may be subject to one's own interpretation. Unlike the ethical code for lawyers, which contains several provisions tailored to address some of the possible predicaments in which lawyers might find themselves, the *Code of Medical Ethics* (only seven principles) anticipates few such situations for doctors, leaving much of the principles' interpretation up to physician discretion.

The primary and overriding principle of medical ethics is to do good for the patient. The patient's welfare and best interests must be the physician's main concern. For 2,000 years physicians have sworn by the Oath of Hippocrates:

> I will follow that system of regimen which, according to my ability and judgment, I consider for the benefit of my patients, and abstain from whatever is deleterious and mischievous. . . . Into

whatever houses I enter, I will go into them for the benefit of the sick, and will abstain from every voluntary act of mischief and corruption.

The AMA code affirms this precept: "The interest of the patient is paramount in the practice of medicine, and everything that can reasonably and lawfully be done to serve that interest must be done by all physicians who have served or are serving the patient."

There are now four integrated primary sources comprising the corpus of the *AMA Code of Medical Ethics* (the code): (1) "Principles of Medical Ethics," consisting of seven imperatives introduced by a preamble; (2) "Fundamental Elements of the Patient-Physician Relationship"; (3) *Current Opinions,* published annually by the AMA Council on Ethical and Judicial Affairs; and (4) periodic reports of the council on various topics of current interest.

AMA WITHDRAWAL POLICY

The AMA has a withdrawal policy, which states that a physician may not abandon a patient once a therapeutic relationship has been established, although the doctor-patient relationship may be terminated voluntarily if adequate notice is given and a reasonable time is allowed for making other arrangements. The stricture against patient abandonment was first (and most poetically) expressed in the original *AMA Code of Ethics* of 1847:

> A physician ought not abandon a patient because the case is deemed incurable; for his attendance may continue to be highly useful to the patient and comforting to the relatives around him, even in the last period of the fatal malady, by alleviating pain and other symptoms and by soothing mental anguish.

All subsequent revisions of the AMA code have included the principle of nonabandonment.

With the advent of managed care and a dilution of the fee-for-service physician base, these ethical standards have been challenged as many interesting scenarios have unfolded. For example, what happens when a physician in a gatekeeper managed care environment is denied requested services? Can he or she withdraw from the patient's care? Is this a fiduciary duty of reasonable care to the patient, or is it usurped by the contractual obligations to the managed care company?

Physicians are bound not only by ethical considerations but by common law. There is an ethical and legal duty to provide reasonable care to the patient. Reasonable care relates to the standards of the community and how procedures and care are delivered to patients within a given geographic region. These standards are flexible and are different for doctors at a major center versus doctors in a rural community. Though flexible, failure to comply with a standard of reasonable care will subject the physician to liability, even when there are limited resources or financial incentives or constraints. Although escalating health care costs may make the corporate management of medicine inevitable, under no circumstances should it require physicians to compromise their professional and ethical obligations to their patients. The legal code of ethics (1.2c) requires independent judgment from the third-party payer.

There is also a fiduciary duty to act within the best interests of the patient. Some states have statutes in which punitive damages may be imposed if the physician violates this fiduciary duty—when to limit care—in order to promoted financial incentives.

The ethical basis of medicine arises from several directives, but all are directed at the welfare of patients: to do good and avoid harm. Also, the establishment of the relationship between doctor and patient creates a fiduciary duty. These characteristics encompass the contractual, tort, and fiduciary foundations of the physician-patient relationship.

CONTRACT LAW

Whether expressed or implied, the physician-patient relationship is a contract, governed by contract law. According to the present AMA code, "the creation of the physician-patient relationship is contractual in nature." The advent of managed care in the physician-patient relationship has altered the nature of two essential elements of classic contract law as they relate to medical treatment, namely, voluntary behavior and mutual consent. Both the physician and the patient are free to enter into or decline the therapeutic relationship; however, the patient's choice may be limited through insurance and managed care options.

In a purely contractual relationship the parties themselves establish the terms of their relationship and can agree to any arrangement that suits them regarding the performance to be expected from each other. In theory, the physician would be held only to a standard of "reasonable care" if the parties agreed on that standard, and the parties could even decide that the physician did not owe the patient a fiduciary duty.

TORT LAW

Once the relationship is created by mutual assent, tort law establishes the standard of care owed by the physician. The physician owes the patient a duty of care, and if that care dips below the appropriate standard and causes injury, the physician must compensate the patient. Because physicians are members of a highly learned profession, that standard has traditionally been set by physicians themselves rather than by the courts, with specific duties identified largely by prevailing practices.

The duty of care is not proportional to pecuniary expectations; that is, physicians are expected to provide the same basic quality of care to every patient they accept for care, regardless of ability to pay. Physicians may refuse to accept a patient because of indigence or other reasons, but acceptance triggers fairly uniform obligations. Efforts by managed care to contain health care costs by forcing physicians to take into account economic concerns undercuts the notion that physicians have sole authority to define appropriate health care outcomes for society.

Many disputes arise over the necessary approach to treatment in the managed care environment. The meaning of competent medical care must be expanded to include *vigorous patient advocacy.* A physician should not feel coerced into silence when the patient's health is at issue, particularly when it is the physician, not managed care organization, who is the patient's doctor, fiduciary, and confidante. This seems fair, since the physician may well be liable for any undertreatment of the patient. A physician's "ethical duty" includes any *lobbying* efforts taken on behalf of a patient. The physician should maintain independent judgment but inform patients of their options through their managed care contract. *Legal Ethics,* 1.8, provides that an insurer must inform the insured that his or her contractual obligations are with the company policyholder.

FIDUCIARY LAW

The physician-patient relationship also has foundations in fiduciary law, since physicians have a duty to act primarily for their patients' benefit. Fiduciary duties are implied in the physician-patient relationship because of the high degree of trust and loyalty mandated by the relationship and because a physician traditionally possesses superior knowledge of the art of medicine. The duty imposed on physicians by their fiduciary status helps minimize the differences in their bargaining power. Fiduciary rules limit the fiduciary's freedom of action by prohibiting him from using superior power to take advantage of the patient and by requiring the fiduciary to act in the patient's best interest. A physician shall be dedicated to providing competent medical service with compassion and respect for human dignity.

The physician may avoid tort liability merely by acting reasonably but may still be liable for breach of fiduciary duty if he or she fails to act loyally. The fiduciary may be required to do more than merely compensate the patient for the loss suffered as a result of a breach of fiduciary duty; punitive damages may be imposed on the fiduciary. There have been several bad faith insurance cases exposing insurers to personal liability.

Initially, patient care was provided on a fee-for-service basis. This held true even with the advent of health insurance companies that indemnified the cost of medical care. As the rate of reimbursement increased, the rate of utilization of services provided increased as well. Physicians had exclusive control of the treatment plan as well as service to be provided. There was no incentive for the physician or patient to contain costs.

Escalating health care costs have fueled the drive for increasingly competitive managed health care. The concentration of health care providers, services, and facilities in the hands of managed care organizations has had an ever expanding effect on the way medical treatment is both administered and received in this country. This forced insurers, policymakers, and employers to consider a new method for the delivery of health care. In 1973, Congress passed the Health

Maintenance Act, promoting the growth of the first managed care organization, the HMO.

The managed care concept was initiated over 50 years ago with the advent of the Kaiser Permanente group. Initially, the logging company wanted to lower its costs by involving gatekeeper physicians who would examine patients and determine whether to treat them or refer them to a specialist. This system, while effective with a young and healthy population base, has found limitations with an elderly population, many of whom require continued care by a specialist.

Managed care plans generally ration health care by giving the gatekeeper physicians financial incentives to reduce their referral rates to specialty care and hospital use. The financial incentives penalize physicians for using high-cost hospital and specialty care. Most individuals who enroll in managed care plans typically have no idea that these rationing incentives exist, generally because managed care organizations have no legal obligation to disclose such information. Many health plans take strict control over resources, and physicians also have varying levels of resource control that carry important obligations to patients.

Health plans and self-insured corporations place stringent controls on health care resources, limiting the physician's freedom to practice medicine as the physician sees fit. There are clinical guidelines from a wide variety of sources, including managed care organizations, medical subspecialty societies, and malpractice insurers. Guidelines purport to tell physicians the best way to practice, but there is often conflict with traditional practice patterns and with patients' expectations.

Because medical decision making has become a multilevel process involving not only the provider but also the third-party payer for health services, courts have begun to examine the potential liability of the third-party payer itself. This trend applies across the board to health maintenance organizations (HMOs), independent physicians associations (IPAs), preferred provider organizations (PPOs), traditional fee-for-service insurance companies, and/or separate utilization review companies contracted to approve or deny medical services.

Under the fee-for-service arrangement, physicians' overutilization of medical services severely increased the cost of medical care. Cost-containment mechanisms, such as utilization review, capitation, and financial incentives have been utilized by managed care to curb the rising cost of health care.

Some evidence suggests that managed care, with its cost-containment mechanism, helps to contain the cost of quality medical services. However, with these constraints inherent in the managed care system, there is a conflict of interest between physician and patient. Managed care provides an incentive for primary care physicians to limit their medical services and time spent with patients. Cost-effective measures encourage physicians to underutilize medical services, which thereby strain the physician-patient relationship. Because managed care organizations place an emphasis on cost control, they will have an obvious incentive to direct hospitals and providers. There have been many cases of legal malpractice, where lawyers followed insurance company directives and exposed physicians to personal liability.

Although escalating health care costs may make the corporate management of medicine inevitable, under no circumstances should physicians be required to compromise their professional or ethical obligations to their patients. The ethical issues presented by managed care revolve largely around its intrusion into the autonomy of physicians and their interactions with patients. The most fundamental question, though, may be which principles of ethics apply regarding this economic reality and the adherence to certain immutable ethical standards regardless of different financial arrangements. This business element of health care may challenge existing notions of the parties' ethical responsibilities. *Do we keep or discard the existing notions?*

Some commentators try to incorporate existing ideas into the new framework. For example, physicians traditionally have had an ethical obligation, recognized in law, to treat established patients within the physician's competence regardless of the patient's ability to pay. Patients now are treated under a special kind of physician-patient relationship, governed by new rules and understandings, whereby the obligation to treat ends when the managed care arrangement ends. Some even go so far as to say that the physician has an obligation *not* to treat the patient, because doing so would violate both the letter and spirit of the patient–managed care relationship.

The traditional standard of medical care is defined as: "the level of knowledge, skills, and diligence that the physician owes each patient." The new element might be redefined as the *standard of resource use,* which encompasses the physical and fiscal resources that the physician should use in treating a patient. This standard varies between patients and is determined by "the specific resource arrangement in force for that patient"—the insurance or other reimbursement plan that will pay for the patient's care. Application of the standard of resource use places on physicians a duty of advocacy on behalf of patients to obtain the resources needed for whatever care is determined necessary and to disclose to patients economic incentives and resource constraints and to minimize conflicts of interest.

Physicians typically contract with managed care entities on an *at-will* basis. There are financial incentives to limit the use of medical treatment, services, and procedures. If a physician nevertheless continues to prescribe treatment the managed care entity feels is unwarranted, then the company can terminate the contract. The same result can occur when the physician must serve as a patient's advocate, pleading to managed care review boards on the patient's behalf for treatment approval. Recognizing a new ethical obligation that permits physicians to stop short of full treatment, it may legitimize actions based on conflicts of interest. No managed care company would ever acknowledge providing anything less than coverage for all medically necessary care. On its face managed care coverage does not vary in the nature or range of treatments covered. Virtually all managed care contracts provide that patients will receive whatever care they need.

Most physicians will not discover the resource constraint simply by reading the terms of a patient's insurance contract but rather by seeing the denial of coverage for a treatment, in a specific case or series of cases, by the managed care reviewers. At that point, physicians must decide whether to proceed with treatment against their financial incentives or acquiesce in the managed care's decision. When public policy commands adequate medical care and a physician feels ethically bound to prescribe a particular treatment, perform a certain procedure, or lobby for treatment approval, termination of an at-will managed care employment contract should entitle a discharged physician to a cause of action.

CONCLUSION

Physicians should not have to compromise their medical and ethical practices to participate in a managed care health system. The consideration of a new standard of medical care, based on resource use, is sure to be a contentious issue in the future. With the advent of liability for the insurance companies, managed care entities will have to defocus their perception of delivering care in a cost-effective system, with ethical considerations in mind

ACKNOWLEDGMENTS

Special appreciation is given to Professor Francis Morrissey and Professor Corrine Morrissey for their assistance in the preparation of this chapter.

REFERENCES AND READINGS

American Medical Association. Council report on ethical and judicial affairs: Ethical issues in managed care. *Journal of the American Medical Association*, 273:330 (1995).

Blackhall, L. J., Murphy, S. T., Frank, G., Michel, V., & Azen, S. Ethnicity and attitudes toward patient autonomy. *Journal of the American Medical Association*, 274:820 (1995).

Buchanan, S. F. Medical ethics at the millennium: A brief retrospective. *Colorado Lawyer*, June 1998.

Caresse, J. A., & Rhodes, L. A. Western bioethics on the Navajo reservation. *Journal of the American Medical Associations*, 274:826 (1995).

Clements, E. Systems ethics and the history of medical ethics. *Psychiatric Quarterly*, 63:367 (1992).

Field, R. I. *Balancing act: The new medical ethics of medicines new economics*. Washington, DC: Georgetown University Press, 1995.

Green, R. Minimizing malpractice risks by role clarification. *Annals of Internal Medicine*, 109:234 (1988).

Hall, M. A. The ethics of health care rationing. *Public Affairs Quarterly*, 8:33, 34 (1994).

Health Matrix 187, 208-7 (1998).

Jurgeleit, P. S. Physician employment under managed care: Toward a retaliatory discharge cause of action for HMO-affiliated physicians. *Ind. Law Journal*, 73:255–273.

Laine, C., & Davidoff, F. Patient centered medicine. *Journal of the American Medical Association*, 275:152 (1996).

McClellan v. H.M.O., 604 A.2d 1053, 1058 (Pa. Super. Ct. 1992) (determining that the theory of corporate negligence could be extended to determine whether such HMOs have a nondelegable duty to select and retain only competent primary care physicians).

Mehlman, M. J. The patient-physician relationship in an era of scarce resources: Is there a duty to treat. *Conn. Law Review*, 25:349, 367–371.

Meisel, A. The "exceptions" to the informed consent doctrine: Striking a balance between competing values in medical decision making. *Wisconsin Law Review,* 413:414–415 (1979).

Morreim, E. Haavi. Medicine meets resource limits: Restructuring the legal standard of care. *University of Pittsburgh Law Review,* 59:1, 41–45 (1997).

Morreim, E. Haavi. Redefining quality by reassigning responsibility, *American Journal of Law and Medicine,* 20:79, 80–81 (1994).

Pulvers v. Kaiser Found. Health Plan, 160 Cal. Rptr. 392, 393 (Cal. Ct. App. 1979) McClellan, 604 A.2d at 1060-61.

Walsh, A. F. The legal attack on cost containment mechanisms: The expansion of liability for physicians and managed care organizations. *John Marshall Law Review,* 31:207, 219–221 (1997).

Wickline, 228 Cal. Rptr. at 670.

Williams v. HealthAmerica, 535 N.E.2d 717, 720 (Ohio Ct. App. 1987).

Wilson, 271 Cal. Rptr. at 883 (explaining that the test for joint tort liability applied).

## CHAPTER 23

Ethical Issues in Managed Medicine

Decision Making, Choice, and Moral Principles

Render S. Davis

> The dogmas of the quiet past are inadequate to the stormy present. The case is piled high with difficulty, and we must rise with the occasion. As our case is new, so we must think anew and act anew.
>
> —Abraham Lincoln, 1862
>
> The times, they are a-changing.
>
> —Bob Dylan, 1962

A century separates the eloquence of Lincoln and Dylan, yet both were witnesses to trying, turbulent times that left our society profoundly changed. There are few who would doubt that the practice of medicine today is both dramatically changing *and* piled high with difficulty. The standards that stood vanguard a generation ago no longer appear to drive the rapidly evolving relationship between physicians and patients. Others entities, most notably payers and regulators, have interposed themselves into the relationship, and the result is a radically different approach to health care.

Yet the ethical principles of beneficence, respect for autonomy, and justice that served as a foundation for the healing professions since the age of Hippocrates remain as important today as two millennia ago. Ethical dilemmas arise, not from clear choices between good and evil but when there are no clear choices between competing goods. Often these issues surface when ethical principles themselves are weighed in relationship to each other. When a physician's obligation to treat conflicts with a patient's right to self-determination or when an individual's demand for autonomous choice offends our society's sense of justice and fairness—these are but two examples of ethical principles in conflict.

EVOLUTIONARY SHIFTS IN THE PRIMACY OF ETHICAL PRINCIPLES

For nearly 2,000 years, the principle of *beneficence*, the profession's obligation to be of service to others, was the foundation of the practice of medicine. In taking the Hippocratic Oath, physicians swore that they would "perform their art solely for the cure of patients," and patients viewed their doctors as wise, caring, and paternalistic healers unwaveringly committed to their welfare. Until the era of modern medicine dawned in the early 20th century, sincere caring and compassionate service probably were the most effective instruments in the physician's meager armamentarium.

World War II and the decades that followed saw an unprecedented explosion in medical knowledge and technology. As a direct consequence, physicians were called upon to become increasingly sophisticated technicians and specialists, demands that pulled them farther from the bedside and diminished the close, personal relationship with patients they once enjoyed. This increasingly impersonal relationship, combined with the starkness and technically intimidating nature of hospitals, led to a dramatic shift in the traditional patient-physician relationship. No longer did the patient see the family doctor as the caring, paternalistic figure who held his or her interests foremost. Instead, an overwhelming array of specialists appeared before the patient to explore illness etiology or examine a particular body part, too often appearing more interested in the malady than in the person afflicted with it.

The covenant of trust that once bonded physician and patient was rapidly eroding, and amid the social turmoil of the 1960s, patients began to demand that physicians treat them as equal partners, both informing them of the nature of their disease and seeking their permission to initiate treatment. After all, patients reasoned, they should have the final say regarding what was done to their own bodies.

Consequently, the principle of *respect for autonomy*, an acknowledgment of an individual's right to self-determination, slowly took precedence over but did not eclipse beneficence. Physicians still cared for their patients, but now they were obligated to take extra steps to bring patients directly into the decision-making process by explaining treatment options and requesting *informed consent* on the plan of care from the patient.

Both principles were supported in the prevailing system of fee-for-service, private-practice medicine. There were few constraints on physicians' clinical autonomy, and their professional judgment remained, for the most part, unquestioned. In this climate, physicians reasoned that patients would likely benefit from more tests and procedures; patients, especially the well-insured, demanded almost unregulated autonomy over their health care choices. For those with the means to pay, access to nearly all that medicine had to offer was considered an unquestioned right.

This proved to be a formula for potential economic disaster. There was an explosion in new and expanded facilities and unwavering demand for the latest technological innovations, much of it supported by the government as vital to a healthy economy. Nonetheless, a fundamental problem existed because health care was being delivered in a financial vacuum, where both physicians and patients had only a vague understanding of or interest in the economic consequences of the services they felt either obligated to provide or entitled to receive.

Both beneficence and respect for autonomy could be invoked to support this nearly unbridled use of health care resources in the care and treatment of individual patients. Insurers, both private and governmental, paid "reasonable and customary" charges, almost without argument, while, as patients' advocates, physicians could garner six-figure incomes from fees generated in providing virtually unlimited care.

The inevitable financial fallout from medicine guided by these laissez-faire rules eventually led to an unsustainable inflationary spiral in medical costs. In the 30 years following the passage of the Medicare Act in 1965, the health care sector of the American economy soared from 4% of Gross Domestic Product (GDP) to over 14%, and there was no clear end in sight to the upward trend. Yet a growing number of Americans actually saw their access to medical care diminish due to rising costs of employer-paid insurance and tightening restrictions in eligibility requirements for Medicaid and other government safety-net programs. Even as the nation continued to increase spending for medical care, many Americans were losing access to the system.

Alarm over rising health care costs began to spread in the early 1970s, as both private and government payers sought any means possible to stem the hemorrhaging outflow of dollars. President Richard Nixon tried unsuccessfully to implement wage and price controls to slow it; a few years later, President Jimmy Carter attempted to cap Medicare expenditures. Both efforts failed for two primary reasons. First was a fundamental misunderstanding of the nature of health care competition. Health care providers did not compete directly for patients but rather for physicians who held the legal authority to admit patients. As independent contractors, physicians could, for the most part, choose to join the staffs of institutions that provided the latest technology, the most-up-do-date facilities, and even the most luxurious amenities. Consequently, hospitals competed fiercely for doctors, a process that actually caused prices to rise, not fall.

Second, the dominant, indemnity-based, fee-for-service approach to medical care remained fundamentally intact, continuing to insulate both physicians (the consumer's agent) and patients (consumers of care) from the true costs of the services provided. But economic concerns arising from double-digit inflation and business downturns in the late 1970s assured that fundamental and inevitable changes in the financing and practice of medicine were on the horizon.

The first major initiative to have a significant cost-constraining effect occurred in the early 1980s with the implementation of the Medicare prospective payment system (PPS) and its health care provider payments pegged to diagnosis related groups (DRGs). This system ushered in a new era of controlled, predetermined prices for health care services. The inflationary spiral of government payments for health care slowed, and soon private payers also were considering adopting alternatives to traditional insurance. Slowly, the concept of prepaid, managed health care provided by health maintenance organizations (HMOs), a concept developed by the Kaiser Foundation and other organizations on the West Coast in the 1940s (and strongly opposed by organized medicine), began to spread nationwide as a possible answer to the country's health care ills.

By the early 1990s, HMOs and other types of managed care organizations (MCOs) that provided integrated health care services and financing through insurance or other means had gained a serious foothold and were moving to positions of dominance in American medical care. The growth in the popularity of managed care signaled the next evolutionary change in the predominance of the key ethical principles.

Just as respect for autonomy superseded beneficence, the principle of *justice*, representing a new approach of balancing the health needs of an individual with the availability of finite resources for the larger population, rose to take its place as the primary principle, becoming the vanguard force driving the movement toward managed care. Physician-ethicist John LaPuma, in his book *Managed Care Ethics,* writes that managed care has gone so far as to "sever the link between autonomy and justice that once existed to support the care of individuals."

Embedded within this drive toward a fairer distribution of health care resources was the urgent but highly controversial desire to rein in costs. Despite years of active suppression and condemnation by health professionals and providers, the hard economic realities of American society's love-hate (love to have it, hate to pay for it) relationship with health care had finally reached the bedside. The result has been an irrevocable sea change in the landscape of American medicine.

THE PHYSICIAN'S DILEMMA: CARING FOR PATIENTS AND POPULATIONS

In today's health care environment, physicians face a myriad of dilemmas in their daily practice. Time constraints, diminished professional autonomy, declining incomes, explosive growth in technology, and deteriorating public trust, *combined with* increasing public demands, are only some of the more obvious problems plaguing practitioners. Although some who have been adversely affected by these changes are quick to lay blame at the feet of managed care, this anger may be both premature and to some extent misdirected.

While there are ample faults in managed care as it is practiced, its theory and principles are ethically sound. Health care should be "managed"—for continuity, quality, value, and optimal outcomes—regardless of the mechanisms by which the caregivers are paid. Practicing medicine within managed care still entails obligations to care for patients and to respect their autonomy, but now providers have been placed in a disquieting role as resource managers, requiring a new approach to finding better, more cost-effective ways to meet these obligations while being held accountable to a larger community to which the individual belongs (e.g., a health plan or employee group) for the costs incurred in delivering care. An article in a recent issue of the *Hastings Center Report* summed up this new approach by noting that managed care is based "on the foundation of a philosophy of care that, however well or poorly articulated, responds to the needs of individual patients in the context of population-based mechanisms to assess needs and distribute resources."

In light of the above-referenced ethical principles, an examination of the current practice of managed care reveals an uneven and troubled landscape. Although the emphasis on health promotion and illness prevention is viewed as very good, there remain many highly publicized instances where the health of individual patients has been jeopardized by apparently arbitrary policies and decisions made by MCOs, ostensibly in the name of cost containment. The following are among especially notable issues:

- Delayed referral of patients to specialty physicians or denials of access to specialized services, primarily based on resource allocation and cost consider-ations.
- Rigidly enforced practice guidelines that potentially penalize a physician's exercise of his or her clinical judgment.
- Crafting of incentives that encourage physicians to withhold clinically perti-nent information from patients *and* to discourage physicians from serving as advocates for their patients.
- Declining consumer choice of health plans and providers.
- Failure of many MCOs, especially those operated as proprietary entities, to acknowledge an obligation to improve community health and broaden access to services.
- Apparent subordination of quality considerations in access and treatment to cost containment in delivery of services.

These issues, according to LaPuma, make managed care "morally vulnerable" and fraught with public suspicion regarding its core values. Consequently, physi-cians practicing medicine today are faced with very real dilemmas in such areas as patient advocacy, access to and scope of care, informed consent, conflict of interest, continuity of care, and patient choice.

In a speech given at Georgetown University in 1993, Marcia Angell, MD, executive editor of the *New England Journal of Medicine*, described the physician's primary dilemma within the framework of managed care practice as one of "double agency," where physicians are being asked to be "both advocates for individual patients *and* allocators of finite health care resources to the larger populations of enrollees of health plans." This is a role that seems to impinge on the fundamental tenets of patient advocacy articulated in the Hippocratic Oath. By the terms of many managed care insurance plans, a physician's income is directly related to savings generated in the delivery of care, a tactic criticized by former surgeon general C. Everett Koop, MD, when he wrote: "Something is wrong with a system that spends more and more each year to provide less and less service."

Many of the proprietary (for-profit) MCOs acknowledge that their primary business objective is the return of value to shareholders, with obligations to provide expanded access and broader health care coverage to plan enrollees a secondary consideration. While Speaker of the Oregon State House, Governor John Kitzhaber (a physician) addressed this concern when he wrote of the insidious problem permeating our health care system . . . the perverse set of incentives that leads health care providers to act as isolated economic entities focused on their own well-being, instead of viewing themselves as community resources whose primary role is—or should be—to promote the health of the nation.

In light of this troubled environment, let us examine some specific dilemmas confronting physicians in their daily practice.

Patient Advocacy

Few areas of life are as personal as an individual's health, and people have long relied on a caring and competent physician to be their champion in securing the medical resources needed to retain or restore health and function. For many physicians, patient care was the foundation of their professional calling. However, in the contemporary delivery organization there may be little opportunity for a generalist physician "gatekeepers" to form relationships with patients, and their personal values may be affected by substantial bonuses, withholds, and other financial incentives that may directly conflict with their advocacy role, especially if a patient is in need of expensive services.

Conflicts of Interest

Conflicts of interest are not a new phenomenon in medicine. In the fee-for-service system, physicians controlled access to medical facilities and technology, and they benefited financially with every order or prescription they wrote. Consequently, there was an inherent temptation to overtreat patients. Even marginal diagnostic or therapeutic procedures were justified on the grounds of both clinical necessity and legal protection against threats of negligence. While it could be construed that this represented a direct conflict of interest, it could also be argued that most patients were well served in this system because the emphasis was on thorough, comprehensive treatment where cost was rarely a consideration. A well-known adage was that physicians "could do well by doing good."

In managed care the potential conflicts between patients and physicians take on a completely different dimension. By design, in health plans where medical care is financed through prepayment arrangements, the physician's income is enhanced not by doing more for his or her patients but by doing less. Patients, confronted with the realization that their doctors will be rewarded for the use of fewer resources, no longer could rely with certainty on the motives underlying a physician's treatment plans. One inevitable outcome has been the continuing decline in patients' trust in their physicians.

Communications

In contemporary medicine, ethical dilemmas in communications are increasingly common and come in many different forms:

- Physicians failing to communicate necessary clinical information to patients in terms and language the patients can truly understand.
- Physicians offering only limited treatment choices to patients because alternatives may not be covered by the patient's insurance plan.
- Failures to disclose financial incentives and other payment arrangements that may influence the physician's treatment recommendations.
- Time constraints that limit opportunities for in-depth discussions between patients and their doctors.
- Lack of a continuing relationship between the patient and physician that fosters open communications.

While so-called gag clauses, implemented by some MCOs to prohibit physicians from informing their patients about noncovered treatment alternatives, have been declared illegal in several states, the duty of physicians to be fully truthful and informative in their communications with patients remains under considerable suspicion.

Confidentiality

Whether it is an employer interested in the results of an employee's health screening; an insurer trying to learn more about an enrollee's prior health history, the media in search of a story, or health planners examining the potential value of national health databases, the confidential nature of the traditional doctor-patient relationship is seriously threatened by new demands for clinical information and increasing reliance on electronic records that may be susceptible to tampering and unauthorized access.

Clearly, employers and insurers are interested in the status of an individual's health and ability to work; but does this *desire* to know, combined with their role as payers for health care, constitute a *right* to know? The patient's right to privacy remains a volatile and unresolved issue.

Access to Care

In his book *Back to Reform*, author Charles Dougherty wrote that "cost containment is the goal for the healthy. Access is the goal for the sick." So, for an increasing number of Americans, the concerns described above are almost meaningless because they are, for the most part, outside the structure of the current health care system. Employers are downsizing staff or cutting out health insurance benefits in an effort to be financially successful in a global economy; while demands for greater government accountability in the expenditure of tax dollars have brought about increasingly more stringent eligibility requirements for safety net programs like Medicaid. As insurance becomes more expensive or government programs undergo budget cuts, people are being excised from the system.

At the same time, new competitive demands have fostered unprecedented consolidations, mergers, and closures of health care facilities. This shake-out may have greatly reduced the overcapacity that plagued the system, but it has been done with greater emphasis on cutting costs than on fostering efficiency and effectiveness in creating a true system of care delivery.

Those who view health care as little different from any other commodity available through the free market see the present access concerns as simply a by-product of the inevitable restructuring of the system. While they argue that we must adhere to market solutions to solve our health care access problems, others demand a different approach, calling for governmental national health insurance or some form of subsidized care providing at least a basic level of treatment for all citizens. While Americans continue to proudly tout that we do not explicitly ration care as do some other countries (notably Great Britain), we tacitly accept a health care system that implicitly excludes citizens who are unable to overcome financial barriers to access.

Access to care represents the most visible issue at the very foundation of the ethical principle of justice. In their text *Principles of Biomedical Ethics*, authors Thomas Beauchamp, PhD, and James F. Childress, PhD point out that justice is subject to interpretation and may even be evoked to support the positions of parties in direct opposition. For example, those who support the predominant principle of *distributive* justice—the fair allocation of resources based on laws or cultural rules—still must decide on what basis these resources will be used. *Utilitarians* argue for resource distribution based on achieving the "greatest good for the greatest number." *Libertarians* believe that recipients of resources should be those who have made the greatest contributions to the production of those resources—a free market approach to distribution. And *egalitarians* support the distribution of resources based on who is in greatest need, irrespective of contribution or other considerations. Consequently, developing a system of access based on "justice" will be fraught with enormous difficulty.

Professional Autonomy

Not so long ago, a physician's clinical judgment was virtually unquestioned. Now, with the advent of clinical pathways and case management protocols, many of the aspects of treatment are outlined in algorithm-based plans that allied health professionals may follow with only minimal direct input from a physician. Much about this change has been good. Physicians have been freed from much tedious routine and are better able to watch more closely for unexpected responses to treatments or unusual outcomes and then utilize their knowledge to chart an appropriate response.

What is of special concern, though, is the restrictive nature of protocols in some care plans that may unduly limit a physician's clinical prerogatives to address a patient's specific needs. Such plans may prove to be the ultimate bad examples of "cookbook" medicine. While some may find health care and the practice of medicine an increasingly stressful and unrewarding field, others are continuing to search for ways to assure that caring, compassionate, and ethically rewarding medicine remains at the heart of our health care system.

FOSTERING ETHICALLY SOUND MEDICINE WITHIN THE FRAMEWORK OF MANAGED CARE

In *Managed Care Ethics*, LaPuma notes that "just as physicians helped society get into an over-spent, over-built, over-utilized health care rut; physicians should help society get out." While the patient-physician relationship has undergone significant erosion, it still remains somewhat tenuously at the center of the medical care universe. There is much that physicians may do within the framework of managed care to restore their role as both patient advocates and compassionate caregivers.

To do this successfully, it is important to recognize that irrevocable changes have occurred but the future evolution of managed care is not yet established. It is much like a pendulum that has swung from one extreme (unregulated, fee-for-service medicine) and is now on an arc toward another, as yet, undetermined destination. Will it be a government-controlled national health care system? A market-driven service bought and sold like any other commodity? Or something in between? Physicians and other health care providers still have the power to influence the answer.

Managed care may yet prove to be a highly functional and effective system committed to providing cost-efficient and clinically effective care, as articulated by William Steinman, MD, who teaches his students at Tulane University Medical School to "order only tests and perform screening procedures that will help provide a diagnosis and treatment plan . . . do the right things, at the right time, and for the right reasons." Renowned physician-ethicist Edmund Pelligrino of the Kennedy Center for Ethics at Georgetown University goes on to note that "what our health policies do to the individual patient serves as a reality check to what values we hold most dear and the ethical foundation of the policies we develop and impose." So those who truly believe that we can still have a caring and compassionate system of managed care must actively work within the system to bring it about.

Physicians must not abdicate their central role in patient care to others but must work within the framework of managed care to foster its development as a means of delivering care that is clinically justified, in a setting that respects the values of individual patients and at the same time recognizes the finiteness of society's resources. The following represent some beginning steps in this process.

Being a Patient Educator, Coach, and Mentor

Never has the well-worn adage "patient heal thyself" been more true. With their emphasis on health promotion and disease prevention and their tightening restrictions on access to expensive acute care, HMOs practically scream at patients to take charge of their own health and well-being. It is no longer enough for physicians to be healers, intervening when a patient appears at their door with an acute or chronic illness. They must be proactive educators, even coaches, providing patients with the information needed to change poor health habits like smoking, drinking, and overeating and encouraging them to adopt healthier lifestyles. Unfortunately, this task is more difficult than it appears. Historically, Americans have refused to accept the consequences of their poor health habits, preferring to seek medicine's help in repairing the damage after it has been done. Results from *America's Health Report Card 1998*, a study recently completed by the Gallup organization, showed that, while Americans express concern over such things as cholesterol levels, high blood pressure, cancer, and weight reduction, many do little to reduce their risks. George Gallup Jr. noted in the report's conclusion that

> some of the messages aren't getting through, although people are very much under a constant bombardment of information. It's ironic in a sense that some of the diseases have been conquered, but people have not done their share to stay healthy because they are indulging in habits that are self-destructive.

Even when confronted with the time constraints and discontinuity inherent in frequently changing health insurance plans, it is clear that physicians must be diligent in assessing their patients' health habits and helping them articulate their health goals, assuring that patients understand the terms, limitations, and costs associated with their health plan and serving as mentors and partners to provide them with the knowledge and self-motivation to change for better long-term health.

Instead of being gatekeepers charged with limiting access to the system, physicians should view their roles as that of "navigators"—guiding patients through an increasingly confusing maze of treatment alternatives and leading them in the direction of informed choices and optimal outcomes. In today's health care environment, the principle of beneficence is inextricably woven into the premise that physicians must do more to help patients help themselves.

Becoming Quality Driven

Whether care should be managed is no longer a legitimate question. The fundamental question now is for what purpose is care to be managed? The present moral vulnerability of managed care rests with its apparent overriding concern with cost reduction, possibly at the expense of clinical appropriateness, quality, and the health needs of the individual patient.

If physicians are to be credible advocates for their patients, they must unwaveringly stand for quality and against arbitrary and unjustifiable limitations in access to needed care. This does not imply a return to unregulated, fee-for-service medicine but rather a demand that MCOs be held accountable for both cost-effectiveness *and* quality. The earliest HMOs were established for this purpose, and it has been only in the past decade that managed care has become the de facto tool for driving down cost and squeezing excess capacity out of the system.

Unfortunately, this has not taken place in a coordinated fashion with any clear goal of establishing a cohesive, seamless health care system. Consequently, we have a fragmented, patchwork system, described by Marcia Angell, MD, as a "hodgepodge of temporary alignments, existing independently, often working at cross purposes" that leaves many patients and providers with inadequate tools and information to make truly informed health care choices. Physicians, other care providers, and MCOs should work in concert to develop a system of care that is integrated and coordinated, epidemiologic data–dependent, consumer-driven, and clearly responsive to the legitimate health care needs of enrollees and the general population.

We as a nation can have a health care system that embraces compassionate, clinically appropriate, cost-effective care, with universal access to basic services, if we are willing to make difficult but publicly informed and debated choices regarding our health care priorities. Physicians must be proactive and central to this process.

Demanding High Professional Moral Standards of Both Yourself and of MCOs

It has been argued that physicians have abdicated the "moral high ground" in health care by their interest in seeking protection for their high incomes, their highly publicized self-referral arrangements, and their historical opposition toward any reform efforts that jeopardized their clinical autonomy. In his book *Medicine at the Crossroads*, Emory University professor Melvin Konnor, MD, notes that "throughout its history, organized medicine has represented, first and foremost, the pecuniary interests of doctors." He goes on to lay significant blame for the present problems in health care at the doorstep of both insurers and doctors, stating that "the system's ills are pervasive and all its participants are responsible."

To reclaim their once esteemed moral position, physicians must actively reaffirm their commitment to the highest standards of the medical profession and call on other participants in the health care delivery system also to elevate their values and standards to the highest level. Daniel Callahan, PhD, former executive director of the Hastings Center, articulated this concern when he wrote, "The change cannot only be in our health care system, in its mechanisms, institutions, and practices. It must be no less a change in our values and goals, our ideas of good health and the good life. The change must, moreover, come from inside ourselves."

In the evolutionary shift toward managed care, physicians have been asked to embrace business values of efficiency and cost-effectiveness, sometimes at the expense of their professional values.

While some of these changes have been inevitable as our society sought to rein in out-of-control costs, it is not unreasonable for physicians to call on payers, regulators, and other parties in the health care delivery system to raise their ethical bar. Harvard University physician-ethicist Linda Emmanuel notes that "health professionals are now accountable to business values (such as efficiency and cost effectiveness), so business persons should be accountable to professional values including kindness and compassion." Within the framework of ethical principles, LaPuma writes that "business's ethical obligations are integrity and honesty. Medicine's are those plus altruism, beneficence, non-maleficence, respect, and fairness."

Physician practice groups should consider proactively developing mission and values statements that clearly articulate the group's collective beliefs and the ethical principles that govern their delivery of care. When they consider joining MCO practitioner panels as either contractors or employees, the physicians should carefully examine the organization's mission and values statements, read its access policies and procedures, review for fairness its denial and grievance processes, and inquire about its internal and external ethics forums, evaluating the degree to which they complement the practitioner group's established values. If it is not a good fit, the group may choose to not join the panel. If that is not a reasonable business option, the group's physicians may work from within the organization to strengthen and enhance the MCO's moral position.

A study by the Rand Corporation identified seven key components of a quality managed care plan: financial accessibility, organizational accessibility, continuity of care, comprehensiveness of treatment, coordination of services, interpersonal accountability, and technical accountability. These and every other facet of the health care delivery system should reflect a commitment to honesty and integrity that provides clear assurance to payers, providers, and patients that the system is designed to offer compassionate care, clear communication, explicit fairness in distribution of resources, and a commitment to the highest organizational values and ethical principles.

Incumbent in these activities is the expectation that the forces that control our health care delivery system—the payers, the regulators, and the providers—will reach out to the larger community, working to eliminate the inequities that have left so many Americans with limited or no access to even basic health care. Charles Dougherty clarified this obligation in *Back to Reform*, when he noted that "behind the daunting social reality stands a simple moral value that motivates the entire enterprise. Health care is grounded in caring. It arises from a sympathetic response to the suffering of others."

Developing Skills Needed for the New Health Care

Medical practice today is vastly different from a generation ago, and physicians need new skills to be successful. To balance their obligations to both individual patients and to larger groups of plan enrollees, physicians now must become more than competent clinicians. Traditionally, the physician was viewed as the "captain of the ship," in charge of nearly all the medical decisions, but this changed with the new dynamics of managed care. Now, as noted previously, the physician's role may be more akin to the ship's navigator, utilizing his or her clinical skills and knowledge of the health care environment to chart the patient's course through a confusing morass of insurance requirements, care choices, and regulations to achieve the best attainable outcome. Some of these new skills include the following:

Negotiation: working to optimize patients' access to services and facilities beneficial to their treatment.

Being a team player: working in concert with other caregivers, from generalist and specialist physicians to nurses and therapists, to coordinate the delivery of care within a clinically appropriate and cost-effective framework.

Working within the limits of professional competence: avoiding the pitfalls of payer arrangements that may restrict access to specialty physicians and facilities by clearly acknowledging when the symptoms or manifestations of a patient's illness require this higher degree of service, then working on behalf of the patient to seek access to them.

Respecting different cultures and values: inherent in the support of the principle of respect for autonomy is acceptance of values that may differ from one's own. As the United States becomes a more culturally heterogeneous nation, health care providers are called on to work within and respect the sociocultural framework of patients and their families.

Seeking clarity on what constitutes marginal care: within a system of finite resources, physicians will be called on to communicate carefully and openly with patients regarding access to marginal and/or futile treatments.

Exercising decision-making flexibility: treatment algorithms and clinical pathways are extremely useful tools when used within their scope, but physicians must follow the case-managed patient closely and have the authority to adjust the plan if clinical circumstances warrant.

These represent only a handful of examples to illustrate the myriad of new skills that today's and tomorrow's physicians must master in order to meet their timeless professional obligation of patient care.

CONCLUSION: FOSTERING A SOCIALLY RESPONSIBLE HEALTH CARE SYSTEM

The erosion of trust expressed by the public for the health care industry may be reversed only if those charged with working within or managing the system place community and patient interests ahead of their own. We must foster an ethical corporate culture within health care that rewards leaders with integrity and vision, leaders who encourage and expect ethical excellence from themselves and others and who recognize that ethics establishes the moral framework for all organizational decision making.

In an article published in the *Journal of the American Medical Association*, authors Ezekiel Emanual, MD, and Nancy Dubler, LLB, cited what they call the "Six C's" of the ideal physician-patient relationship: choice, competence, communications, compassion, continuity, and (no) conflict of interest. Physicians who accept a seventh "c", the challenge, and are imbued with the moral sensitivity embodied in their solemn oath, have an obligation to serve as the conscience of this new system dedicated toward caring for all Americans.

Writer and ethicist Emily Friedman said it best when she wrote:

> There are many communities in health care. But three to which I hope we all belong are
> the communities devoted to improving the health of all around us, to achieving access to
> care for all, and to providing our services at a price that society can afford. These interests
> are, of course, expressions of the deeper community of values that states that healing, justice,
> and equality must guide what we believe and do.

ACKNOWLEDGMENTS

The author acknowledges the technical assistance of Ms. Kathy Kinlaw, M.Div.,
in the preparation of this chapter.

REFERENCES AND READINGS

American Medical Association, Council on Ethical and Judicial Affairs. Ethical issues in
managed care. *Journal of the American Medical Association*, vol. 273, no. 4 (January
25, 1995).

Angell, M. The doctor as double agent. *Kennedy Institute of Ethics Journal*, vol. 3, no. 3
(September 1993).

Beauchamp, T. L., & Childress, J. F. *Principles of biomedical ethics.* New York: Oxford
University Press, 1989.

Carefoote, R. L. Managed care and quality management; Medical management: Practice
guidelines; Medical management: Oversight. (Medical Management Signature Series).
Chicago: Managed Care Resources, 1997. Website: www.mcres.com

Dougherty, C. J. *Back to reform: Values, markets, and the healthcare system.* New York: Oxford
University Press, 1989.

Duffy, J. A. Poll: Health advice ignored. *Atlanta Journal-Constitution*, November 20, 1998.

Emanual, E. J., & Dubler, N. N. Preserving the physician-patient relationship in the era
of managed care. *Journal of the American Medical Association*, vol. 273, no. 4 (January
25, 1995).

Friedman, E. *The right thing: Ten years of ethics columns from the* Healthcare Forum Journal.
San Francisco: Jossey-Bass, 1996.

Konnor, M. *Medicine at the crossroads.* New York: Vintage Books, 1994.

LaPuma, J. *Managed care ethics: Essays on the impact of managed care on traditional medical
ethics.* New York: Hatherleigh Press, 1998.

LaPuma, J. Understand guiding principles when mixing business, medicine. *Managed
Care Magazine*, July 1998.

Managed Health Care: A Brief Glossary. Pleasonton, CA: Integrated Healthcare Association,
1997. Website: www.iha.org

Pelligrino, E. D., Veatch, R. M., & Langan, J. P. *Ethics, trust, and the professions: Philosophical
and cultural aspects.* Washington, DC: Georgetown University Press, 1991.

Philip, D. J. Ethics of managed care. *Medical Group Management Journal*, November–
December 1997.

Principles of Managed Healthcare. Pleasonton, CA: Integrated Healthcare Association, 1997.
Website: www.iha.org

What could have saved John Worthy? *Hastings Center Report*, Special Supplement, Vol.
28, No. 4, July–August 1998.

Wicclair, M. R. *Ethical issues in managed care.* Paper presented at Fifth Annual Retreat of the Consortium Ethics Program, Jackson Hole, WY, October 1995.

Zwolak, J. Outside the box. *Tulane Medicine*, September 1995.

Interviews: Frank Brescia, MD, professor, Medical University of South Carolina, Charleston, SC; Joseph DeGross, MD, professor, Mercer University School of Medicine, Macon, GA; David DeRuyter, MD, pulmonologist, Atlanta; Daniel Russler, MD, vice-president, HBOC, Inc. Atlanta.

## CHAPTER 24

Asset Protection Strategies for Physicians

Defining a Personal Liability Protection Plan

Edward J. Rappaport

> I advise you to go on living solely to enrage those who are paying your annuities.
>
> —Voltaire

The concept of personal responsibility has been under assault for the past 30 years, depending on one's view of history. Society's victims subordinate personal responsibility to blame if the victim can place that blame elsewhere. As a result, individuals and corporations in the United States with deep pockets are being pursued by professional victims. Those who are mindful of these occurrences may remember well the multimillion-dollar verdict in favor of the individual burned by the spill of a hot cup of coffee.

Based on the foregoing, propertied individuals, such as physicians and other learned health care professionals, have every reason to protect their accumulated wealth from professional victims. This chapter will address asset protection planning techniques and strategies currently available to those concerned with the potential claims of creditors both known and unknown.

WHAT IS ASSET PROTECTION PLANNING?

Asset protection planning is the thoughtful and deliberate use of a variety of means both to protect an individual's assets from the claims of creditors and also the creation of barriers to an individual's assets that have the effect of discouraging claims against the individuals owning those assets. These techniques and strategies run the gamut from simple to elaborate and will also identify sources of claims that propertied physicians need to address.

Interestingly, one of the collateral benefits of asset protection planning is *estate planning*. Clients delight in discovering that the pursuit of estate planning very often means the accomplishment of asset protection planning and vice versa.

ASSET PROTECTION STRATEGIES

Prior to discussing actual techniques, we should first consider the sources from which claims may arise in the conduct of a medical practice. These claims can be subdivided into claims from the provision of medical treatment and claims arising out of the conduct of a medical practice.

Delivery of Professional Services

Physicians are acutely aware that they are liable for claims arising from their professional activities if they deliver medical treatment that falls below the applicable standard of care and that causes injury to their patients. Moreover, managed care's influence on both the number and frequency of claims is unknown. However, with the interweaving of treatment provided by the health care industry inherent in managed care, plaintiffs will attempt to cast a wide liability net over physicians, hospitals, insurers, health maintenance organizations (HMOs), nurses, physician assistants, and any other person or entity involved in the treatment of the patient. Furthermore, lawyers will attempt to expand theories of recovery and liability in every jurisdiction.

The most obvious method of preventing malpractice claims from resulting in personal liability to the physician is through malpractice insurance coverage with a reputable carrier. Unfortunately, malpractice insurance itself may not be sufficient to completely protect a physician against professional liability claims. First, as verdicts increase, they may exceed policy limits. Second, as claims become more innovative, insurance companies may argue that the insurance contract does not embrace such risks and as a result may deny coverage.

Another crucial strategy in this regard is the organization of the physician's practice through an entity that protects the equity owner from individual liability. For a number of years, physicians conducted their practice under the umbrella of a professional corporation. A common strategy for physicians practicing together was to organize a professional corporation whose stockholders were also professional corporations. Such structures minimized the risk of vicarious liability being imposed from one physician stockholder to another.

The recent proliferation of *limited liability companies* (LLCs) and *limited liability partnerships* (LLPs) as operational entities allows for more flexibility to minimize physician-owner liability. Along these same lines, physicians conducting their practice through one of the above-described entities should also carefully manage the operational entity. For instance, the operational entity should own a minimal amount of assets, as it will be at risk in the event of a malpractice suit. Thus, if physicians own a building used by the practice, that building should be owned by a different entity to prevent it from being subject to the claims of creditors.

Conduct of Professional Practice

Independent physicians, like any business owners, are subject to a host of liabilities by virtue of the conduct of their business. These liabilities include workers' compensation for work-related injuries, employment liability, and taxes. While these liabilities exist with the conduct of any business, the physician tends to focus more on potential liability for the delivery of patient care, even though liabilities arising out of the conduct of their business arise more frequently and are potentially disruptive.

These types of risks can be addressed through the use of appropriate insurance and through careful documentation of all matters pertaining to the operation of the office. The purchase of insurance would include workers' compensation and general liability and property insurance.

The documentation of office matters is worthy of further discussion. Documentation is useful in providing evidence of the intention of the parties in the event of a dispute. Thus, if the practice employs any individual (whether a physician or physician assistant or otherwise), an employment contract is useful to determine the rights of the parties in the event of a dispute.

Documentation is vital in the event that a dispute exists and the parties differ as to the underlying facts. Creating a paper trail may be the means through which the physician prevails in a dispute. Additionally, sensitive documents and information must be safeguarded and accordingly marked. Every physician should maintain a stamp that will mark such documents as *personal and confidential*.

Documentation is also useful to set expectations of employees. This can be achieved with a well-constructed employee handbook outlining procedures and policies. Such a handbook could be the difference between a positive result and a negative outcome in a sexual harassment lawsuit brought by an employee.

ASSET PROTECTION OUTSIDE THE CONDUCT OF PROFESSIONAL ACTIVITIES

Once the physician is satisfied with his or her protection from liabilities associated with the practice, he or she may concentrate on asset protection planning on a personal level. These types of claims include (1) family-oriented claims, (2) investment-related claims, and (3) tort claims.

1. *Family-oriented claims* include not only the breakup of the marriage of physician and spouse but also claims of illegitimate children and the divorce of children of the physician. These claims constitute the most serious risk that propertied individuals face with respect to their assets, given the current high divorce rate in the United States. Many physicians considering asset protection planning are surprised to learn, for example, that even antenuptial agreements are not a silver bullet, even with respect to assets acquired outside a marriage. They can be effective, but unforeseen circumstances may result in these agreements being set aside. Also, antenuptial agreements are not always practical

or appropriate as they can poison the relationship of a married couple. For these reasons, many of the asset protection techniques discussed herein will not always achieve the objectives sought through the creation of an antenuptial agreement.

2.   *Investment-related claims* include liability that arises through the conduct of investment activities. These liabilities include personal guarantees and director and officer liability in connection with a corporation. In fraud claims, particularly, an individual serving on the corporation's board may be subject to liability.

3.   *Tort claims* arise most frequently from the ownership and use of a family home, automobile, or pleasure craft. Umbrella liability insurance can help to protect against these types of risks.

Other types of claims include environmental liability attributable to owning land containing toxic waste and liability to a tenant in the capacity of a landlord. Liability insurance can often protect an individual against these claims, and broad, umbrella coverage should always be considered. Needless to say, personal guarantees should be given only when absolutely necessary.

PRELIMINARY PLANNING CONSIDERATIONS

To protect against all of the liabilities and risks described above, propertied individuals can engage in both simple and complex planning techniques that will protect their assets from the claims of creditors. Prior to discussing the specific techniques, several points should be addressed initially.

The expression "timing is everything" is a bedrock principle of asset protection planning. The earlier the planning tool is implemented prior to the occurrence giving rise to liability, the more likely that the planning technique will be respected by the court in the event of a judgment against the individual. Asset protection planning is not an exact science. Creditors will make the universal argument that the implementation of the asset planning tool is a *fraudulent conveyance* (i.e., the transfer of assets by the debtor made him insolvent and in the process defrauded the debtor's creditors) and that the court should set it aside. The court will weigh relevant facts in deciding this issue. Thus, the sooner that a given technique is implemented, the more likely it is that a court deciding the issue of fraudulent conveyance will rule in favor of the debtor. The fraudulent conveyance rules must always be considered when evaluating asset protection planning tools.

Propertied individuals also must bear in mind that no technique by itself will protect his or her assets from the claims of creditors. In other words, one should not put all of one's eggs in the same basket. The starting point for asset protection planning must always be insurance. Insurance will protect an individual against catastrophic claims and give a variety of creditors some meaningful recovery in the event that liability arises. Of course, insurance will not protect an individual against certain claims (e.g., divorce), and other methods must be employed for asset protection. Generally speaking, a variety of asset protection techniques implemented as part of a customized asset protection plan will be the most effective means of protecting an individual's assets from the claims of creditors.

One additional preliminary point must be addressed. In devising an asset protection plan the individual, with professional assistance, must evaluate his or her potential liabilities. Physicians engage in a relatively high-risk profession, and any asset protection plan should reflect the level of risk. Propertied physicians must assess their relative risk and conduct a cost-benefit analysis to determine the extent to which they engage in asset protection planning.

SIMPLE ASSET PROTECTION TOOLS

One cannot underestimate the importance of insurance. It is the first line of protection an individual should seek.

One useful and simple tool is the qualified retirement plan. The plan can be an IRA or an employer-sponsored plan. While turnkey plans are readily available in the professional marketplace, any plan must be carefully considered and implemented because relevant law regarding the protection of these types of assets from the claims of creditors varies from state to state and in many jurisdictions is either unclear or highly dynamic. Additionally, the Employee Retirement Income and Security Act (ERISA) generally protects retirement plan assets from the claims of creditors, adding another layer of complexity to this issue. IRAs are not generally treated in the same manner as employer-sponsored plans and their treatment vis-a-vis creditors may vary depending upon whether they are set up as trust accounts or custodial accounts. Prior to implementing any retirement plan, one should seek professional advice from an expert in the qualified plan arena.

Another simple technique is the transfer of assets to an individual's spouse. Because of fraudulent conveyance concerns, any transfer of assets to a spouse should occur well before any claim arises against the transferor. Most commonly, physicians transfer ownership of their homes to their spouses. This usually protects the home from the claims of the transferor's creditors. However, such a transfer could be problematic in the event of a dissolution of the marriage. Divorce notwithstanding, if the spouse then dies and leaves the home outright to the physician, the physician's creditors can make claims against it. Thus, the couple's estate plan must be structured to make sure that no assets pass outright to a surviving spouse physician who may be subject to the claims of creditors.

An individual may also make gifts to his or her descendants, either outright or through an irrevocable trust containing enforceable spendthrift provisions, indicating that the trust is intended to protect the trust beneficiaries from wasting their interest in the trust. Such gifts in trust are generally effective (unless deemed fraudulent conveyances) but have the following disadvantages: (1) the transferor cannot retain control of the trust assets, and (2) the transferor no longer has beneficial use of the property. These disadvantages often discourage individuals from making gifts.

The purchase of life insurance contracts and annuity contracts by residents of certain states can also be a simple and effective asset protection tool, as the cash value is protected from the claims of creditors. As an example, Florida has liberal provisions with respect to the protection afforded such assets when the owner and beneficiary of such instruments are residents of the state. For individuals outside Florida or some other jurisdiction that affords similar treatment to such assets, the ownership of life insurance by an irrevocable trust provides asset protection but limits the ability of the physician who creates the trust from accessing its cash value.

COMPLEX ASSET PROTECTION PLANNING TECHNIQUES

These techniques are complex, elaborate, expensive, and generally very effective. Unlike insurance, which is used to satisfy a creditor's judgment, the rationale underlying the implementation of these techniques is to create huge obstacles for potential creditors seeking to satisfy their judgment against a debtor. These techniques are intended to discourage creditors from enforcing judgments against debtors who have used them. Additionally, the following frequently work effectively when used in combination.

The first complex technique is relocation to a *debtor-friendly state*, such as Florida. Not only are the cash values of annuities and life insurance contracts protected, but Florida residents enjoy a liberal homestead exemption and a home ownership doctrine called *tenancy by the entirety*. This exemption shelters 160 acres of rural property, located in the state of Florida, together with any improvements, from the claims of the homeowner's creditors. The homestead exemption for nonrural property is roughly one-half acre, with improvements. In this context, a homeowner facing a sizable judgment would declare bankruptcy, have all of his or her debts discharged, and then pull out his or her equity in the home. This is a technique that has been used with great success by prominent businesspeople facing financial ruin.

Tenancy by the entirety is a concept that is not unique to Florida but not available everywhere. It is a form of ownership of property between a husband and wife that protects the residence from the claims of a creditor against one of the spouses. It will not be effective against the claims that any creditor may have against both spouses, however. Also, once one of the spouses dies, the surviving spouse receives the property outright and must rely solely on the homestead exemption for protection against creditors. Thus, establishing residency in a state like Florida which is debtor-friendly, has significant advantages.

The *family limited partnership* (FLP) (and in some states, the family limited liability company) is also an estate planning technique that can result in both minimizing an individual's federal estate and gift tax liability and protecting an individual from the claims of creditors. An FLP is designed to own assets accumulated by the physician so that assets will not be exposed in the event of the personal liability of the physician or any other family member who is a limited partner of the partnership. Additionally, since the physician and spouse are either the general partners or control the general partner, the physician retains control over the FLP and its assets.

To better understand the FLP concept, a physician should know a bit of the workings of a limited partnership. A limited partnership is an entity that conducts a trade or business or owns investments and has two types of owners. The first type of owner is a general partner. The general partner manages and controls the partnership and makes, in its own discretion, distributions to all of the partners. A general partner is subject to unlimited liability for the acts of the partnership. A limited partner is a passive owner of the partnership and has no managerial control over partnership operations.

The FLP is commonly established to own business and/or investment assets contributed primarily by the physician and spouse for their children and is a palatable alternative to antenuptial agreements. The FLP achieves asset protection because if a claim arises against any individual who is a partner and the creditor attempts to satisfy its claim by foreclosing on such individual's partnership interest, the creditor's only legal remedy is to obtain a "charging order" against the individual's partnership interest. This charging order will generally be insufficient to allow the creditor to cause the dissolution of the partnership. If the partnership were dissolved, the partnership would distribute to each partner their pro rata share of partnership assets, which the creditor could then use to satisfy its claims against the individual. Instead, the charging order permits the creditor to step into the shoes of a limited partner, meaning that the creditor is a passive owner of the limited partnership.

This situation is particularly unappealing to the creditor since the general partner could manage the partnership in such a way as to generate income tax to the creditor without making a partnership distribution to the creditor. Because the creditor's ownership of the limited partnership interest is an albatross, the creditor will attempt to negotiate a settlement with the debtor for some percentage of the original liability. Due to complex income and transfer tax considerations, this tool should be implemented with the careful assistance of professional advisors.

The final asset protection tool to be considered is the *asset protection trust*. Traditionally, asset protection trusts were available only in foreign jurisdictions. Recently, the states of Alaska and Delaware have enacted similar legislation. Both domestic and foreign trusts will be considered.

The *foreign asset protection trust* (FAPT) is an irrevocable trust that an individual establishes in a foreign jurisdiction to protect the assets contributed to the trust from the claims of the creditors of both the creator of the FAPT and any of its beneficiaries. The primary distinction between an FAPT and any of the irrevocable trusts discussed earlier is that the creator of an FAPT may specify in the trust document that he or she may receive discretionary distributions of trust principal and income. In all other irrevocable trusts, the trust is ineffective against the claims of creditors if the creator of the trust reserves any right to principal or income for himself. The FAPT is frequently funded with interests in an FLP.

The FAPT offers a considerable degree of asset protection because the barriers for making claims in jurisdictions such as the Cook Islands, Cayman Islands, and the Bahamas can be severe. These and other favorable jurisdictions do not recognize the judgments of US courts. Thus, a creditor must bring its case in the court of the foreign jurisdiction, usually with a local attorney. Often, the laws of the foreign jurisdiction require that a creditor filing suit post a sizable bond. Furthermore, in some of the most favorable jurisdictions, the creditor cannot use the fraudulent conveyance doctrine to make its claim. These factors have the effect of discouraging creditors from pursuing remedies against individuals whose assets are owned in an FAPT. Nevertheless, some US courts have disregarded the creation of the FAPT by a debtor; therefore, like any other tool, it be must carefully implemented and conceived.

The FAPT possesses other disadvantages as well. While escaping tax in the jurisdiction in which it is established, the FAPT is disregarded with respect to an individual's US income tax liability. Because US citizens have used FAPTs to hide assets in an attempt to evade US taxes, the IRS now requires taxpayers with any interest in an FAPT to report the existence of the FAPT in excruciating detail. Additionally, the FAPT can be very expensive both to establish and to maintain. The control over the FAPT is in the hands of the trustee of the FAPT, who cannot be the creator of the FAPT. Thus, the creator of the FAPT must yield some control over the FAPT to an institution located outside the United States, making some individuals uncomfortable. Thus, the stability of the government of the foreign jurisdiction and the institution holding the assets of the FAPT is of great importance.

A *domestic asset protection trust* (DAPT) is similar to the FAPT in almost every respect but differs by virtue of the laws of the United States. Unlike the FAPT, no reporting to the IRS is necessary. An individual can set up a DAPT without disclosure to the IRS. Additionally, individuals considering an asset protection trust take comfort in knowing that the institution involved in administering the DAPT is subject to U.S. laws. Likewise, DAPTs should prove to be less expensive to establish and maintain than FAPTs.

However, the inherent barriers to creditors present in the most favorable foreign jurisdictions are not present with respect to DAPTs. DAPTs have very rigid fraudulent conveyance provisions so that creditors may avail themselves of this doctrine for several years following the creator's transfer of assets to the DAPT. Additionally, the state in which the DAPT is located is required under the US Constitution to respect the judgments of other states under the *full faith and credit doctrine*. Arguably, a creditor may take its claim to a court in either Alaska or Delaware, and the local court is required to enforce the out-of-state judgment. Since no cases have been decided under either the Alaska or Delaware statutes, no one can be absolutely certain what will occur if a creditor makes a claim against a DAPT beneficiary. However, a recent IRS ruling in PLR 98370007 determined that a DAPT with the creator entitled to receive discretionary distributions of principal and income was a completed gift. Generally speaking, this means that the DAPT has the provisions appropriate for protecting its assets against the claims of creditors of any DAPT beneficiary. The DAPT is worth watching as it evolves in the next few years.

CONCLUSION

Asset protection planning can be crucial in protecting the physician from a catastrophic lawsuit. However, to be most effective, the plan must be carefully implemented with the supervision of a team of professional advisors and ideally must occur well in advance of the catastrophic event giving rise to the initial cause of liability.

## CHAPTER 25

Choosing the Practice Management Consultant That's Right for You

Understanding Advisory Roles, Processes, Fees, and Credentials

---

Hope Rachel Hetico

> MCOs must recruit and train more good physician managers if they are going to grow and be successful. The current dominant role of physician managers supervising other clinicians, in a hierarchical structure, will be replaced by physician leaders who facilitate 'self managing' teams of clinicians and staff. Physician leaders will do this by helping areas of communications teamwork, conflict resolution and quality management.
>
> —David B. Nash, *Physician's Guide to Managed Care*

There are a plethora of self-help publications and management gurus purporting to impart business information to their readers and physician clients. Within the current managed care climate, medical business advisors are currently all the rage. However, in the same vein, physician bankruptcies are mounting, medical student loan delinquencies are increasing, and medical and ancillary practices are closing at record numbers. What gives?

Perhaps the answer lies in the lack of real business, accounting, and financial acumen of the average practitioner. This growing concern is prompting more and more MDs to seek the help of a business advisor or management consultant. But just what does a practice management consultant do, what credentials are needed to be in the business, and how can an advisor help you coordinate all aspects of your practice's life? More important, can your consultant help you achieve your economic goals while still practicing medicine in an enjoyable and actice

Rex Haber
Consultant in Mpls

stress-fr⋯ ⋯llow, and the hallmarks of
successf⋯ .

THE C⋯IEW PROCESS

Medica⋯ ⋯nd focuses on the business
factors⋯ ⋯ to separate personal from
profess⋯ ⋯nt review provides a short-
term a⋯ ⋯every aspect of your office
situatio⋯ ⋯e your objectives. Although
constar⋯ ⋯ng field, the office management r⋯ ⋯undation on which to build
a secur⋯ ⋯here are several distinct steps
in the d⋯ ⋯hich should be considered by
every business advisor.

1. *Clarification of your present financial circumstances* by gathering all relevant financial data, such as a list of corporate and/or personal and financial assets and liabilities, tax returns, records of securities transactions (stocks, bonds, mutual funds, real estate, and other partnerships), insurance policies, wills, trusts, IRAs and pension plans.

2. *Identifying your practice goals and objectives* through a careful review of your personal attitudes and values. These may include more new patients to increase market share, increased or decreased frequency of existing patients, more revenue per patient, spending more time with patients or for charity work, or just generating more gross revenues or profits. Some MDs may have overlapping or conflicting goals, but there are some considerations, such as your net worth statement, that may be important in determining your best management strategy.

3. *Identifying special problems that may stymie you from achieving your goals.* These might include too few paying patients or inappropriate payer mix, improper practice location or access, or inadequate cash flow or deflation. All must be identified before solutions can be explored.

4. *Constructing a written business and/or marketing plan*, which can vary in length according to the complexity of your current practice situation.

5. *Implementation of the plan*, since theoretical formulation is often easier than the actual execution of a plan. Why? Execution often delays current gratification in favor of future consumption. This may be hard to swallow in society's current attitude of immediate gratification and conspicuous consumption.

6. *Periodic review* of the plan and the data used to create it. Just as health care is a rapidly changing environment, decreasing profits, marriage, divorce, or poor managed care contracting strategies may signal a need for the reformation of your plan.

ELEMENTS OF GOOD MANAGEMENT REVIEW

Generally, although the presentation and style may vary, a well-thought-out and comprehensive management review should contain at least the following 10 elements. This should be obtained by completing a confidential business financial or data gathering questionnaire or by personal interview. Remember the adage "garbage in, garbage out," and recall that the review will be only as good as the information used to perform it.

1. *Goals and objectives with practice data:* business data and a prioritization of your goals, with estimated time line, and economic benchmarks for achieving them. For example, you may not expect to jump-start your practice over night, but it is not unreasonable to improve its efficiency and profitability over time.

2. *Special problems and issues* may include illness, practice continuation, or buy/sell agreements. Especially noteworthy, according to Dr. Rex Huber, MBA, a professional practice management consultant in Minneapolis, "are the myriad concerns involving practice mergers, acquisitions, MSO, IPA, PPMC or regional network contracting issues."

3. *Business assumptions* will change over time but usually include such items as specialty type, geographic location and demographics, reimbursement rates, inflation, economic indicators, training, age, and sex, as well as personal risk tolerance or aversion.

4. *Consolidated financial statements* should include at least the last three annual corporate financial statements (balance sheet, net income statement, and statement of cash flows) and tax returns. According to Dr. William P. Scherer, MS, executive of a computer-based testing firm in Ft. Lauderdale, Florida, "financial software such as Quicken® now makes the creation of consolidated financial statements a pleasure, rather than a chore."

5. *Net worth statement:* Net worth on the balance sheet represents practice equity levels obtained by subtracting short- and/or long-term liabilities from assets at a particular point in time, as well as future estimates and projections. Practice net worth, however, is not income, and professional expenses are paid out of cash flows, not net worth. Nevertheless, more is usually better, except when assets are overstated or liabilities underreported. Physician practices are particularly prone to high gross incomes but low profit margins and net worth because of this problem.

6. *Income taxation and planning* should include but may not be limited to a review of corporate income tax statements for all relevant years, with deductions, credits, tax liability, and rates.

7. *Insurance planning and risk management* minimally should include an analysis of your personal and corporate financial exposure, relative to malpractice liability, morbidity, property, casualty, health, life, annuity, long-term care, and disability insurance. It also should include an analysis of corporate buy/sell agreements and a review of all current polices in force.

8. *Benefits and retirement planning* contains an evaluation of all IRAs, SEPs, 401-Ks, 403-Bs, annuities, social security projected benefits, and personal pension and profit-sharing plans, of both the defined-contribution and defined-benefit types. A comparison also should be made of the taxable and tax-exempt rates of returns for these investment vehicles.

9. *Operational audits* generally should include a review of most of the following: processes; patient flow and controls; accounts receivable and cash management;

fee schedule review, with CPT and ICD-9 coding and compliance; cost expense analysis; practice financial ratio creation and analysis; marketing and advertising plans and stationery; profit maximization and reimbursement issues; insurance and third-party payer processing and controls; personnel policies, administration, job structure, benefits, and productivity reviews; as well as any special concerns of the practice.

10. *Recommendations, implementation, and follow-up*: Oral and written communication between you and your consultant is important for understanding, executing, and achieving your management goals and the costs associated with them, as well as the risks and benefits of each. A prioritized schedule and action list is used to implement or reject recommendations, as described in all of the above.

In short, the practice management planning process denotes the method for meeting business goals through proper management of resources. It is a broad-based approach, distinguishing the exceptional management consultant from other professional and nonprofessional advisors, who typically focus on only a single area of the management picture.

CREDENTIALS AND CRITERIA FOR CONSULTANT SELECTION

> No legacy is so rich as honesty.
>
> —William Shakespeare

As you begin your search for a business advisor, call the consultant and ask for a short initial meeting, which should be free of charge. Just as you would select a physician or clergyman, you should base your decision about an advisor on comfort, credentials, experience, and especially education. Fee schedules are probably of least importance. By asking the following questions, you stand the best chance of finding a advisor that's right for your budget, practice, and personality.

Business Designations

What designation(s) does the advisor possess? Realize that the absolute terms *business advisor, practice management consultant,* and *business planner* have no real meaning, credentials, education, or standards associated with them. Anyone can use these terms and get into the advisory business—your brother, neighbor, or the engineer down the street! They are increasingly used by stockbrokers, bankers, and insurance agents, who may or may not add value to your practice and are really commissioned salespeople. Therefore, it is worthwhile to know the following nomenclature.

CPE/CHE

The *certified physician executive* (CPE) or *certified healthcare executive* designations, from the Certifying Commission in Medical Management (CCMM: 4890 West

Kennedy Blvd., # 200, Tampa, Florida 33609-2575; 813-287-8944), may be earned by those physicians or lay professionals with the requisite requirements in education and demonstrated special competence and professional experience in the field of medical management. Specific requirements for certification include (1) current stature as a physician (MD/DO) or working lay professional; (2) completion of the American College of Physician Executive's Graduate Program in Medical Management (GPPM) *or* completion of an accredited graduate management degree program (i.e., MBA, MHA, MPH, etc.), *or* completion of 200 hours of management education with 120 hours of a core curriculum from the GPMM; (3) at least 1 year of medical management experience; and (4) completion of an approved weeklong CPE tutorial program. Upon receipt of the CPE designation diplomate, fellowship and distinguished fellowship status may sought.

FACPE

The American College of Physician Executives offers several educational programs over the entire field of medical management, such as certification curricula, master's degree programs at Tulane and Carnegie Mellon universities, continuing education units (CEUs) and other advanced-standing or fellowship educational programs. A similar program for nonphysicians may lead to the designation Fellow American College of Hospital Executives (FACHE).

CLU/ChFC/NAPFA

A *chartered life underwriter,* as granted by the American College, or *chartered financial consultant*, is a valid insurance designation demonstrating a focused expertise in the insurance business. These are typically commission sales *agents* who work for their respective firms or for themselves but not necessarily you. They sell all sorts of personal and business insurance. Most recently, according to Beverly Brooks, president of the American Society of CLU and ChFC, in Bryn Mawr, Pennsylvania, the society is rethinking its own strategy of insurance agents as the organization has changed its name to the Society of Financial Services Professionals to appeal to a broader base of financial practitioners beyond the insurance products it has traditionally provided. Finally, the National Association of Personal Financial Advisors was formed in the 1980s, and the more than 800 NAPFA members are compensated on a fee-only basis.

Registered Representative

A retail or discount stockbroker, regardless of compensation schedule, is also known as a registered representative. Typically, the rigorous national test known as a Series 7 (General Securities License) examination and the state-specific Series 63 license is needed, along with Securities and Exchange Commission (SEC) registration through the National Association of Securities Dealers (NASD), to become a stockbroker. Since a commission may be involved and performance-based incentives are allowed, be aware of costs.

Registered Investment Advisor

This securities license, obtained after passing the Series 65 examination, allows the designee to charge for giving unbiased securities advice on retirement plans and portfolio management, although not necessarily to sell securities or insurance products.

CPA/EA/CMA

A *certified public accountant, enrolled agent*, or *certified managerial accountant* provides retroactive tax and financial accounting and proactive cost accounting information, respectively. Increasingly, in the medical managed care environment, the role of the CPA is yielding to the CMA or MBA; EAs (usually former IRS agents with comprehensive knowledge of the tax code) can file your tax returns and are licensed to practice before the IRS. Do not expect EA fees to be necessarily lower than CPA tax rates.

CFA

A *chartered financial analyst* will usually work for a brokerage house and follow one or a few publicly traded companies. These analysts may manage institutional money or run a mutual fund. Unfortunately, the previously unbiased nature of these Wall Street experts has been questioned lately with the collapse of such stocks as MedPartners, Oxford Health Plans, Coastal Physicians Group, Inc., and others. Some authorities now feel that CFAs have become merely promoters of the followed company, since sell recommendations are rarely made and CFAs cozy up to insiders and corporate executives as they curry their favor. As always, *caveat emtor* is a good rule to follow.

CFP

The premier personal financial planning designation of choice for the International Association for Financial Planning (IAFP), located in Atlanta and founded in 1969, is board certification in financial planning (CFP). This independent designation represents a professional who has completed a grueling 24-month course of study at an accredited institution and passed the exhausting 2-day, comprehensive Certified Financial Planner Board of Standards Examination. This test encompasses all aspects of the financial planning process, including insurance, economic principles, taxation, investments, and retirement benefits planning. CFPs may also work with JDs (see below) on estate planning or business continuation issues. An ethics, continuing education, and confidentiality requirement is also mandated for this designation.

Health Care Quality Designations

ABQAURP

The American Board of Quality Assurance and Utilization Review Physicians (Professionals) certifies diplomates who are either MDs, DOs, DDSs, DMDs,

DPMs, or other human service or health care professionals, such as RNs or PhDs. The board is accredited by the American Council for Continuing Medical Education (ACCME) to sponsor such programs. Holders of the designation are distinguished by their knowledge of such diverse fields as case and risk management, managed care, credentialing and physician profiling, worker's compensation and medical ethics, Employee Retirement Income Security Act (ERISA), Omni Budget Reconciliation Act (OBRA), Clinical Laboratory Improvement Act (CLIA) and Stark II antitrust laws, as well as National Committee on Quality Assurance (NCQA), Health Plan Employer Data Information Set (HEDIS), and total quality assurance (TQA) principles and practices (48900 W. Kennedy Blvd., # 260, Tampa, Florida 33609; 813-286-4411).

CPHQ

The mission of the National Association for Healthcare Quality (NAHQ) is to improve health care by advancing the theory and practice of quality management in health care organizations and by supporting the professional growth and development of quality health care management professionals. The association has about 10,000 members and was established in 1976. It has specialties in infection control, medical and staff records, nursing, risk management, utilization review, and CQI/TQM. Annual educational conferences are available, along with integrated educational courses, the quarterly newsletter *NAHQ News*, and the bimonthly publication *Journal for Healthcare Quality.*

The NAHQ certification program, confers the designation *certified professional in healthcare quality* (CPHQ) to members and is accredited by the National Organization for Competency and the National Commission for Health Certifying Agencies. It has certified more than 5,000 individuals. The NAHQ has liaison relationships with allied organizations, such as the American Hospital Association, the JCAHO, the National Health Council, and the National Association of Medical Staff Services. It has working relationships with the American Health Information Management Association, the Healthcare Financial Management Association, and the US Department of Health and Human Services. Corporate headquarters are at 5700 Old Orchard Road, 1st Floor, Skokie, Illinois 60077; (708) 966-9392.

Professional Education

What education and degree(s) does the consultant possess and in what field? The following nomenclature is worthwhile to know.

MBA/MHA

One of these graduate degrees (master's degree in business/healthcare/hospital administration) is probably the ideal complement to real-life experience, especially when combined with other insurance, investment advisory, and securities licenses. In fact, a subspecialty in finance, management, cost accounting, or health or hospital administration provides exceptional planning and investment advisory credentials.

JD

Attorneys with a health and managed care background may provide valuable advice on such topics as antitrust and corporate compliance, health care transactions, contracts and litigation, credentialing and peer review, federal and state fraud and abuse, elder care law, professional liability and malpractice defense, ERISA and welfare benefits, and third-party payments. They may also work with CFPs or MBAs on investment, retirement, and estate planning issues.

Expertise

Remember, there are only two types of experience, *good* and *bad.* Therefore, it may be worthwhile to recall that experience does matter but only in the context of appropriate information and performance. After all, all physicians had to treat that *first* patient before a professional career was begun. For example, you may feel that an advisor who specializes in working with physician clients represents a real value-added service, or you may not. Admittedly, more and more advisors are beginning to understand the plight of the modern physician in this new era of capitated health care, so it might behoove you seek a consultant familiar with the risks and benefits of managed medical care.

Medical Management Education

The Center for Education in Medical Practice Management (CEMPM) is the source of all educational development and programming for the Medical Group Management Association (MGMA), American College of Medical Practice Executives (ACMPE), and the Center for Research in Ambulatory Healthcare Administration (CRAHCA). The CEMPM comprises the knowledge base of all facets of the MGMA, ACMPE, and CRAHCA and is an experienced provider of education, focusing on the management and leadership of medical group practices and their strategic partners.

The Financial Management Society (FMS) was created by the MGMA in 1986 to meet the needs of managers/administrators involved in the financial aspects of a medical group practice

The Managed Care Assembly (MCA) of the MGMA was previously known as the PrePaid Healthcare Assembly. The MCA was founded in 1981 to respond to the needs of MGMA members participating in capitated health care contracts.

Bankers

Bankers are very conservative by nature and generally do not charge a fee for their advice. It may be increasingly difficult to borrow money, however, especially since modern bankers know that a medical degree is no longer the guarantee of a steady and high income that it once was. As more than one banker has opined, "We don't usually lend money to doctors who really need it."

They also may not have a clue about what the practitioner can do to compete more successfully in the managed care arena. Bankers do have a good concept of local community politics, however, for those not familiar with a practice venue. They frequently can provide references to more focused advisors and credible consultants.

Networks

A business advisor should work with a host of trusted and competent other professionals, such as those described above, for the best results. In the final analysis the MD is considered captain of his or her practice. It also goes without saying that your advisor should have errors and omissions (E&O) insurance, since he or she is creating and maintaining a chart on your case, just like the medical chart you create for your patients. In cases of dispute, items not documented in the chart likely do not exist.

ADVISOR FEE SCHEDULES

Most management consultants charge for their services in one of three ways: (1) fee only, (2) commission only, or (3) a blended schedule. Typical hourly fees range from $100 to $350 per hour. Insurance and brokerage commission rates vary from 1% to 10%, and cost efficiency experts may garner one-third of all cost savings the first year. Most clients prefer the blended approach so that they can pick and choose among products and services, depending on personal circumstances. An honest consultant will not only inform you of his or her fee schedule and scope of work but empower you to produce the best outcome for the least cost. For example, a CPT compliance audit may cost $1,000–$5,000 per full-time equivalent (FTE) physician but return 5–10 times that amount. Remember, it is perfectly reasonable to compensate a business consultant who works with you to achieve your practice's business goals.

"HOT" HEALTH CARE CONSULTING FIELDS FOR PHYSICIANS AND GROUP PRACTICE MANAGERS

> One shortcoming of many physician organizations is that they aren't willing to compensate their leaders for [their] efforts.
>
> —Thomas M. Gorey, Policy Planning Associates, Crystal Lake, Illinois

If you are a medical practitioner with specific expertise in a particular administrative area and are interested in working as a management consultant, the following health care facilitators and fields are on the upswing, according to Susan A.

Cejka, president, Cejka & Co., a national health care search firm for physician executives. Usually, real-world experience is as important as advanced degrees or designations.

- *Assemblers:* Organize physicians and physicians' organizations in a single- or multispecialty group practice setting.
- *Care managers:* Triage leaders for fields such as nursing, physical therapy, oncology, and electronic data interchange.
- *Financial/capitation analysts:* Review financial ratios and crunch capitation numbers, utilization rates, and other economic numerics on a large scale.
- *Integrators:* Serve to decouple the recent wave of practice mergers and acquisitions, since some have failed and experts are needed to undo the damage, especially in the hospital or PHO setting. Efficiency, capacity utilization expertise, and reengineering are included in this employment model.
- *Insurance experts:* Require large-scale capitation contracting experience and negotiating skills to integrate the myriad of existing, networked managed medical care products of the future.

Moreover, you must have the flexible mindset to bridge the gap between the clinical world of medicine and the administrative world of business. According to the Medical Group Management Association (MGMA), the following chart modification represents a descriptive contract between physician-clinicians and physician-administrators (Table 25.1).

Contemporaneously, the just released *Management Compensation Survey* (1998), of the MGMA, reported that compensation was essentially unchanged for many key medical group practice manager positions. For example, compensation rose about $2,000 for CEOs, increased $373 to $77,373 for administrators of groups with seven or more FTE physicians, and rose $1,100 to $57,000 for administrators with six or fewer FTE physicians. Compensation for other core management positions marginally increased, from about 1% to 4%; for example, as chief operating officer (COO), $81,000; chief financial officer (CFO), $71,346; business office manager, $39,619; and medical office manager, $35,900.

TABLE 25.1   Clinicians versus Administrators

PHYSICIAN-CLINICIAN	PHYSICIAN-ADMINISTRATOR
Physiologic and anatomic disorders	Health organization with finite budgets
Defined specialty and scope	Generalists in business knowledge
Individuals and patients	Trends and cohorts
Science and medicine	Finance, accounting, and business
Slow change with flexibility	Rapid change with flexibility
Short-term goals	Long-term strategic plans
One-to-one interactions	Group dynamics/organizational structure
Independent	Dependent
Performer (action)	Delegator (assignor)

Moreover, according to Jerome T. Henry, MBA, MSHA, of the MGMA, "with more physicians participating in MSOs, PPMCs or other outside management entities, there is a significant demand for qualified managers. When an MSO or PPMC wants to hire proven talent, they appear willing to pay a top salary." Accordingly, compensation for physician executives who spend at least 50% of their time in administrative duties saw minor pay increases last year. CEOs made $253,940, and medical directors made $186,720, up 5% and 4.3%, respectively.

For those physicians serious about developing a consulting career, a variety of insurance products may be required for their protection. These might include the following policies, as offered by Executive Risk (860-408-2000 or www. execrisk.com).

1. Health care consultants professional liability insurance.
2. Medical directors and officers liability insurance (private and public companies) for health care and managed care organizations.
3. Employment practices liability insurance for health care organizations.
4. Managed care errors and omissions liability coverage.
5. Employment practices, crime, and fiduciary liability insurance.
6. Antitrust, staff privilege discrimination, and restraint of trade conspiracy insurance.
7. Credentialing, peer review, and miscellaneous professional liability insurance.
8. Diversified errors and omissions insurance.

Additionally, be aware that several states (Maryland, Mississippi, New Jersey, Ohio) are now considering legislation to make certain decision-making or -denying medical directors/consultants responsible for care. In effect, such bills make physician executives/consultants as responsible as attending physicians when action, or lack of it, causes patient harm. Therefore, malpractice liability riders are important in this regard.

CONCLUSION

Despite the fact that some physicians and other medical professionals believe that they can employ all aspects of the practice management planning process without professional guidance, history seems to suggest otherwise, according to Rachel Pentin-Maki, MHA, nationally known health care consultant in Atlanta. Therefore, hire the appropriate consultant when needed. Your medical practice may just depend on it!

REFERENCES AND READINGS

American College of Medical Practice Executives Index. MGMA Item # 1327.
Cook, R. Leveling the field: States try to make medical directors liable for care decisions. *Modern Physician*, November 1998.

Dunevitz, B. Compensation flat for group practice managers. *MGMA Update*, vol. 37, No. 20., 1998.

Dunevitz, B. Three worlds of healthcare move together; not separately. *MGMA Update*, December 1998.

Financial Management Society & Managed Care Assembly (4th. Annual Conference), 1999.

Gorey, T. F. Consultant says physician leaders need to be strong and visionary entrepreneurs. *Practice Options*, December 1998.

Krill, M. A. Successful Partnerships for the Future: The Administrator-Physician Dynamic. MGMA Item # 4819.

Longo, T. Goodbye, alphabet soup. *Financial Planning*, November 1998.

Patterson, H. Take Charge of your Healthcare Career: Successful Job-Search Strategies for the Health Care Professional. MGMA Item # 5142.

Epilogue

In his dictionary, Webster defines the word *visionary* as, "one who is able to see into the future." Unlike some pundits, prescience is not a quality we claim to possess. To the purveyors of health care gloom and doom however, the future for physicians is a bleak *fate accompli*. If you were of this same philosophical ilk prior to reading this book, we hope that you now realize the bulk of impending activity for physicians, payers and patients will take place at the physician-management level; as doctors take back their place as maestro of the medical care symphony. In the future, this doctor-manager dichotomy will blur as physicians control their professional and economic lives through Medical Provider Service Networks (MPSN) that obviate the need for broker-middlemen-agents sucking huge profits out of the system at the expense of all concerned. By a true MPSN, we mean a medical care organization run by physician managers who contract directly with employers, rather than managed care intermediaries. For this to occur, physicians will need to consider the example of our contributing authors and graduate from law school and business school; or take management, accounting or technology courses to re-engineer their practices with the needed organization tools of the new millennium. Hopefully, this book will prove useful in this regard and serve as a valuable resource for every medical, business and graduate school library.

Do not be complacent, for as onerous as it seems, we may not survive autonomously as a profession without utilizing this sort of information, because the bar to a new level of medical care has been raised in this decade. Although we still need actuarial and accounting data, working capital, marketing techniques and correct product pricing, we believe that all physicians will look back on the year 2001 and recognize it as the turning point in the current health care imbroglio.

Therefore, as practicing physicians, please realize that we all face the same managed care issues as you. And, although the multi-degreed experts of this textbook may have a particular business expertise, we should never loose sight of the fact that, above all else, medical care should be delivered in a personal and humane manner, with patient interest, rather than self-interest, as our guiding standard.

Good medicine, good business, good day!

Fraternally,
David Edward Marcinko
Hope Rachel Hetico

Index

Electronic medical claims submission:
    cost of, 85
    overview, 83–84
    paperwork, 84
Employee(s), generally:
    benefits, 50
    leasing, 48, 215
    outsourcing advantages, 51
    risk management strategies, 159–160
Employee Retirement Income Security Act
        (ERISA), 17, 153–154, 371
Employment contracts, covenant not to com-
        pete, 35
Empowerment model HMO, 15
Enurement, 338
Environmental Protection Agency (EPA),
        risk management, 160
Equity financing, PPMCs, 337–338
Equity value:
    acquisitions/mergers and, 256
    determination factors, 256–263
Established patient:
    billing guidelines, 106
    defined, 108
Ethical issues:
    access to care, 357–358
    communications, 356–357
    confidentiality, 357
    conflicts of interest, 356
    ethical principles, evolutionary shifts in,
        352–354
    managed care framework:
        moral standards, professional, 361–362
        patient education, coaching, and men-
            toring, 359–360
        quality–driven, 360–361
        skills development, 362–363
    patient advocacy, 355–356
    physician's dilemma, 354–356
    professional autonomy, 355, 358
    social responsibility, 363–364
Evaluation and management services:
    billing guidelines, 106–107, 109
    defined, 109
Excess earnings method, practice valuation,
        272–273
Exclusive provider organization (EPO), 18
Executive Risk, 387
Expense models:
    breakeven analysis and profits, 184–186
    cost analysis, equipment payback method,
        186
    cost structure and behavior:
        controllable costs, 179–180
        differential costs, 179

direct costs, 179
economic order quantity cost (EOQC),
    181–182
fixed costs, 176–177
indirect costs, 179
marginal costs, 182–184
marginal revenues, 182–184
mixed costs, 178
opportunity costs, 180
relevant costs, 180–181
sunk costs, 180
variable costs, 176–178
Extended care providers, 9
Externalities, defined, 7

Facility & Activity Center Tracking (FACT)
    Service, 308
Fair market value, 260
Family limited partnerships (FLPs), 372–373
Family-oriented claims, 369–370
FASB Statements, PPMCs, 333
Federal False Claims Act, 315–316
Federation of Physicians and Dentists (FPD),
    28
Fee-for-service market, 8
Fee-for-service methodology:
    traditional, overview, 18
    tracking managed care plans, 133–134
Fee-for-service system, overview, 129–130
Fees, *see* Fee-for-service methodology; Fee-
        for-service system
    advisors', 385
    medical and insurance, 91–93
    in trend analysis, 247
Fiduciary law, 346–349
Financial Accounting Standards Board
    (FASB), 170, 256
Financial guidelines:
    accountant, function of, 252–253
    avoiding wasting money, 251–252
    bankers *vs.* medical practitioners, 253–254
Financial profiles and trends, 132–133
Financial ratios:
    asset management, 226–228
    debt management, 228
    equity value and, 257
    liquidity and solvency:
        current liabilities to net worth, 226
        current ratio, 226
    profitability, 228–229
Financial statements:
    balance sheet (Statement of Financial Posi-
        tion), 168–169
    equity value and, 256–257

Springer Publishing Company

Telemedicine and Telehealth
Principles, Policies, Performance and Pitfalls

Adam William Darkins, MD, MPH, FRCS
Margaret Ann Cary, MD, MBA, MPH

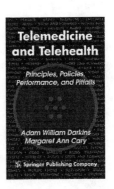

"The most comprehensive resource on telehealth. Clearly a must read for those who feel telehealth can rebuild the physician-patient relationship."
—**Charles Safran,** MD
Chief Executive Officer
Clinician Support Technology

"This is the thinking person's gateway to the world of telemedicine...these authors set the stage for nearly everyone involved in planning or evaluating a telemedicine program, policy, or research project."

—**Douglas A. Perednia,** MD
Founder and President
Association of Telemedicine Service Providers

Telemedicine and telehealth are changing the face of health care delivery and becoming a multi-billion dollar industry. The authors provide practical insights and advice on transforming telemedicine programs into successful clinical services.

Contents: Introduction • Definitions of Telemedicine and Telehealth and a History of the Remote Management of Disease • Telehealth: A Patient Perspective • Telehealth and Relationships with Physicians • Using Telehealth to Make Health Care Transactions • Telehealth Services • Regulatory, Legislative and Political Considerations in Telehealth • The Market for Telehealth Services • Contracting for Telehealth Services • The Business of Telehealth • The Management of Telehealth Services • Choosing the Right Technology for Telehealth • Other Important Influences on Health Care that Affect the Future of Telehealth • References • Glossary of Terms and Abbreviations

2000   328pp.   0-8261-1302-8   hard   www.springerpub.com

536 Broadway, New York, NY 10012-3955 • (212) 431-4370 • Fax (212) 941-7842

Springer Publishing Company

Preventing and Managing Osteoporosis

Sarah Hall Gueldner, DSN, FAAN
M. Susan Burke, MD
Helen Smiciklas-Wright, PhD, Editors

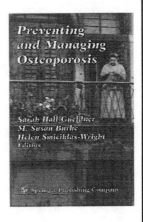

Written by a team of authors from medicine, nursing, nutrition, exercise physiology, and physical therapy, the volume provides an overview of the disease process—discussing its epidemiology, strategies for prevention and treatment, as well as the clinical implications of osteoporosis across disciplines.

Contents:

- Epidemiology: The Magnitude of Concern
- Living With Osteoporosis: The Personal Experience
- Nutritional Considerations
- Exercise: A Prescription for Osteoporosis?
- Bone Remodeling and the Development of Osteoporosis
- Osteoporosis: Patient Identification and Evaluation
- Therapeutic Strategies for Prevention and Treatment
- Osteoporosis and Fall Prevention
- Relief of Pain
- Adapting Clothing to Accommodate Changes in the Body
- Target Groups for Prevention and Early Detection
- Osteoporosis: Clinical Implications Across Disciplines

2000   216pp.   0-8261-1318-4   hard
www.springerpub.com

536 Broadway, New York, NY 10012 • (212)431-4370 • Fax: (212)941-7842